MacArthur's ULTRA

Modern War Studies

Theodore A. Wilson
General Editor

Raymond A. Callahan
J. Garry Clifford
Jacob W. Kipp
Jay Luvaas
Series Editors

MacArthur's ULTRA
Codebreaking and the War against Japan, 1942–1945

Edward J. Drea

 University Press of Kansas

For my mother, Joan Lavene Drea

Published by the University Press of Kansas (Lawrence, Kansas 66049), which was
organized by the Kansas Board of Regents and is operated and funded by Emporia State
University, Fort Hays State University, Kansas State University, Pittsburg State University,
the University of Kansas, and Wichita State University

Library of Congress Cataloging-in-Publication Data

Drea, Edward J., 1944–
    MacArthur's ULTRA : codebreaking and the war against Japan,
  1942–1945 / Edward J. Drea.
        p.   cm. — (Modern war studies)
    Includes bibliographical references (p.   ) and index.
    ISBN 0–7006–0504–5 (alk. paper)   ISBN 0–7006–0576–2 (pbk.)
    ʹ1. World War, 1939–1945—Campaigns—Pacific Area.   2. World War,
  1939–1945—Cryptography.   3. World War, 1939–1945—Military
  intelligence—Pacific Area.   4. MacArthur, Douglas, 1880–1964—
  Military Leadership.   5. Pacific Area—History.   I. Title.
  II. Series.
D767.D66   1991
940.54′26—dc20   91–16842

British Library Cataloguing in Publication Data is available.

Printed in the United States of America

10 9 8 7 6 5 4 3 2

The paper used in this publication meets the minimum requirements of the American
National Standard for Permanence of Paper for Printed Library Materials Z39.48-1984.

Contents

Illustrations and Tables

Preface

In this book I assess the relationship between special intelligence and the campaigns of General Douglas MacArthur in the Pacific. During World War II, special intelligence, commonly referred to as ULTRA today, meant information obtained through monitoring, intercepting, and decoding enemy radio communications.[1] The British used the code word ULTRA from mid-1940 to alert the initiated that special intelligence was the source of what they were reading.[2] Americans in the North African and European theaters adopted the British intelligence practice and this code word. In the Pacific and Southeast Asia, no uniform policies governed the use and distribution of special intelligence, and ULTRA as a code word did not gain currency in the Pacific until March 1944. For reasons of clarity and simplicity, I use the terms "special intelligence" and "ULTRA" interchangeably.

The task I have set for myself is to do for ULTRA in the Pacific what Ralph Bennett did for ULTRA in Europe—to analyze its significance for military operations.[3] I focus on ULTRA, decrypted radio intercepts of Japanese military traffic, in one theater of operations, MacArthur's Southwest Pacific theater. I treat only in passing the well-known American efforts (MAGIC) that penetrated Japanese diplomatic codes. The triumphs of U.S. Navy cryptanalysis receive attention only as they relate to MacArthur's operations. The comprehensive story of the U.S. Navy's success against Imperial Japanese Navy codes still awaits an author. My goal is to add the ULTRA dimension to MacArthur's campaigns in New Guinea and the Philippine Islands.

When Japanese carrier aircraft attacked the American naval base at Pearl Harbor, Hawaii, on December 7, 1941, the U.S. Army was unable to decrypt a single Imperial Army message. Not until September 1943 did American codebreakers read their first Japanese army message. By February 1944, however, U.S. analysts were deciphering more than twenty thousand Japanese army messages per month.

This remarkable achievement and its effects on MacArthur's campaigns form the core of this book.

The labor that preceded the break into the Japanese army codes is also important, because that "campaign" established parameters for the flood of information U.S. Army intelligence exploited in 1944 and 1945. Nevertheless, the focus here is on the application of ULTRA to a military campaign, not on the techniques of cracking codes and ciphers. Technical information appears solely for illustrative purposes, and any purist will object to my use of the words "code" and "cipher" as synonyms. Throughout, I pose three fundamental questions: What did American or Allied commanders know about their Japanese counterparts' capabilities? When did they find out? And what did they do as a consequence? Answers to these questions often remain vague because ULTRA cause and operational effect usually cannot be fully documented. The sensitive nature of intelligence from deciphered Japanese radio messages precluded extensive note taking and recorded minutes during planning or decisionmaking sessions. Nevertheless, sufficient circumstantial and limited documentary evidence does exist to permit logical inferences about the influence of ULTRA on MacArthur's operations.

MacArthur's ULTRA unit, Central Bureau, was born and matured during the Pacific war. It originated from a cadre of codebreakers brought out of the Philippine Islands in early 1942, supplemented by a handful of cryptanalysts from Washington. From those humble beginnings, Central Bureau developed the capability to read the highest-level Japanese army secret communications and evolved into MacArthur's personal and independent cryptologic organization. Much has been made of the friction that existed between Central Bureau, the War Department in Washington, and the U.S. Navy's signal intelligence organization; however, overemphasizing this aspect diminishes an appreciation of the remarkable accomplishment of MacArthur's people, of the degree of cooperation, and of the exchange of ULTRA intelligence among the three parties.

Any examination of MacArthur's ULTRA must describe, however briefly, the state of the U.S. Army cryptanalytic arts in the years preceding Pearl Harbor. Thus in Chapter 1, I discuss the complex Imperial Japanese Army codes and summarize the American army and navy signal intelligence efforts in East Asia in early 1941. I introduce key personalities in MacArthur's headquarters and describe the origins and evolution of Central Bureau from 1942 to 1945. Finally, I analyze the relationship of Central Bureau to MacArthur's theater intelligence services, the War Department, and the U.S. Navy.

In Chapter 2, I examine ULTRA in MacArthur's theater of operations in 1942. I highlight the role of intelligence in the Papua New Guinea campaign. The progress of ULTRA during 1943, particularly its use in the Battle of the Bismarck Sea and the reduction of the Japanese fortress at Rabaul, forms the centerpiece of Chapter 3. MacArthur's most spectacular use of ULTRA, its role in the plan and execution of his leap to Hollandia, Netherlands New Guinea, is dealt with in Chapter 4. In Chapter 5, I examine MacArthur's drive into western New Guinea and scrutinize the claims made for ULTRA during the Aitape operation in North-East New Guinea. In chapters 6 and 7, I offer an analysis of ULTRA intelligence and MacArthur's operations on Leyte and Luzon, Philippines. In Chapter 8, I compare the ULTRA-derived Japanese order of battle for the defense of the Japanese home islands in 1945 with the actual Japanese deployments. ULTRA's role in this case was more than academic. ULTRA monitored the massive Japanese mobilization for the defense of the home islands, and this detailed knowledge of Japanese preparations, in turn, may have contributed greatly to the decision to use the atomic bomb. In the concluding chapter I assess MacArthur's codebreakers and the general's use of ULTRA.

As British historian and former intelligence officer Peter Calvocoressi has observed, World War II featured many ways to gather intelligence, but only ULTRA was "prompt and authentic."[4] However, the intercepted and decrypted message alone was merely an impressive display of the technical craft of codebreaking. Intelligence analysts provided a "context and background" that gave the intercepted message significance without which the decrypted information could not be fully exploited.[5] Context did not come overnight. It resulted from a labor-intensive recording, organizing, analyzing, and filing of thousands of seemingly inconsequential tidbits of information that, much like a jigsaw puzzle, only made sense when fitted together.

For instance, if unit X at Singapore becomes associated with unit Y in the Palaus, which, in turn, transships supplies and reinforcements to Rabaul, New Britain, then perhaps unit X will appear shortly at Rabaul. If one knows that the Shipping Headquarters in Manila has secretly announced that the former head of Army Transport Services has been appointed to command Thirty-Fifth Army in the Philippines, then Lieutenant General Suzuki Sosaku has just taken command of a previously unidentified army in the Philippines.[6] The same associations suggested the further possibility of additional Japanese forces, heretofore unsuspected, augmenting already identified formations in the Philippines. Analysts then had to determine the implications of this intelligence. Did the Japanese now have two separate army commands in the islands? If so, what did this fact portend? Were more reinforcements en route? Each answer was another small solution to the overall mystery.

It took time to organize the outlines of the puzzle, connect similar pieces of ULTRA within the framework, and finally assemble the discoveries in a coherent manner that revealed the otherwise fragmented picture of Japanese deployments. ULTRA was the key to the solution because it provided accurate data based on discussions among Japanese units. And, in the vast Pacific region, ULTRA uniquely provided impeccable intelligence about Japanese forces hundreds or even thousands of miles away. Without ULTRA, great distances shrouded Japanese units behind an impenetrable security barrier. Furthermore, by early 1944 in both Asia and Europe, intercepted Japanese and German messages could be read with celerity—within hours of the time they were put on the air—and the enormous advantages ULTRA bestowed are perceived as self-evident.[7]

It was not that simple in practice. As complex as it was, deciphering enemy radio communications was only the first step in a larger process designed to translate ULTRA-derived knowledge about one's opponent into action while simultaneously concealing from him that his secret communications were being deciphered. The translated decryption passed to commanders or intelligence specialists, who evaluated and decided its significance. ULTRA then had to be disseminated to field commanders, who determined how this new intelligence modified existing plans and deployments. The chief story in this book is how MacArthur and his commanders used ULTRA.

Many people in Japan and the United States generously assisted my research for this book, which began several years ago at Fort Leavenworth, Kansas. The staff of the Military History Department, National Institute for Defense Studies, Tokyo, allowed me access to their unique archive of World War II documents. Professor Takahashi Hisashi was always helpful, as were his colleagues Professor Hatano Sumio, now at Tsukuba University, and Dr. Akagi Kanji, now at Keio University. Professor Akagi was particularly helpful by pointing out or sending me pertinent articles about military intelligence in Japan. In the United States, Thaddeus Ohta of the Japan Section, Library of Congress, was unfailingly considerate in helping me locate Japanese language books and periodicals. Eugene Carvalho, director of the East Asian Library, University of Kansas, Lawrence, made the extensive collection of Japanese language materials on World War II housed there available to me and also took time from his busy schedule in Japan to secure otherwise unobtainable books and magazines for this study.

The primary sources in English that I used for this book are found in Record Group 457, U.S. National Archives and Records Administration, Washington, D.C. There I relied on John Taylor's expert advice and guidance for more than a decade. The National Security Agency (NSA), Fort Meade, Maryland, has been offering these documents to the Archives since the mid-1970s, and I have benefited over the years from the knowledge and first-hand experience of several NSA historians who prefer anonymity. Staff members at the Washington National Records Center, Suitland, Maryland, helped me through the massive collection of World War II unit records.

Edward Boone and Jeffery Acosta made my visits to the MacArthur Memorial Bureau of Archives, Norfolk, Virginia, both productive and enjoyable. Mr. Boone always discovered new leads that helped me clarify my thinking about the war in the Southwest Pacific. I had the good fortune to work with the excellent staff at the U.S. Army Military History Institute, Carlisle Barracks, Pennsylvania, from 1983 to 1987. At the risk of slighting some, I must thank Louise Arnold, Katherine Davis, Nancy Gilbert, David Keough, John Slonaker, Dr. Richard J. Sommers, Dennis Vetock, Michael Winey, Randy Hackenburg, and Lieutenant Colonel Martin Andresen for their assistance. At the U.S. Army Center of Military History, Washington, D.C., the historical resources staff—Hannah Zeidlik, Jim Knight, Geri Harcarik, and Steve Hardyman—were also helpful. I am also indebted to Michael Briggs and Michele McTighe Kendall of the University Press of Kansas.

I am grateful to Dr. Abraham Sinkov, Taro Yoshihashi, and Joseph E. Richard for sharing their first-hand experiences with me. Fellow historians Louis Allen, Robert Berlin, Carl Boyd, Martin Blumenson, John Carland, Ray Callahan, Harold Deutsch, Jack Finnegan, Colonel David Glantz, Michael I. Handel, William Leary, Ray Skates, Roger Spiller, and Theodore Wilson in one way or another encouraged me to complete this book. My wife, Kazuko, and daughter, Rika, deserve thanks for their support and understanding during this project. Finally, I am indebted to Dr. Stanley L. Falk for his patience in reading several earlier versions of the manuscript. Without his constructive criticism, insights, and unparalleled knowledge of the war in the Southwest Pacific, I could not have written this book. The opinions and interpretations herein are, of course, my own. So too are any errors.

1
MacArthur's Codebreaking Organization

Since antiquity armies and navies have resorted to codes and ciphers to conceal sensitive information from prying enemies. Twentieth-century developments in radio communications speeded a commander's messages to his dispersed units, but they lacked security. An enemy could, theoretically, intercept and read any message transmitted over airwaves. To protect themselves from unwanted eavesdroppers, military establishments used a wide variety of codes or ciphers.[1] The Imperial Japanese Army employed a book-based, hand-written encipherment system. It had three distinct steps.

Picture a one-star private in the General Affairs Section of the Army Department of Imperial General Headquarters (IGHQ) in Tokyo who was handed a *Kimitsu* (Top Secret) message to encipher. First he looked up in the Army Code Book *(Rikugun angosho)* each word he wished to conceal. A code substitutes a word or number for another word or phrase. For example, the private located the word *"daitai"* in the left-hand column of the codebook. Opposite *daitai* in the right-hand column appeared a four-digit number 3472. He encoded *daitai* as 3472 and proceeded to the next word until all the words in the message had been encoded.

In step two, he enciphered each code number. A cipher transforms individual letters, or in this case numbers, into gibberish. In the Japanese army a separate key register, a random series of four-digit numbers displayed in column form, was used for encipherment. The key identified the random number from which the code clerk had begun to encipher his four-digit code. It changed daily. Based on the key for that day, the private opened the register to the assigned page and located the proper column and line. Reading down from the first number, say 6982, he encrypted the message by adding the key numbers to his basic code numbers.

The third step employed false, or noncarrying, addition to further confuse would-be codebreakers. The sum of 3472*(daitai)* and the key 6982 equaled 9354, the encrypted form of *daitai*. As he encrypted all his code numbers *daitai* had metamorphosed from 3472 to 9354.

At the other end, in this case Davao, Philippines, a corporal reversed the process to decrypt the message. First he identified the two four-digit numbers, called discriminants, that always preceded the message text. The first set of four-digit numbers, say 2345, told the informed reader the code system in use. The second, perhaps 6966, directed him to the key register, specifying the exact page, column, and row from which to begin decrypting the message.

His substitution table told the private that 2345 equated to 3155, the code in effect. Likewise 6966 equated to 2999, or page 29, column 9, row 9 in the key register. Starting from the specified row, he found 6982. He subtracted 6982 from 9354, without carrying tens to the next column, to get 3472. He did this for the remaining code groups in the message. Finally, in a second codebook, arranged numerically, he looked up 3472.[2] Opposite it appeared the word "*daitai*." With practice an average communications code clerk could encrypt or decrypt perhaps fifteen words a minute.

This cumbersome system needed two codebooks, one arranged by Japanese characters to encode and the other by digits to decode. Each contained ten thousand four-digit groups from 0000 to 9999, offering 9,500 meanings. The remaining 500 entries were blanks to confuse potential codebreakers. The numerical cipher was a book of one-hundred pages, each containing one-hundred random four-digit groups arranged in ten columns and ten rows.[3] The Army Code Book was prepared and distributed by the General Staff. Higher-echelon units, such as Imperial General Headquarters, employed a four-digit system for concealing messages. Units below division level used a three-digit one. Codebooks were valid for one year, the one-hundred-page key registers for one to three months, and substitution tables for five to thirty days.

After a corporal supervising his section nodded perfunctory approval of the encipherment, the one-star private carried the message to the signal message center. There he handed the documents to the communications officer, who logged in yet another message destined for transmission to Japan's far-flung armies.

Administrative details completed, the officer ordered a sergeant to take the message to the radio room. There he passed the message to a superior private, who quickly added the discriminants in effect that day. The sergeant then walked over to a wireless operator and handed him the enciphered message. This technician disguised the plain-text address prefixed to the message by a series of encipherments. For this step, he used yet another set of codebooks, the geographic place name lists. He found that the address—DAI NI HOMEN GUN SAMBOCHO (Second Area Army, chief of staff)—was 1887, 1773, 3972. At the same time, he converted the place of destination and place of origin. According to his geographic

00	完了(ノ)豫定	34	電信課	68	荒
01	(519)	35	承命服務	69	大阪(海軍)運輸部神戸支部
02	(ア)以テ	36	セ ラ レ	70	エ ー
03	完成(况)	37	暗礁ニ觸(况)	71	儲備券
04	鐵	38	聲退(况)	72	逼迫(况)
05	送水ポンプ	39	減(况)	73	豫定(ノ)期日
06	全力ヲ擧ゲテ	40	改編(况)	74	後報(况)
07	紫電	41	擲彈	75	鋲
08	大角度(ノ)	42	座席	76	18
09	0300	43	9月	77	(108)
10	(ク	44	換装(况)	78	マー
11	(ト)看[見]做(况)	45	下關	79	タルモノ
12	騰貴(况)	46	ツツイラ	80	基地員
13	大冶	47	自爆(况)	81	タテ
14	推力	48	惰力	82	タズ
15	綠燈	49	省	83	(=)資(况)
16	當直(况)	50	乘客(…名)	84	造兵
17	ラルル	51	禀申(况)	85	給粮船(…隻)
18	送院(况)	52	分解檢查(况)	86	(315)
19	大型	53	基準(况)	87	(8)
20	狀	54	232	88	(=)接續(况)
21	(ヨセ	55	機密	89	有望(况)
22	富津埼	56	(346)	90	櫻
23	(ノ)海面	57	上旬	91	マル
24	佐渡	58	電波探知機	92	(ヲ)連送(况)
25	從軍	59	(ヲ)掃蕩(况)	93	內外
26	爆發(况)	60	三原	94	(ノ)途(=)
27	上海	61	差當リ	95	偵察第…飛行隊
28	詳細不明	62	湊	96	手動
29	錨地(ヲ)指定(况)	63	ボ	97	良質(况)
30	炎	64	目下	98	118
31	グリーニッチ	65	伺早(况)	99	(ヲ)徵發(况)
32	60	66	(198)		
33	(49)	67	メツ		

Figure 1.1. A sample page from the Japanese Army Code Book TEN (Receiver) Series No. Nine. The recipient of a coded message would match the four-digit number with the corresponding term. Number 8127, for example, is ''Shanghai, China''; 8158 is ''radar''; and 8169 is ''Osaka (Naval) Transport Division, Kobe Branch.'' The large ''8'' centered on the right-hand margin is a tab that enables a user to flip directly to the ''8000'' series of code groups. (Courtesy of U.S. National Security Agency)

Figure 1.2. A Typical Japanese Army Message Enciphered for Transmission

57[a]   491[b]   48[c]   12022240[d]

1887 1773 3972[e]

DD 6635 = 4761[f]

2345[g]	6966[h]	2804	6249	4481	2424	8376	6135	7994	9570
1115	0312	2284	6870	6683	5207	1397	3689	7290	1861
8944	1980	3848	8428	9292	7802	1864	7499	3588	8585
1199	6952	9759	3102	1750	0646	7871	5765	6085	9415
1489	8410	4835	5340	9436	3943	0900	6249		

[a] Circuit number
[b] Originating message center number (Army Operations Department, IGHQ)
[c] Group count (forty-eight four-digit groups of numbers in the message)
[d] File date and time (December 2/10:40 P.M. (Tokyo time)
[e] Disguised address (Second Area Army, Chief of Staff)
[f] Disguised points of origin and destination (DD = *den' dai* or telegraph address) (Tokyo = Davao)
[g] Discriminant code (3155 when converted from substitution table)
[h] Key indicator (2999 when converted from substitution table)

Source: *History of the SSA*, Vol. 3: *The Japanese Army Problem: Cryptanalysis, 1942–45*, 21–22, Record Group 457, U.S. National Archives and Records Administration, Washington, D.C.

codebook, Davao in the Philippines became 6635 and Tokyo 4761. The message was now ready for transmission (see Figure 1.2).

It took three enlisted men twenty minutes to prepare a message for transmission over a Japanese military radio channel to Davao. Before sending this message, a Tokyo radio operator at Imperial General Headquarters contacted the signalman at Headquarters, Southern Army, Manila, Philippines, which had overall command of Imperial Army forces spread from New Guinea to Burma (see Figure 1.3). It relayed radio messages carrying orders and instructions from Tokyo to subordinate units in regularly scheduled broadcasts. If transmission readability and signal strength were good, the Tokyo operator tapped out his message manually, using a system of abbreviated numerals of Morse Code. The substitution for each of the ten digits is as follows:

1 = N	4 = M	7 = R	0 = O
2 = Z	5 = A	8 = W	
3 = S	6 = T	9 = V	

The receiving Japanese radioman at Headquarters, Southern Army, copied the numerical equivalents of the Morse Code. He entered them on his prescribed

Figure 1.3

The Mainline Radio Network, Imperial General Headquarters

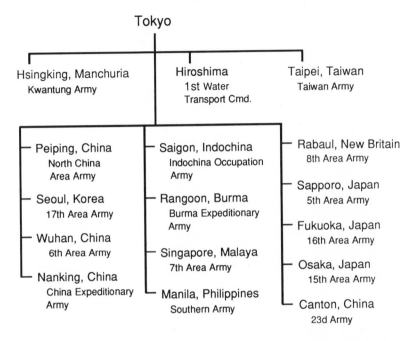

Tokyo

Hsingking, Manchuria	Hiroshima	Taipei, Taiwan
Kwantung Army	1st Water	Taiwan Army
	Transport Cmd.	

Peiping, China
North China
Area Army

Seoul, Korea
17th Area Army

Wuhan, China
6th Area Army

Nanking, China
China Expeditionary
Army

Saigon, Indochina
Indochina Occupation
Army

Rangoon, Burma
Burma Expeditionary
Army

Singapore, Malaya
7th Area Army

Manila, Philippines
Southern Army

Rabaul, New Britain
8th Area Army

Sapporo, Japan
5th Area Army

Fukuoka, Japan
16th Area Army

Osaka, Japan
15th Area Army

Canton, China
23d Army

Source: Nakamura Fumio, "Gunji tsushinshi hanashi: Daihon'ei to tsushin" [Stories about the history of military communications], Denpu to Juken (September 1982): 105.

message form and marked it for retransmission at Manila's next scheduled transmission to Second Area Army at Davao.

Half a world away, Americans listened at United States Intercept Station Number 2, Petaluma, California. The station, just 35 miles north of San Francisco on Highway 101, was responsible for intercepting IGHQ radio transmissions to Manila. For that reason, Traffic Analysis and Control personnel routinely monitored known and suspected Japanese army radio frequencies. They overheard the Tokyo-Manila radio test and informed the American intercept operator to monitor a schedule between Tokyo and Manila on frequency 7190-6720 kilocycles at 2330 Tokyo Time.

The intercept operator, a U.S. Army private first-class, intercepted the dots and dashes from Tokyo to Manila and recorded them on a prescribed form. The

Figure 1.4. The Japanese Army Message in Figure 1.2
Transmitted in Morse Code

(RONSE/RONSE)[a]

7190/6720[b]   12022343[c]   (A)[d]   US00298367[e]

MA[f]   57[g]   MVN[h]   MW[i]   NZ/ZZMO[j]

NWWR NRRS SVRZ[k]

DD 6635 = 4767[l]

[m]ZSMA TVTT ZWOM TZMV MMWN ZMZN WSRT TNSA RVVM VARO
NNNA OSNZ ZZWM TWRO TAWS AZOR NSVR STWV RZVO NWTN
WVMM NVWO SWMW WMZW RWPZ NWTM RMVV SAWW WAWA
NNVV TVAZ VRAV SZON ZRAO OTMT RWRN ARTA TOWA VMNA
NMWV WMNO MWSA ASMO VSMT SVMS OOVO TZMV VE[n]

[a]Circuit call between Tokyo and Manila
[b]Kilocycles to 7190 kilocycles from 6720.
[c]Day, month, and hour of interception (Tokyo time)
[d]Classification of quality of intercept
[e]Intercept station number and teletype transmission number
[f]Routing instruction indicating relay
[g]Circuit number
[h]Originating message center number
[i]Group count
[j]File date and time
[k]Enciphered address
[l]Geographic code indicating point of origin and destination
[m]Text of message including discriminant and key cipher groups
[n]Prodedure signal indicating end of message

Source: History of the SSA, Vol. 3: The Japanese Army Problem: Cryptanalysis, 1942–45, 23,
    Record Group 457, U.S. National Archives and Records Administration, Washington, D.C.

enciphered Japanese message was gobbledegook to the American (see Figure 1.4).
Its contents bespoke the mind-numbing tedium that characterized any intercept
operator's eight-to-twelve-hour workday. Intercept operators never learned the
meaning of the messages they intercepted. The intercept site commander sent all
intercepts to the U.S. Army Signal Security Agency at Arlington Hall in the
Virginia suburbs just outside Washington, D.C., for decryption and analysis. Day
in and day out intercept operators all over the world copied seeming gibberish in a
monotonous yet absolutely vital job.

    When the Signal Security Agency broke the Japanese four-digit code numbers,
the message did not revert to the Japanese ideographs. Since few Americans could

read these ideographs, the Signal Security Agency transliterated them into Roman letters *(Romaji)*.

DAI ICHI. DAI JU YON SHIDAN WO DAI SAN HOMEN GUN NOO HENSO YORI WO NOZOKU DAI NI GUN SENTO JORETSU HENNYU SHI DAI NIJU KU SHIDAN WO KANTOGUN HENSO YORI WO NOZUKU DAI HACHI HOMEN GUN SENTO JORETSU HENNYU SHI.

The translation of this decryption was:

Paragraph 1. The 14th Division is deleted from the Third Area Army Order of Battle and enrolled in the Second Area Army Order of Battle. Paragraph 2. The 29th Division is removed from the Kwantung Army Order of Battle and enrolled in the Eighth Area Army Order of Battle.

This routine transmission confirmed previously announced unit transfers of the 29th Division to the Marianas in February and the 14th Division to the Palaus in March 1944. The extraordinary significance of this ordinary administrative signal lay in the U.S. Army's ability to decipher and translate it. However, American ability to decrypt the Imperial Army's most secret communications was far from a miracle. Rather, it was the result of years of heartbreaking and sometimes mind-shattering effort.

No intelligence was gained from decryptions of Japanese army communications from December 7, 1941, to June 1943.[4] Even after mid-1943, routine Japanese army changes to the key register quickly frustrated further American exploitation of that initial ephemeral advantage. American cryptanalysts could not simply reverse the encryption process to break the message without all of the cryptographic materials the Japanese army message centers employed. Rather, they had to attack the cipher by stages. Thus cryptanalysts searched for clues to the fundamental connections between the multifarious cryptographic elements.

Besides these cryptanalytic problems, the Japanese language itself posed a barrier to most American intelligence analysts. An official document described Japanese as "amounting almost to a cryptologic system."[5] Translation difficulties not found in its Axis German or Italian counterparts persisted with the Japanese language. The prevalence of homonyms in Japanese could bedevil the erstwhile translator. For instance, *"kaisen"* might mean "decisive engagement," "sea battle," "opening of hostilities," "ghost ship," "barge," "rotation," "reelection," or "itch." If the U.S. translator had access to Chinese ideographs, upon which the Japanese written language is based, the meaning could quickly be understood, but since only the *Romaji* was at hand, the translator had a problem. A spelling was easy to find in the dictionary, but the translator still had to use his or her imagination to select the suitable word within the context of the message to render "*kaisen*" accurately.[6] Although intelligence analysts might recognize key words in a message, they might not be able to render the context of the signal into intelligible English. Some knowledge, no matter how limited, of Japanese was desirable at a very early stage of code solution. It was almost indispensable at many other stages before the actual translation.

The special characteristics of Japanese military communications also hampered attempts to exploit them. Abbreviations and code words abounded in Japanese military messages. Second Area Army was "KI" (brilliant), so Message 98 from Second Area Army chief of staff would appear as "KI HO SAN DEN DAI KUJUHACHI GO," a shortened form of KI HOMENGUN DENPO SANBOCHO DAI KUJUHACHI GO (Second Area Army chief of staff signal number 98). Cloaked behind the double veils of sophisticated ciphers and complex language, the Japanese army believed its radio communications codes were unbreakable. Japanese communications officers were convinced that they had learned much from their earlier rude initiation into the perils of using insecure codes.

The U.S. War Department, Military Intelligence Division (MID), was the G-2 (Intelligence) directorate for the General Staff from 1918 to 1942. One of its branches, MI-8, was the army cryptanalytic service. MI-8 had broken Japanese naval and diplomatic codes in the early 1920s. Led by Herbert O. Yardley, a short, balding, hugely egotistical cryptanalyst, the handful of civilian and military code-breakers in MI-8 basked in praise. The State Department used the resulting intelligence windfall to great advantage during the Washington Peace Conference of 1921-22. Afterward, State and MID both funded Yardley's so-called Black Chamber. Then a series of parsimonious budgets, capped by the State Department's decision in 1929 to withdraw all funding, put Yardley out of business. Yardley was a ladies' man always in need of money for his amorous adventures. Thoroughly disgruntled and anxious to recoup his finances, Yardley exposed the exploits of his small group in a sensational best-seller, *The American Black Chamber,* published in 1931.[7]

Meanwhile, a similar U.S. Army organization, the Code and Cipher Section, Office of the Chief Signal Officer, was compiling codes and ciphers for the army. Since 1921, William F. Friedman had directed its efforts. If Yardley depended on inspiration to crack codes, Friedman relied on precision. Everything about this stylishly dressed man, including his tiny mustache, announced a fastidious nature. In early 1929, the army transferred its cryptanalytic functions from the G-2 to the Signal Corps. That December Friedman took charge of the newly created Signal Intelligence Service (SIS), which was under the control of the Signal Corps. His small band worked in the rear wing of the second floor of a decrepit wooden structure, the Munitions Building, on Constitution Avenue in Washington, D.C.

Yardley's revelations caused the Japanese Foreign Ministry to replace their exist-ing manual encoding systems with a newly developed cipher machine. In effect, the Signal Intelligence Service, thrown back to square one, had to begin anew to solve Japanese communication ciphers.[8]

As director of the SIS until mid-1935, Friedman brought three brilliant young mathematicians—Frank Rowlett, Solomon Kullback, and Abraham Sinkov—into the organization from his Code and Cipher Section. In 1930 a congressman looking for a job for his nephew approached the Signal Intelligence Service. Although he had never set foot west of the Mississippi River, the politician's nephew, John Hurt, was a superb natural linguist with an excellent command of Japanese.[9] These men, and a handful of other men and women, spent the next decade attacking the complex and sophisticated Japanese mechanical ciphers that followed in Yardley's wake.

Another of Yardley's legacies was the Federal Communications Act of 1934, which prohibited government agencies from intercepting messages between foreign countries and the United States. At this time the Signal Intelligence Serv-ice operated under the War Department's assistant chief of staff, G-2 (Intelli-gence). To comply with the law, the War Department emphasized that Friedman's group decrypted intercepted messages for purposes of training, not intelligence. However, General Malin Craig, U.S. Army chief of staff, was uncomfortable about this ambiguity and allocated only minimum funds from a depression-era budget for army codebreakers.[10] Friedman's select few pressed their attack on foreign codes and ciphers in spite of these obstacles.

By 1933 Kullback and Hurt were already solving and translating Japanese encoded messages (in the older, previously compromised code system) in a "few hours." These two men were a strange pair. Hurt was a lively, witty, rather eccentric man, the notable exception to Friedman's quest for order. Kullback was gregarious, with an ever-present smile and a football player's build. Friedman's codebreakers were generalists who increased their expertise by attacking a variety of foreign codes. Thus by the mid-1930s, Kullback headed G Section, which targeted German diplomatic messages. The tall, powerfully built Rowlett was in charge of J Section, responsible for Japanese diplomatic traffic. Sinkov worked against Japanese commercial codes and later tracked Italian ciphers. He was a short, stocky man with twinkly eyes who looked more like the high school math teacher he had been than an expert codebreaker. During the mid-1930s, Sinkov developed signal intercept sites in the Panama Canal Zone with the help of the U.S. Army signal officer in Panama, Lieutenant Colonel Spencer B. Akin. In the decade preceding the Japanese attack on Pearl Harbor, the Signal Intelligence Service, despite its diverse targets, managed to identify thirty-three Japanese coding systems. In 1935 it supplied the first translation of Japanese diplomatic traffic since the Yardley fiasco. That same year, Friedman's group attacked the "RED Machine," a machine-encrypted Japanese diplomatic system, which it solved the following year.[11]

In 1939 the Japanese Foreign Ministry introduced the famous "PURPLE Machine." Eighteen months of intensive effort were invested in solving this latest Japanese diplomatic code.[12] Akin, recently promoted colonel, returned to Washington in August 1939 to command the Signal Intelligence Service and headed the organization during the heady, hectic days of breaking PURPLE. When he reported for duty, the chief signal officer, Brigadier General Joseph O. Mauborgne, emphasized to Akin that the solution of the Japanese diplomatic system between Tokyo and Washington was the Signal Intelligence Service's most important mission.[13] General George C. Marshall, the new chief of staff, was willing to overlook the restrictive Federal Communications Act. The outbreak of war in Europe in September 1939 pitted Japan's German ally against Great Britain, which enjoyed a special relationship with the United States. It was imperative to discern Japanese intentions, ideally by reading their coded cables. Tight budgets and limited personnel, however, still dictated that the army attack only one Japanese code at a time. Consequently, the SIS aimed almost its entire decryption effort at solving the Japanese diplomatic ciphers, though at the expense of extensive study of the Imperial Army's codes.

SIS cryptanalysts did crack PURPLE, but the enormous intellectual strain involved overwhelmed Friedman, who succumbed to a nervous breakdown. The effort continued without him. Mauborgne told the U.S. Navy of the breakthrough, and together the services developed a system for sharing PURPLE and other diplomatic material. Within the army, the resulting decryptions of Japanese diplomatic traffic were known as "MAGIC" because General Mauborgne referred to his cryptanalyic team as "magicians."[14]

The PURPLE solution depended on an "analog" machine that decrypted machine-enciphered Japanese diplomatic traffic. A mechanical solution facilitated breaking the code, but the Japanese changed the key to the code each day. They altered the set of keys in ten-day increments. A twenty-seven-year-old navy lieutenant (j.g.), Francis A. Raven, solved the master key. His insight meant that cryptanalysts had to uncover the new keys only every ten days. The PURPLE Machine could then decipher encrypted Japanese diplomatic messages for the next nine days, at which point the cycle began again.[15] The U.S. Army built eight PURPLE Machines. By October 1941, four machines remained in Washington, two each under army and navy auspices; three were in London; and one, under navy control, was on the island of Corregidor.[16]

This cryptanalytic effort was one element of the U.S. Army's preparations for war. In February 1941 Colonel Akin had departed the SIS for Third Army. He served as Major General Walter Krueger's chief signal officer during the Louisiana

Maneuvers of 1941. That summer General Douglas MacArthur, commanding general of the newly established U.S. Army Forces in the Far East, personally requested Akin for his chief signal officer.[17] Akin maintained communication channels at MacArthur's headquarters in Manila and was not involved with any interception or decryption work. However, Akin was aware from his SIS days that Station 6, just outside the gate of Fort McKinley in the Manila suburbs, intercepted Japanese radio traffic. He also knew that a PURPLE Machine was operating on Corregidor. Yet he had no authority over these hush-hush units.

Instead, the U.S. Navy operated its own signal facility in the Philippines. Under the command of Lieutenant Rudolph J. Fabian, ten officers and fifty-one enlisted men maintained a PURPLE Machine at Monkey Point, Fort Mills, Corregidor. Fabian's men broke Japanese diplomatic systems in a specially constructed, air-conditioned tunnel. Only MacArthur and Admiral Thomas C. Hart, commander of the U.S. Asiatic Fleet, Manila, received decrypted Japanese intercepts from this source.[18] In late July 1941, Lieutenant Colonel Richard K. Sutherland, MacArthur's new chief of staff, who was promoted directly to brigadier general in August, was placed on the distribution list for MAGIC, which special couriers hand-carried to his office.

The U.S. Army's Station 6, manned by two officers and sixteen enlisted men of the 2d Signal Service Company, communicated directly to the Signal Intelligence Service. It, too, was exempt from Akin's control. Major Joe T. Sherr, the station commander, at first reported exclusively to MacArthur. Sherr's men focused on intercepting PURPLE and other Japanese diplomatic systems, not military communications. They then sent the reenciphered, transcribed intercepts to the Munitions Building in Washington, D.C. Station 6 also provided copies for Fabian's U.S. Navy detachment, called "CAST." CAST was about 30 miles from MacArthur's headquarters across Manila Bay. It might as well have been 30,000 miles away. Rigid security procedures created a three-day delay between the time Sherr's men intercepted a Japanese message and Fabian's unit made a decrypted translation available for delivery to MacArthur.[19] One of Sherr's men, for example, might intercept a Japanese message on Monday. On Tuesday a Station 6 courier exchanged the intercept at the Manila docks with the CAST courier for decrypted traffic. On Wednesday Fabian's courier returned the decrypted Monday intercept. Then the intelligence went to MacArthur. Sutherland normally first read the MAGIC file. If he thought that it contained items of interest to the general, he sent the Station 6 courier into MacArthur's office. Security considerations excluded MacArthur's G-2 officer, Colonel Charles A. Willoughby, from MAGIC distribution. This anomaly continued after the outbreak of hostilities with Japan.

The War Department purposely limited the dissemination of MAGIC in order to conceal from the Japanese that Americans were reading their encrypted diplomatic messages. The theory assumed the fewer people privy to a secret, the fewer chances existed to reveal the secret. Commonly referred to as "need to know," it worked well enough in peacetime, but the added pressures of wartime decision-making required more timely access to such special intelligence. Before Pearl Harbor, the Signal Intelligence Service achieved security by sacrificing timeliness and with it the operational needs of the theater commanders at Pearl Harbor and Manila. If an intelligence officer's cardinal sin was to reveal the source of his information to other than the select few, then his second deadly sin was to bring a commander a highly classified report that had just been broadcast over a commercial radio network.

Second Lieutenant Howard W. Brown faced just that mortification when he handed General Sutherland a decrypted Japanese diplomatic message breaking off negotiations with the United States. Five hours earlier, somber announcers on Manila's commercial radio station had shocked listeners with news of the devastating Japanese attack on Pearl Harbor. Sutherland sarcastically noted the timeliness of the message and demanded that Brown explain how such an important message could have been delayed by intelligence channels to the point of uselessness.[20] The wartime debut of special intelligence in MacArthur's headquarters was a clumsy gaffe.

As mentioned earlier, the U.S. Army had made sporadic efforts to monitor and intercept Imperial Army communications during the 1930s, but insufficient funds, equipment failures, and lack of interest soon terminated those half-hearted attempts.[21] The Signal Intelligence Service instead invested its talents and budget in the solution of Japanese diplomatic ciphers. However, success against this one machine cipher did not translate into penetration of all Japanese ciphers because the Imperial Army and Navy each employed entirely different cipher systems than the Foreign Ministry.

The Japanese naval code relied on a five-digit encryption method. A petty officer first looked up the word he wished to encode in the navy codebook. Say the petty officer wanted to encode "battleship." Opposite "battleship" was a five-digit numeral, 52194. He replaced "battleship" with 52194. Next the petty officer reached for a key register. He located the proper page, column, row, and line according to the daily key in effect. Then, reading down, he randomly selected five-digit numbers. The petty officer, like his army counterpart, used "false" addition to add this number, say 39682, to 52194 for a total of 81776. Now enciphered, "battleship" had changed from 52194 to 81776.[22]

The U.S. Navy, besides assisting the army in the solution of diplomatic codes, had consistently monitored the Imperial Japanese Navy's codes since the 1920s. With no other potential naval adversaries during most of the interwar years, the U.S. Navy could afford to concentrate its intelligence resources on Japan. From the late 1920s, it frequently eavesdropped on Imperial Navy peacetime fleet exercises. During the 1920s and 1930s, the U.S. Navy intercepted extensive Japanese naval message traffic. It analyzed the voluminous signal patterns to deduce Japanese naval tactics during fleet exercises. The navy also studied JN-25, the main naval operational code. In short, by the time of the Japanese attack on Pearl Harbor, the American navy had a cryptanalytic infrastructure with extensive practical experience against Japanese diplomatic and naval codes with perhaps forty officers capable of reading Japanese.[23] This groundwork allowed U.S. Navy codebreakers during the opening months of the Pacific war to far outpace their army counterparts. For instance, navy cryptanalysts first penetrated JN-25 in September 1940, nearly three years earlier than the U.S. Army's initial break into Japanese army ciphers.[24]

This condition paralleled the Japanese military intelligence experience. During the Russo-Japanese War (1904–1905), the Imperial Navy had intercepted Russian fleet messages. In 1923, Japanese navy intercept operators aboard the cruiser *Yuhara* had listened in on American fleet exercises off Hawaii. Exactly when the Imperial Army entered into the arcane world of signal intelligence remains a mystery, but documents from 1920 clearly show that the army was monitoring the broadcasts of the U.S. Navy's China Fleet as well as Nationalist Chinese communications from a series of listening posts in China. Like their future opponents, the Japanese divided codebreaking responsibilities between the army and navy. The Japanese army effort targeted the Asian continent, with emphasis on solving Soviet ciphers. The navy took over the Pacific, centering its activities on the U.S. Fleet. The huge signal intercept sites at Jaluit, in the Marshall islands, and at Owada, just northwest of Tokyo, eavesdropped on U.S. Fleet and American diplomatic communications, respectively. By November 1940, a five-man Japanese intercept team in Mexico was listening in on the radio message traffic of the U.S. Fleet stationed on the West Coast of the United States. In contrast to this well-developed network, at the outbreak of the Pacific war the Imperial Army found itself without a comprehensive technical knowledge of U.S. Army communications systems or sufficient personnel to meet the heavy demands of combat operations.[25]

As for the Americans, a decade of restrictive security practices proved impossible to surmount overnight. MacArthur's subordinate field commanders in the Philippines were unaware of the advantages signal intelligence offered. The notion of capitalizing on information derived from reading enemy communications seemed to many of them hopelessly exotic and unreliable. When Akin, Sherr, and Brown unveiled their previously restricted intelligence treasures to Army Air Corps and Air Warning Service officers, they encountered disbelief. They were, after all, asking operational commanders to make major tactical decisions on the basis of electronic dots, dashes, and blips that only a skilled communications or signal intelligence operative could interpret. The technological ignorance of U.S. Army officers was staggering. Akin spent much time reassuring air commanders

Willoughby visits Akin's headquarters, Bataan, 1942. Left to right: Charles A. Willoughby, Spencer B. Akin, unidentified officer, Joe R. Sherr, unidentified officer. (Joe R. Sherr Collection, MacArthur Memorial Bureau of Archives)

that radar and radio signal intercepts did, in fact, provide legitimate early warning of impending air raids.[26]

The outbreak of war in the Pacific redirected the efforts of the Signal Intelligence Service and Station 6 to Japanese military traffic. Station 6 shifted priorities from monitoring Japanese diplomatic radio frequencies to intercepting tactical military circuits. Its primary mission now was to support MacArthur, so Station 6 was incorporated into his headquarters under Akin's control. Entirely new Japanese military radio networks blossomed almost overnight. An enormous volume of operational Japanese radio message traffic became available to intercept operators at Station 6, enabling them to reconstruct quickly the Japanese naval air force's communications network. Station 6 also provided early warning of the approach or targets of Japanese aircraft by intercepting plain-text Japanese air-ground messages. These scattered successes created a few believers among skeptical field commanders.

Following the major Japanese landings and the rapid Japanese advance toward Manila in December 1941, Station 6 redeployed to Corregidor on a grim Christmas

Eve. From Corregidor, it continued to intercept Japanese tactical circuits in the Philippines, monitor Japanese army air force communications, and listen to Japanese weather station broadcasts.[27] The ability to understand Japanese was at a premium, so Sherr turned to second-generation Japanese-Americans (nisei) for help. In the months just before Pearl Harbor, several FBI-trained nisei had been dispatched from Hawaii to spy on the Japanese population in the Philippines. These Japanese-Americans now found themselves pressed into service as translators of plain-text Japanese voice transmissions intercepted by Station 6. G-2 also used nisei to interrogate Japanese prisoners of war and to translate captured documents. When MacArthur retreated from Manila to Corregidor in February 1942, he took these nisei to Station 6, which was already ensconced on "the Rock."[28]

As the Japanese army bottled up the American and Philippine defenders on Bataan and Corregidor, it was foreordained that without reinforcements and supplies the Philippines were doomed. Senior intelligence officers determined that the U.S. Army and Navy signal intelligence units had to be evacuated from Corregidor. The detachments had acquired irreplaceable combat experience against Japanese radio traffic during the Japanese offensive in the Philippines. U.S. Army intelligence would capitalize on this bittersweet circumstance throughout the war. Station 6, for example, had identified the Japanese air-ground communications system and the principal Japanese army and navy air force communications networks from a captured codebook. It had also demonstrated that signal intelligence provided early warning about enemy air raids and aircraft movements. This rudimentary effort was the wedge that opened operations for MacArthur's cryptanalysts in Australia later on.[29] For the navy, Fabian's unit represented a significant portion of the limited number of signal intelligence personnel who had combat experience in cryptanalysis and decryption, radio intercept, as well as radio direction finding, against the Japanese.

Besides the loss of cryptanalytic expertise, another factor drove the decision to evacuate American codebreakers from Corregidor: the possibility that the Japanese would capture and torture the American cryptanalysts, forcing them to betray codebreaking successes. This might have been disastrous to the American war effort, for such revelations would have alerted the Japanese to the porous state of their diplomatic and naval ciphers and codes. Wholesale changes would have followed, just as happened after Yardley's exposé, and a decade's worth of American cryptanalytic toil would have gone for naught. Thus the U.S. Navy started the evacuation of Fabian's group and the PURPLE Machine for Australia by submarine on February 4, 1942. MacArthur announced on March 8, from Corregidor, that Fabian's detachment, an Australian unit, and a small British communications intelligence unit from Singapore would establish themselves in Melbourne, Australia. The conglomeration became Fleet Radio Unit, Melbourne, or FRUMEL.

Fabian and the last of his men from Corregidor arrived at Melbourne in April. By May 1942 FRUMEL had plunged once again into the world of deciphering Japanese naval and diplomatic signals.[30]

The army acted more slowly. It began an aerial evacuation of Station 6 personnel on March 27. This tardiness enabled the Japanese, when they overran Corregidor in May 1942, to capture six enlisted men from the intercept station. Only one lived through the Japanese routine of brutality meted out to all prisoners of war, although their captors apparently never suspected the intelligence role performed by these captives.[31] Station 6's survivors reassembled in Australia and formed the nucleus of General MacArthur's combined U.S.-Australian signal intelligence organization then being organized in Melbourne.

MacArthur himself arrived in Melbourne to a hero's welcome on March 21, 1942. He quickly set to work establishing his new command, General Headquarters, Southwest Pacific Area (SWPA). He organized his forces into four subordinate commands designated as Allied Land Forces, Allied Air Forces, Allied Naval Forces, and United States Army Forces in Australia.[32] Except for three officers, MacArthur's General Headquarters staff consisted of men who had served with him on Bataan. Among this Bataan Gang, Akin produced signal intelligence, Willoughby analyzed it, and Sutherland normally determined whether nor not MacArthur saw it. Two outsiders also became involved in the intelligence chain. They were Brigadier General Stephen J. Chamberlin, MacArthur's G-3 (Operations) officer, and General Thomas A. Blamey, commander of the Allied Land Forces.

Sutherland was, by his own admission, the Southwest Pacific theater's "S.O.B." or hatchet man. MacArthur's chief of staff was the exacting taskmaster every commander needs, and Sutherland enjoyed the role. His foul temper, large ego, and autocratic manner offended nearly every officer who crossed his path. Lieutenant General Robert L. Eichelberger, a corps and army commander for MacArthur, and no shrinking violet, described Sutherland as an untrustworthy "natural climber." Eichelberger wrote to his wife that Sutherland "will cheerfully cut our throats if we present him any advantage." The chief of staff was a brilliant loner and an indefatigable worker on a sixteen-hours-a-day basis. Sutherland's intensity complemented the perfectionist strain in MacArthur. He was closest to MacArthur and cast the operational recommendations for the general's final approval. But Sutherland's habit of running roughshod over other officers, treating them with contempt or condescension, left him without the respect of his peers. Learning of Sutherland's death, General Walter Krueger, himself seriously ill, remarked that "it was a good thing for mankind."[33]

Willoughby, the G-2, was neither as bright nor as competent as Sutherland. He fluctuated between emotional extremes, shifting from melancholy brooding to temper tantrums. The sight and sound of Willoughby venting his anger in hall-

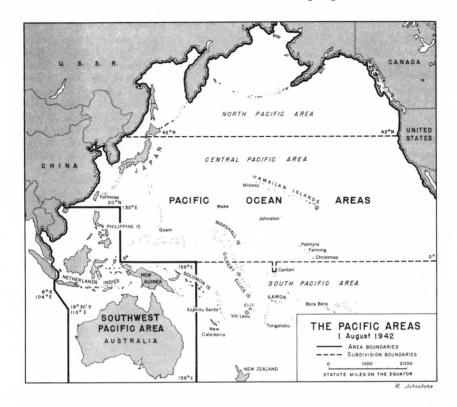

R. Johnstone

Source: Samuel Milner, *United States Army in World War II: The War in the Pacific: Victory in Papua* (Washington, D.C.: Government Printing Office, 1957).

ways, punctuating his curses with the code word "ULTRA," made the special security officers cringe and question his appreciation and understanding of ULTRA.[34] (The War Department had sent these junior officers to MacArthur's headquarters to safeguard ULTRA.) Willoughby's explosive personality, coupled with a physically intimidating 6-foot-3-inch, 220-pound frame, struck terror into field-grade staff officers. He ruled the G-2 shop with an iron hand and seemed paranoid about any outside interference. He was intimidated by Sutherland (who usually snubbed him) and disliked Chamberlin, who he felt either made unreasonable demands or ignored G-2's advice.

Willoughby had been born in Germany and affected the mannerisms of a Prussian officer, earning for himself the nickname "Sir Charles." Like many Germans of the time, Willoughby was critical of Eastern Europeans, irrationally anti-Communist, and easily dismissed as a racist. Yet when the U.S. Army was rounding up Japanese-Americans on the West Coast, Willoughby demanded that the War Department assign Japanese-Americans to his sensitive intelligence outfit. He never questioned nisei loyalty or directed racist outbursts their way. This complex officer served MacArthur unquestioningly, and in exchange MacArthur tolerated Willoughby's uneven intelligence appreciations throughout the Pacific war.[35]

Akin was the technical expert, schooled in decryption and the craft of signal communications. With extensive practical experience in both realms, he assumed the dual roles of chief signal officer of the Southwest Pacific theater and head of MacArthur's codebreaking bureau. Akin was never content to confine himself to windowless offices. Instead, he visited the front lines and rear areas to see for himself that vital communications links were properly maintained. Willoughby noted that the tall, gangly Akin looked like a younger Abe Lincoln with the same dry grass-roots wit. Sinkov saw him as stern and hard working, but nonetheless easy to get along with. Akin's men saw him differently. They claimed his signature, "S. B. Akin," should be changed to read "S.O.B. Akin." A man of few words, Akin was a demanding overseer who once relieved an entire signal company on the spot for ineffectiveness. He enjoyed unique access to MacArthur, but because of his codebreaking work, he always lurked in the shadows.[36]

Chamberlin, the G-3, was an outsider by virtue of not having served with MacArthur on Bataan. MacArthur selected him as operations chief because of Chamberlin's excellent work as chief of staff for United States Army Forces in Australia where he had devoted most of his effort to moving supplies to the Philippines. Chamberlin was a talented officer and superb planner who was able to translate MacArthur's often ethereal concepts into reality. A man who did not suffer fools, Chamberlin guarded his domain closely and resented unsolicited recommendations. Sweat not inspiration was his trademark. He pored over details to ensure success. MacArthur praised Chamberlin as "a master of tactical detail and possessed of bold strategic concepts."[37] Once MacArthur decided on an operation, Chamberlin, Sutherland, and the appropriate army or corps commanders worked out the details to implement his concept.

Australian Thomas Blamey was MacArthur's only foreign senior subordinate. This short, stout man, sporting a neatly trimmed white mustache, looked anything but a fighting general. However, many officers who judged him only by his appearance left his office nonplussed, for Blamey had a quick mind and dominating personality. Far from a caricature of an overaged, doddering fool, Blamey was a crude, blunt, and effective soldier. He was both tough and competent enough to stand up to MacArthur and the Bataan Gang.[38]

These key staff officers were the ones who produced, analyzed, and delivered ULTRA to MacArthur and shaped the course of the war against Japan. Like any staff, their commander was the unifying force who demanded their loyalty and made the final decision on their recommendations.

In March 1942 MacArthur was already larger than life, and he remains a controversial figure seemingly wrapped in contradictions. A legitimate hero, he craved ever-greater glory and recognition. Brilliant, articulate, and imaginative, he also displayed paranoia, arrogance, and such a sense of histrionics that one of his army commanders derided him behind his back as "Sarah," after the famous French actress Sarah Bernhardt. Always fearful of Washington or a "European clique," MacArthur shielded his staff from outsiders, even when they were wrong. In return he demanded, and received, unquestioning loyalty. He inspired worship or revulsion, but not affection. The general was a perfectionist who together with Sutherland outworked lesser mortals on his staff. MacArthur's sense of destiny propelled his staff and made them work together despite their aberrations.[39] In the spring of 1942, a defeated MacArthur was already planning for his return to the Philippines. In his path was a powerful opponent, flushed with victory, whose offensive remained unchecked. MacArthur's foremost task was to stop the advancing Japanese.

One of the general's first appeals to the War Department was for cryptanalytic support. On April 1 MacArthur requested that Washington send trained cryptanalysts to Australia to supplement the "few individuals that I have brought from the Philippines."[40] Delays and transmission uncertainties occasioned by the great distances between Washington and Melbourne, he told the War Department, mandated local control over the interception and decryption of Japanese signals. Indeed, Allied forces were already organizing such a decryption center. Two days later Chief of Staff Marshall advised MacArthur that ten officers and eight enlisted men of the Signal Intelligence Service would depart by air for Australia at "an early date" to establish a communications intelligence unit. He also instructed MacArthur to let the War Department know his headquarters' IBM equipment needs and additional personnel estimates. Marshall's choice of words acknowledged that MacArthur would have his own independent signal intelligence center.[41] This apparently casual decision later proved controversial.

The first contingent of American signal intelligence personnel, six officers and eight enlisted men of the 837th Signal Service Detachment, departed the United States in mid-April. The group took several days to reach Australia. They encountered numerous delays traveling as passengers without special priority on military aircraft. Kullback, who had prewar experience in Hawaii, was originally selected to command the unit, but he turned down the assignment to stay in Washington with his wife and family. Sinkov, who had gotten married only a few weeks earlier, had twice worked with Akin and so went in Kullback's place. He left in June with the second American group of three officers and twelve enlisted men, and when they arrived at MacArthur's headquarters in Melbourne, Major Sinkov took command of the 837th Detachment, the American component of Central Bureau, the Southwest Pacific theater's codebreaking organization.[42]

The first American cryptanalysts in front of the Henry Street headquarters of Central Bureau, 1943. Abraham Sinkov is in the middle of the front row. Joseph E. Richard is on the extreme right of the front row. (U.S. Army Signal Corps photo, courtesy of Joseph E. Richard)

Central Bureau was activated by MacArthur on April 15, 1942, after a conference of all services. This signal intercept organization comprised U.S. and Australian Army and Royal Australian Air Force signal units.[43] Veteran intercept operators of the Australian Special Wireless group (who had worked against General Erwin Rommel's Afrika Corps in North Africa) and members of a British signal detachment evacuated from Singapore formed the Australian Army contingent. They joined Lieutenant Brown's survivors of Station 6, who pooled their talents with the 837th contingent and the first Operating Platoon, 121st (later redesignated 126th) Signal Radio Intelligence Company, from Fort Dix, New Jersey.[44]

Central Bureau was directed by Akin and had a fourfold mission. First and foremost, it was a cryptanalytic agency charged with providing MacArthur with radio intelligence derived from Japanese military signals. Second, the bureau was responsible for Allied communications security throughout MacArthur's domain. Third, Central Bureau worked closely with the Signal Intelligence Service at Arlington Hall just outside Washington, D.C., to solve Japanese army codes by daily exchanging data about the Japanese cryptographic system. Finally, it supplied and exchanged intelligence with the U.S. Navy and the British in adjacent theaters as appropriate.[45]

Akin's relationship to Willoughby, whom he outranked, was originally patterned on the prewar Station 6 model. Under that procedure, the G-2 was excluded from seeing the results of cryptanalysis. Central Bureau bypassed Willoughby by sending a courier with the daily siftings of Japanese radio traffic to Akin's office. He determined which items were significant enough to warrant MacArthur's attention. As Central Bureau's chief, Akin enjoyed the prerogative of passing important raw (unanalyzed) decryptions directly to MacArthur, although he was bureaucratically shrewd enough always to inform MacArthur's alter ego, Sutherland, first. With Sutherland's approval, Akin transmitted pertinent intelligence from the decryptions directly to field commands over Southwest Pacific Headquarters' signal channel. Akin's unique, unscheduled, direct access to MacArthur continued throughout the war. As late as October 1944, for instance, a War Department representative reported to Washington that Willoughby received only delayed information copies of ULTRA. In brief, the Southwest Pacific theater's G-2 exercised no operational control over Central Bureau.[46]

Willoughby's job was to analyze raw decryptions and data that Central Bureau produced—in other words, to place the decryptions into a military context, thereby transforming data into processed ULTRA. The setup was similar to the relationship between the War Department G-2 and the Signal Intelligence Service. Arlington Hall was supposed to intercept, decipher, and translate into English any enemy message it could read. Thereafter, the translation passed from it into the hands of intelligence analysts in the War Department G-2 across the Potomac River. This division of labor between highly technical cryptanalytic competence and specialized knowledge of Japanese characteristics persisted in MacArthur's theater during the war, although in December 1944 the War Department centralized the production of ULTRA under the control of the assistant chief of staff for intelligence.[47]

Converting Morse Code dots and dashes into military intelligence in the Southwest Pacific theater began at one of the scattered intercept sites. An intercept operator copied a coded Japanese radio broadcast and transmitted his reenciphered results to Central Bureau. Cryptanalysts in Melbourne attempted to decipher the code system or, if they were unable to do so, glean technical data from the message. In either case, Central Bureau radioed all its technical findings to Arlington Hall. During peak periods, such as just before Allied invasions, Central Bureau might borrow members of Willoughby's Allied Translator and Interpreter Section (ATIS) or the U.S. Navy to ensure complete coverage of decrypted Japanese radio messages.[48] Translated decryptions went through Sinkov, who determined the items that a courier would hand-carry from Central Bureau to Akin at Southwest Pacific Headquarters. The Signal Corps's responsibility ended when Akin passed the English language version of the Japanese message to Sutherland and MacArthur, who decided what to do about the information. As a rule, Central

Bureau's cryptanalysts did not learn the results of their work. Sinkov passed word of major successes, such as torpedoed Japanese ships, but otherwise the process of cryptanalysis was all-consuming and totally compartmentalized.

The analysis of Central Bureau's ULTRA fell to Willoughby, who received rather than produced special intelligence. His intelligence specialists analyzed raw decrypts and intercepts that Central Bureau, the U.S. Navy, and Allied signal intelligence units provided. G-2 integrated ULTRA with other intelligence sources—aerial reconnaissance, agent reports, captured Japanese documents, prisoner of war interrogations, and so forth—to prepare theater estimates and intelligence appreciations for MacArthur.

Willoughby organized G-2's Order of Battle Section in August 1942. At that time Central Bureau was unable to decipher Japanese army codes, so the only ULTRA available to MacArthur's headquarters was produced by the U.S. Navy. Members of the Order of Battle shop initially tracked Japanese ground and army air forces in the Southwest Pacific Area by traditional intelligence methods—prisoner of war interrogations, captured documents, and air sightings. Later, in mid-1943, when army-produced ULTRA became available in quantity, Central Bureau regularly sent the Order of Battle Section intelligence it had obtained from decrypted Japanese army radio messages. By early 1944 Sutherland gave Central Bureau blanket authority to route ULTRA messages with intelligence about Japanese army units directly to Captain (later Lieutenant Colonel) George L. Magruder, head of the Order of Battle Section. Magruder took cryptic notes for his section's use in order to conceal the exact source of the intelligence. He then returned the messages to the Central Bureau courier.[49]

Magruder was a Princeton graduate who had worked with the New York City Bank in Singapore before the war. Endowed with a photographic memory and the ability to analyze materials quickly, accurately, and seemingly effortlessly, he possessed the ideal qualities demanded of an order of battle specialist. He also had an impressive supporting cast: A certified public accountant made out order of battle lists, and a former librarian at Harvard University assisted him. A prewar attorney for CBS worked with two Ivy League enlisted men to collect organizational data about Japanese ground forces. A nisei warrant officer with a degree in psychology from UCLA and three enlisted men tracked the movements of Japanese army units from the Aleutians to Burma. They entered any changes affecting a unit on an itemized card index that listed unit designation, code name, code number, commanding officer, and other pertinent information. At a glance, they could compare and contrast new intelligence with known data. Over months and years, Willoughby's Order of Battle Section constructed an accurate assessment of Japanese ground forces and air forces by unit location, strength, and equipment.[50]

The Operational Section, G-2, originally included ULTRA in its secret-level

"Daily Intelligence Summary," which was distributed throughout MacArthur's command. As greater amounts of ULTRA became available to the Southwest Pacific theater, Willoughby responded by inaugurating a "Special Intelligence Bulletin" (SIB) whose distribution was limited to Willoughby himself, MacArthur, Sutherland, Chamberlin, and a G-2 file copy. The name "Special Intelligence Bulletin" lasted until mid-April 1945 when the daily report became known as the "ULTRA Intelligence Summary." Regardless of name, the report was Willoughby's vehicle to appraise decryptions, offer comments, and make pronouncements. Willoughby also published special bulletins as warranted by theater demands. Except for a few spectacular and well-publicized occasions, the Special Intelligence Bulletin was informational not operational in nature.

Comments on a particular decrypt often revealed that MacArthur had already set forces into motion based on the raw intercepts that formed the basis for a specific paragraph in the SIB. On one occasion, a Central Bureau courier brought Akin a decrypt that directed the Japanese air commander at Hollandia to evacuate all his aircraft immediately because the Japanese suspected an Allied air raid was imminent. Akin promptly took the message to MacArthur's air commander, who, in turn, ordered the schedule for the attack accelerated. Allied pilots had already bombed the airfield by the time the ULTRA appeared in Willoughby's March 31, 1944, report.[51]

Less spectacular but in the long run more important was the work of the Plans and Estimates Section (later Plans and Estimates Group). It used ULTRA to prepare G-2 estimates (intelligence annexes) for MacArthur's operational plans. It also published a monthly summary of Japanese dispositions that was heavily laden with ULTRA. The Plans and Estimates Section often found itself in the middle of controversy because Willoughby grumbled that Chamberlin always waited until the last minute to summon him to furnish an intelligence estimate for an impending operation.[52]

External distribution of Central Bureau's labors depended upon whether the information was technical (that is, dealing with cryptanalysis) or analytical (that is, concerning intelligence). The two paths rarely crossed. Cryptanalytic aspects (Japanese codebook additive numbers, code numbers, and so on) were disseminated horizontally from Central Bureau to Arlington Hall as well as to British cryptanalysts in India. Intelligence analysis traveled vertically, going up from Southwest Pacific Headquarters to the War Department's Military Intelligence Service and down from both agencies to MacArthur's subordinate commands. (General Marshall had reorganized the War Department General Staff in March 1942, reducing it to a planning role. A separate, subordinate Military Intelligence Service [MIS] was established under MID to conduct MID's previous functions of collecting and producing intelligence.)

Central Bureau also had a liaison arrangement with Fabian's naval cryptanalysts at Melbourne, the FRUMEL outfit. Willoughby later alleged that FRUMEL forwarded selected ULTRA to MacArthur's headquarters only when it suited the navy. The record suggests otherwise. Technical distinctions between Japanese naval, ground, and air code systems made joint cryptanalytic cooperation unprofitable. Because each system had its own cipher characteristics, knowledge of the naval system might not be helpful in solving the ground or air codes. In fact, Central Bureau and FRUMEL did not exchange technical cryptanalytic material but instead—with a few notable exceptions, such as navy assistance to the army in traffic analysis techniques—worked on their separate cryptographic problems as if the other did not exist. MacArthur was satisfied with a liaison arrangement between the navy cryptanalysts at Melbourne and his codebreakers at Central Bureau because Melbourne did relay ULTRA to his headquarters.[53]

Throughout the war, naval ULTRA reached MacArthur via several channels. In 1942 Fabian reported daily to MacArthur's office and briefed the general and his chief of staff on "all information obtained or received" from Japanese diplomatic and naval communications.[54] Fabian also carried the MAGIC Diplomatic Summary, a synopsis of decrypted Japanese diplomatic message traffic, to Sutherland and MacArthur. Willoughby was initially excluded from MAGIC. Once, after showing the MAGIC Summary to MacArthur, Fabian ostentatiously burned it in a wastebasket next to Willoughby's desk. Such theatrics hardly improved the mercurial G-2's receptivity to ULTRA.[55] Willoughby had little recourse because MacArthur did not control Fabian's unit. It reported to the director of Naval Intelligence, Seventh Fleet, and the Office of Naval Intelligence, Washington, D.C.

When MacArthur moved his headquarters forward during his campaigns, Fabian stayed in Melbourne. From that site he transmitted a daily summary of naval ULTRA to the naval staff officer with MacArthur's Southwest Pacific Headquarters. This officer conducted the navy's daily briefing to MacArthur. As a theater commander, MacArthur also received the U.S. Navy's ULTRA summaries and daily bulletins, which were transmitted to his headquarters in encrypted form. In early 1942 naval ULTRA went to the Combined Operational Intelligence Centre (COIC) in MacArthur's headquarters. It then made its way to MacArthur and his staff, either directly or via the G-2's Daily Intelligence Summary. An unintentional consequence was that the navy saw its own intelligence reappearing in Southwest Pacific theater reports to the War Department.[56]

As for army ULTRA, the Military Intelligence Division (MID) at the War Department forwarded raw decryptions of Japanese radio messages, with or without comment, to Sutherland, who determined appropriate action and dissemination. Such intelligence usually did not reach Central Bureau because it was nontechnical in nature. Willoughby was the more likely recipient, and Sutherland showed him War Department ULTRA in the privacy of the chief of staff's office. By early 1944, after special security officers had arrived in the Southwest Pacific theater, the War

Department dispatched the MAGIC Summary to them and they delivered it personally to Willoughby. Central Bureau was not on distribution for this report. Intelligence derived from traffic analysis, discussed in the next chapter, went to the chief of staff, who passed it to the G-2. Sutherland later eliminated himself from this chain. Willoughby too designated several recipients in his operations section for traffic analysis.

Thus MacArthur routinely had access to a variety of naval, ground, and diplomatic ULTRA intelligence, though the quality varied. Southwest Pacific Headquarters gradually institutionalized procedures to ensure that MacArthur or his key staff were promptly apprised of significant ULTRA. Simultaneously, his own cryptanalytic agency was growing dramatically. Augmented with IBM equipment, operators, and technicians sent from Washington, Central Bureau expanded from a handful of cryptanalysts in April 1942 to more than a thousand men and women by late 1943. As it evolved, the American contingent became the Signal Intelligence Service, which replaced the 837th in May 1943. The change reflected the close ties between MacArthur's American cryptanalysts and their colleagues back home, who had moved in July 1942 from the Munitions Building to Arlington Hall. It also emphasized that both groups concentrated solely on codebreaking and did not engage in analysis of their decryptions. Sinkov became the head of Central Bureau's SIS in the fall of 1943.

Throughout the war the organization, control, and dissemination of ULTRA in MacArthur's command constantly evolved and adapted to meet the Southwest Pacific theater's operational requirements. Central Bureau itself displaced five times during the war. It followed MacArthur from Melbourne to Brisbane (September 1942). As MacArthur's offensive drew him from Australia, a core Central Bureau remained in Brisbane while advance detachments moved to Hollandia, Netherlands New Guinea (late summer 1944), to Leyte, Philippines (October 1944), to San Miguel, Luzon, Philippines (May 1945), to Tokyo (September 1945). By war's end, Central Bureau boasted more than four thousand men and women.

As more and more decrypted Japanese messages flowed into Central Bureau, three concerns impelled a reorganization. First, effective control over all intercept and direction-finding units in the vast operational area was necessary to establish effective coverage of Japanese targets. Second, the various electronic listening posts had to coordinate their efforts to avoid duplicating each other's work. Third, with so many Japanese signals filling the airwaves, priority had to be assigned to particular types of frequencies. In late August 1942 General Blamey proposed a realignment to MacArthur.[57] However, Central Bureau's relocation to Brisbane the next month preempted an immediate reorganization.

Central Bureau, Brisbane (CBB), was unimpressive in appearance. Perhaps twenty quonset huts were ensconced behind the stables of Ascot Racetrack. This site was about 5 miles east of MacArthur's Southwest Pacific Headquarters, which was located in an old insurance building on Queen Street in downtown Brisbane. Each hut housed thirty-five to forty cryptanalysts. Overaged Australian territorial militia stood guard outside a barbed-wire fence that surrounded the compound. A tent city covered the racetrack infield and served as home for enlisted troops assigned to Central Bureau. Two and a half blocks from the racetrack through Ascot Park stood Twenty-One Henry Street. This large, two-story building, encircled by a veranda, housed the cryptanalytic chiefs who directed and analyzed the technical work accomplished in the huts. Australian codebreakers worked on the first floor and Sinkov and the Americans on the second.

Akin organized Central Bureau much like its British counterpart, the Government Code and Cipher School, located at Bletchley Park about 50 miles northwest of London. At both places, each hut had a specialized cryptanalytic task and operated on the principle of strict, functional compartmentalization. Cryptanalysts of Hut A attacked Japanese air force signals, Hut B army message traffic, Hut C the Army Water Transport Code, and so forth. Overseers in a traffic-sorting office directed Japanese intercepts to the responsible hut where cryptanalysts broke the cipher message.

Cryptanalysts neither translated nor analyzed the results of their decipherments. Trained to recognize a few significant Japanese words in *Romaji*, they scanned each decrypt. If a cryptanalyst spotted a telltale word or phrase, he or she hand-carried the decrypt to the duty officer, who passed it to one of Central Bureau's Japanese language specialists working at Twenty-One Henry Street. If the duty officer and Henry Street experts deemed an intercept significant or containing perishable intelligence, it went by courier directly to Akin at the downtown headquarters. Akin rarely visited Central Bureau because he did not want to draw attention to the link between his work and that of the cryptanalysts. He occasionally called Sinkov to the headquarters to discuss technical aspects of their craft and to keep himself apprised of the direction of Central Bureau's work. Sinkov remained unaware, however, of exactly what Akin did with Central Bureau decryptions. He presumed that Akin circulated them to MacArthur and Willoughby (but he saw Willoughby only once during the entire war).[58]

During those early days, Lieutenant Colonel Sherr served as Akin's executive officer and ran the American portion of Central Bureau's daily intercept and cryptanalysis efforts, much like he had Station 6 in the Philippines. Sinkov, Wing Commander H. Roy Booth, Royal Australian Air Force, and Major Alastair W. Sandford, Australian Army—all experienced codebreakers—were the three assistant directors who provided technical guidance to the cryptanalysts. Lieutenant Brown headed an advanced section of Central Bureau that deployed to intercept sites at Townsville in northeastern Australia.[59]

Central Bureau's opening days exemplified the American rush to mobilize for total war and all the problems attendant upon such a massive undertaking. For the first six months, no more than thirty American and a like number of Australian cryptanalysts worked to solve Japanese codes at Central Bureau. According to Sinkov, the Australians, though well advanced in traffic analysis, had little cryptographic experience. For expediency's sake, the Americans assumed most of the codebreaking workload.[60]

Assignment of Signal Corps personnel to Central Bureau was at first a hit-or-miss proposition. Newly arrived American cryptanalysts reported to a nearby replacement depot, but they were just as likely to be assigned to another Signal Corps unit as to Central Bureau. Some lucky replacements ran into old friends who were working in Central Bureau and liberated them from the depot's clutches. Equipment arrived in the same haphazard way.

Following MacArthur's April 1942 request, state-of-the-art IBM equipment, including a collator, tabulator, printer, and card punchers, was shipped from the American West Coast to Sydney. In their haste to send the precious cargo, no one remembered to tell Central Bureau that it was on the way. A few months after the IBM equipment had left the U.S. mainland, a clerk discovered the shipping invoices. Akin dispatched an officer to the Sydney docks. After considerable searching, he discovered some large, grimy wooden crates on the end of a pier in Sydney harbor. The machines were quickly shifted to Brisbane, where American officers and enlisted men stripped and overhauled the sensitive machines, removing the corrosion accumulated from long exposure to salt air. These Americans, incidentally, had all been IBM employees in civilian life. After reconditioning, the IBM equipment was shifted to the newly air-conditioned and insulated three-car garage of Twenty-one Henry Street. By early 1943 Central Bureau's codebreakers were using two banks of IBM tabulators to decipher Japanese military communications.[61]

Sophisticated machinery and additional skilled technicians enabled Central Bureau to soak up greater quantities of Japanese army signals. Throughout 1942 MacArthur insisted on seeing all pertinent messages through the COIC, "regardless of the sources from which the messages are derived."[62] As the number of ULTRA items arriving at the COIC increased, so did the possibility that they might fall into the wrong hands. At this time the U.S. Army and Australian handling of ULTRA was somewhat slipshod, further diminishing security. Widespread disclosures that the allies were reading Japanese radio messages transmitted from Rabaul jeopardized the entire codebreaking effort. The U.S. Navy complained often and loudly in 1942 about Southwest Pacific Headquarters's casual treatment of ULTRA while the army lambasted the navy's apparent indifference to security.[63]

These deficiencies made evident the need for a standard system for handling ULTRA within Southwest Pacific Headquarters and disseminating it to field commanders promptly and securely. On the basis of the April agreement with Marshall, MacArthur believed that Central Bureau was *his* agency and he was reluctant to see outside controls imposed. Nonetheless, mounting pressure from Washington to implement War Department regulations governing the use and dissemination of ULTRA seemed to leave him little choice.

MacArthur reorganized Central Bureau on January 30, 1943. A few days later Sutherland told Blamey that the COIC would no longer process ULTRA for distribution. Willoughby would henceforth disseminate ULTRA to Blamey's command.[64] This decision formalized the existing division of labor between the technical functions of Central Bureau and the analytical ones of Willoughby's intelligence section. It did not resolve the larger issue of centralized control over ULTRA.

In late March 1943 the War Department alerted overseas theater commanders of forthcoming changes with regard to ULTRA procedures. The Signal Intelligence Service would hereafter assign specific missions to theater signal units and communicate directly with the theater signal officer, who would send all intercepts to Arlington Hall for translation and analysis. This struck at the heart of Akin's domain. MacArthur, by nature suspicious of outsiders, needed little encouragement from Akin to protest to Marshall about this attempt to impose external controls on Central Bureau. The Southwest Pacific commander's forceful intervention stymied "this fallacious procedure from being placed in effect."[65]

Centralized procedures had long governed the use and dissemination of ULTRA in the European war; indeed, that code word identified the source of intelligence as decrypted Axis signals. This was not the case in the Southwest Pacific theater where MacArthur consistently rejected War Department initiatives to institute similar centralized controls over his ULTRA. He thwarted successive attempts by Washington to dominate Central Bureau, insisting that the theater commander needed the independence to "produce intelligence from sources that are available locally."[66] In July 1943, for example, Major General George V. Strong, the War Department's G-2 (May 1942–February 1944), dangled the bait of direct access to decrypted Japanese intelligence in front of MacArthur. The hook was Strong's insistence that War Department special security officers handle ULTRA in each theater. MacArthur welcomed the intelligence but not the officer. He emphasized that any officer assigned to his theater had to be assigned to his command, not to the War Department. Strong tried again. In December 1943 he managed to dispatch special security officers to the Southwest Pacific theater through the efforts of Brigadier General Carter W. Clarke, chief of the Special Branch, Military Intelligence Service (MIS), War Department. MacArthur again had the last word because the officers came under his control for administration and discipline.[67] This left the War Department special security officers, usually a captain or major, at Sutherland's or Akin's mercy. As low-ranking officers trying to penetrate Southwest Pacific Headquarters' bureaucracy, they did not lead happy lives.

Letters from special security officers to General Clarke in early 1944 revealed their plight. They were excluded from Central Bureau. Sutherland refused to allow them to communicate by radio with anyone without his permission. Akin ordered Central Bureau analysts not to talk to them, and they were generally treated with suspicion. Clarke's efforts in April 1944 to remedy this situation through intelligence channels ran into a stone wall.

Willoughby saw no need for the War Department to interfere with local organizations like Central Bureau. Consequently, he rejected Clarke's proposal to allow special security officers access to the bureau because they were "simply guardians of certain codes," not codebreakers. When the newly arrived special security officers observed that General Headquarters had no arrangement for passing ULTRA to field commanders, Willoughby countered that G-2 immediately passed operational messages to U.S. Sixth Army and distributed ULTRA to the corps. Since the G-2 was already taking steps to institutionalize a dissemination process for ULTRA, he regarded recommendations by special security officers unfamiliar with the Southwest Pacific theater as unnecessary.[68]

It is true that through the summer of 1944 Southwest Pacific Headquarters had no uniform system for distributing ULTRA to its ground commanders. It is equally true that MacArthur did not need one until the Leyte invasion in October 1944. The reasons were technical, organizational, and tactical. On the technical side, until February 1944 there was not enough intelligence gained from decrypted Japanese army messages to warrant distribution to ground commanders. Between February and October 1944 MacArthur's troops fought as task forces, usually of regimental size, over widely dispersed areas. ULTRA's strategic intelligence was inappropriate for such small formations. Because the jungles of New Guinea fragmented large forces, this was tactically the only way to fight, but it precluded the need for extensive ULTRA dissemination to ground commanders. Only one corps-size grouping occurred during this period and most of its units were kept as reserves.

By October 1944 conditions had changed. Army ULTRA was available in quantity; two corps of two divisions each were initially engaged at Leyte; and the more-open terrain permitted multidivision tactical maneuvers. By that time as well a standardized system existed to disseminate ULTRA from Southwest Pacific Headquarters to Sixth and Eighth armies, Fifth, Thirteenth, and Far Eastern Air Forces, and the X and XXIV Corps. Not coincidentally this was the first time such a multitude of large units operated together in MacArthur's theater.

The absence of army regulations governing ULTRA procedures in the Asiatic theaters further strengthened Southwest Pacific theater's assertions of autonomy. British and American signal intelligence chieftains had voiced concern over the absence of any standard policy for the handling and use of Japanese signal intelligence in operational theaters. Not until May 1944, however, did they propose uniform draft regulations and central control over the products of Japanese

ULTRA.[69] This time Sutherland amended the War Department draft to conform with existing ULTRA policies in MacArthur's command and thereby emasculate the War Department's special security officers. Central Bureau continued to generate ULTRA locally and to exchange technical intelligence with Arlington Hall; Akin continued to dispatch locally produced ULTRA directly to MacArthur's commands over his own radio channels without Washington's approval; and Willoughby distributed similar ULTRA to field commands.

That November, Clarke's Special Branch requested that MacArthur establish a secure channel in Central Bureau to transmit locally produced ULTRA to Washington. This was a preliminary step toward effecting the new ULTRA regulations in the Southwest Pacific theater.[70] Clarke would personally visit Central Bureau to establish the new communications channel. MacArthur played on his seniority and carefully crafted popularity to deflect this latest challenge. He refused to allow General Clarke to inspect Central Bureau. Clarke had journeyed as far as Hawaii when he was ordered back to Washington. The Special Branch chief blamed Akin and Sutherland for preventing him from seeing MacArthur, even though Clarke carried a personal message from General Marshall for the Southwest Pacific Area commander.[71]

In December 1944 a chief of staff directive placed Major General Clayton Bissell, the War Department's G-2 (February 1944–January 1946), in full control of the intercept and cryptanalytic work at Arlington Hall, thereby transferring these functions from the Signal Corps to the Military Intelligence Division. Bissell drafted a letter to MacArthur explaining the strict new guidelines for using ULTRA in overseas theaters. Before Marshall agreed to sign Bissell's draft, however, he told the deputy chief of staff, Lieutenant General Thomas T. Handy, to tone it down. Handy's aside that "while ULTRA was important there were lots of other things just as important" exemplified the kid-gloved treatment accorded Mac-Arthur.[72] Marshall further agreed that unclear lines of authority and duplication of codebreaking efforts necessitated an independent cryptanalytic agency directly under the chief of staff's control but postponed its effective date until after the defeat of Japan.[73] Only MacArthur's stature stood in Marshall's way, but that enormous shadow allowed Central Bureau to maintain its peculiar relationship with the War Department throughout the war in the Pacific.

Advocates of centralized control of ULTRA criticized Central Bureau's independence and General Headquarters's procedures for distributing ULTRA to its commands. Certainly a local decryption service, not answerable to Washington, resulted in some duplication of the total cryptanalytic effort. Independent distribution and lax security, critics charged, imperiled secrecy and efficiency. Systematically, however, the Southwest Pacific Area's ULTRA arrangements worked, though perhaps neither as well as General Headquarters claimed nor as poorly as critics alleged. Willoughby asserted that Central Bureau's "top-flight cryptanalysts" produced intelligence that "proved extremely useful to high Allied echelons throughout the campaigns" and was "of great importance" for planning future operations. On the other hand, Bissell observed, "Akin has built a signal intelligence empire in Central Bureau which in my opinion, judged by results in other areas and by other agencies, is not very efficient."[74]

Yet Central Bureau could generate ULTRA locally by intercepting, decrypting, translating, and analyzing Japanese army radio messages. It received and exchanged technical data with other Allied cryptanalytic centers. Southwest Pacific Headquarters also received and exchanged ULTRA intelligence with various American and Allied intelligence agencies. It developed procedures during the war to disseminate ULTRA to its field commanders in a timely, secure fashion. The system was sound, although controversial. The following chapters relate how MacArthur and his commanders used ULTRA, the product of this unique system.

2

ULTRA's Trials and Errors, 1942

MacArthur's forlorn defense of Bataan temporarily delayed the Japanese military timetable in the Philippines. Elsewhere, Japanese ground and naval forces spread rapidly throughout the Pacific. In January 1942 Japanese troops seized the massive natural harbor at Rabaul, New Britain, and by March they held small enclaves on the northern New Guinea coast, which protected Rabaul's southern approaches. Meanwhile, the Japanese army captured the British bastion at Singapore and with it the resources of British Malaya. They then extended their conquests to encompass the oil-rich Netherlands East Indies. Caught up in the euphoria of a string of unbroken victories, Imperial General Headquarters staff officers were drafting ambitious plans for invasions of Australia, Hawaii, and even the continental United States. Still invincible in battle, the Imperial Japanese Navy's carrier strike forces prowled the Indian and Pacific oceans, leaving havoc in their wakes. At the nadir of Allied fortunes in the Pacific war, a defeated MacArthur had fled the Philippines in March for Australia.

MacArthur's arrival in Australia coincided with an influx of American air and ground reinforcements that Washington had set in motion well before the general's move. Still the available Allied forces were few in number, largely untrained, and poorly equipped for the impending struggle against the tenacious and determined Japanese. Furthermore, General Marshall had made it clear to MacArthur that the Anglo-American Combined Chiefs of Staff viewed Nazi Germany as the opponent whose defeat took precedence over Japan's destruction. With this objective in mind, the Combined Chiefs, on March 24, 1942, further agreed on a worldwide division of strategic responsibilities that made the United States accountable for the conduct of the war in the Pacific. Six days later, the U.S. Joint Chiefs of Staff (JCS), in turn, placed MacArthur in command of the Southwest Pacific Area. During the three weeks required for America's other Pacific allies to concur with the JCS directive, MacArthur organized his new headquarters and selected his key staff officers.[1] Interestingly, the establishment of Central Bureau in Melbourne on April 15, 1942, predated Southwest Pacific Headquarters by three days.

This early period of the Pacific war witnessed the U.S. Navy's greatest cryptographic triumphs. Decryption and analysis of Japanese naval messages proved operationally decisive at the Battle of the Coral Sea in May and gave the strategic advantage at Midway just one month later. For Central Bureau, however, these were the worst of times. It could not unravel any Japanese army ciphers and lacked expertise analyzing enemy naval radio traffic networks. Australian traffic analysts were gradually reconstructing Japanese radio networks by studying the formats of the Imperial Army's radio messages. Unable to read the enciphered text itself, they scrutinized call signs, message priorities, and addresses as a means of identifying the organization and operation of the Japanese communications system. Together with direction finding, which located radio transmitters, traffic analysis could reveal the disposition of troops and their potential deployment as well as offer valuable data to intelligence specialists before cryptanalysts rendered an encrypted message into readable form.[2] The Australians concentrated on analyzing Japanese army, army air force, and land-based naval air communications from their main intercept site at Townsville on the northeastern Australian coast. Sherr's men from the Philippines brought valuable cryptanalytic experience about the Japanese air force's communications system and Sinkov's contingent from Washington brought cryptanalytic expertise. Central Bureau's ambitious mission was to tackle and ultimately to decipher the whole range of Japanese army radio communications. This had to be accomplished more or less from scratch.[3]

In theory, the assignment was simple. A radio station had to be established where an enemy commander located his headquarters so he could communicate with other units. Direction-finding techniques could locate the headquarters's transmitter. Identifying and monitoring Japanese military radio frequencies could then expose the relative importance of major headquarters, trace the pattern of their radio transmissions, and assemble sufficient encoded messages to lay the groundwork for a cryptanalytic solution of the Japanese army code. Central Bureau's American cryptanalysts first attacked the Japanese army's low-level, three-digit, regimental code. Because it was used to encipher messages intended for minor units, they assumed that it would prove less secure and therefore easier to solve than the four-digit, mainline cipher used by divisions and higher levels of command.[4] The cryptanalysts' reasoning was sound, but their efforts encountered a peculiarity of the Japanese army's radio communications system that stymied them throughout the war.

The three-digit cipher used by Japanese regimental and battalion radiomen for secure communications worked vertically, not laterally. This meant that a Japanese regiment could communicate with its parent division but not exchange radio messages directly with another regiment in the same division. All subordinate unit signals went up to the division, and only the division could communicate with all its units. Because each regiment had its own cipher system, Central Bureau could never amass enough signals from a single regiment to discern patterns that might help to break the code. Even if Central Bureau cracked one regiment's code, cryptanalysts would not have been able to read the messages of other regiments unless they went through the same painstaking process for each unit.

If the 78th Infantry Regiment, for example, wanted to communicate with the 79th or 80th Infantry regiments, the 78th's signalman transmitted the message up the chain of command to his parent 20th Division (see Figure 2.1). The division signal unit retransmitted the 78th's message down the chain in a different code to the 79th and in still another code to the 80th. Replies from the regiments followed the same route in reverse. Instead of four messages in one code back and forth from the 78th to the other two regiments, there were now six messages relayed in three separate codes from the 78th Regiment via the division to the other two regiments.

Japanese techniques for sending low-level messages also discouraged eavesdropping. Signalmen observed radio discipline by transmitting the three-digit messages on minimum power because of the units' proximity to one another. A radio operator tuned to high power just long enough to establish contact with the receiver and then tuned down to minimum power to dispatch the message. Transmitting on minimum power made it extremely difficult for Central Bureau's distant intercept operators to overhear or to record the very weak signal. Paradoxically, Japanese high-level communications were less secure than the low-level ones. Larger Japanese units, such as divisions, armies (two or more divisions), and area armies (two or more armies), were usually deployed across a wide area. Thus a radioman had to transmit a stronger signal to reach the intended recipient and ensure clear reception and readability on the other end. The stronger, louder signal was easier for an intercept operator to overhear. As Japanese units proliferated on Rabaul and New Guinea, so did the number of radio messages among the units. The rapid expansion strained the security of the main army system by allowing Central Bureau to collect huge amounts of intercepts. This circumstance improved the possibility of discerning relationships in the ciphers that might compromise Japanese secrets. In April 1942 these accomplishments still lay in the future. The present beheld a Japanese war machine poised to seize Port Moresby.

The Imperial Navy's preparations to occupy Moresby precipitated the Battle of the Coral Sea. MacArthur's cryptanalysts contributed little to the intelligence preparation of this unprecedented sea battle in which capital ships never exchanged surface fire. However, U.S. Navy codebreakers and traffic analysts were reading sufficient portions of Japanese naval messages to forewarn Admiral Chester W. Nimitz, commander in chief of the Pacific Fleet, of the impending Japanese offensive.

Figure 2.1

Abbreviated Army Chain of Command

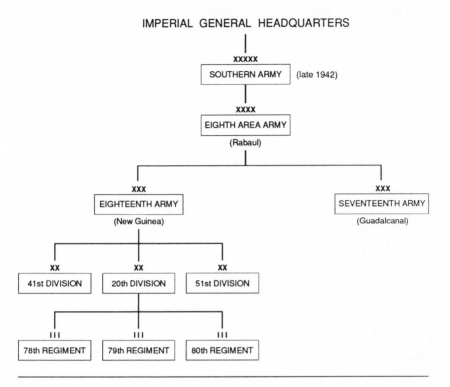

IMPERIAL GENERAL HEADQUARTERS

XXXXX
| SOUTHERN ARMY | (late 1942)

XXXX
| EIGHTH AREA ARMY |
(Rabaul)

XXX
| EIGHTEENTH ARMY |
(New Guinea)

XXX
| SEVENTEENTH ARMY |
(Guadalcanal)

XX
| 41st DIVISION |

XX
| 20th DIVISION |

XX
| 51st DIVISION |

III
| 78th REGIMENT |

III
| 79th REGIMENT |

III
| 80th REGIMENT |

LATERAL COMMUNICATIONS NETWORK

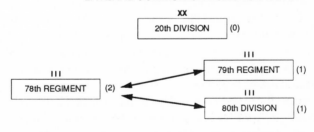

XX
| 20th DIVISION | (0)

III
| 79th REGIMENT | (1)

III
| 78th REGIMENT | (2)

III
| 80th DIVISION | (1)

VERTICAL COMMUNICATIONS NETWORK

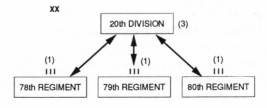

XX
| 20th DIVISION | (3)

(1)
III
| 78th REGIMENT |

(1)
III
| 79th REGIMENT |

(1)
III
| 80th REGIMENT |

(Number of messages in parentheses)

Naval intelligence uncovered the outline of Japanese plans against Australia and passed it to the Intelligence Branch, Military Intelligence Division, in Washington. The branch chief, Colonel Hayes A. Kroner, notified Sutherland, who warned Lieutenant General George H. Brett, the Allied Air Forces commander in Australia, on April 16 that Port Moresby might be attacked by sea on April 21. Based on this navy ULTRA, MacArthur ordered an immediate aerial reconnaissance of Rabaul Harbor. Returning pilots reported no concentrations of Japanese shipping that would tip off a major amphibious operation. Five days later in Hawaii, Admiral Nimitz listened intently as his fleet intelligence officer, Commander Edwin T. Layton, explained his deductions about an imminent Japanese offensive in the New Guinea–New Britain–Solomon area. Layton did not know the exact Japanese target, but he surmised that enemy predelictions to move under the cover of land-based aircraft suggested an attack against Port Moresby.[5]

Willoughby had received the same ULTRA but produced a radically different intelligence assessment. He questioned the rationale for a Japanese attack on Port Moresby. The presence of four carriers, exposed by ULTRA, suggested to him that the Japanese were about to attack somewhere beyond the range of their land-based aircraft. As Willoughby saw it, the Japanese aimed to occupy the northeastern Australian coast or New Caledonia in order to strategically outflank northern Australia and interdict the Allied line of communication between Hawaii and Australia.

Sutherland relied on U.S. Navy appraisals when he briefed MacArthur's high command that the Japanese had probably postponed their attack against Moresby until the first week of May. Shortly thereafter, Willoughby reversed himself and predicted a one-division Japanese landing at Port Moresby between May 5 and 10.[6] On May 7 the Battle of the Coral Sea commenced. Forewarned of enemy intentions, a naval task force, organized around the U.S. carriers *Lexington* and *Yorktown,* intercepted the Japanese invasion force. The resulting battle produced a revolution in naval warfare, a tactical draw, and a strategic victory for the Allies. For the first time in naval history, a battle had been fought entirely between carrier aircraft of opposing fleets that never came within 100 miles of each other. At the tactical level, Japanese carrier pilots sank *Lexington* and damaged *Yorktown,* but American airmen sank the carrier *Shoho* and seriously damaged *Shokaku.* Realizing that without air cover an invasion was impossible, the Japanese recalled their armada to Rabaul.

Initial contradictory interpretations by Willoughby and Layton of the same ULTRA data illustrated the ambiguities that accompanied decrypted Japanese messages. Rarely were the enemy's intentions self-evident. Analysis and evaluation of the decryptions were central to exploiting full advantage from codebreaking. ULTRA's role in the battle also highlighted MacArthur's almost total reliance on naval cryptanalysts at this stage of the war. Nimitz recognized the need to keep

MacArthur informed about U.S. Navy plans and operations in the Pacific if the two theater commanders were to work together. As a step in that direction, he had ordered Vice Admiral Arthur S. Carpender, commander of the Southwest Pacific Force, the theater's American naval commander, to pass naval ULTRA to MacArthur.[7] Thus it was through navy ULTRA that MacArthur learned of the bold Japanese overland attempt to seize Port Moresby.

On May 18 Fabian's naval analysts at Melbourne intercepted and decrypted a Japanese navy message which revealed that the Japanese had abandoned plans for a seaborne invasion of Port Moresby but were accelerating studies for an overland invasion. The message mentioned a land route to Port Moresby, although translation difficulties left the exact purpose of such a road open to conjecture. That same day, at Pacific Fleet Combat Intelligence Center, Hawaii, Lieutenant Commander Joseph J. Rochefort penned his longhand estimate of the Japanese plans and their order of battle for the Midway operation. In the same report he predicted that about June 15 an overland attempt would commence to occupy Moresby. The Japanese advance would originate from their bases at Lae and Salamaua, which were located on the northern coast of New Guinea about 200 miles northwest of Port Moresby.[8]

Within ten days of Rochefort's coup, the Japanese effected a routine change to their main operational naval code that temporarily blinded American cryptanalysts. During July and August 1942, analysis, not decipherment, of Japanese message traffic, accounted for practically all of the ULTRA furnished to Pacific commanders.[9] Nevertheless, skilled naval traffic analysts continued to pass accurate intelligence derived from enemy radio communications to MacArthur's headquarters.

Because Japanese naval communications often concerned joint operations undertaken with the army, U.S. Navy intercept operators grew familiar with specific Japanese army call signs. The army employed a four-digit cipher to encode message addresses that differed completely from other military cipher systems. (The Japanese army had initially employed a three-digit cipher to encode message addresses but soon changed to a four-digit one for the duration.) The radio operator transmitting the signal enciphered the message preamble from a separate codebook to conceal the message's points of origin and destination. Fortunately, Layton's earlier solution of the Japanese naval message routing system, the "WE WE" code, could help to break the call sign cipher.

Early in 1941 Layton had discovered that addresses on Japanese naval messages, especially newly organized units or task forces, often did not have official call signs in the call sign codebooks. Instead, their messages were addressed in a simple *kana* (Japanese syllabary) substitution code that was always bracketed by the Japanese vowel "WE." A typical address might read: WE RA "KA TE MU NU SO HO RU" MU WE. Simple substitution yielded: "RA BA U RU TSU SHIN TAI," or, translated into English, "Rabaul Communications Unit." This insight was especially important as Japanese expansion into the Southwest Pacific in 1942 outpaced existing unit call signs. Until up-to-date codebooks were issued, radiomen had to rely on this insecure "WE WE" code to guide Japanese naval radio messages to and from Rabaul. In the early months of the war, the American navy took full advantage of the excellent crib to identify the proliferating Japanese units. Once the revised codebooks described above appeared, however, cryptanalysts had to solve a new place-name code.[10]

The British Far East Combined Bureau, New Delhi, India, and the Signal Intelligence Service had the responsibility for unraveling the address code. Captured message forms disclosing the external structure of a Japanese army message gave the first clues in solving the place-name code. With this opening, the Signal Intelligence Service in June 1942 assigned a handful of analysts to work on solving the army address system. They matched intercepted army messages, collected by the expanding network of U.S. Army intercept sites, with those relayed on Japanese navy radio links picked up by U.S. Navy stations. In September, when only twenty-three people at Arlington Hall were analyzing Japanese army cipher systems, cryptanalysts solved the Japanese message center place-name code. They shared the techniques with the thirty to forty people who were similarly engaged at Central Bureau.[11]

From that point MacArthur's cryptanalysts deciphered address code numbers in the intercepted Imperial Army messages. Solution of the place-name code identified locations, not units. Thus the call signs DD 4421-9834 equated with the Palau islands (4421), the place of destination, and Rabaul (9834), the place of origin. The specific unit addressed in the Palaus, say 3008, was encrypted in yet another and more secure cipher that Arlington Hall eventually solved. This opening wedge into the army codes enabled traffic analysts to identify radio transmitter and message center place names. By associating these locations with the broadcasts of particular military units, they could infer deployments and forthcoming operations. The following example illustrates the methodology of traffic analysis. (The italicized information in parentheses was unknown at the time analysts received the intelligence.)

On July 5, 1942, navy traffic analysts at Melbourne identified the 6433 Akatsuki (army) detachment at Rabaul (*Anchorage Unit 45*). The same call sign again appeared in communications on July 12 amid numerous radio broadcasts. Heavy bursts of messages indicated that a major operation was impending. About a month later, in mid-August, the commander of Akatsuki Detachment 2943 (*Major General Yamada Eizo, commander of Shipping Group 1*), was an addressee on a message sent to the Palaus. Although traffic analysts could not relate this code name to a specific type of Japanese army unit, they understood that the message's high precedence and multiple routings to and from 2943 stamped it as a major headquarters. The characteristics of its radio communications were those of a Japanese army controlling two or more divisions. Akatsuki 2943's span of command stretched from the Palaus to Rabaul. Both places were known to be major Japanese bases.

Radio messages in November from an Akatsuki unit betrayed its presence on Rabaul to Central Bureau monitors. A few weeks later they discovered the Rabaul unit communicating with Akatsuki detachments in the Philippines, Formosa, and Japan. This incidence of Japanese radio activity coincided with ULTRA indications of possible renewed Japanese attacks against Port Moresby. By late November Akatsuki Detachment 6168 (*units of Shipping Transport Command, Moji*) was transmitting and receiving radio messages at Buna, Papua New Guinea. Central Bureau traffic analysts overheard Akatsuki 6169 (*Shipping Group 2*) transmitting messages from Buna in mid-December. The same day, they intercepted radio messages of Akatsuki 6170 (*Shipping Engineer Regiment 1*) addressed to the chief of staff, Eighteenth Army, on Rabaul.[12] In no instance had Central Bureau deciphered the text of an Akatsuki unit message.

Yet the repetitive radio traffic patterns involving Akatsuki units had disclosed significant intelligence. Code name Akatsuki appeared during periods of unusually heavy radio traffic, itself a significant indicator that the Japanese were embarking on an operation. The appearance of Akatsuki 6433 in July preceded the Japanese landings at Buna. The presence of a general officer commanding Akatsuki in the Palaus in mid-August corresponded to Japanese efforts to rush additional ground troops to Guadalcanal and New Guinea. The November connections coincided with Japanese reinforcements for Buna. An experienced traffic analyst might conclude, as Central Bureau did in late December, that Akatsuki traffic in December among stations at Buna, Rabaul, and the Palaus likely was associated with the movement of army troops from one of those places to the other.[13] However, analysts could reach this seemingly self-evident conclusion only after identifying and isolating Akatsuki call signs and frequencies amid the thousands of daily radio messages that cluttered the airwaves.

This oversimplified example illustrates that even without the ability to decipher a Japanese message, traffic analysts provided commanders with enormously useful, and otherwise unobtainable, intelligence. Code name Akatsuki did designate a specific, if unidentified, Japanese army unit. Solution of the Akatsuki mystery unit depended upon an extensive, carefully constructed, and cross-referenced intelligence data base. Intercept operators collected such information from monitoring repetitive call signs, unit designators, addressees, associated communications, and personalities. It was the first step in compiling an accurate Japanese order of battle. When the Japanese struck again at Port Moresby in July 1942, this sort of traffic analysis was MacArthur's main source of signal intelligence.

Imperial Headquarters commenced planning for a Japanese overland attack on

Port Moresby on June 7, just three days after their disastrous naval defeat at Midway. MacArthur did signal Blamey on June 9 that "minor forces" might attempt an attack against Port Moresby through Kokoda. Otherwise, the Southwest Pacific commander was preoccupied with his own plans to deploy Allied forces to Buna in early August in order to establish an air base there.[14] Simultaneously, MacArthur's forces were constructing an airfield at Milne Bay, on the southeastern tip of New Guinea, to forestall another Japanese seaborne invasion of Port Moresby.

In late June, Japanese navy pilots lazily circled and recircled their Zero fighters over the Buna-Kokoda sector searching for a suitable trail for vehicle traffic. They could not find one because the thick jungle canopy obscured the ground about 6 miles inland from the coast. The brazen reconnaissance, however, alerted MacArthur's command to the enemy's interest in Buna. The pilots' inconclusive reports also complicated the task of Major General Horii Tomitaro's five-thousand-man South Seas Detachment. Originally selected for the amphibious assault on Port Moresby, the detachment now had orders to attack Moresby overland on extended lines of communication through uncharted jungle and mountainous terrain. Horii voiced concern that the logistics for the attack were beyond his unit's slender sustainment capabilities.[15] Nonetheless, on July 1, Seventeenth Army Headquarters at Rabaul ordered the operation to proceed.

Within five days, Allied analysts noted radio messages from new units addressed to Seventeenth Army. The most frequent call signs were from a composite group at Davao, Philippines. Meanwhile, an Australian guerrilla unit, the Kanga Force, had captured numerous Japanese documents in a raid against a camp near Salamaua. The papers disclosed that the 14th Construction Detachment would accompany the 5th Special Naval Landing Force to the eastern coast of New Guinea. Naval landing forces were specialized amphibious assault units whose presence in New Guinea presaged that an operation of that sort was coming.[16]

Also in early July, U.S. naval intelligence deciphered a Japanese navy message, apparently in a superseded code, that disclosed that the Japanese were likely to land at Buna on July 21 and then push south over the Owen Stanley mountain range to Moresby. By July 11 the appearance of new message addresses in radio communications portended a strengthening of the Japanese Third Fleet preparatory to offensive action against northern Australia or Port Moresby. Large-scale troop movements from the Philippines and China to Truk and Rabaul also emerged from radio traffic. The Melbourne naval intercept station disclosed on July 12 that the Japanese were passing intelligence on Allied deployments before launching their New Guinea campaign. Central Bureau reported that, based on previous experience in the Philippines, the gradual buildup of Japanese radio traffic signaled an operational crescendo within thirty days.[17]

ULTRA kept Willoughby apprised of Japanese moves. On July 13 he predicted that the enemy destination was Buna or possibly Milne Bay and recommended to Chamberlin that he concentrate his reconnaissance efforts at those points and be ready to repulse any landings. Central Bureau underlined the likelihood of an impending Japanese landing when they detected sizable increases in fighter activity characteristic of earlier Japanese offensives in the Philippines. Just three days later, however, Willoughby reversed himself and declared that the Japanese purpose was to consolidate areas they already held, not to invade new ones.[18] This turnaround was reminiscent of his April 1942 Port Moresby appreciation.

By this time, the U.S. Pacific Fleet Intelligence Summary was warning about a forthcoming Japanese operation in the New Guinea–Solomons area. Naval intelligence foresaw likely Japanese expansion into new areas, perhaps Guadalcanal and the eastern coast of New Guinea. Radio messages addressed to the Sasebo 5th Special Naval Landing Force and 8th Base Force implied that future air or naval base development would follow the Japanese transports. Troop ships were already under way from Truk, having departed there on July 10. In the face of this array of intelligence indicators of a Japanese invasion, MacArthur remained inactive. His passivity resulted in part from a lack of strategic direction from Washington and in part from a paucity of resources.[19]

MacArthur's air force was in shambles with perhaps eighty to one hundred operational aircraft. Heavy losses of pilots and aircraft had drained its morale; its leadership ebbed, as did the general's confidence in his air commander's ability. The theater's two American infantry divisions, the 32d and 41st, needed more training before facing battle, and the Australian brigades under MacArthur's command had just completed their deployment to Milne Bay in late June. Available intelligence did point to a Japanese offensive but could not identify the enemy objective. On July 18, for example, Allied pilots reported a large concentration of Japanese transports anchored at Rabaul. Willoughby told MacArthur that the ships might just as well be headed for Guadalcanal or Lae as Buna.[20] Unsure of the Japanese target, MacArthur was reluctant to concentrate his weak forces at a single location.

Naval intelligence analysts also hedged their conclusions about the exact destination of a large convoy detected by traffic analysis. By July 19, the Melbourne unit had tracked the commander of the Sasebo 5th Special Naval Landing Force to Rabaul, where he was in radio contact with his unit at Salamaua. The Fleet Intelligence Summary disclosed that Cruiser Division 18 and three destroyers were also near Salamaua escorting a four-transport convoy. An imminent Japanese landing, the summary continued, ''may indicate the near completion of preparations for an overland attack on Port Moresby or, more probable, the strengthening of bases in this area.''[21]

Japanese troops splashing ashore at Buna on July 22 temporarily united Willoughby and the U.S. Navy. The two services joined forces to disparage the

Southwest Pacific theater's air arm. Willoughby editorialized, "For the record
. . . in spite of our advance notice, our Air Force was unable to prevent this
landing." The Japanese landing "in spite of our land based air," the navy commented with acerbity, showed the need for "land based torpedo and dive bombers
against surface ships."[22] Willoughby had never unequivocally singled out Buna as
the invasion point. For its part, the navy was guilty of special pleading because
they alone had the trained pilots and aircraft specifically designed to attack shipping. These comments were unfair. Bad weather, not inefficiency, had grounded
MacArthur's air force. Heavy rains had drenched the Allied air base at Port
Moresby, preventing Allied aircraft from taking off to strike the convoy.

The capricious weather more than anything else allowed Colonel Yokoyama
Yosuke and his three-thousand-man advance force to land in daylight without
opposition. They immediately fanned out to reconnoiter the feasibility of a proposed mountain crossing for the overland advance on Port Moresby. Then the
weather shifted. A storm front sweeping over Rabaul forced the Japanese to
suspend flight operations later that morning. Meanwhile, the skies had cleared
over Moresby, and Allied aircraft promptly attacked the Japanese beachhead,
setting afire a Japanese transport that finally beached on a sandbar.

Decrypted naval message addresses let MacArthur evaluate the latest enemy
landing. A message addressed to a naval air group commander at Lae was evidence
that the Japanese were shifting air strength from Rabaul to New Guinea to protect
their forces at Buna. On July 25 intercept operators overheard call signs of unidentified army units being broadcast to the New Guinea–Solomons area and listened
to Cruiser Division 18, active in the first landing, again shuttling reinforcements to
the New Guinea beachhead. Despite the pace of the Japanese buildup ULTRA
revealed and the rapid enemy advance inland, Willoughby judged that they aimed
only at securing an airfield at Buna. He espoused that interpretation throughout the
bitter campaign.[23]

Only the much-maligned Allied Air Forces carried the fight to the Japanese.
Naval ULTRA assisted them in their attacks. A July 27 intercept, for instance,
predicted a convoy would arrive at Buna two days later. A two-ship convoy with
destroyer escort did indeed depart Rabaul on July 29, bringing supplies and
reinforcements for Buna. Alerted, Allied airmen attacked the ships forcing one
transport to beach itself and the other to hurry its unloading so that it might flee to
Rabaul and safety. A subsequent night bombing attack crippled the surviving
transport, which limped into Rabaul Harbor.[24] Such successes were few and far
between for MacArthur.

Japanese infantrymen were steadily hacking their way through the New Guinea
rain forest toward Port Moresby, and rumors of another Japanese invasion
abounded. In this crisis atmosphere MacArthur welcomed his new air chieftain,
Major General George C. Kenney, to Australia. The 5-foot-6-inch, crew-cut

Kenney enjoyed a well-earned reputation as a pioneer airman and an innovator. Perhaps because of his willingness to innovate, Kenney became one of the most receptive "clients of ULTRA." Within two weeks of his arrival in MacArthur's theater, Kenney relied on navy-supplied ULTRA to strike a Japanese resupply convoy headed from Rabaul to Buna.[25]

Based on a deciphered enemy dispatch available August 11, Kenney knew that the Japanese had scheduled a convoy with air escort to depart Rabaul the following morning. Armed with this advance information, he carefully plotted his attack and confidently dispatched reconnaissance aircraft to the vicinity where he knew the Japanese convoy was likely to appear. After his air patrols sighted the ships, an air strike soon followed. Twenty-eight American bombers launched four unsuccessful raids against this small convoy. The Japanese landed the 14th and 15th Naval Construction units and their supplies—damp but otherwise little the worse for wear.[26] (Five days afterward, Fabian's Melbourne outfit announced that these naval construction units had restored the airfield at Buna to operating condition.) Kenney's attack, however, foreshadowed the future integration of ULTRA into his operational planning. Although the first results were disappointing, the potent combination of ULTRA in the hands of a willing commander would prove its value throughout the air war in MacArthur's theater.

Japanese air strikes against Kenney's airfields at Port Moresby preceded another Buna reinforcement convoy carrying Major General Horii and the South Seas Detachment Headquarters, the bulk of the 144th Infantry Regiment, as well as a mountain artillery battalion. The convoy slipped safely into Buna on August 18, undetected either by ULTRA or aerial reconnaissance. Three days later, the 41st Infantry (minus) repeated the feat. Recently altered Japanese unit call sign codes and improved communications security temporarily shrouded the movement of Japanese reinforcements and enabled them to secure their lodgement for the attack on Port Moresby.[27]

U.S. Navy analysts attributed this newfound Japanese security awareness to American press leaks. They were convinced that newspaper accounts of the recent Battle of Midway—particularly the *Chicago Tribune*'s version, which had specifically mentioned codebreaking—had alerted the Japanese that the Americans were reading their codes. In fact, Japanese naval intelligence was unaware of the *Tribune* story. The fortuitous timing of the code changes, however, seemed to fall into a sinister pattern.[28]

The latest Japanese landings at Buna did not alter Willoughby's earlier estimate of their intention. He discounted any Japanese overland advance in strength because the nearly impassable jungle and mountains precluded sufficient logistics and communications' support for other than minor units. ULTRA confirmation of an operational Japanese airstrip at Buna convinced him that the air base explained the Japanese seizure of the beachhead.[29] From Willoughby's vantage point, the

Japanese were executing a mirror image of MacArthur's plan to construct a series of airfields at strategic points along the New Guinea coast to secure control of the southern end of the Owen Stanley range. The coincidence of Japanese and Allied plans suggested that the Japanese were reading Allied codes.[30]

Willoughby's penchant to attribute or superimpose his own concept of tactics and strategy on his opponents in intelligence appreciations had appeared earlier when he predicted a Japanese attack on mainland Australia. It was another tendency that would reappear throughout the war and partly accounts for the sometimes erratic nature of his forecasts. In his defense, Willoughby made his estimates under great pressure, based on available and sketchy intelligence. In the larger military theater context, Buna was only one of several Japanese thrusts. No one could identify precisely the main axis of the enemy offensive because the Japanese were pushing simultaneously at Port Moresby, Guadalcanal, and Milne Bay.

MacArthur had not originally envisioned defending Milne Bay, about 180 miles southeast of Buna, against a land attack. In late June he did dispatch combat reinforcements to protect the engineers constructing the airfield. His action was grounded in sound, strategic principles and not based on intelligence revelations. Because Milne Bay anchored the southern flank of the Owen Stanleys and guarded the sea approach to Port Moresby, Southwest Pacific intelligence believed that Milne Bay was a natural target for the next enemy push even before the Japanese had considered it. With that predisposition, Willoughby interpreted Japanese aerial reconnaissance of Milne Bay in early July as presaging amphibious operations against the newly created Allied air base. Numerous radio messages between special naval landing forces on New Ireland and at Rabaul throughout July also foretokened another Japanese invasion. A likely objective was on the southeastern New Guinea coast, and Willoughby surmised that the Japanese had definite designs on Milne Bay.[31]

On July 31, two days after Willoughby's speculation, Seventeenth Army ordered the occupation of Milne Bay. A few days later, Japanese naval pilots flew over the area, snapping preinvasion photographs. Runways cleared from the jungle leaped out at Japanese photo-interpreters in Rabaul. Further study identified two small aircraft that proved the Allied base was in operating condition. These overflights and the fragmentary recovery of a July 21 Japanese radio message mentioning occupation forces dovetailed with captured documents that marked Port Moresby and Milne Bay as the targets. Taken together, the evidence confirmed earlier Allied suspicions about a forthcoming attack against Milne Bay.[32]

Japanese intelligence, conversely, remained ignorant of the strengthened Allied defenses at Milne Bay. Seventeenth Army staff officers reasoned that since the base was newly operational, it did not yet have a large defensive garrison. Japanese naval signal intercept operators were preoccupied with making sense of the marked increases in American radio messages transmitted from Hawaii to the

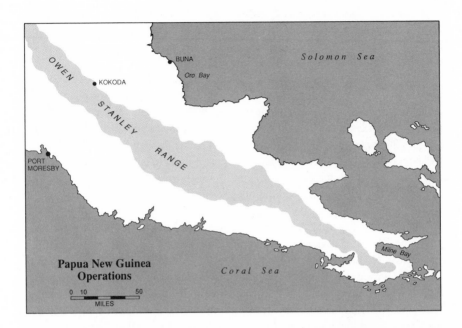

Papua New Guinea
Operations

Pacific and Southwest Pacific fleets. They also monitored extensive radio communications from Allied aircraft active over the Solomon Islands. Agents reported a large convoy sailing from the American West Coast. With this evidence, Japanese naval intelligence warned fleet commanders on August 4 to be on the alert for an imminent Allied operation. They expected that the Japanese force advancing on Port Moresby was the likely target.[33] Three days later, U.S. Marines landed on Guadalcanal.

Imperial Headquarters judged the Marine landing a nuisance, nothing more than a reconnaissance in force, and decided to go ahead with the Milne Bay landing. Navy ULTRA disclosed the formation of a Japanese submarine picket line blockading the approaches to Milne Bay, a characteristic Japanese tactic preceding invasions. In response MacArthur rushed more reinforcements to the threatened area. The arrival of the 18th Australian Infantry Brigade on August 21 brought the Milne Bay garrison to almost ten thousand men, including more than sixty-four hundred combat troops. That same day, MacArthur and Kenney devised countermeasures to check the Japanese attack on Milne Bay that ULTRA had uncovered. Japanese air attacks on Allied installations at Milne Bay gave added urgency to their discussions. One result of their meeting was that Kenney stepped up his air patrols over the likely routes any invasion convoy might pass. Presently, an American flier radioed a sighting of a small Japanese convoy heading south toward Milne Bay with a battalion-sized landing force.[34] At this time MacArthur's entire navy consisted of only one destroyer because all the other Southwest Pacific fleet warships were committed to the Guadalcanal campaign. Only the infantrymen already at Milne Bay and Allied airmen stood between the Japanese and the loss of the strategic tip of southern New Guinea.

Timely advance warning supplied by ULTRA let Kenney marshal his slender air forces. He launched preemptive air strikes against Japanese airdromes at Rabaul and Buna, reasoning that without air superiority the Japanese incursion was bound to fail. Air battles over Buna on August 24 and Kenney's attacks the next day left only six Japanese fighter aircraft to protect the Milne Bay landing force.[35] Kenney had hoped to strike the invading Japanese convoy at sea, but few pilots could pick their way through a violent storm front to attack the rain-shrouded ships. This enabled the Japanese troops to land unopposed at Milne Bay at a critical time in Allied fortunes in the Pacific.

Japanese attacks in the Solomons had sorely hurt the Allied navies and compelled the American fleet to withdraw from Guadalcanal. This reduced the Marines on the island to half rations. On August 24/25, the indecisive Battle of the Eastern Solomons played out. The U.S. Navy sank one light Japanese carrier and temporarily blocked Japanese ground reinforcements for Guadalcanal. During the action, *Enterprise* suffered three bomb hits that put the carrier out of action until October. That same sultry August night, the Japanese landed their Milne Bay force.

MacArthur's headquarters was silent about the Japanese landing. This concerned naval intelligence analysts, who speculated that the Japanese had already captured Milne Bay. The silence also had implications for Central Bureau and Melbourne intercept operators. In World War II, radio communications usually reached a peak during preparations for an upcoming operation. Commanders had to get together to discuss plans; units had to be assembled; fleets had to be gathered; orders had to be issued; logistics and support and provisions had to be arranged; liaison and coordination had to be accomplished. After this preparatory period passed, usually about ten days before launching the operation, radio communications dropped off precipitously. For intelligence operatives, a radio standdown, or communications' silence, was a red flag of imminent action.[36]

When the fighting started, the volume of radio messages again increased dramatically. Standard procedure for American units under attack was to transmit a steady stream of radio messages to higher headquarters. This practice kept commanders informed about battlefield developments and allowed them to make informed tactical decisions. The Australian defenders at Milne Bay, however, did not file operational reports as frequently as Sutherland or MacArthur expected, which left the Americans without word on the Japanese invasion. Frustrated and angry, Sutherland fired off several curt signals to the Australian commander demanding an account of the Milne Bay action.[37]

The curtain of silence that dropped on Milne Bay owed as much to the natural surroundings as to Japanese action. New Guinea was an eerie battleground, and soldiers there had to overcome the foulest terrain of any World War II theater. Torrential downpours intermingled with streaming humidity, blazing sun, and thick jungle foliage conspired to convert the routine into an ordeal. High-explosive shells, lobbed by a Japanese cruiser offshore onto the defenders, occasionally tore through the curtain of rain. Whenever the sun broke through, so did Allied fighter aircraft. Unable to distinguish friend from foe in the lush jungle vegetation, pilots strafed both sides impartially. Night was the worst time. The Japanese rose like phantoms from the darkness and rain to strike. Confusion reigned. Japanese light tanks, headlights ablaze, drove into and through Australian defenses, only to disappear into the jungle. Radios failed, defeated by humidity and rot. Rain and mist obscured the action from higher headquarters on both sides.

As the fighting raged back and forth, the heavily outnumbered Japanese were getting the worst of it. Allied air strikes on the morning of August 27 had destroyed almost all Japanese stores stacked on the beachhead. Low on ammunition and with heavy casualties, the Japanese called for help. A reinforcement convoy arrived at Milne Bay the evening of August 28, and despite torrential rains followed by Allied air strikes, it unloaded 567 officers and men of the 3d Kure Special Naval Landing Force.[38] These naval infantrymen floundered through jungle swamps, saw their light tanks bog down forever in the mud, and met death from snipers hidden in the jungle gloom. Their bleak situation report read: "We attacked as expected. When we drew near the enemy front, their crossfire from prepared pillboxes cut us to pieces. I called for my reserves, but by dawn they had not yet arrived. Any breakthrough will be difficult."[39]

MacArthur relied on decrypted Japanese naval radio messages to keep abreast of the perilous Japanese situation. They disclosed that the commander of the 5th Kure Special Naval Landing Force had been killed in action; that the commander of the 3d Kure Special Landing Force had been seriously wounded; and that only about one-third of the Japanese force remained combat effective. In short, Australian troops were slowly destroying the invading Japanese. Yet after a week of vicious fighting, the Japanese clung stubbornly to their beachhead. Moreover, intercepted radio broadcasts located Cruiser Division 18, the Japanese covering force, lurking nearby. Analysts suggested that more Japanese reinforcements were en route to Milne Bay. In this atmosphere of uncertainty Fabian's Melbourne unit broke two significant Imperial Navy messages. The first was from the commander in chief of the Eighth Fleet and promised relief was on the way. The second, issued just a few hours later, ordered Japanese forces to evacuate Milne Bay. Melbourne passed this naval ULTRA to MacArthur, who ordered Kenney to attack the evacuation convoy.[40] Horrendous weather again frustrated Allied pilots, and the Japanese were able to withdraw their badly mauled naval landing forces. Still, the Allied victory at Milne Bay had checked the Japanese advance and the immediate Allied crisis had passed. Vice Admiral Ugaki Matome, chief of staff of the Combined Fleet, penned the Milne Bay force's epitaph. "The Guadalcanal situation is out of control because we rashly dispersed our forces on three fronts," he concluded. "Our landing forces couldn't take the enemy-held airfields [at Milne Bay]. Our landing force personnel weren't any good because they were overaged, (30 to 35 year old) recalled reservists lacking tenacity and fighting spirit."[41]

The Japanese campaign against Milne Bay had collapsed, but they were determined to hold Guadalcanal. Traffic analysts in early September discerned from radio message addresses that more Japanese reinforcements were streaming from the Philippines to Rabaul. Troop convoys from Davao and the Palaus heading toward New Guinea also appeared prominently in radio communications. By mid-September, intercepted signals were keeping the Allies informed about the large-scale Japanese air redeployments in progress to the Southwest and South Pacific and the "considerable" army movements from the Philippines to the Southwest Pacific.

This disturbing intelligence led MacArthur to radio General Marshall in Washington on September 27 about the War Department's responsibility to support the Southwest Pacific theater's counterstrokes. MacArthur had earlier envisioned an Allied drive up the northern New Guinea coast to seize Buna and thereby parry the Japanese thrust. Simultaneously, an enveloping movement by small units of infantry "over the trails of the Owen Stanley Mountains" would isolate the Japanese. Washington had rejected that plan. Now MacArthur urged the Joint Chiefs to reverse themselves and provide him with landing craft, logistics support, and American "trained amphibious combat teams" for his proposed maneuver.[42]

MacArthur relied on ULTRA to bolster his claims about the gravity of the Japanese menace and consequent need for Marshall to reconsider the Southwest Pacific theater's case. Japanese radiograms themselves provided irrefutable evidence to Washington that MacArthur, unlike other theater commanders, faced an immediate threat. Although his requests went unanswered, MacArthur's willingness to use ULTRA when it suited his needs or strengthened his contentions would continue throughout his campaign.

Even as MacArthur planned his counteroffensive, Imperial Headquarters in Tokyo made far-reaching decisions about the New Guinea front. The Japanese high command ordered the South Seas Detachment to strengthen its defenses near Buna while simultaneously holding its gains inland. Japan's military leaders underwrote their commitment to fight for New Guinea by dispatching the 51st Infantry Division from South China with additional air defense, logistics, and service support troops to Seventeenth Army at Rabaul.[43] By late September, exchanges of radio messages among the affected Japanese units alerted American intelligence that they were again on the march.

For the next two weeks, Nimitz's headquarters traced the flow of army reinforcements from Japan, China, and Malaya to New Britain. Most of the troops were destined to sail from Rabaul for the terrible struggle on Guadalcanal, but on November 2 two Japanese transports safely reached Buna where they unloaded ammunition and supplies. Meanwhile, Australian counterattacks against the South Seas Detachment in the Owen Stanley range had broken Japanese defenses and sent the enemy retreating in disorder toward their Buna perimeter. On the morning of November 16, a Japanese naval pilot on a routine picket patrol spied an Allied convoy about 10 miles south of Buna in Oro Bay. Two hours later the Buna garrison radioed an emergency message to Rabaul announcing that the Allies were landing in the bay.[44]

As outlined in his September message to Marshall, MacArthur wanted to cut off the Japanese retreat from the Owen Stanleys. His plan hinged on landing the 32d Division in the Japanese rear to destroy their lodgement at Buna. The officers and men of the "Red Arrow" Division anticipated little Japanese resistance. Willoughby was less sanguine, doubting that the Japanese would evacuate Buna voluntarily until the Solomons campaign was decided. He publicized his concern that the Japanese had an "enormous concentration of first-class troops" capable of major operations in MacArthur's theater.[45] A War Department estimate of Japanese ground forces in the South Pacific was the source of Willoughby's wariness. Because ULTRA was the basis for this appreciation, it provides a gauge to measure the quality of U.S. Army intelligence about its Japanese opponent in late 1942 (see Table 2.1).[46]

The "division" that Washington was unable to identify on New Guinea was Horii's South Seas Detachment. Allied frontline fighting troops provided the intelligence about the division's subordinate units. They confirmed individual formations from captured documents taken from enemy dead and interrogations of Japanese prisoners of war. The three-thousand-man discrepancy between Washington and Brisbane over the number of Japanese troops on New Guinea resulted from Southwest Pacific Headquarters' decision to factor Japanese casualties into their strength equations. As for ULTRA, it portended that another five thousand troops were destined for the island.

ULTRA mistakenly located three divisions—the Guards, 16th, and 48th—on New Britain when they were at Singapore, in the Philippines, and in the Netherlands East Indies, respectively. Consequently, the War Department located a total of six divisions on New Britain; the Guards, 16th, 38th, 48th, and 65th, and one unidentified division, or forty-seven thousand troops. Willoughby more accurately counted only three divisions on New Britain, the 48th, 16th, and 65th, or a total of twenty-four thousand troops, although he acknowledged another thirty-six thousand troops were moving into the theater. He suspected that the unidentified division was the Akatsuki Force, a corps-level formation, and identified the

Table 2.1. Japanese Units Identified by SWPA in the Southwest Pacific
as of November 1, 1942

Units	Estimated Location	Remarks (SWPA)	Actual Unit	Actual Location
2d Division	Solomons		2d Division	Solomons
18th Division	Solomons/in transit		124th Infantry, 18th Division	Solomons[a]
7th Division	Solomons/in transit		28th Infantry, 7th Division	Solomons
Special Naval Landing Force (SNLF)	Solomons		5th Sasebo SNLF	Solomons
Unidentified division	New Guinea	Horii Force	144th Infantry, 55th Division	New Guinea
38th Division	New Britain		38th Division	New Britain
Unidentified division	New Britain	Akatsuki?	1st Shipping Group	New Britain
Guards Division	New Britain	Yamagata Force	21st Independent Mixed Brigade[b]	New Britain
48th Division	New Britain/in transit		—	Netherlands East Indies
16th Division	New Britain	unconfirmed		Philippines
65th Division	New Britain	previously reported	65th Separate Brigade[c]	New Britain

Strength Summary

Location	War Department Estimate	In Transit	SWPA, G-2, Estimate	In Transit
New Guinea	10,000	—	7,000	5,000[d]
New Britain	47,000	—	24,000	36,000[e]
Guadalcanal	17,000	—	17,000	19,000[f]

[a]Detached from 18th Division; arrived from Philippines
[b]Sailed November from French Indochina for Rabaul
[c]From Philippines (reduced to 141st Infantry Regiment)
[d]SWPA note: Horii Division = 12,000 men
[e]SWPA note: 38th Division, Akatsuki Division, and Guards Division = 36,000 men
[f]SWPA note: 2d Division, 18th Division, and 7th Division = 36,000 men

Source: SWPA, Daily Intelligence Summary, 5/6 November 1942, in MacArthur Memorial Bureau
    of Archives, Norfolk, Virginia.

Guards Division as the Yamagata Force, which was actually the 21st Independent
Mixed Brigade.

Both army intelligence agencies mistook two brigades—the 21st and 65th—for
divisions. Intelligence analysts did not yet completely understand the Japanese
army's predilection to routinely form task forces or detachments of individual

infantry regiments. The presence of one of a division's three assigned regiments did not necessarily mean that the other two were either nearby or even en route to the same location. Analysts who credited lone regiments as full divisions ended up with highly inflated figures of enemy strength. In sum, because ULTRA's identifications of Japanese ground forces were tenuous at best and unreliable at worst, any analysis of ULTRA was subject to wide variances and outright misinterpretation.

American troops moving cautiously forward to engage the Japanese at Buna were unaware of what awaited them. Neither ULTRA nor traditional battlefield intelligence had penetrated the cloak of secrecy that surrounded Japanese operations and obscured their deployments. The November 6/7 Intelligence Summary noted that the bulk of the 5th Special Naval Landing Force was at Buna and commented lamely that such forces had been used as "shock troops" for previous operations in New Britain and the Solomons. The November 12/13 summary reported, without further elaboration, that "usually reliable sources" indicated possible renewed Japanese attacks against Port Moresby. Willoughby simultaneously maintained that "it was known" that Horii had orders to hold Buna until the contest for Guadalcanal was decided while he doubted that the Japanese would reinforce Buna.[47] A reader might fairly conclude that Horii had to make do with the few troops Southwest Pacific credited to him at Buna.

Willoughby underestimated the Japanese defenders holding the Buna sector as a depleted combat regiment and its supporting units, perhaps numbering fifteen hundred to two thousand troops capable only of conducting a delaying action. About six thousand Japanese actually garrisoned Buna. This was not, however, a critical error because only nine hundred of the Japanese were trained infantrymen still able to fight. The remainder were convalescents or service and support troops. Willoughby's error was to declare that further reinforcement of Buna was improbable because of Japanese commitments in the Solomons, logistics difficulties, and the high risks of such a gamble. By November 16 he predicted that even if reinforcements did arrive, they could not save the garrison, whose seizure was "practically assured."[48] Instead, the Japanese response to the American landing at Oro Bay was as swift as it was violent.

Japanese land-based naval aircraft from New Britain bombed the American landing site a mere six hours after Rabaul received the initial report of the invasion. The next morning a convoy sailed from Rabaul and landed one thousand Japanese reinforcements at Buna that night. Although concealed by darkness, they were not hidden from alert intercept operators, who reported the unfolding Japanese reinforcements. With this information, Southwest Pacific G-2 increased the total Japanese at Buna to between twenty-five hundred and twenty-seven hundred troops. Later, ULTRA uncovered a second convoy bound for Buna with a destroyer escort. It managed to disembark five hundred replacements near Buna destined for the grievously depleted 144th Infantry Regiment. That night Kenney's fliers, aiming by moonlight, slightly damaged two destroyers on their return voyage to Rabaul.[49]

When the U.S. 32d Division attacked Buna on November 19, the GIs expected to meet perhaps one thousand starving and battle-weary Japanese troops. Instead, there were at least thirty-five hundred fresh, tough reinforcements with orders to fight to the death to hold their positions. Overcoming their initial shock at the American landing, the Japanese in just forty-eight hours had reversed the tactical situation at Buna and now surprised their attackers. Confronted with an opponent unwilling to accommodate his assessments, Willoughby declared that it was "expedient for the enemy to withdraw. . . . [B]ut his bull-headed tendency may well cause him to continue [the struggle] in spite of losses entailed."[50] A Janus-faced assessment pattern, another G-2 trademark, later allowed Willoughby to claim prescience and conveniently overlook his less clairvoyant estimates.

The anticipated American walkover degenerated into a grinding battle of attrition in natural elements that nearly defied description. The 128th Infantry Regiment stumbled into a verdant hell.

> The first opposition from the enemy here was a surprise and shock to our green troops. The enemy positions were amazingly well camouflaged, and even seemed to have excellent fields of fire in the close quarters of the jungle. . . . Snipers were everywhere. . . . The enemy habitually allowed our troops to advance to very close range—sometimes four or five feet from a machine gun post—before opening fire; . . . . It was impossible to see where the enemy fire was coming from; consequently our own rifle and machine gun [fire] was ineffective during the early stages.[51]

Later in the campaign, on the other side of the line, a Japanese officer recorded: "Of the 6000 troops at Buna and Giruwa, 2000 have been killed in action. Another 500 or 600 are hospitalized. Everyone else has malaria. . . . [T]he daily ration is a half cup of cooked rice. Troops in support positions refuse to fire at the enemy for fear of being bombed. Each day twenty men perish. Patients cannot be evacuated."[52]

Cryptanalysts fought the war on another level, not as lethal but at times as nerve-racking and filled with uncertainty. Their war involved sorting and sifting through piles of irrelevant ULTRA material to uncover nuggets of valuable data. They worked under constant pressure because every day the Japanese military broadcast thousands of radio messages. A former Japanese signal officer estimated that each army division transmitted about forty messages a day, or roughly fourteen thousand a year. Imperial Army Headquarters in Tokyo routinely dispatched five hundred messages a day; Southern Army perhaps four hundred, and Seventeenth Army between two hundred and three hundred daily. Japanese forces in the Southwest Pacific likely transmitted fourteen hundred messages a day, excluding army air and Imperial Navy communications.[53]

Distance, signal strengths, frequencies, atmospherics, weather, and equipment affected Central Bureau's ability to intercept Japanese broadcasts. It was of course impossible to copy every single radio message, so traffic analysts and crypt-analysts had to assess unprocessed and fragmentary material. They passed these incomplete data, usually vague and often contradictory, to Allied intelligence analysts whose interpretations and evaluations placed the data into a context that rendered them meaningful to others. The exhilaration of a correct deduction accompanied the despair of ever penetrating the Japanese army cipher system.

In early December 1942, American signal intelligence caught glimpses of Japan's newly formed Eighteenth Army, which Imperial General Headquarters had organized on November 18 to conduct ground operations on New Guinea. Naval intelligence analysts in Hawaii pinpointed this new headquarters at Rabaul and identified it as the 18th Army Division. Central Bureau pursued that lead and determined that this was the unit responsible for furnishing reinforcements from Rabaul to Buna. By December 6 Central Bureau had identified Eighteenth Army as the controlling headquarters for the Buna forces.[54] Thus within two weeks of its formation, ULTRA had verified the creation of a major new Japanese army-level headquarters in the Southwest Pacific theater.

At Rabaul Eighteenth Army's commander, Lieutenant General Adachi Hatazo, ordered his 21st Independent Mixed Brigade taken by destroyers to Buna beginning on November 28. By November 26, U.S. naval intelligence in Hawaii predicted further Japanese attempts using destroyers to reinforce Buna within three to four days.[55] In short, navy ULTRA had revealed the impending Japanese joint operation within hours of Adachi's orders. Like the Port Moresby operation, intelligence gleaned from reading Japanese naval codes exposed the plans of participating army units. The Imperial Navy's less secure cipher system had again compromised both services' intentions.

The first Japanese serial of four destroyers departed Rabaul Harbor as scheduled on November 28. B-17 heavy bombers damaged two ships, forcing the convoy to reverse course and return to port. Two days later another four-destroyer convoy sailed for Buna protected by twenty Zeros. It reached its destination during the early morning hours of December 1, but then Allied aircraft dropped flares over the landing area, illuminating the ships. The ensuing attacks so disrupted the landing that only an infantry company and part of a signal unit got ashore.[56]

Constant Allied aerial attacks on Japanese shipping failed to arouse Japanese suspicions about the security of their operational ciphers. They believed that routine changes to key registers and the issuance of new codebooks frustrated potential codebreakers. During August and September 1942, for instance, the Japanese had changed practically every one of their naval codes and ciphers, although difficulties in distributing copies of new codebooks and call signs to fleet units scattered halfway around the world delayed the major call sign change until October 1, 1942.[57] Secure that such changes ensured the sanctity of their codes, the Japanese looked elsewhere for possible explanations of Allied attacks on their shipping.

One likely source of advance warning on Japanese convoys departing from Rabaul was the Allied coastwatcher network. The Directorate of Intelligence, Royal Australian Navy, had established the Coastwatcher Service before the war. Adventurous, independent, and undisciplined, most coastwatchers lived in the wild, remote regions of the islands of the Bismarck Archipelago, New Guinea, and the Solomons. The Allied Intelligence Bureau (AIB) cultivated these coastwatchers, who operated deep behind Japanese lines, and also dispatched its own agents to the islands to spy on Japanese air and ship movements. When the coastwatchers transmitted their reports about Japanese air and sea movements to Allied headquarters in Australia, their radio broadcasts simultaneously betrayed their presence to the Japanese just as Japanese radio signals had revealed their operations to the Allies. Japanese patrols hunted down and killed or brutally tortured coastwatchers and the locals who helped them. Beyond their tactical reports, perhaps the coastwatchers' finest service was to shield, albeit unknowingly, the ULTRA secret in the Southwest Pacific Area.[58]

Coastwatchers augmented MacArthur's growing intelligence network, but even at this early date, much to Willoughby's chagrin, Southwest Pacific Headquarters was relying heavily on ULTRA.[59] Only ULTRA routinely provided the Allies with advance and reliable notification of Japanese deployments. Hawaii warned MacArthur on December 2, for example, that Japanese fighters staging from southern New Britain would escort the next Buna convoy scheduled for December 8. Forewarned of the fighter escort, American B-17 pilots altered their tactics. The big, four-engine bombers struck the convoy in successive waves, raining bombs on the destroyers. When the Zero pilots wheeled after one wave of bombers, another wave arrived to bore in on the ships. At the undeground communications' center at Rabaul, Adachi studied radio messages from the convoy describing the attack. Judging the risks too great, he ordered the naval commander to abort his run and return to the base.[60]

The Japanese regrouped for another resupply effort and naval ULTRA again detected their preparations. Concealed by darkness and heavy rain from air observation but not from ULTRA, five destroyers were able to unload supplies at Buna on December 12. Naval intelligence recorded the successful reinforcement, and Kenney's fliers harassed this convoy on its return route to Rabaul.[61]

Kenney's aerial gauntlet and relentless ground attrition did compel the Japanese high command to reconsider the protracted defense of Buna. Instead of pouring more reinforcements into Buna, they opted to strengthen their rear areas in New Guinea and thereby create a formidable defense in depth. When Imperial Headquarters charged Eighteenth Army with the New Guinea campaign, it simultaneously created Eighth Area Army, also located at Rabaul. This newest area army controlled Eighteenth and Seventeenth armies, the latter directing operations in the Solomons. Tokyo ordered Eighth Area Army to occupy Madang and Wewak on the New Guinea coast as the first steps to consolidating a defense in depth.[62] The three infantry battalions from the 5th Infantry Division that were assigned the mission departed Singapore on December 2 bound for Rabaul. Coordination for the shipment among the scattered army and navy units was accomplished through numerous radio messages and this sudden surge in communications tipped the Japanese hand to Allied signal intercept monitors.

Navy analysts in Hawaii predicted on December 13 that a major offensive was forthcoming in New Guinea. A partially decrypted Japanese naval message from Rabaul the next day ordered the occupation of Madang, Wewak, and other points on the northern New Guinea coast. A later, more complete, decipherment of this intercept disclosed that the Japanese would first occupy Madang and then take Wewak on December 18. By December 17 U.S. naval ULTRA had uncovered the scope of the Japanese force aimed at Madang; the next day, pilots sighted the convoy moving toward Madang. U.S. radio intelligence facilities on Guadalcanal deciphered the name of the convoy as the "Wewak-Madang Occupation Force."

This latest convoy berthed at Madang after escaping with light damage from attacks by Allied bombers. Off-loading proceeded smoothly as two infantry battalions of the 5th Division quickly captured Madang and its nearby airstrip. In the midst of the occupation, however, the USS *Albacore*, forewarned of the convoy's destination, torpedoed and sank the convoy flagship, the light cruiser *Tenryu*, whose loss decrypted Japanese messages unwittingly confirmed for the Americans. At Wewak the occupation force also suffered air attacks, but all its ships landed safely at their destination late on the afternoon of December 18.[63]

Intercepted Japanese naval messages to the Eleventh Air Fleet on December 17, available to U.S. intelligence the next day, had already unmasked Japanese plans to construct a series of airfields at Madang, Wewak, Hollandia, Wakde, Moemi, and other enclaves along the northern New Guinea coast. On Christmas Eve, cryptanalysts detected a convoy carrying the 19th Pioneer Unit, 24th Special Base Force, and an airfield construction outfit leaving the Palaus for Hollandia.[64] Only ULTRA could penetrate 300 to 400 miles into Japanese-held territory to identify these units accurately and with celerity. MacArthur's headquarters might have discovered the Japanese buildup at Madang and perhaps even at Wewak without ULTRA, but not in such specific detail. The air base construction program at Hollandia and points west might have escaped Allied notice entirely because it was in a region where Allied reconnaissance aircraft and ships ventured at their peril. ULTRA, then, was the sole means Southwest Pacific Headquarters had to discern the outlines of this major shift in Japanese strategy in New Guinea.

The diversified Japanese network of air bases also betokened the arrival of greater numbers of Japanese aircraft in the Southwest Pacific theater. Heretofore only Japanese naval aircraft had contested the control of the skies over MacArthur's theater. By mid-December, numerous Japanese army air force messages and new air-ground controllers at Rabaul denoted a forthcoming increase in army aircraft. Analysis of coded message addresses and partially decrypted messages disclosed that a convoy from the Palaus to Rabaul was carrying the Japanese army air force 11th Air Regiment, which was somehow associated with a 6th Army Air Force Division. Navy ULTRA made known a December 17 message from Truk warning Rabaul not to mistake the fifty-seven army aircraft flying to Rabaul the next day for enemy planes. Two days later, the 6th Air Division appeared for the first time in radio communications as its controllers directed orientation flights for the recently arrived fighter-pilot reinforcements. New army radio stations along the New Guinea coast at Wewak, Aitape, and Madang began broadcasting around the same time. [65] All the activity involving these army air force reinforcements left a trail of electronic footprints for Allied intelligence to track their movement into the theater.

At the time Imperial Headquarters organized Eighth Area Army, it also formed the 6th Air Division and dispatched it to New Guinea. On December 10, the first unit of the new air army, the 76th Independent Air Squadron, flew into Rabaul. Within days ULTRA discovered thirty-seven more fighters of the 11th Squadron landing at Rabaul. These aircraft had deployed from bases in Burma and loaded aboard an auxiliary carrier at Singapore that transported them to Truk. From there, they flew with a naval air escort to Rabaul. The 1st Squadron joined them at Rabaul in January 1943. A third echelon, consisting of the 45th Squadron, a light bomber outfit, flew from Manchuria to Japan.

The 6th Air Division's command group and the 45th's pilots, mechanics, and equipment sailed from the great naval base at Yokosuka, Japan, for Truk on the light carrier *Ryuho*. Decrypted Japanese naval signals, available December 4 and 6, unmasked *Ryuho*'s departure date, scheduled noontime positions, and lack of escort until the entire convoy formed on December 14. On December 12 the USS *Drum* torpedoed *Ryuho* off the Japanese coast. *Ryuho* survived, but forty-five pilots did not, and the damaged carrier limped back to Yokosuka. [66]

Submarine Force in Hawaii had used ULTRA to vector *Drum* across *Ryuho*'s path. The result denied much-needed aircraft and pilot reinforcements to the Japanese fighting on New Guinea. Allied submarine interdiction of Japanese sea-lanes of communication, at distances far from the fighting fronts, depended in great measure on ULTRA revelations. *Ryuho*'s fate was a harbinger of the full fury that Allied submarine commanders would presently unleash against Japanese shipping.

ULTRA occasionally gave tactical warning of Japanese air raids. For example, on December 23 an urgent dispatch alerted Southwest Pacific Headquarters to a forthcoming twelve-plane Japanese raid on Buna scheduled for the next afternoon. Follow-up intercepts of naval Eleventh Air Fleet messages disclosed that the Japanese planned two separate raids, involving a total of thirty-seven aircraft, to support an infantry counterattack. After further postponements, also detected by ULTRA, twenty to thirty Japanese fighters and several dive-bombers did attack Buna on December 28. They killed three Allied soldiers and wounded seven others, but in exchange the waiting American P-38s shot down eleven Japanese aircraft.[67]

During 1942, naval ULTRA enjoyed spectacular success in the Pacific war from the Coral Sea to Midway to the Solomons and New Guinea. In contrast, army ULTRA was still in its formative stages. Arlington Hall and Central Bureau had made measured gains that year in reading message addresses and in traffic analysis, but these owed much to the navy's technical assistance. In short, MacArthur was dependent on the U.S. Navy for ULTRA.

A yardstick of the success of army ULTRA is the intelligence appreciation of Japanese ground forces arrayed in MacArthur's theater on the final day of 1942 (see Table 2.2). Available army ULTRA predicted that the 3d, 4th, 5th, and Guards divisions were headed to Rabaul. In fact, none of these units was slated for Rabaul. Neither was the 21st Division at Rabaul; it remained at Hanoi, French Indochina. Thus the mistaken location of these five divisions became a planner's nemesis that had to be taken into account because no one at Southwest Pacific Headquarters could ignore the possibility that ULTRA was correct. Just as significant, neither Central Bureau nor Arlington Hall had detected the movement of the 51st Division into the theater in November. Nor was there any advance warning that the 20th and 41st divisions had received orders in December to deploy to Rabaul. Army ULTRA, like the swelling Allied counteroffensive in the Southwest Pacific, was still in its embryonic stage.

Allied victories on the grim battlegrounds of the Solomons and New Guinea in 1942 were the first steps on the road to Tokyo. ULTRA also made opening gains against Japanese military communications that year. But just as powerful Japanese forces barred the way to Tokyo, so the Imperial Army's ciphers blocked Central Bureau and Arlington Hall codebreakers' attempts to ferret out their secrets. The U.S. Navy overstated the case, however, when it complained that "the Army has accomplished practically nothing whatsoever in obtaining operational radio intelligence."[68] Navy assertions that "all radio intelligence of concern to the Army had come from the Navy" were similarly exaggerated. Naval signals intelligence experts did share techniques of traffic analysis with Allied intercept operators.

Table 2.2. U.S. Army Intelligence Estimate of Japanese Forces in the
Southwest Pacific, December 31, 1942

	Location			
Unit	New Guinea	New Britain	Solomons	Remarks
Eighth Area Army		X		Captured documents
3d Division		X		ULTRA
4th Division		X		ULTRA
5th Division		X		ULTRA
Guards Division		X		ULTRA
21st Division		X		Rabaul or en route
Eighteenth Army	X			Recently established
21st Independent Mixed Brigade	X			
170th Infantry Regiment	X			
229th Infantry Regiment	X			One battalion at Buna
144th Infantry Regiment	X			Previously identified
41st Infantry Regiment	X			Previously identified
Seventeenth Army			X	
2d Division			X	
38th Division			X	
35th Brigade			X	

Source: SWPA, Daily Intelligence Summary, 30/31 December 1942, in MacArthur Memorial Bureau
of Archives, Norfolk, Virginia.

They did provide information about the idiosyncratic "fist" or transmission techniques of certain Japanese naval operators; each operator had a particular touch
and rhythm as he tapped out Morse Code, and this was used to identify naval
units.[69] The navy also supplied some equipment and data-sorting machines to the
army that materially assisted Central Bureau's assault on Japanese military
ciphers.

As mentioned earlier, the roots of the navy's predominance are found in the
prewar years when naval intelligence had monitored and deciphered Japanese
naval radio communications. The U.S. Navy's radio intelligence effort was
grounded in extensive theoretical and practical experience. Naval cryptanalysts
also had the advantage of solving Japanese naval ciphers that were not as sophisticated as those employed by the Imperial Army. At the outbreak of war, the U.S.
Navy already had operational interception and decryption facilities in Melbourne,
Hawaii, and Washington targeted against Japanese naval communications. In
contrast, the U.S. Army had to construct its interception and decryption service
against Japanese military communications while fighting the war.

Central Bureau's foundation was an intercept network with sites at Brisbane,
Townsville, Port Moresby, and other detachments scattered over northeastern
Australia and southeastern New Guinea. Cryptanalytic successes against Japa-

nese army call signs were balanced by the maddening inviolability of the army's three-digit code. Limited victories against air-ground communications systems were offset by the failure of direction-finding efforts at Townsville. Successful traffic analysis as in the Akatsuki case was counterbalanced by the failure to decipher the Japanese army's four-digit mainline code. Even so, a cryptanalytic organization with hard-won operational experience existed. On the technical side, Central Bureau and Arlington Hall (the cryptanalysts, the intercept operators, the IBM sorters—in short, the paraphernalia of codebreaking in World War II) had established the nucleus of the decryption center targeted specifically against Japanese military radio communications. Central Bureau's constant exchange of technical data with Arlington Hall was building the basis for a solution to some codes in 1943. In the meantime, the U.S. Navy supplied most of MacArthur's ULTRA and it would retain a prominent role in his headquarters throughout the war.

On the intelligence side, the process of analysis and evaluation of ULTRA during 1942 exhibited Willoughby's idiosyncrasies, particularly his disconcerting habit of reversing major interpretations overnight for no apparent reason. Such contradictory assessments allowed Willoughby's critics—of whom there were many—to point to his hedging as confirmation of the G-2's incompetence or mendacity. In addition, Willoughby often projected his military appreciation of events onto opponents, a cardinal sin for an intelligence chieftain who aims to understand, not transform, the enemy. These traits resurfaced throughout the war in the highly personalized brand of intelligence assessments that were characteristic of MacArthur's campaigns. Another emerging pattern was MacArthur's willingness to execute scheduled plans despite what ULTRA or other intelligence might reveal about the Japanese. He launched the drive against the northern New Guinea coast in November exactly as he had outlined in his September message to Marshall despite intelligence warnings that massive Japanese reinforcements were headed for the region.

The Southwest Pacific theater's development was Central Bureau's writ large. In April 1942 MacArthur had the equivalent of twelve divisions, including the U.S. 41st Division and the 32d Division en route from the United States. Among his five hundred aircraft, only eighty-five were able to fly combat missions. MacArthur's navy numbered four cruisers, ten lesser warships, and eleven submarines. By January 1943 he had the equivalent of fifteen and two-thirds divisions with two more scheduled to arrive from the United States during 1943. His one thousand aircraft, five cruisers, sixteen lesser warships, and twenty-three submarines gave him greater striking power. Following a year of terrible attrition, MacArthur had attained rough parity with the Japanese and stood poised to wrest the strategic initiative and push forward to the Philippines.[70]

If 1942 was a year of learning for MacArthur's Central Bureau, 1943 became a year of exploitation. Japanese and Allied commanders in the Southwest Pacific entered the new year locked in a stalemate. The Japanese could not oust the Allies from Papua, but neither could the Allies eject the Japanese from the Bismarcks. Both sides were checked, and the belligerents seemed destined to fight a protracted struggle in forbidding swamps and rain forests. ULTRA provided the signposts that guided MacArthur through the Japanese defenses in this "Bismarck Barrier."

3
Breaking into the Japanese Army Codes, January 1943–January 1944

Four events highlighted the role of ULTRA in MacArthur's headquarters from January 1943 through January 1944. First, the Battle of the Bismarck Sea in March 1943 witnessed the almost complete annihilation of the Japanese Imperial Navy's Convoy Number 81. ULTRA had uncovered Japanese intentions to convoy the 51st Divison to Lae, New Guinea, and this intelligence allowed General Kenney to mastermind a gigantic aerial ambush that smashed the hapless clutch of Japanese transports and destroyers. Destruction was so complete that the strategic initiative in New Guinea passed forever from Japanese hands. Henceforth the Japanese found themselves condemned to defend coastal enclaves against a growing Allied counteroffensive capability in the Southwest Pacific.

The second event in which ULTRA proved significant was the destruction of Japanese air power in New Guinea. If the Battle of the Bismarck Sea nullified Japan's ability to send major reinforcements by sea to eastern New Guinea, Kenney's air assault on the Japanese airdromes at Wewak in August 1943 wrested air superiority over New Guinea from Tokyo's grasp. Kenney and his deputy, Brigadier General Ennis C. Whitehead, relied on the ULTRA intelligence harvested from Japanese army air force communications to plan their deadly raids. ULTRA kept the Allies apprised of the buildup of Japanese air bases on the northern New Guinea coast, and Kenney countered by secretly constructing advance airfields from which he launched strikes against Japanese planes identified by ULTRA as massed at vulnerable airdromes. The raids crippled Japanese air power just days before the Allied amphibious assault on Lae and subsequent paratroop drop on Nadzab.

The third event was a series of major codebreaking successes in 1943 against several Japanese military cipher systems. The first break into an imperial Army mainline code came in April. Central Bureau and the Signal Security Agency (SSA), the redesignated Signal Intelligence Service, were able to read a few hundred Japanese military messages per month. Of greater immediate significance was the U.S. Army's mastery of the Japanese army's Water Transport Code and penetration into the Japanese military attaché cipher system.

The U.S. Navy had originally worked on solving all water transport codes. Study revealed that the Japanese divided such codes between the army and the navy. The Imperial Army's Shipping Transport Command, for example, coordinated the movement of Japanese army units by sea and relied on army codes to encrypt its radio messages. According to the American cryptanalytic division of labor, the U.S. Navy continued to work on naval water transport codes but passed the army water transport system to U.S. Army cryptanalysts for solution. Central Bureau and Arlington Hall almost simultaneously pried open the secrets of the army water transport system code in April. Decrypted water transport messages revealed convoy sailing times, noon positions, cargoes, and a host of other related details hitherto unavailable to the Allies. A seemingly minor administrative code allowed Southwest Pacific Headquarters to identify with precision many of the Japanese ground forces moving by sea into the theater. ULTRA was the key to undersea ambushes that ultimately destroyed the Japanese merchant marine.

In September 1943, U.S. codebreakers solved the Japanese military attaché system of encryption. From then until March 5, 1945, nearly half the army attaché messages intercepted were available for translation within hours of receipt.[1] Decrypted attaché messages usually dealt with high-level strategy or military/political affairs but also contained valuable operational intelligence about the status of recent or ongoing Japanese army operations in theaters of war throughout Asia.

The fourth ULTRA milestone was a piece of good fortune bestowed on the allies. Australian troops mopping up the retreating Japanese near Sio, New Guinea, in January 1944 unearthed the complete cryptographic library of the Japanese 20th Infantry Division. When their find reached Central Bureau, Akin's cryptanalysts were able to read Japanese army messages with precision and immediacy in heretofore undreamed of quantities. From deciphering a few hundred Japanese army radio messages a month, Central Bureau almost overnight began solving more than twenty thousand messages a month. MacArthur reaped the accompanying intelligence windfall during his steady advance along the northern New Guinea coast.

Nineteen forty-two had closed on a grim note. After the Allied capture of Buna, both adversaries had to reconstitute their battered forces. Japanese losses were perhaps 13,000 killed of 20,000 engaged, but American and Australian troops suffered more than 8,500 battle and 27,000 malaria casualties. The U.S. 32d Division was wrecked and required almost a full year for retraining and rehabilitation before its next operation. The 163d Infantry Regiment, 41st Division, lost only 361 troops to the fighting but was ravaged by malaria; the Australian 7th Division endured about twice the battle casualties (5,698 to 2,848) of their American allies. The Japanese accepted the bitter loss of Buna, but they continued to hold a network of mutually supporting Japanese air and naval bases. These strongholds, deployed in depth, ran in two converging arcs through New Guinea and the Solomons to Rabaul.[2]

From January to June 1943, a stalemate existed in eastern New Guinea. Shipping shortages plagued the adversaries. The fighting on Guadalcanal drained Japanese transports away from Buna just as Allied operations in Europe and the South Pacific drew Allied vessels away from MacArthur. Aircraft were also in short supply. The U.S. Army Air Forces (AAF), mesmerized by the prospects of a strategic bombing campaign against the Nazi Reich, gave priority to Europe. In the Pacific, carrier air forces remained firmly under navy control. The Japanese too felt the aerial pinch because the Imperial Navy could not make good its carrier losses from Midway and the Solomon campaigns. Both belligerents ran their New Guinea operations on a shoestring and neither had the resources in 1943 to produce a decisive victory. This did not mean that the fighting stopped. The Southwest Pacific theater degenerated into a war of attrition. It was a contest that the Japanese could not win because they could not replace lost equipment, matériel, ships, and aircraft as fast as the American industrial giant could make good U.S. losses. It was a warfare that guaranteed heavy casualties, a warfare the Allies did not want to fight.

Lieutenant General Imamura Hitoshi, commander of Eighth Area Army at Rabaul, learned on January 1, 1943, that Imperial Headquarters had reported to the emperor its decision to suspend operations on Guadalcanal. The news especially troubled Imamura because during his imperial audience only two months earlier, the emperor had charged him with retaking the island. A sober, reflective, somewhat bookish officer, Imamura had helped to revise the Imperial Army's "Field Service Regulations." In a sense, Imamura had written the book, and the situation he faced on New Guinea seemed to have a textbook solution.[3]

In January 1943 Japan still held preponderant air, naval, and ground strength in the Southwest Pacific and retained the strategic initiative in New Guinea. With these advantages, Imamura's overall plan was to carve out a defensive perimeter in eastern new Guinea. Behind this bulwark, Eighteenth Army would fight a delaying action designed to buy time to complete the buildup of Japanese bases in western New Guinea. Despite the loss of Buna, Imamura pushed ahead with his earlier plans to secure Lae and capture Wau. Wau, located about 150 miles west-northwest of Buna, was defended only by the small Australian Kanga Force, which depended on aerial resupply for survival. This advance guerrilla outpost was hemmed in by cloud-draped mountains that made routine aerial resupply flights harrowing experiences. Isolated and weakly defended, Wau seemed ripe for Imamura's picking. He ordered the 102d Infantry Regiment, 51st Division, from Rabaul to New Guinea to spearhead the attack. Eighth Area Army staff officers expected that their offensive would trigger a decisive battle near Wau in July or August 1943.[4]

Under the command of Major General Okabe Tooru, the division infantry group commander, the 102d Infantry and a battalion of field artillery represented the largest single Japanese reinforcement effort to date in New Guinea. Okabe expected to land at Lae and then move rapidly inland to Wau. A convoy sailing as far east as Lae ran the risk of Allied air attacks. On the other hand, if Imamura selected a safer port farther to the west for the landing, the rugged, uncharted terrain between the port and Lae would delay Okabe's move inland and upset the timetable for the Wau offensive.

Japanese troop transports moved at barely 8 knots per hour. At that rate they needed fifty hours to cover the 400 nautical miles from Rabaul to Lae. In order to protect the Lae convoy from air attack, each pilot of the newly arrived 6th Air Division had to fly two sorties per day. Each sortie involved four hours transit time and four hours escort—a prohibitive sixteen-hour flight day on the pilot's shoulders. Eighth Area Army, Eighteenth Army, 6th Air Division, Eighth Fleet, and Eleventh Naval Air Fleet staff officers met on December 25 at Rabaul to work out details for the convoy's route. Although the navy pledged to bomb the Allied air bases at Port Moresby before the convoy's departure, naval aircraft maintenance facilities at Rabaul lacked spare parts, and mechanics could not overhaul enough fighters and bombers in time for the promised attack. The convoy still sailed for Lae on schedule.[5]

Central Bureau passed General Kenney a warning that a Japanese reinforcement convoy was destined to depart Rabaul for Lae on January 6. Although neither cryptanalysts nor intelligence specialists knew that this was the Okabe Force, its imminent arrival fit with known Japanese efforts to strengthen their newly constructed airdromes dotting the northern New Guinea coast. U.S. Navy radio intercept operators at Melbourne also detected increased Japanese radio traffic associated with troop movements into the Southwest Pacific Area. Japanese units from China, the Philippines, and the home islands were heading into MacArthur's theater via the major staging area in the Palaus.[6]

Acting on this ULTRA, Kenney had stepped up attacks on Japanese shipping in Rabaul harbor and intensified reconnaissance of the New Britain coast in the hope of locating the convoy. On January 6, reconnaissance pilots sighted the enemy ships as predicted off the south-central coast of New Britain. American and Australian pilots fought the convoy for two days. Repeated high-altitude attacks by Kenney's B-24 heavy bombers and twin-engine P-38 long-range fighters inflicted no damage the first day. Kenney stubbornly kept up the pressure with

B-25s attack a Japanese transport during the Battle of the Bismarck Sea, March 1943. (Official photo USAAF, courtesy of U.S. Army Military History Institute)

night attacks that finally left one transport on fire and adrift. Japanese destroyers rescued six hundred survivors from the sea.

Japanese aircraft and destroyer escorts managed to shelter the convoy from damage during Allied strikes the next day. The repeated heavy air attacks forced the Eleventh Air Fleet to switch its plans from defending the convoy to attacking Port Moresby. The transports steamed into Lae on January 8 in time to see the still-smoldering debris of a dawn air strike on the Lae airdrome and the charred frames of fifteen Japanese aircraft littering the dispersal area. Around noon, American fighters and bombers returned to damage a transport, which later beached. Captured Japanese diaries testified to the deadly effect of the American bombs on the soldiers aboard the crowded transports. One admitted: "Night and day the enemy bombings have become more and more active despite the continuous air cover given by our fighters. Bombs come down like rain and explode around the ships. . . . Despite the constant attack of our fighters, enemy planes carry out their dreadful bombings on as large a scale as they prefer." A second noted: "At 1900 hours yesterday [January 6], enemy planes commenced dropping flares. Soon afterwards, bombing of the convoy was carried out. Several tens of enemy planes coming in rapid succession made their intensive attacks which were utterly indescribable."[7]

As Allied airmen punished the New Guinea–bound ships, Naval Communication Intelligence Center, Washington, decrypted Japanese messages on January 8 that mentioned a Lae reinforcement force. Two American submarines, *Grampus* and *Argonaut*, took up the hunt. On January 10 *Grampus* sank two more merchantmen on their return course from Lae to Rabaul. However, Japanese destroyers cornered *Argonaut*, depth-bombed it to the surface, and finished off the American submarine with gunfire.[8]

Operation 18, the Japanese code name for this convoy, cost the Japanese two troop transports sunk and another damaged. These losses were confirmed for MacArthur by ULTRA. About 600 soldiers perished along with the stricken ships. Allied airmen shot down six aircraft and destroyed another seventeen on the ground at Lae. Twenty percent of the 6th Air Division's pilots were killed in action. Only one-third of the Okabe Force safely reached shore at Lae, with just one-half its supplies and equipment. The Japanese high command was so desperate to get fresh troops to New Guinea that it accepted these frightful losses and declared the operation a success.[9] Eighth Area Army issued commendations to the units involved in Operation 18, and Imperial Headquarters reported the action to the emperor. Awards and rhetoric aside, the full-fledged Okabe Force could not be committed to the Wau offensive. Given the near-success of the Japanese attack, the remaining two-thirds of Okabe's troops might have made a decisive difference. They never arrived because ULTRA alerts enabled the Allies to disrupt the effort.

Imamura, unaware that his radio messages were betraying his schemes to the Allies, pushed ahead with plans to reinforce the New Guinea redoubts. On January 15 and 16, ULTRA revealed that two army transports were scheduled to reach Wewak two days later. Submarine Force, Pacific, passed the convoy's noon positions, escorts, and arrival time at Wewak to the USS *Triton*, which attacked and sank one transport and damaged the other.[10]

ULTRA did not, however, catch the mid-January move of ten thousand men of the 20th Division from the Palaus to Wewak. Japanese dispatches of January 13 intercepted in Washington withheld their secrets as a new cipher key temporarily stymied navy cryptanalysts. Ten days after the original intercept, codebreakers finally read the message about the 20th Division's deployment on January 17 to Wewak. About the same time, naval cryptanalysts at Melbourne broke a January 14 message announcing the division's passage to Wewak. By February 1, naval ULTRA confirmed that ninety-five hundred troops of the 20th Division, including personnel of the division headquarters, had been transported to Wewak. By that time, navy cryptanalysts in Hawaii had already spotted the arrival of Japanese army fighter planes at Wewak and anticipated further deployments by units of the 20th Division from the Palaus to Wewak.[11] The 20th's unhindered arrival at Wewak was a quirk brought about by a temporary blackout of Japanese codes. Its success encouraged Imamura's plans to convert Lae into a redoubt to block further Allied advances along the northern New Guinea coast.

Imamura had to reinforce the tiny Eighteenth Army garrisons near Lae to accomplish his design. Staff officers in Tokyo confidently jabbed at maps as if the jungle trails of New Guinea were the same as the road network on the China front and asked why Imamura wasn't moving. Distances appeared deceptively close on the maps decorating Tokyo's walls. In reality, the jungle terrain sapped the troops. For example, it took an infantryman forty grueling days to traverse the 240 miles between Wewak and Lae. Construction units and engineers from Eighteenth Army were supposed to be widening trails along the coast, but they needed four to five months to corduroy a road suitable for army vehicles. The sea offered the only avenue to move infantrymen and their equipment quickly to Lae.

After the evacuation of Buna, Adachi planned to ship his 51st Infantry Division to New Guinea. Adachi was an experienced campaigner from the China front. A round face, drooping mouth, and receding hairline masked Adachi's ironlike determination. He revered the traditional Japanese warrior values of patience, perseverance, and uncomplaining endurance. The general was a simple, tough, hard-drinking soldier who could conceive of no greater glory than sacrificing himself for his emperor. This flinty leader passed the time in New Guinea's jungles writing Japanese poetry (*tanka*).[12]

At the beginning of February 1943, senior Eighth Area Army officers huddled on Rabaul to consider alternatives on New Guinea following the loss of Guadalcanal. Imperial Headquarters favored sending reinforcements to New Guinea in May, but Imamura and Adachi argued that they were needed by March. The sooner Lae was reinforced, their argument ran, the greater the chances for success. Allied air power was increasing and the Japanese air forces were unable to replace their terrible losses over Guadalcanal and New Guinea. To postpone the convoy until May simply handed the Allies time to muster additional aircraft to attack the ships. The scheduled evacuation of Guadalcanal by early February would permit the Japanese to use all their aircraft to defend the New Guinea convoy.

Imamura had confronted the same dilemma in January when he dispatched the Okabe Force to Lae. Staff officers heatedly debated the 51st Division's destination. Was it better to ship the reinforcements to Lae where they were within range of Allied aircraft or to Madang where they were not? Madang was about 140 miles, as the crow flies, from Lae. Troops would have to march along narrow coastal tracks that meandered through the great swamp between the Sepik and But rivers; this nearly doubled the distance. Okabe's shattered remnants retreating after their repulse at Wau needed reinforcements immediately. Eighth Area Army staff officers estimated that a convoy bound for Lae had at best a 50-50 chance of success. War games involving a ten-ship convoy to Lae projected losses along the route of four transports and thirty to forty aircraft, or 40 percent of the ships and 33 to 50 percent of their aerial escorts. Eighteenth Army's chief of staff, Lieutenant General Yoshihara Kane, recalled that the battlefield situation left "no alternative to Lae."[13] Without options, Imamura on February 14 ordered the 51st Division to Lae.

The Japanese set out to locate and neutralize Kenney's airfields. Aerial photographs taken on February 12 told the 6th Air Division commander, Lieutenant General Itabana Giichi, that Allied air bases in New Guinea held ninety-seven bombers and eighty-one fighters. Reconnaissance flights two weeks later uncovered no other concentrations of aircraft. Itabana determined that he could not attack Port Moresby because the airdromes there were too well defended; the aircraft too dispersed; and Japanese air power too weak to destroy the fields. Hard lessons learned over Guadalcanal suggested that the 6th Air Division had better conserve its limited air strength to protect the convoy. Another Guadalcanal lesson was that Allied bombers favored high-altitude attacks. Itabana accordingly ordered his pilots to fly at high altitudes in order to intercept any bombers.[14]

MacArthur's headquarters expected Rabaul to reinforce the Japanese on New Guinea, but the Americans were uncertain when or where this might occur. The first tip-offs of a forthcoming convoy appeared in early February when Kenney's air intelligence branch discerned Japanese deployments characteristic of preparations for a major convoy. The sighting of a Japanese floatplane off New Britain on February 7 coincided with the known enemy habit of deploying these planes for antisubmarine patrols in advance of convoys. Kenney ordered more patrols over Rabaul. Photographs taken on February 14 displayed a concentration of seventy-nine vessels, including forty-five merchantmen and six transports, a surprisingly high number when there was no sign of the Imperial Combined Fleet in the area.[15] Rabaul Harbor was once again jammed with shipping, but photographs alone could not tell MacArthur or Kenney the Japanese destination. The situation recalled the indecision of the previous July when Willoughby and the navy were uncertain of the intended Japanese target. This time U.S. Navy cryptanalysts provided the answer.

On February 19 Fabian's Melbourne unit handed MacArthur ULTRA that the Japanese planned to land at Lae in early March. Since February 8, navy cryptanalysts in Washington had labored to decipher an intercepted Japanese naval message. Eight days later, despite difficulties in translation, the broken message revealed that the convoy schedule to RZM—the Japanese designation for Lae—had to be changed to add more destroyer transports. Seventeen hours later, a better translation clarified Japanese plans to dispatch three separate convoys, one each to land at Madang, Wewak, and Lae. The CINCPAC (Commander in Chief, Pacific Fleet) Intelligence Bulletin for February 19 reported the forthcoming simultaneous reinforcement and noted that the 20th and 41st divisions would be taken to Madang and Wewak in transports while transports and destroyers would carry troops to Lae. Washington needed three days to decrypt a February 21 Eleventh Air Fleet message that pinpointed a six-ship convoy destined to land the 51st Division about March 5 at Lae. ULTRA later announced that the Japanese had ordered destroyers and six transports to reach Lae sometime before March 12.[16]

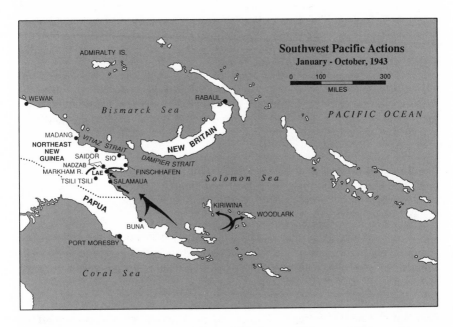

Allied aerial reconnaissance of Rabaul Harbor on February 22 showed a new high of fifty-nine merchant vessels, totaling nearly 300,000 tons, anchored there. This was far above the 200,000 tons of merchant shipping normally at anchor in the vast harbor. Given the inactivity in the Solomons, Willoughby warned, this increased shipping might be used to reinforce New Guinea. Three days later, MacArthur and Kenney set in motion the destruction of the Lae convoy. Mac-Arthur gave the mission highest theater priority, and Kenney called on his aircrews for a maximum effort. By February 26, Southwest Pacific Headquarters knew from navy ULTRA that the six ships would arrive at Lae about March 5. The same day, Kenney and Brigadier General Ennis Whitehead, deputy commander of the Fifth Air Force, carefully planned the execution of Number 81 Convoy. Dissatisfied with the inaccuracy of medium- and high-altitude bombing against Japanese shipping, Kenney determined to improve precision by using modified twin-engine B-25 medium bombers for daytime low-level skip-bombing and strafing attacks against Japanese vessels. On February 27, the two airmen choreographed dress rehearsals of the new tactics.[17]

With Whitehead's aircrews already practicing for a low-level attack on a large convoy, rumors that something big was up swirled through the command. Mac-Arthur and Kenney faced the classic predicament of mounting an operation based on intelligence from broken enemy codes without revealing to their adversary that they were reading his secrets. Because air patrols were routine, they used aerial reconnaissance to locate the Lae convoy without revealing the advance knowledge available from the broken codes. The pilots were, of course, not privy to ULTRA. They flew reconnaissance patterns where higher headquarters ordered them to fly. On any given day, several crews might be airborne. Only one, however, would locate the target. When Japanese lookouts on the destroyers escorting the Lae convoy spotted Allied reconnaissance planes on their first two days out of Rabaul, they had no reason to suspect that the Allies already knew their destination. After the sighting, other reconnaissance aircraft shadowed the sixteen-ship convoy as it wound its way slowly around the northern coast of New Britain toward New Guinea.

Willoughby disclosed the convoy's destination with a mixture of aerial sightings and "analysis." Although the daily Intelligence Summary acknowledged that the convoy's exact terminus was uncertain, it presented an intelligence appreciation that was, to the uninitiated, almost clairvoyant. According to Willoughby, if the Japanese destination was Wewak or Madang, they were taking too hazardous a southern route and exposing themselves needlessly to Allied air power. With these ports ruled out, aerial sightings of the convoy supported the notion that the Japanese intended to break south toward Lae under cover of darkness.[18]

Even with the two weeks' advance notification of the Lae convoy that ULTRA provided, the actual intercept was touch and go. A pilot spotted the convoy off the northern coast of New Britain on March 1, but darkness soon enveloped the ships. The next morning American pilots rediscovered the convoy around 8:30, but poor weather delayed their attacks until nearly 10:00 when long-range B-17s and B-24s attacked it from high altitudes. They managed to sink one transport and damage two other ships. As Number 81 Convoy pressed on for Lae, it came within the range of American medium bombers.

Japanese airmen were circling over the convoy at 7,000 feet because they were expecting a repeat of the earlier high-level bombing. B-25s and scores of fighter aircraft roaring in at low levels caught the Japanese totally off guard. Their reaction was slowed further by the incompatible radios used in Japanese army and navy aircraft, which made radio communications between the services impossible. Radio communications between the army's 6th Air Division and its 12th Air Brigade were also inadequate because of incompatible receiving equipment. Eleventh Air Fleet naval pilots arrived above the convoy just in time to witness the carnage.[19]

Allied pilots shouted over their radios about Japanese ships "burning and exploding" or "smoking and burning amidships." They flew so low that Japanese sailors believed the enemy aircraft would smash into the bridge of their ships. Under interrogation a survivor of the *Aiyo* Maru told a harrowing tale: "A bomb exploded between Number 3 hatch and the engine room about nine A.M. on March 3rd. Fuel caught fire and ammunition exploded turning the hold into a flaming hell. Troops who could rushed up to boat deck. Crowded together like cattle on the open deck they were machine gun strafed and many were killed and wounded."

Distress calls from stricken Japanese ships filled the airwaves. Throughout the three-day air-sea battle, Allied intercept operators overheard uncoded Japanese broadcasts like "Proceed to rescue the survivors" or "Drop rubber boats at the scene of the disaster." The survivors needed every bit of help because the official American report recorded that "life rafts and debris of the stricken convoy were thoroughly strafed and the number of enemy personnel that reached land safely appears to have been negligible."[20] This was no "clean" or impersonal air war from 10,000 feet. Pilots saw closeup the devastation they wrought.

Their cannon shells and bullets tore into Japanese clinging to life rafts, floating in the water, and huddling together in lifeboats. The water was whipped and churned into a bloody froth, the blood mixing with chunks of flesh and the oil from sunken ships. There was no respite for the survivors, who now floated defenseless, naked and exposed to machine-gun fire. The grisly business lasted into the night. When nothing was seen to move in the water, the strafing runs ended.[21] Pilots and aircrews gagged and vomited at the sight of the mangled human remains in the bloody sea. PT-boats moved in to finish off crippled transports and pluck a few lucky Japanese from the water for intelligence officers to interrogate.

Eight Japanese transports were lost along with four destroyers. Of 6,912 Japanese troops, about 3,900 survived. Only 1,000 reached Lae on their own; the remainder were returned to Rabaul aboard destroyers that had rescued them from the water. Eighth Area Army officially listed 3,000 men as missing. Losses proved heaviest in the division's 115th Infantry Regiment—51 officers and 1,206 enlisted men from the nearly 2,000-man regiment had perished. Adachi himself had to be rescued from the sea. When the disaster was reported to the emperor, he questioned why Lae was used instead of the port at Madang and urged the military to learn suitable lessons from the experience for future convoys.[22]

Even though MacArthur's triumph was total, he was not satisfied. The general's March 4 press release claimed that the Allied Air Forces had destroyed twenty-two Japanese ships (fourteen transports and eight destroyers) and killed 15,000 troops. However, ULTRA provided to MacArthur and the War Department confirmed the loss of at most ten transports. These major discrepancies between MacArthur's claims and the losses acknowledged in decrypted Japanese naval messages raised eyebrows in AAF Headquarters in Washington. After a thorough six-month study, Washington bluntly told Kenney that MacArthur's claims were exaggerated and that eight transports and four destroyers had been sunk with the loss of about 2,900 troops. MacArthur and Kenney bitterly contested the findings long after the war ended.[23] Both commanders ignored ULTRA confirmations of results not to their liking. In other words, they exploited ULTRA when it supported their operational preference, but this did not necessarily mean that they regarded this intelligence as definitive, particularly when the ULTRA version of events conflicted with their own perceptions.

Tokyo had counted on the 51st Division to hold Lae, and its virtual destruction critically weakened the southeastern approach to Rabaul. A hurried revision of Japanese joint policy, embodied in the Army-Navy Central Agreement on Southeast Area Operations of March 25, shifted priority from the Solomons to reinforce New Guinea in order to protect the endangered flank of their base at Rabaul.[24]

These circumstances governed the decision of the diminutive commander in chief of the Imperial Combined Fleet, Admiral Yamamoto Isoroku, to launch Operation I. The opportunity for a ground offensive in New Guinea had vanished, but future Allied advances there would eventually menace Rabaul. The Imperial Navy could no longer sustain the heavy losses it had suffered defending the New Guinea and Solomon fronts. For Yamamoto, a massed aerial onslaught against Allied air and shipping in the Solomons was his best opportunity to retard the swelling enemy counteroffensive. On April 3 Yamamoto, Vice Admiral Ugaki, and their respective staffs flew from the great Japanese naval bastion at Truk, Caroline Islands, to Rabaul to implement Operation I.[25]

Yamamoto massed a total of 350 naval aircraft, 160 planes from the Third Fleet's four carriers, and 190 aircraft from the Eleventh Air Fleet. U.S. Navy intercept operators overheard the two fleet headquarters in communication with each other, which alerted the Allies to an impending, large-scale air attack. The exact targets and dates of the attack remained unknown. Then an April 6 decryption announced X-day against Guadalcanal as April 7, and the U.S. Navy promptly warned the targeted commands to take precautionary measures. With this forewarning, Allied units on Guadalcanal dispersed shipping and braced for the air assault. On April 7 Allied coastwatchers on New Britain signaled news of Japanese aircraft heading south for targets previously identified by ULTRA. This combination of human and technical intelligence enabled 67 Allied fighter interceptors to meet the air armada of about 100 Japanese aircraft, roughly divided between fighters and bombers. The Japanese forced a fleet oiler to beach, sank a New Zealand corvette and a U.S. Navy destroyer, and damaged several other vessels. Allied airmen claimed 48 Zeros and 12 dive-bombers shot down, but later intercepts revealed actual Japanese losses as 12 fighters and 9 bombers.

Yamamoto had divided Operation I into four phases: the X-day phase against Guadalcanal; the Y phase against Port Moresby; the Y-1 phase against shipping in Oro Bay; and the Y-2 phase against Milne Bay and its airstrip. Another deciphered message, dated April 9, had identified the Y-1 and Y-2 phases and dates, but not the Y phase against Port Moresby. That base was hit by 45 bombers and 60 fighters on April 12 but it managed to escape major damage because of poor marksmanship on the part of the Japanese. U.S. Navy intelligence reported more raids likely the next day against Milne Bay. Nearly 90 Japanese aircraft struck Milne Bay as predicted, but they inflicted scant damage against the alerted defenders. Nonetheless, the inexperienced Japanese aircrews reported sinking 1 cruiser, 2 destroyers, and 25 transports and shooting down 134 Allied aircraft and destroying another 20 on the ground—all for the loss of forty-nine Japanese aircraft. Actual Allied losses amounted to 1 corvette and 1 destroyer, in addition to 2 transports sunk and 12 aircraft lost. Unaware of the wildly exaggerated battle damage claims, Yamamoto was jubilant, more so because he received a congratulatory telegram from the emperor exhorting him to build on the success.[26]

To pass on this news with a morale-raising visit to his frontline pilots, Yamamoto scheduled a flight to Ballale and Shortland islands. His exact itinerary was learned from a deciphered message three days before the trip.[27] Determined to get the man who had planned the attack on Pearl Harbor, the Office of the Secretary of the Navy made a decision. On April 18 American P-38s intercepted and shot down the bomber carrying Yamamoto to his troops.

Yamamoto's death sent shock waves throughout the Imperial Navy. Vice Admiral Kusaka Jin'ichi, commander of the Eleventh Air Fleet, suspected that the Allies were reading Japanese ciphers and ordered an investigation. Communications officers, however, disagreed. The navy's key register, they pointed out, had been changed on April 1 and it was impossible that Allied cryptanalysts could have so quickly solved the new cipher. In the end, blame was assigned to the Ballale army guard unit commander, who, it was alleged, had signaled Headquarters, Seventeenth Army, in a minor, insecure code about Yamamoto's planned visit. For whatever reasons, the Japanese navy refused to consider that the Allies had broken the five-digit mainline naval operations code. Their self-delusion continued to cost them dearly as MacArthur's counteroffensive gained momentum.

Another side effect of the Battle of the Bismarck Sea occurred on Goodenough Island. An Allied patrol captured a Japanese in a lifeboat that had washed ashore. They learned that their prisoner was a ship's master who took along his navigation charts to plot his course as well as several confidential documents entrusted to his care. In the abandoned lifeboat, they discovered the current "Japanese Army List," a register of forty thousand active duty Japanese officers, by rank and assignment, as of October 15, 1942. This invaluable reference document was turned over to MacArthur's Allied Translator and Interpreter Section where Japanese linguists worked day and night to translate every name and its accompanying data. Within two months, the translation, entitled *Alphabetical List of Japanese Army Officers,* had been printed by the Australian Government Printer on emergency order and distributed to Allied units from Alaska to India.[28]

Henceforth MacArthur's order of battle specialists could correlate the personal names of Japanese officers with specific Japanese units. For instance, a captured document might refer to a Lieutenant Ogawa at Finschhafen. Reference to the

Alphabetical List quickly identified him as First Lieutenant Ogawa Takeshi, Commander, 9th Company, 115th Infantry Regiment, 51st Division. This information located Ogawa's unit at a given time. Names of high-ranking Imperial Army officers appearing in naval ULTRA could be cross-checked and verified from the *Alphabetical List*. As Central Bureau gathered more and more ULTRA, comparing Japanese officers' names in deciphered communications against those in the register became a convenient and reliable means to verify an order of battle. The list filled a void because the information on Japanese formations provided to MacArthur's theater by the War Department was so elementary it was useless.[29]

The army register coup was followed in April by the first break into the Japanese Army Water Transport Code. Shortly after the outbreak of the Pacific war, U.S. Navy divers had salvaged the Japanese navy's water transport "S" code books from a submarine that had been sunk off Darwin, Australia, in January 1942. With these documents in hand, navy cryptanalysts were able to read Japanese naval shipping messages and use the resulting intelligence to interdict some Japanese navy convoys. The Imperial Army also controlled a major portion of Japanese shipping in order to transport its forces to their Pacific garrisons. The army used a separate code to communicate its convoy plans that had so far stymied Allied cryptanalysts. In the summer of 1942, the Japanese army reorganized its shipping command organization to meet the demands of its far-flung armies. A Shipping Command and a Shipping Force reported directly to the chief of staff of the Imperial Army. The Shipping Command controlled the 1st Water Transport Command (Japan), organized in August, and the 2d (China) and 3d (Southern Region) Water Transport commands, formed the next month. Each Water Transport Command was located at a major port where it regulated shipping schedules and priorities. It controlled various shipping transport sector units that had their own subordinate anchorage commands located on islands occupied by the Japanese army. The anchorage director controlled the arrivals and departures of ships and barges. He reported directly to his respective Water Transport Command.

The Shipping Force controlled the 1st Shipping Group Command, which had its own water transport construction regiments, debarkation units, and independent shipping engineer and construction units. Shipping group units provided the stevedores and construction personnel who built bases and maintained port facilities. Army shipping units proliferated along the northern New Guinea coast in order to support Eighteenth Army's expansion and the concomitant development of air bases and supply dumps. All of these shipping units were independent commands and communicated directly with each other and with their higher headquarters in a private code, the Army Water Transport Code, which was known by its discriminant, 2468. This simplified version of the mainline army code was a four-digit cipher that first appeared in December 1942. Rushed into operation to support the spreading network of anchorages, it lacked the carefully designed security of the mainline army code.

Internal flaws in the water transport system caught the attention of a U.S. Army sergeant (T-4) at Central Bureau named Joseph E. Richard, who was there merely by chance. Richard had been at the Signal Intelligence Service in the Munitions Building in January 1942 when he volunteered for overseas duty. He asked to be sent to Europe, but the only openings were in Australia. In July 1942, he joined the second cryptanalytic contingent that went to Australia. Richard soon became one of a handful of analysts who worked in vain against the Japanese three-digit cipher. In February 1943, a frustrated Richard asked Sinkov for permission to reexamine the four-digit message intercepts that had been recorded but that had not been sorted according to code or analyzed.

Richard began sorting all the intercepts in the 2468 series (the Japanese designation for the Water Transport Code) and others going back to mid-December 1942 in the hope that code changes may have been ordered around January 1, perhaps offering clues about the cipher. Arlington Hall had previously run the nonrandom 2468 on an IBM index (Central Bureau was still searching the Sydney docks for its IBM equipment), but the printout had shown no links between 2468 and previously recovered codebook entries. When Central Bureau's IBM sorters became available, they displayed the same disappointing conclusions. Richard noticed that the Water Transport Code underwent periodic changes and reported his find to Sinkov. Once 2468 was separated into the appropriate three-week periods marking the changes, relationships between the two code groups emerged. Sinkov signaled the discovery to Arlington Hall where cryptanalysts, using IBM runs that accommodated the three-week rule, saw further connections that helped to penetrate 2468 on April 6, 1943. IBM runs at Central Bureau had detected the same similarities, and a few hours after their colleagues at Arlington Hall, Sinkov and Richard also broke into 2468. It was a purely cryptanalytic solution, and contrary to Japanese beliefs, the deciphering of the Army Water Transport Code never depended on a captured codebook.[30]

It was no coincidence that Central Bureau and Arlington Hall discovered the wedge that broke the Water Transport Code "almost at the same hour" because they had been exchanging technical cryptanalytic intelligence daily. Besides the exchange of respective Japanese codebook meanings and additive book recoveries, from March 1943, Central Bureau supplemented the daily reports with a typed monthly progress report and summary of significant events. Akin and Sinkov had worked for the Signal Intelligence Service before it was renamed the Signal Security Agency, so sharing technical data with another army cryptanalytic agency was natural. Other Central Bureau personnel had also served as cryptanalysts in Washington and their personal relationships and ties facilitated cooperation between the two army organizations.

Two months after the initial break into the system, Central Bureau and Arlington Hall were routinely passing translations of decrypted water transport messages to the Military Intelligence Service (MIS) in the War Department. ULTRA from deciphered 2468 encoded messages enabled the U.S. Army to develop a broad picture of the Japanese army's shipping organization and activities as well as occasional data related to specific naval operational movements. The volume of messages was staggering. By August 1, 1944, U.S. Army intercept operators had recorded nearly 750,000 water transport messages. Roughly 10 percent—75,000 messages—contained significant intelligence that merited a complete translation of the signal. Among these, 34 percent—25,550—were shipping related, with 5 percent—3,750—convoy related.[31]

Assessment of ULTRA and any action taken on it remained separate issues reserved for the Southwest Pacific commander. Akin's active role ended when he handed a significant Army Water Transport Code decryption to Sutherland or MacArthur. Based on their decision and approval, Akin would transmit a summary of the message to submarine headquarters in Hawaii and to Seventh Fleet submarines at Perth and Brisbane.[32]

Submarine headquarters then rebroadcast "eyes only" radio messages to submarine commanders patrolling the Pacific. The submarine skipper used a special codebook to decipher the message. Afterward he steered his boat on the course most likely to intercept his oblivious victim. The Japanese never suspected that their Water Transport Code leaked, and they made only routine and well-anticipated changes to the code throughout the war.[33] Time and again, U.S. submarines, guided by ULTRA from decrypted Water Transport Code messages, sank Japanese merchantmen or warships.

Allied codebreaking successes of 1943 continued with the solution by U.S. Army cryptanalysts of the Japanese military attaché codes. Initial breaks into the attaché code occurred in the fall of 1942, and by September 1943 U.S. codebreakers were regularly reading radio messages between the attachés and Tōkyo. The military attachés received uniformly high-quality, strategic intelligence via Imperial Headquarters's weekly intelligence circulars that often included Tokyo's appraisal of Japan's battlefronts in China, the Pacific, and Europe. The daily messages Tokyo dispatched to its military attachés kept them apprised of current policy and unwittingly handed American codebreakers the Japanese perspective and interpretation of wartime events. Between July 1, 1943, and August 15, 1944, Arlington Hall translated more than five thousand attaché messages, and the War Department considered twenty-one hundred of these of the greatest strategic importance. Small wonder that the Signal Security Agency described Japanese military attachés as the most efficient spies working for the United States in Europe.[34]

PURPLE Machines, operating in Arlington, Brisbane, and London regularly pried open the secrets of the Japanese Foreign Ministry cables. Perhaps the most spectacular examples of operational intelligence obtained from diplomatic codes were the decrypted messages of the Japanese ambassador to Berlin, General Oshima Hiroshi, to the Foreign Ministry that detailed German defensive preparations on the so-called Atlantic Wall.[35] By early 1944, both military attaché and diplomatic reports were incorporated into the Military Intelligence Section's "Daily Intelligence Summary" and distributed to Southwest Pacific Headquarters.

However, as long as the Japanese army's four-digit codes defied compromise, an accurate assessment of Japanese forces in New Guinea eluded MacArthur's headquarters. The April 1943 "G-2 Summary of Enemy Dispositions," for instance, carried three Japanese divisions—20th, 41st, and 51st—in New Guinea but could identify only one of the nine infantry regiments subordinate to these divisions. The solitary identification hinged on battlefield intelligence collected by Australian infantrymen while fighting the 102d Regiment, 51st Division, during the grim, protracted battle at Wau. From that four-month-old information, Willoughby estimated that between 26,600 and 31,200 Japanese troops were on New Guinea. A month later, he believed that 4,000 reinforcements for the 20th Division and 8,000 for the 41st had increased Japanese strength on New Guinea to between 43,800 and 45,900 men. The 78th Infantry Regiment, 20th Division, was thought to be en route to New Guinea from the Palaus and analysts suspected that the entire 41st Division had concentrated at Wewak.[36]

In May, Central Bureau noticed additional Japanese reinforcements had landed at Wewak (May 3, 6). (The dates in parentheses refer to when the intelligence appeared in SWPA's Special Intelligence Bulletin [SIB].) In fact, the 61st Field Antiaircraft Battalion had just arrived. Anticipated troop convoy movements between the Palaus and Wewak materialized when another antiaircraft battalion as well as logistics and service units arrived at the New Guinea port. Telltale radio messages allowed Central Bureau to follow two naval transports to Wewak where they disembarked four labor companies to improve anchorage and airfield facilities there (May 16). Intercepted messages also revealed that Japanese troops were moving from the Netherlands East Indies and the Philippines toward New Guinea (May 7, 12, 18, 22).

ULTRA was not uniformly successful. It erroneously "confirmed" that the 40th Division had arrived in New Guinea during May because codebreakers mistook the presence of the 40th Field Road Construction Unit at Wewak for a subordinate unit of the 40th Division (May 6). This error led intelligence specialists to spend weeks speculating on what role the 40th Division would play in New Guinea when the formation was actually located in China.

An alert intercept operator could follow a convoy's progress, like the one of May 16 from the Palaus to Wewak. There the trail went cold because Allied air superiority rendered Hansa Bay so dangerous for large transports that the Japanese switched to smaller barges and trawlers to meet the resupply needs of forward units.[37] They used low-powered, short-range radio signals to manage the barge traffic that steadily moved men and supplies from Wewak to Hansa Bay and Lae. In most instances, the shifting tactics of the Japanese frustrated Central Bureau's eavesdroppers whose intercept stations were too far away to detect the weak radio signals that directed the stream of barges stuffed with troops and supplies to Lae. Over short distances, Japanese field telephone landlines made communications secure unless an agent could physically reach the phone line wire to tap it for Central Bureau. (A landline can be wire strung on telephone poles or wire laid on the ground to connect field telephones. The latter method was more common because it was easier to string the wire along the ground.) Thus Southwest Pacific Headquarters knew the approximate location of the enemy's divisions but could positively identify only those Japanese regiments actually fighting Allied forces. That was the state of intelligence on May 6, 1943, when MacArthur inaugurated Operation CARTWHEEL to reduce the Japanese bastion at Rabaul.

CARTWHEEL was a joint Southwest and South Pacific undertaking that originally envisioned thirteen amphibious operations, over six months, culminating in the seizure of Rabaul. As South Pacific forces under Admiral William Halsey climbed the Solomon Island chain, MacArthur's forces would seize Lae and Finschhafen. Next they would capture Madang. After that, MacArthur would cross the Dampier Straits to land on New Britain. For CARTWHEEL, MacArthur created the Alamo Force, an independent operational command but in truth nearly identical to his newly created U.S. Sixth Army.[38] The fiction did allow MacArthur to remove American troops from General Blamey's Allied Land Forces and place them under an American commander. The man MacArthur personally selected for this new army was Lieutenant General Walter Krueger.

Krueger started his army career as an enlisted man during the Spanish-American War (1898–1899). He served in the Philippines fighting Filipino guerrillas, and his outstanding soldierly skills in that brutal little war earned him an officer's commission. Hard working, detail oriented, and intensely curious about military affairs, Krueger also had a good sense of humor and enjoyed an entertaining story. He was a voracious reader of French, German, and English literature whose love of strategy and military history meshed naturally with his career.[39] By nature deliberate, methodical and somewhat of a perfectionist, Krueger was a patient, sometimes overly cautious commander.

Vice Admiral Arthur S. Carpender commanded the Allied Naval Forces, which included the U.S. Seventh Fleet. His aggressive assistant was Rear Admiral Daniel E. Barbey, who commanded the VII Amphibious Force. Barbey's command was the most important component of MacArthur's navy because the general's strategy and the geography of the Southwest Pacific mandated a series of amphibious operations.[40] Barbey built his command by scrounging matériel and precious landing craft from wherever he could find them. MacArthur also placed

Barbey in charge of all amphibious training in the Southwest Pacific Area. By June 1943, Barbey, Krueger, and Kenney, were ready to turn CARTWHEEL planning into operational reality.

CARTWHEEL began without fanfare. Around midnight on June 30, Japanese sentries on a hilltop overlooking Nassau Bay heard the roar of PT-boats above the crashing waves and heavy rain. A sergeant atop a crudely built observation tower focused his binoculars through the darkness toward the sound but could see nothing. Shortly after, two flares popped over the far side of the bay. The Japanese outpost was witnessing a mistake. The leading PT-boat of a three-boat serial, each carrying seventy troops, had overshot the designated landing beach. The signal flares were meant to warn the first wave of landing craft to turn back. When the misguided first wave did return to the proper landing area, they nearly collided with the second assault wave now bearing on the beach. Of eighteen boats, only one returned from the beachhead to open waters. Others broached and filled with water or lost their way and ran aground in the blackness. The U.S. Army's 1st Battalion, 162d Infantry, had landed at Nassau Bay.

From a small thatch hut, the commander of the 280 defenders sent an emergency message to 51st Division Headquarters requesting immediate air support. The continuing rain throughout the gloomy dawn made air attacks impossible. That night a series of uncoordinated and confused ground attacks left eighteen Americans dead and twenty-seven wounded, but only a handful of Japanese survived to flee into the jungle. By the time the Japanese mounted fighter and bomber raids of forty to fifty planes against Barbey's shipping, they were too late to stop the consolidation of MacArthur's latest foothold on New Guinea's northern coast.[41]

General Blamey was the brain behind the seizure of Nassau Bay. MacArthur had wanted to grab the major Japanese airdrome and supply point at Lae. The 80 miles separating Lae from the nearest Allied staging area exceeded the limited (60-mile) range of the Allied landing craft available to the Southwest Pacific command. Blamey then recommended the seizure of Nassau Bay, roughly 40 miles from Lae. He had two reasons. First, it could serve as an intermediate staging base. Second, it forced Adachi to defend Salamaua, a village about 20 miles north of Nassau Bay that guarded the overland approach to Lae. Success at Nassau Bay provoked MacArthur and his staff, especially Kenney, to clamor for the immediate capture of Salamaua. Blamey stood firm against a haphazard push toward Lae and reminded the Americans that the overall plan depended on Australian ground forces siphoning off Japanese units to defend Salamaua, thereby leaving Lae's northern back door wide open.[42] Any assault on Lae, however, invited Japanese aerial retaliation from their nearby web of air bases.

ULTRA had kept Kenney and MacArthur continuously informed of the pace of Japanese army air force reinforcements into the theater since it had alerted them to the Imperial Headquarters' plan to develop air bases in New Guinea. Central

General Thomas A. Blamey visits the codebreakers at Twenty-One Henry Street, February 1943. Back row, left to right: Captain Porter, aide to Blamey; Lieutenant Colonel Harold Doud, Central Bureau; Wing Commander H. Roy Booth, Royal Australian Air Force, Central Bureau; Lieutenant Colonel Alastair W. Sandford, Australian Army, Central Bureau. Front row, left to right: Brigadier General John D. Rogers, director of intelligence, Allied Land Forces Headquarters; Blamey; Spencer Akin. (U.S. Army Signal Corps photo, courtesy of Joseph E. Richard)

Bureau's traffic analysis and voice intercepts of Japanese air-ground communications disclosed that Japanese planes were flying from newly operational air bases at Hollandia, Netherlands New Guinea (May 8), and that the 45th Air Regiment, equipped with Type 99 twin-engine light bombers, was at Rabaul (May 14). Armed with this data, Willoughby suggested that the 45th's sister regiments, the 24th, a fighter unit, and the 61st, heavy bombers, would soon appear in the theater.

Impending reinforcements made Kenney's job of neutralizing Japanese air power in New Guinea—before MacArthur's Lae operation, which was set for early September—potentially much more difficult. If Kenney could catch the enemy air force defenseless on the ground, he could destroy the force at one stroke and thus assure local air superiority for the air, ground, and sea phases of MacArthur's plan. The Fifth Air Force commander's destruction of the Japanese airdromes at Wewak in mid-August was a masterpiece of tactical planning, deception, and surprise. Yet he could not have accomplished the mission without ULTRA's advance notice of Japanese aerial deployments. Kenney learned that heavy bombers of the 14th Air Regiment had deployed to Wewak on May 27 (June 4). As the ongoing buildup unfolded, decrypted air-ground communications mentioned a new airfield at Manokwari in western New Guinea (June 5) and large convoys destined for Wewak. Among the new units was the 14th Air Brigade at Rabaul.

The 14th Air Brigade was organized in Manchuria in April 1942 and was one of those proverbially unlucky units. Its two fighter regiments, the 68th and 78th, had Type 3 fighters that sported a modified, liquid-cooled engine notorious for its breakdowns. Imperial Headquarters ordered the brigade to Rabaul in March 1943 to replace the 12th Air Brigade whose pilots rotated to Japan for reconstitution.

A well-escorted auxiliary carrier took the 68th Air Regiment and its aircraft from Yokosuka to Truk where the 68th's pilots were supposed to fly directly to Rabaul. Japanese army pilots lacked training in the complex art of long-distance overwater flights. Their air-speed indicators were calibrated in miles, not nautical miles, per hour, which made precise navigation over water difficult. To compensate for these deficiencies, the pilots were supposed to rendezvous with a navy Type 100 reconnaissance aircraft that would shepherd them to Rabaul. They missed the rendezvous, and only one of the twenty-seven aircraft reached Rabaul. Eight were able to make emergency landings, but eighteen ran out of fuel and plunged into the sea.[43] A second replacement group arrived in the theater in June.

American voice-intercept operators listened to conversations between pilots and between pilots and airfield controllers as the 14th Air Brigade from western New Guinea changed places with the 12th Air Brigade in eastern New Guinea (June 15). Radio messages from the Palaus addressed to the commander of the 12th Air Brigade uncovered his presence at Wewak (June 16). Decrypts and traffic analysis all pointed to increasing Japanese army control over air operations in New Guinea (June 28). At the time of the Nassau Bay and New Georgia landings, ULTRA let Kenney plot the deployment of 7th Air Division units to Wewak from as far away as Burma (June 30). The large numbers of Japanese aircraft hurled against the New Georgia and Nassau Bay landings confirmed the air reinforcements that ULTRA had already detected.

The Japanese air buildup threatened Fifth Air Force on two fronts: from Rabaul to the northeast and from Wewak to the northwest. Kenney concentrated on taking out Wewak. The Japanese air base lay safely beyond the range of Allied fighter aircraft where unescorted bombers in daylight risked prohibitive losses to the strong air and ground defenses at Wewak. An attack at night sacrificed accuracy. Besides, bombers alone were insufficient for the knockout blow Kenney had in mind. He envisioned fighters strafing the airfields, the runways, the parked aircraft, the antiaircraft gun crews, and, in his words, ''really liquidating the place."[44] To bring his fighters within striking range, an advanced air base was constructed about 60 miles west of Lae at Tsili-Tsili. From there fighters could escort bombers all the way on the 600-mile round-trip to Wewak.

Great secrecy surrounded the work at Tsili-Tsili, a name, incidentally, that Kenney changed to Marilinan to avoid the inevitable jibes of "Silly-Silly" should his plan fail. Meanwhile, American and Australian engineers ostentatiously labored on another airfield near Bena Bena about 90 miles as the crow flies west-northwest of Marilinan. Heavy equipment threw up clouds of dust to distract snooping Japanese reconnaissance aircraft and to divert Japanese attention from the Marilinan works.

Few Imperial Army officers aspired to a career in intelligence. Those who did studied Russian to prepare for the showdown with the Soviet Union that the Japanese army believed was inevitable. The rapid expansion of the air force during the war brought home the years of neglect as hastily cobbled-together intelligence units reported for frontline duty. The 4th Air Intelligence Detachment's situation in New Guinea was typical. It was formed in November 1942, but aside from its commander none of its officers or enlisted men were trained or experienced intelligence personnel. They also lacked up-to-date equipment and any sense of urgency about the situation. Two radar sets, for example, were brought from Rabaul in May 1943, but enlisted men of the intelligence detachment were still trying to site one radar on a hill overlooking Wewak three months later.

This left Wewak dependent on the naked eye for early warning of approaching Allied aircraft. Air defense doctrine called for a series of about twenty air lookout posts, connected by field telephone, to cover about 450 miles. The 4th Air Intelligence Detachment had to guard twice that distance on New Guinea. Nor did Japanese special intelligence compensate for these deficiencies. Shortages of trained intercept operators and linguists plagued special intelligence until August 1943 when the army's General Staff ordered a wholesale expansion and reorganization of intercept and decryption efforts against the Americans. Eighth Area Army on Rabaul had just organized a three-hundred-man Special Intelligence Detachment and positioned forward intercept stations at Wewak and Ambon when Kenney's blow fell.[45] Like blindfolded chess players, the Japanese at Wewak fumbled with their pieces, ignorant that their opponents could see and attack the entire chessboard.

In early July the 45th Air Regiment flew into Wewak. Allied electronic eavesdroppers overheard the 76th Independent Air Squadron ground controller calling his reconnaissance aircraft pilots from Wewak a few days later (July 8, 10). Thirty-six Type 99 bombers of the 14th Air Regiment landed at Hollandia soon afterward. Coupling Willoughby's earlier deduction with recent ULTRA, Kenney thought the fighter units of the 24th Air Regiment and the bomber units of the 61st were also stationed at Wewak fields (July 11, 15). A light-bomber unit, the 75th Air

Regiment from China, and a fighter regiment, the 58th from Java, next appeared at Babo. The latter raided Darwin, Australia, on July 17. The 10th Air Regiment's reconnaissance planes staged to Hollandia in late July, the first appearance of that unit in New Guinea (August 2). Another new fighter unit, the 78th Air Regiment, flew into Wewak in mid-August. Only ULTRA allowed Kenney to know that Japanese army air activity centered on the Wewak-Hollandia hub with frequent flights between those major air bases.

Japanese air doctrine predicated aircraft dispersal to avoid destruction on the ground. A typical air division had a headquarters and two or three flying regiments of thirty-six aircraft each, or between seventy-five and one hundred aircraft. Usually one-third of these aircraft were located at a forward airfield, another third at the main headquarters base, and the remainder at a rear area base safely out of harm's way. Proper dispersal obliged the Japanese to construct scores of airfields in the New Guinea wilds. Considerable heavy construction equipment was needed to build this network of air bases, but Japanese industry produced a paltry eighty bulldozers in 1943 and 1944. Manpower alone could not carve sufficient airdromes out of the thick, often trackless jungle growth. Pilots detested the New Guinea runways, which they regarded as primitive, poorly maintained, and too short and too dangerous for heavy-bomber take-offs and landings.[46] The increasing number of aircraft coupled with the shortage of fields compelled the Japanese Fourth Air Army, activated on July 28 at Rabaul, to risk concentrating two air divisions at Wewak. It was a bad gamble against an opponent as ruthless as Kenney.

Around the beginning of August, Kenney ordered General Whitehead to prepare an all-out attack on Wewak. Marilinan was nearing completion and was still undetected by the Japanese. On August 11 the two-man crew of a Mitsubishi twin-engine reconnaissance aircraft (nicknamed "Dinah" by the Allies) on their first combat mission photographed the Marilinan airstrip. Incredulous officers of Fourth Air Army's staff at Rabaul were dumbfounded when they examined the crew's photos. The commander, Lieutenant General Teramoto Noriichi, ordered a prestrike reconnaissance and alerted his combat air units for an attack against the newly discovered Marilinan target.

Japanese reconnaissance flights tipped off Kenney, who shifted thirty-five fighters to defend his now not-so-secret forward base. American radar operators went on full alert. On the morning of August 15, their radar scopes lit up with the blips of approaching Japanese bombers. Fighter control was alerted. The ensuing aerial melee sent six twin-engine bombers and three more Japanese fighters spiraling to earth in flames. Fifth Air Force lost three fighters. In the excitement of combat, the inexperienced Japanese pilots claimed they had shot down eighteen American aircraft and had left Marilinan a smoking ruin.[47]

Meanwhile, at Wewak, ground crews sweated around the clock to repair aircraft damaged in the Marilinan raid and to rearm and maintain planes for Teramoto's

Table 3.1. ULTRA-Identified Japanese Air Units at Wewak, August 1943

Unit	Date Detected[a]
Fourth Air Army	August 28
6th Air Division	August 15
10th Air Regiment	August 2
13th Air Regiment	July 3
14th Air Regiment	June 4
24th Air Regiment	July 15
45th Air Regiment	July 4
208th Air Regiment	May 26
7th Air Division	
5th Air Regiment	
7th Air Regiment	
59th Air Regiment	August 15
61st Air Regiment	July 15
75th Air Regiment	July 19
14th Air Brigade	
68th Air Regiment	
78th Air Regiment	August 18

[a]Wewak raid occurred on August 17, 1943.

Source: SWPA, Special Intelligence Bulletin, July-August 1943, National Archives and Records Administration, Washington, D.C.

planned attack against the Bena Bena field. ULTRA counted the 13th Air Regiment, 6th Air Division, and the 59th and 78th Air regiments at Wewak.[48] American photo reconnaissance of August 16 confirmed that the four airfields near Wewak were packed with all kinds of aircraft. Early the next morning, almost two hundred American warplanes filled the sky.

At Wewak the 4th Air Intelligence Detachment Headquarters' first warning of the raid came while the American planes were over Hansa Bay, about twenty minutes flight time from Wewak. The air intelligence unit was physically separated from both the 6th and the 7th Air Division headquarters but had telephone communications with each. That morning the phone lines failed, perhaps mildewed or chewed through by the large rats that roamed the base. Captain Yamanaka Akira, assigned to the headquarters, darted frantically across the air base to spread the alarm. The roar of aircraft engines drowned out his shouts.[49]

Surprise was total. Four-engine heavy bombers plastered two fields with high explosives. Deadly B-25s roared in 300 feet over the main Wewak base dropping parachute-retarded fragmentation bombs on the rows of parked Japanese aircraft. P-38 and P-39 fighters then swooped down, strafing everything in sight. Billowing clouds of thick, black smoke from burning oil storage tanks cast an appropriate pall over Wewak. Considering the ferocity of the attack, Japanese personnel losses were light, sixty-eight killed or wounded. But American pilots had destroyed 50 aircraft on the ground and seriously damaged another 50. Kenney followed up with an even heavier raid the next day that accounted for another 14 aircraft destroyed and 14 damaged. Of 120 aircraft available thirty-six hours earlier, only 38 remained. American monitors overheard a Japanese army pilot on August 18 trying to contact the four air-ground stations near Wewak. He could raise only one. Kenney had just about put Wewak off the air.[50]

Two weeks later, Allied troops landed about 20 miles north of Lae, unchallenged by Japanese aircraft. The next day, September 5, American paratroopers dropped on Nadzab, 20 miles west of Lae. The converging pincers threatened to surround the beleaguered 51st Division whose main forces were still clinging to Salamaua. Exactly as Blamey had foreseen, Salamaua had pulled the Japanese defenders away from Lae and now left them trapped by the Allied sea and air envelopment. The Allied landing to its rear changed nothing for the 51st Division Headquarters at Salamaua because Lieutenant General Nakano Hidemitsu had already ordered his men to fight to the death. After a month's combat in the disease-infested coastal areas, the division's pitiful infantry companies mustered an average of 40 to 50 men, fewer than one-third of their normal 180-man complement.

Adachi quickly took steps to contain the invaders near Lae. He regarded Finschhafen as the key to defense of the 60-mile-wide Dampier Straits between New Guinea and New Britain. Finschhafen in Japanese hands allowed them to control both sides of the straits and checked an Allied advance into the open Bismarck Sea. Satisfied that Finschhafen was in no immediate danger, Adachi strengthened its garrison. Next he dispatched a regiment to cover the northwest approach from Lae. Finally he reprieved his 51st Division by ordering its withdrawal from Salamaua. A regimental commander, Lieutenant Colonel Matsui Keiji, recalled that "We were determined to sacrifice ourselves fighting to the death, so we were relieved when ordered to withdraw. My worry now was about whether or not we could get across the river on just the two remaining boats under enemy artillery fire."[51]

Colonel Matsui's ordeal was just beginning. The Japanese had to cross the rugged, 12,000-foot-high Saruwaged Range to reach the coast. Some wounded, the lucky ones, were put into barges for transport to Madang. The unlucky ones were shot or blew themselves apart with hand grenades supplied by their comrades. Then about eight thousand Japanese trekked north from Lae into the forbidding mountains. Each man carried enough half rations to last ten days. Officers expected the march to take sixteen days. It took twenty-six. Discipline collapsed as the strongest pushed ahead, picking the land clean of food. The weak were left to die. Two thousand of the marchers never came out. Most of them simply starved to death.[52]

For Adachi and MacArthur, Finschhafen was the next objective. In mid-August, the 80th Infantry Regiment had reinforced Major General Yamada Eizo's

1st Shipping Engineer Group at Finschhafen. Although the regiment's advance party went by barge, the bulk of the unit, roughly 2,350 men, had to march overland from Madang.[53] Japanese air power also reasserted itself in eastern New Guinea. Central Bureau listened as Japanese ground controllers at Wewak coaxed inexperienced Japanese pilots from Hollandia to safe landings. Another unseasoned air unit flew to Wewak from Rabaul (August 24). A few days later, Lieutenant General Teramoto himself was detected in New Guinea (August 28). The constant stream of aerial reinforcements intensified as seventy aircraft arrived at Hollandia in early September (September 8, 9). ULTRA identified the 9th Air Brigade's 7th, 24th, and 61st Air regiments at Wewak. The 13th and 59th Air regiments, which had been decimated at Wewak in August, were also collecting replacements (September 9). By September 10 the Japanese had rebuilt a respectable force of about one hundred aircraft.[54] Headquarters, 61st Air Regiment, a medium-bomber formation, showed up in communications from Hollandia (September 13). All of this activity reflected far-reaching strategic decisions made in Tokyo following weeks of acrimonious talks between the army and navy leadership.

Shocked by the disaster at Wewak, the heavy losses suffered in the central Solomons, and the sudden Italian capitulation, Imperial Headquarters found itself painfully divided on future courses of action. Since the Imperial Fleet's annihilation of the czarist fleet at Tsushima in 1905, Japan's naval General Staff was spellbound by the notion of a decisive naval engagement. In 1943 it argued that the showdown with the American navy should be along the present battle lines of the Pacific. The army General Staff, however, insisted that it made more sense to conduct a delaying action on the Pacific front. Army leaders expected to buy time so they could reinforce rear areas where they anticipated a climactic ground battle against a weakened foe forced to operate on overextended supply lines. While the army favored withdrawing to a line running from the Marianas and the Carolines to western New Guinea, the navy insisted that the Marshalls had to be held to protect the great base at Truk. Similarly, the navy refused to abandon Rabaul. That base, it argued, could be defended from the network of airfields on New Guinea and the Admiralties. Navy dreams were army staff officers' nightmares about overextended lines of communication and isolated garrisons.

MacArthur's now predictable tactics figured in these Japanese calculations. The Allies always operated within the 240-to-300-mile fighter radius of their air bases. From Salamaua to Geelvink Bay in western New Guinea the distance was roughly 1,200 miles, so the Japanese estimated that MacArthur needed a series of four or five amphibious operations to reach the western tip of the long island. Each leap required at least two months' preparation. According to Japanese computations, between eight and ten months were available to convert western New

Guinea into an impregnable fortress. Hard-fought delaying actions at Madang and Wewak might purchase even more time to prepare the defense in depth.[55]

The Japanese Army-Navy Central Agreement of September 30, 1943, embodied these conflicting strategic concepts. Both services agreed to hold the Dampier Straits, thereby blocking MacArthur's approach to the Philippines and granting time to strengthen bases in western New Guinea. The Imperial Navy reluctantly agreed to a primary defensive line running from western New Guinea to the Marianas via the Carolines. To sanction the agreement, it was reported to the throne in the fourth Imperial Conference held since the war began.[56]

As part of the inevitable Japanese compromise, however, the army had agreed on September 11 to send the 17th Division from China to Rabaul. This decision pleased no one. To defend Rabaul the army had to disperse reinforcements needed to bolster forces in western New Guinea. For its part, the navy regarded a single division as insufficient for the agreed-upon delaying action. Although the Allies remained unaware of the new strategy, by early November ULTRA had confirmed Chinese reports that the 17th Division was leaving central China for the South Pacific. Melbourne-based U.S. Navy cryptanalysts funneled this information to MacArthur.[57]

Meanwhile, on New Guinea, General Yamada was transforming Finschhafen from a transshipment point into a stronghold to blunt MacArthur's offensive. By the end of August, Yamada had collected nearly 3,000 troops to defend the next objective on the Allies' timetable. Only one-third of the Japanese were combat troops; the others were the poorly equipped service troops of Yamada's shipping command whom he had organized as a mobile reserve.[58] Adachi did his part by sending the 20th Division to reinforce Yamada. It was making its painful way overland as Southwest Pacific Headquarters put the finishing touches on its Finschhafen operation. Meanwhile, the American and Australian intelligence staffs had prepared conflicting versions of enemy strength—they worked on different principles and often reached different conclusions.[59] On August 31 Willoughby declared that 1,000 Japanese defended Finschhafen, mainly from the 8th Shipping Engineer Regiment. After the fall of Lae, he reduced this figure to 350 defenders. Australian intelligence painted a different assessment, anywhere from 1,500 to 4,000 Japanese at Finschhafen. ULTRA could not settle the argument because of the paucity of radio message intercepts emanating from the area. An American long-range reconnaissance team, the Alamo Scouts, landed near Finschhafen during the night of September 11/12, but they could not determine the extent of Japanese defenses.[60] Australian troops came ashore at Finschhafen on September 22 expecting little opposition and, after meeting initial sharp resistance, they quickly cleared the coastal enclave.

Yamada dug in on Satelberg Heights, a ridge overlooking the entire coast, and

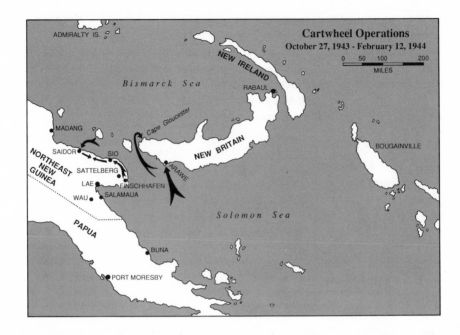

barred any northward Allied advance toward Sio. By the end of September, 2,400 reinforcements from the 20th Division had augmented Yamada's troops. From their dominating heights, the Japanese fought with stoical courage as the Australian 9th Division again and again bored into the ridge-line defenses. MacArthur's amphibious hook had promised a quick knockout; instead, it turned into an alley brawl. For two months Australian and Japanese infantrymen fought a series of deadly small-unit combats that measured gains in yards. Ultimately, 12,500 Japanese troops were fed into the maw of the New Guinea portal to the Dampier Straits. At least 5,500 lost their lives, but they clung to Satelberg Heights until November 27. Yamada had slowed MacArthur's advance to the pace of an infantryman's crawl.

ULTRA's contributions to the prolonged battle were negligible. Reports that Japanese radio traffic from Finschhafen decreased because of their evacuation to Satelberg hardly impressed the dog-tired Australian infantrymen who had just taken that stronghold (October 4). Direction finding did isolate the 41st Division's radio transmitter, but it was somewhere around Madang, far away from the fighting (October 21). Shortly after the Australian 9th Division offensive opened, traffic analysts reported that the transmitter for the 20th Division had been shifted to Sio (November 19). This was the first scrap of ULTRA that pointed to a Japanese withdrawal, but the Japanese defense of Satelberg held out until December 8. Army ULTRA had yet to assert itself in MacArthur's ground campaign.

Navy ULTRA did uncover impending Japanese operations. Fleet Radio Unit, Melbourne, intercept operators stayed tuned to enemy naval air radio frequencies to follow operations from Rabaul. By early September Kenney was aware of the "strenuous effort to build up [naval] air strength in the Bismarcks" (September 13). ULTRA made known that the Japanese 1st Carrier Division had detached some of its aircraft to supplement land-based operations by the 25th and 26th Air flotillas defending Rabaul. Kenney also knew through ULTRA that these Japanese air units at Rabaul maintained their strength by regularly refitting on Formosa (September 9, 30).

Rabaul was a hive of Japanese air activity. However, aside from nuisance raids, the Japanese citadel was relatively safe from Allied air power. Until Allied fighters could escort bombers to Rabaul, the Japanese could rebuild or reinforce their air forces with impunity. American reconnaissance aircraft routinely appeared in the skies over Rabaul, so the B-17 pilot snapping high-altitude photographs on October 11 did not stir much attention on the ground.

Photographs of 294 Japanese aircraft concentrated around Rabaul's airstrips did create great excitement at Port Moresby because they gave Kenney the lucrative targets he wanted. Ever the improvisational leader, Kenney had forged new airstrips at Nadzab, Lae, and Finschhafen that placed Rabaul within range of Fifth Air Force's improved twin-engine P-38 fighters. The quarry sighted, Kenney sent everything "that could fly that far" against Rabaul on October 12. Nearly 350 planes, ranging from huge four-engine B-24s to Australian Beaufighters, swept over the four Japanese naval air bases, bombing and strafing the installations. Excited crew debriefings recounted great fires, at least 100 aircraft destroyed and half that number damaged, and numerous secondary, or chain reaction, explosions. Air intelligence officers uncritically recorded air crew claims. So did MacArthur, whose communiqués gave a patina of legitimacy on the wildly exaggerated tallies.[61]

Although Kenney's massive attack was successful, it did not knock out Rabaul. Fabian's analysts at Melbourne tracked Japanese aircraft from all four Rabaul fields the day after the big raid (October 13). Within a few days, Japanese naval airmen were again attacking Allied shipping in Oro Bay and near Finschhafen. The strike did, however, inaugurate a vicious, four-month air war for possession of the skies over Rabaul. Representative of the ferocity of this fighting was the second big Rabaul raid.

On November 2, B-25s attacking Rabaul ran into the veteran pilots of the 1st Carrier Division. The skill and number of these Japanese airmen surprised the Americans because intercept operators did not realize this deployment had occurred until six days after the raid. Japanese Zekes ripped into the first wave of B-25s, knocking down three of them. Dogfighting aircraft careened across the blue skies over Rabaul as trails of smoke or blinding explosions marked victims.

Japanese pilots shot down eight B-25s and nine P-38s. Fifth Air Force grimly listed forty-five pilots or crewmen killed or missing in action. To Kenney it was "the toughest fight Fifth Air Force encountered in the whole war."[62]

Stung by the losses, Kenney claimed fifty-five Japanese aircraft shot down and 114,000 tons of shipping destroyed or damaged. Actual Japanese losses were twenty aircraft and 500 tons of shipping.[63] Pumped up on adrenalin with only a few seconds to identify their results, American pilots, like all others, naturally exaggerated the damage they had inflicted on their adversaries. Kenney knew better, but he winked at the fanciful claims. So did MacArthur's headquarters. In a feat of mathematical legerdemain, Willoughby concocted a formula to deflate aircrew claims. A G-2-sponsored conference determined that only 86 percent of reported Fifth Air Force claims could be considered real Japanese losses and henceforth claims would be adjusted accordingly to obtain actual damage.[64] Based on the experience from the November 2 raid, 36 percent was a more realistic figure.

Fifth Air Force's raids on Rabaul were part of a joint effort to soften up the island in conjunction with the U.S. Marine landing on Bougainville on November 1. Marines and later U.S. Army reinforcements busied themselves developing airfields within the small enclave on their narrow beachhead. In the meantime, Australian troops were wearing down the stubborn Japanese defenders at Satelberg. Lieutenant General Nakano's shattered 20th Division slowly gave ground northward. In spite of the time-consuming and supply-draining campaign, the word was that MacArthur "is mentally prepared to go on a supply shoestring in order to meet target dates, and he is determined to play his luck."[65] The American general's invasion at Arawe, New Britain, on the opposite side of the straits from Finschhafen showed that he relied heavily on intuition and luck.

The attack on Arawe came after four months of haggling about an often contentious, often contradictory, and often changed objective. Allied intelligence reports of a Japanese buildup by units of the 17th Division near the originally proposed landing site were one cause for delay. ULTRA detected the newly arrived 17th's headquarters at Rabaul on November 23. By December General Krueger had ordered the 112th Cavalry Regiment (Mounted) to land at Arawe in order to divert Japanese attention from the main landing by the 1st Marine Division on the opposite side of the island. Willoughby estimated that five hundred Japanese of the 115th Infantry, 51st Division, were near Arawe. (There were about four hundred Japanese near the landing beach—a reinforced company of the 115th Infantry and a handful of sailors assigned to an early warning observation post.) Of greater concern to MacArthur was the potential Japanese air reaction to his New Britain landings. The Japanese had more than one hundred fighters at Wewak and eighty-two twin-engined bombers at Hollandia.[66] Japanese air strength on Rabaul numbered about three hundred fighters.

The Arawe landings provoked a major air war as planes from the 6th Air Division from Wewak and Eleventh Air Fleet from Rabaul converged on the Arawe beachhead. Forty fighters and bombers from the 6th Air Division bombed the Allied convoy on December 16, and thirty attacked it again two days later. Japanese navy pilots, staging from nearby Rabaul, launched large successive raids against the beachhead, including an eighty-three-plane effort on December 26. Despite the massive effort, Japanese pilots sank only one coastal transport and damaged only eight other auxiliary vessels, including six LSTs (landing ship, tank). Their own casualties were disproportionate to the damage they inflicted. The 6th Air Division lost all its bombers, and Eleventh Air Fleet wrote off nineteen bombers and twenty-two fighters.

An effective air umbrella protected the Arawe task force because Allied pilots usually received thirty to sixty minutes' warning of Japanese aircraft approaching Arawe. Three months before the invasion, a U.S. submarine landed AIB teams to aid coastwatchers already on New Britain. Together they established a chain of air-watcher radio stations across the island. Connected with Fighter Command Headquarters at Nadzab, New Guinea, the agents tapped out warnings when they spotted Japanese aircraft overhead.[67] Fighter Command then vectored its planes across the straits to meet the Japanese. Unable to disrupt the landing or dislodge the invaders, General Imamura eventually opted to leave the Americans their toeholds in southern New Britain and pull his forces back to defend Rabaul.

MacArthur next reversed his field to seize Saidor, New Guinea. Chamberlin had suggested Saidor's capture in September, but no plan appeared until December 11. Saidor's airstrip was valuable, but more important, Saidor stood between Adachi's 41st Division at Madang and his 20th Division near Sio where it was still fighting a desperate rearguard action against the Australian 9th Division. In MacArthur's hands, Saidor could split Adachi's already fragmented army.

Fifty melancholy Japanese soldiers garrisoned a crude outpost at Saidor. On January 2, 1944, shells began crashing down near their position. Explosions quickly severed their field telephone lines with higher headquarters. Once that happened there was no reason for them to remain targets, so the survivors withdrew inland. Just that quickly Japanese forces on New Guinea were split asunder.

Two days later Adachi flew to Sio to oversee the Japanese withdrawal west to defend Madang, surely the next Allied target. Once again the cutoff Japanese units had to move over tortuous inland trails and cross daunting mountains to reach Madang. As on their earlier death march from Lae, the troops were on reduced rations. They moved only after dark to avoid punishment from Allied aircraft controlling the skies during the day. Nightly downpours chilled men to the bone and the heavy rain swelled otherwise torpid streams into overflowing torrents. Many Japanese, already weakened from malnutrition, drowned in the swift currents. Dysentery and starvation stalked the marchers. Lonely gunshots punctuated the falling rain as the Japanese again marked their line of retreat with corpses.[68]

The 20th Division withdrew from Sio in four stages. When the final echelon prepared to move, the headquarters' radio platoon broke down the division's radio for portage through the mountains. Since individual radio parts were quite heavy, no one wanted to be burdened with the large steel trunk containing the division's cryptographic materials as they climbed uphill. It was too wet to burn the codebooks, substitution tables, and key registers page by page. It was also too dangerous because roving Allied aircraft might spy the column of smoke. So the exhausted soldiers resorted to a field expedient. They tore off all the covers of the codebooks and substitution tables to serve as "proof" of their destruction. Then they buried the trunk near a streambed, possibly hoping that rising water would complete their halfhearted efforts. Afterward, they marched into the mountains.

Australian infantrymen and engineers presently came upon the former Japanese headquarters site near Sio. Since the Japanese customarily left booby traps and mines littered about abandoned bivouacs, a young engineer began carefully sweeping the area with his mine detector. He froze when his earphones brayed a shrill warning. Demolitions experts moved in to dig up a suspected land mine and unearthed a treasure in a steel trunk. An anonymous intelligence officer with this advance party recognized its contents as codebooks and sent the entire cipher library of the 20th Division intact to Central Bureau.[69]

The Japanese codebooks, assorted key registers, and substitution tables arrived at Central Bureau still sopping wet. In Australia's mid-summer January heat, Richard and other Central Bureau cryptanalysts spent the day in the closed garage on Henry Street tenderly drying out the priceless pages. Hand-held pages were inserted into a gas oven to speed drying. Other pages were hung on clothesline around the garage so electric fans and heaters could dry them. When the cryptanalysts finished work, Central Bureau had an intact version of the four-digit, mainline Japanese army code. The next step was to photograph each page and immediately send the copies to Arlington Hall. Even as the photographer worked, cryptanalysts and uniformed IBM technicians made punch-card entries for each codebook and additive table. Once they entered this information on the IBM machines, they programmed it to strip off the cipher and print the code number together with the accompanying meaning in *Romaji*. Central Bureau had achieved an electromagnetic machine solution to the Imperial Army code. The immediate result was a case of being overwhelmed by one's success. The IBM printouts spewed forth so many deciphered messages that Central Bureau translators could not keep pace! MacArthur issued an emergency request for the two best translator cryptanalysts available from the U.S. Navy.

On February 4, 1944, Melbourne sent Lieutenant Commanders Thomas R. Mackie and Forrest R. ("Tex") Biard to Brisbane on temporary duty. Both naval officers were veterans of the rigorous prewar U.S. Navy Japanese-language training program. Mackie had worked at CAST and been at FRUMEL since it opened. Biard had first served at Fleet Radio Unit, Pacific (FRUPAC; codenamed "HYPO"), Pearl Harbor, and then worked intercept and decryption aboard the USS *Yorktown*; he had been at Melbourne for only a few months. When they arrived at Central Bureau, they found that several nisei were having difficulty with the idioms, phraseology, and specific military and technical terms peculiar to Imperial Army radio terminology. According to Biard's colorful account, the translators were working their way up in a high stack of decrypted messages. He and Mackie immediately agreed that the latest decrypts should be read first and so they grabbed the top of the pile. What they found was a thirteen-part message that laid out the decisions reached about the New Guinea front at a major conference of high-ranking Japanese army and navy officers.[70]

For Sinkov it was a moment of great happiness because Central Bureau was spared an enormous amount of cryptanalytic work. Under his direction, Central Bureau had succeeded in partially decrypting some Japanese army signals. The initial breaks occurred in June 1943 when the first Japanese army message was read. That September more army codes were solved, but without sufficient consistency or timeliness to influence operations. Now Sinkov literally was handed the solution to the devilish army ciphers that had frustrated Central Bureau for so long. The exciting news of their great prize was radioed to Arlington Hall on January 28 and a microfilmed copy of the documents arrived there on February 20.[71]

Almost overnight the find transformed Central Bureau into a high-quality cryptanalysis agency, an organization capable of producing ULTRA. MacArthur's codebreakers and those at Arlington Hall suffered an embarrassment of riches. In January 1944, Arlington Hall analysts decrypted 1,846 Japanese army messages, most probably in the Water Transport Code. With the Sio documents in hand, Arlington Hall decrypted more than 36,000 Japanese army messages in March 1944.[72] The U.S. Army could now read Japanese military signals with the same speed and precision as the U.S. Navy solved Japanese naval signals.

Even before the breakthrough, ULTRA was instrumental in tipping the strategic balance in New Guinea. Its forewarnings had enabled Kenney to destroy Number 81 Convoy in the Battle of the Bismarck Sea, after which the Japanese never recovered the strategic initiative. ULTRA also set the tone for the undersea and aerial interdiction of Japanese resupply convoys. The strain of doing without proper logistical support was showing on Japanese units in New Guinea just as the loss of ships, men, and equipment stretched Imperial Headquarters to its limit. Finally, ULTRA helped Kenney gain local control of the skies either by allowing him to target unsuspecting Japanese air bases for destruction or by informing him of impending enemy air raids. Although these were significant accomplishments, ULTRA's finest moment in MacArthur's war lay just over the horizon.

4

ULTRA's Great Victory: The Hollandia Operation, January–April 1944

By late January 1944 General Douglas MacArthur could reflect on solid, successful, but hardly spectacular accomplishments against a determined and resourceful opponent. CARTWHEEL had ground its way through New Georgia, but Bougainville was still being contested. In twenty months MacArthur had advanced about 300 miles, or one-third of the way along the northern New Guinea coast. He still faced the daunting prospect of driving stubborn Japanese defenders from their strongholds on the great island.[1]

Although MacArthur favored bypassing and isolating Japanese garrisons so that the defenders might slowly starve to death, Southwest Pacific's advance was moving at a snail's pace compared with Admiral Nimitz's island-hopping campaign, which jumped 2,000 miles from the Gilbert Islands in November 1943 to the Marshalls in February 1944.[2] MacArthur's amphibious flanking maneuvers to date had been too shallow to ensnare General Adachi's entire Eighteenth Army. Twice Adachi's bruised divisions had escaped encirclement. The cost was high, but it preserved Eighteenth Army as a roadblock on MacArthur's highway to the Philippines. If the Japanese could make MacArthur fight his way through western New Guinea in short bounds, they could buy time to strengthen their defenses in the Philippines. At this time Allied resources (especially shipping), military technology (range of aircraft), and military intelligence about the Japanese (limited army ULTRA) made advancing by short bounds along the coast the norm. MacArthur aimed his next leap, spearheaded by Krueger's 24th and 32d divisions, against Hansa Bay about 100 miles up the coast from Saidor. Adachi waited at Hansa Bay, carefully preparing his defenses to seize victory after a year of humiliating defeats.

MacArthur's shining successes—for example, the Battle of the Bismarck Sea and the destruction of the Wewak airdromes—were victories of air power. His ground forces conquered territory only after hard fighting and heavy casualties. If

MacArthur's objective was to reach the Philippines with minimum casualties, he was not doing very well, having suffered eleven thousand American and four thousand Australian army battle casualties in 1943. The grinding attrition had also punished Imamura's Eighth Area Army and crippled the Southwest Area Fleet. CARTWHEEL had claimed the lives of perhaps fifty thousand Japanese soldiers and sailors and taken one hundred fifty merchant vessels, seventy-five warships of all types, and perhaps as many as three thousand aircraft.[3] Japan could not replace matériel losses as quickly as the United States and was critically short of skilled manpower, especially pilots. MacArthur was clearly winning his war, but Manila was a long way off, and Tokyo was even farther in the distance.

At the QUADRANT Conference in Quebec, Canada, August 14–24, 1943, the British and American Combined Chiefs of Staff had approved bypassing rather than capturing Rabaul. Their decision to neutralize Rabaul gave priority to Admiral Nimitz's Central Pacific advance and seemed to leave MacArthur in a strategic backwater. The supply pipeline to the Southwest Pacific Area suggested its relative importance to other theaters. MacArthur's theater lagged a poor third behind the logistics support for the forthcoming invasion of Europe set for the spring of 1944 and the ongoing Central Pacific drive of the U.S. Navy. Nevertheless, the driving force in MacArthur's strategy was the obligation to liberate the Philippines.

MacArthur's schedule naming the Philippines as the final objective of the Southwest Pacific Area campaign first appeared in March 1943, code-named RENO I. Subsequent versions of the plan formed the basis for operations against the Japanese. RENO II, drafted in August 1943, proposed operations after the capture of Rabaul designed to culminate in an invasion of Mindanao, the southernmost island in the Philippine chain, in early 1945. Two months later RENO III, dated October 20, 1943, envisioned bypassing Rabaul but capturing it later and accelerating MacArthur's drive along the northern New Guinea coast. Mindanao would be invaded in February 1945. The plan aimed at the successive occupation of the minimum bases required to advance the land-based bomber line to the Philippines. It emphasized bypassing Japanese garrisons wherever possible, thereby reducing Allied casualties and quickening the tempo of the Allied advance. Accurate intelligence about Japanese defenses was the key to this strategy. When General Headquarters' planners drafted the RENO III concept, they lacked precise information about Japanese deployments along the New Guinea coast. Thus they set RENO III's initial attack for February 1 against strongly defended Hansa Bay. Successive assaults on Hollandia (June 1), Geelvink Bay (August 15), the Vogelkop Peninsula (October 1), and Halmahera or Morotai (December 1) would follow. The campaign objective was to establish major air and naval bases to support the assault on Mindanao contemplated for February 1, 1945. At the SEXTANT Conference in December 1943, the British and American Combined

Chiefs approved the RENO III concepts but made no decision about MacArthur's subsequent advance into the Philippines. His drive seemed to be stopped at the equator when the Combined Chiefs agreed that the defeat of Japan might be accomplished by a sea and air blockade and intensive air bombardment from advanced bases.[4]

Meanwhile, Admiral Nimitz was not convinced either of the wisdom of the Washington-directed two-pronged Pacific advance or of the Marianas as his next target. His inclination toward a single spearhead aimed at Mindanao found a natural advocate in MacArthur. At a January 27, 1944, meeting at Pearl Harbor with Sutherland, Kenney, and Vice Admiral Thomas C. Kinkaid, Nimitz agreed to send two divisions of his fast carriers to support MacArthur's proposed Admiralties and Kavieng, New Ireland, invasions. The Joint Chiefs of Staff, however, overruled the admiral and ordered the approach to the Philippines be made on two axes of advance. They assigned priority to the Central Pacific since that approach appeared to be more strategically decisive.[5]

Faced with permanent second-class status, the Southwest Pacific commander dispatched a long message to Marshall on February 2, 1944. MacArthur stated that he was sending Sutherland to Washington to discuss matters of great concern, namely, Washington's plan to employ "two weak thrusts" instead of uniting Southwest and Central Pacific forces under his command. Moreover, the Combined Chiefs' apportionment of resources upset his RENO III schedule by retarding the Geelvink Bay landing six weeks until October 1 and the invasion of the Philippines four weeks until March 1945. Finally, MacArthur still planned to land at Hansa Bay on April 26, 1944, but even that limited operation depended on getting additional amphibious support—namely, aircraft carriers—from Nimitz.[6] Sutherland's departure for Washington was a last-ditch effort to rescue the Southwest Pacific Area from slipping into a strategic backwater.

ULTRA then came to MacArthur's rescue: it provided the general with the wherewithal to devise a bold, seemingly reckless scheme to strike deep behind Japanese lines. Following the intelligence thread through the planning stages reveals how MacArthur's detailed awareness of unfolding Japanese ground dispositions on New Guinea enabled him to tailor his plans to take advantage of their weakness and force General Adachi to fight at times and places of MacArthur's choosing. Central Bureau's newfound ability to produce ULTRA was the catalyst for MacArthur's daring new timetable.

Comparing a typical intelligence estimate before and after Central Bureau's IBM machines spewed forth decryptions illustrates the quality that the codebreakers brought to the Southwest Pacific Headquarters' planning sessions. On December 31, 1943, Willoughby estimated that between 39,500 and 54,500 Japanese defended eastern New Guinea. The source of confusion was the unconfirmed presence of the 54th Division at Wewak. If the division was there, then 24,000 troops defended Wewak; if not, only 9,000 did, a significant difference. There were 20,000 Japanese holding Madang, and 3,000 at Hollandia.[7] In mid-January 1944, MacArthur provided essentially the same ground order of battle figures, less the unconfirmed division, to the War Department, although he did acknowledge that a yet unidentified division might be near Wewak. Willoughby meanwhile had been analyzing a likely Japanese response to an assault against Aitape. Admitting that "present hostile strength and dispositions at Aitape proper are unknown," he still believed that not more than a regiment defended the area and that reinforcing the small Japanese garrison would be difficult. By January 31, Willoughby carried roughly the same ground order of battle as he had the previous month with the same ambiguities.[8] This was the extent of the intelligence available to MacArthur when he drafted his long plea to Marshall. Two days later, courtesy of Central Bureau and Lieutenant Commanders Biard and Mackie, ULTRA placed in Mac-Arthur's hands a detailed appreciation of the situation sent by the Eighth Area Army chief of staff to Tokyo.

Dated January 19, 1944, the message specified Imamura's intentions to strengthen the Admiralties, New Ireland, and New Guinea. It revealed that rein-forcements were en route for the 41st and 20th divisions defending the Madang–Hansa Bay sector; that the 51st Division was reconstituting at Wewak; and that defenses at Hollandia needed improvement. Since a recently captured Japanese diary spoke of two divisions landing at Hollandia, this was good news indeed (February 4). The same day, an Eighteenth Army message confirmed for South-west Pacific Headquarters that the "enemy intention to cling to Madang . . . also tends to fix his defensive position." Subsequent ULTRA available during February related that the Japanese 41st Division experienced great difficulty in moving into position because of Allied air raids and heavy rain (February 6); that the 20th and 41st divisions were each to receive 2,000 replacements and the 51st Division 4,500 replacements (February 12); that the projected reorganized strength of the 51st Division was about 10,000 men and the 20th Division around 15,000 (February 19); and that the mission of the 51st Division was probably the defense of Wewak (February 12). On February 22, based on further analysis, Willoughby was able to subdivide the strengths of the 51st and 20th divisions according to those engaged in battle, those available at Wewak, and those in transit from Japan. Eavesdropping electronically on enemy radio signals also provided Southwest Pacific Headquar-ters with the strength of reinforcements arriving at Wewak and Hollandia in late February and Japanese troop requisitions for March (February 22).

ULTRA divulged General Adachi's intentions to reinforce Hansa Bay in anticipa-tion of future Allied landings there. Based on the unfolding intelligence picture, Willoughby resurrected an amended version of his earlier Aitape estimate. He now proposed a leap to a weakly garrisoned Hollandia instead of an assault against a well-defended Hansa Bay. Brigadier General Bonner Fellers, planning section

chief for G-3, agreed. Fellers's superior, General Chamberlin, enmeshed in hurried planning for the Admiralties operation, dismissed this latest proposal as a
"wild scheme." Nevertheless, Fellers circumvented Chamberlin and presented
the concept to MacArthur, who gave it his blessing. Stung by this deceit, Chamberlin fired Fellers, who spent the rest of the war as MacArthur's military secretary.[9] Together with his staff, MacArthur accordingly amended the original RENO
III objectives to seize Hollandia six months ahead of schedule. Implementation of
this revised RENO IV plan, however, depended on the immediate seizure of the
Admiralties.

The Admiralties' central location (360 miles west of Rabaul and 200 miles from
the Wewak-Madang coastal area), excellent harbor, and two airfields marked it as
a natural air and naval base to support MacArthur's unfolding 1944 operations.
Control of the Admiralties also protected MacArthur's otherwise exposed right
flank and completed the encirclement of Rabaul. In early February 1944, Southwest Pacific theater plans called for the 1st Cavalry Division to seize the Admiralties by April 1 with the two-division assault on Hansa Bay to follow twenty-five
days later.[10] With that timetable in mind, Kenney's fliers had been softening up
Los Negros, largest of the Admiralties. As an apostle of air warfare, Kenney saw
even greater possibilities.[11] The developing situation in the Admiralties offered
the chance to show that air power alone could drive the Japanese from Los Negros.
Doctrinal blinders shielded Kenney from any evidence that contradicted his pet
theory.

Kenney's stubborn air war of attrition over Rabaul, aided mightily by U.S.
Navy carrier- and land-based dive-bombers as well as U.S. Marine and New
Zealand fighters, had gradually whittled down Japanese defenses. In November
the Japanese could make good their losses to Allied airmen with an influx of
replacements and maintain their air strength in the Southwest Pacific. By December they could no longer replace the aircraft and pilots chewed up in the
Rabaul meat grinder. During January 1944, Japanese air power could no longer
challenge every major Allied air raid. In fact, Fourth Air Army had only sixty
operational aircraft, and only about eighty naval carrier planes were available.[12]

From Central Bureau's intercepted voice communications, decoded call signs,
and traffic analysis, Kenney learned that Japanese fighters and reconnaissance
planes were based at Lorengau Airfield on Manus (January 4, 13). News that an
airfield construction unit was headed to Lorengau set off alarms at MacArthur's
headquarters because any improvement of enemy air capability would affect the
burgeoning RENO IV plan (January 22). Moreover, Fourth Air Army had ordered a
squadron of the 63d Air Regiment to Momote Airfield on Los Negros in order to
protect convoys running between Rabaul and New Guinea ports. By chance the
squadron's arrival on January 22 coincided with a Fifth Air Force photo reconnaissance mission.

Exposed on film, the Japanese were trapped on the ground two days later when Kenney's marauding pilots destroyed all twelve of their aircraft within minutes. Later attacks against the Admiralties encountered almost no Japanese resistance. Kenney saw that his theory about air power was apparently being borne out because thereafter life seemingly stopped in the Admiralties. Allied pilots zoomed past unrepaired airstrips and runway bomb craters filled with water or partially overgrown with grass. No antiaircraft fire greeted the planes. Kenney ordered photographs taken from 200 feet, an almost suicidal height. Photo interpreters at Port Moresby pored over the glossy, high-resolution pictures, pinpointing twenty-four Japanese bunkers around the airstrip. No other signs of life appeared on the photographs. Nor was any activity observed for the ten days immediately preceding the 1st Cavalry's landing.[13]

This stillness fit into a larger pattern of Japanese abandonment of the Bismarcks. Allied air strikes in February against Wewak and the New Guinea coast met little aerial opposition, and ULTRA revealed that Japanese naval air units were pulling out of the Bismarcks. Japanese airfields were generally unserviceable and few fighters rose to challenge Allied pilots. In late February, two U.S. destroyers swept through the Bismarck Sea but drew no Japanese response. The next day, February 23, three B-25s lazily circled the Admiralties, dropping lower and lower with each pass. After ninety minutes the pilots were 20 feet off the ground. They saw no Japanese, no trucks, no laundry, no latrines. No one fired at them. Their report convinced Kenney in Brisbane that the islands were deserted.[14]

Kenney quickly proposed to MacArthur an immediate landing on Los Negros, which air power, Kenney insisted with the certitude of a true believer, had cleared of all Japanese.[15] Chamberlin and Admiral Kinkaid bought Kenney's idea, and Admiral Barbey received orders to arrange naval transport and covering fire for the landing force. MacArthur decided to risk a reconnaissance in force with just five days' preparation. Chamberlin went to Krueger, the Sixth Army commander whose troops would make the assault, to finalize their operational plans.

For the Japanese, the Admiralties were an unwanted stepchild. With excess troops on his hands after the withdrawal from Guadalcanal, General Imamura had ordered the 51st Transport Regiment to Los Negros. They arrived in April 1943 and set to work building an airfield. Six months later Imamura pressed Tokyo to dispatch a full division to defend the islands. Already overcommitted, Imperial Army Headquarters told the general that no unit was available. Eighth Area Army next proposed sending the 66th Regiment, then reconstituting its forces in the Palaus, to defend the Admiralties. As Tokyo saw it, Eighteenth Army needed the 66th more than the Admiralties.

Imamura got no help from the Imperial Navy, which rejected his notion of deploying a special naval landing force to garrison the islands. Vice Admiral Kusuka Jin'ichi, commander of the Southeast Area Fleet, insisted that he had no naval landing detachments available for redeployment. The army then proposed dispatching the newly organized 1st Independent Mixed Regiment to be created from a cadre of the 66th Infantry Regiment. In the midst of this bitter interservice haggling, MacArthur struck at Arawe, New Britain. At a hurriedly called conference, Eighth Area Army and Southeast Area Fleet staff officers wrangled over future Allied intentions as well as countermeasures to stop the inexorable enemy advance toward the Philippines. Among the spate of recommendations to Tokyo that the five-day conference produced was one to send at least a regiment to the Admiralties. MacArthur's landing at Saidor in January finally swayed Imperial Headquarters to order the 66th Regiment to the Admiralties. Imamura was still unable to convey to his naval counterpart at Rabaul any sense of urgency that time was running out for those islands. When he pointed out the likelihood of an Allied invasion during the dark phase of the moon during late January (MacArthur had always landed at such periods), Kusaka expressed interest but refused to let his precious cruisers transport the 66th Regiment from the Palaus to the Admiralites.[16] A deadly game of cat and mouse played out 900 miles north of the Palaus forced Imamura's hand.

On January 16, the USS *Whale* slid under two Japanese destroyers and made ready to fire torpedoes into a three-ship convoy. As *Whale*'s captain lined up his target, a destroyer suddenly darted between the submarine and its intended victim and dropped a depth charge. With the destroyer less than 400 yards away, *Whale* fired one torpedo, then two more eight seconds apart. The destroyer, frantically dropping more depth charges, immediately swerved toward *Whale*'s periscope. The submarine plunged for the safety of the depths, and crewmen heard muffled explosions as their torpedoes hit home. They claimed to have sunk a freighter and tanker. The genesis of *Whale*'s successful ambush was submarine headquarters in Hawaii. From decrypted Japanese radio messages reporting torpedo attacks, Hawaii had steered *Whale* toward its hunting partner USS *Seawolf*, already attacking a convoy. *Seawolf*'s signal had alerted *Whale* to the convoy's course and speed. The Japanese destroyer had also been warned by Japanese intercept operators monitoring calls from nearby merchantmen not under attack on the assumption that the Allied submarine would soon be lining up its next victim.[17]

Whale had torpedoed the *Denmark* Maru nine days out of Pusan, Korea. The stricken transport carried 2,999 troops, who were crammed into every nook and corner of the creaky, old vessel. These replacements were destined for the 66th Regiment cadre in the Palaus. Instead, more than 1,000 Japanese ended their voyage sealed in an underwater tomb. ULTRA did not disclose the cargo of the ship, although by early February Central Bureau had available two partial army references to this disaster. MacArthur knew, for instance, that due to a "sea mishap" 1,300 men of the 66th Regiment were still reported missing (February 4, 8). When the first news of the sinking reached Rabaul, a desperate Imamura ordered his 38th Division to provide immediately a battalion for the Admiralties.

The disaster also stirred Kusaka to promise Imamura the 6th South Seas Detachment, but Imperial Headquarters ordered that outfit to Hollandia instead. Imamura did sneak 750 men of the 1st Independent Mixed Regiment into the Admiralties on the night of January 24/25. Eighth Area Army wanted to dispatch another infantry and field artillery battalion to the Admiralties in early February. The troops boarded two transports, but frequent Allied air attacks forced Eighth Area Army to cancel the effort. On the night of January 30, a submarine torpedoed one of the transports, killing 350 of the 857 troops aboard. On the moonless night of February 2, an additional 530 men from the 1st Battalion, 229th Infantry, 38th Division, stole into Los Negros. The reinforcement, haphazard though it was, monopolized radio frequencies. Unfortunately for Imamura, Central Bureau was listening as Japanese radio operators tapped out their Morse Code messages implementing his plan.

Since April 1943, Willoughby's Order of Battle Section had methodically maintained a card file on Japanese units in the Admiralties. Starting from pilots' sightings of airfield construction and their reports of antiaircraft fire, the section had estimated that about 200 Japanese garrisoned Los Negros. By October, intelligence had identified the 51st Transport Regiment from captured documents and increased the number of Japanese troops in the Admiralties to 1,000 service troops, a figure that held steady until the end of January 1944. Then Willoughby commented circumspectly that according to "recent intelligence," combat reinforcements might have arrived in the Admiralties and more were on the way.[18] Although Willoughby took the credit, ULTRA provided the data for his assertions.

Increased spurts of radio traffic from Los Negros first alerted Central Bureau that further reinforcements were destined for the Admiralties (January 27). The Japanese already in the area amounted to little more than a regiment, but they formed an independent task force. As such, radio communications with Eighth Area Army Headquarters were in the four-digit, mainline army code and not the three-digit one reserved for regiments. This meant that Central Bureau could decrypt the radio messages. Akin's cryptanalysts broke Imamura's radio message to Tokyo, dated January 19, detailing his plans for strengthening the islands with an ad hoc 2,000-to-3,000-man independent mixed regiment (February 4). Central Bureau learned from another decrypted message about the infantry battalion that Imamura transferred to the Admiralties on the night of January 24/25 (February 4). Allied intercept operators monitored the heavy flow of radio traffic to and from the Admiralties that confirmed "known enemy intentions to reinforce the islands as quickly as possible" (February 11). On February 10 Willoughby sent Sutherland and Krueger a memo describing the transport of the 1st Battalion, 38th Division

(550 men), from Rabaul to the Admiralties on two destroyers. ULTRA was so sophisticated that Sutherland could read Japanese complaints that only 300 troops had landed because of a shortage of motorized landing craft.[19]

ULTRA made available messages from Eighth Area Army to the Palaus about the assignment of 1,000 men of the 17th Division replacement depot there to the Admiralties (February 10). Overwhelmed by stacks of suddenly readable Japanese messages, Central Bureau's cryptanalysts naturally overlooked several of importance. A review of dated radio messages discovered one of February 3 concerning 2,000 reinforcements with matériel for the Admiralties. ULTRA also confirmed tht Kenney's air strikes had rendered Los Negros airstrip unserviceable by mid-February (February 22), although the airdrome remained the center of Japanese ground defenses (February 25). Two days before the 1st Cavalry Division's scheduled landing, ULTRA warned Sutherland and Krueger that the Japanese expected imminent large-scale Allied operations. Deciphered Japanese radio messages referred to such giveaways as increased Allied radio messages that suggested new commands were staging their forces in the Buna area; increased radio traffic between MacArthur's and Nimitz's headquarters; and the appearance of Allied submarines near the Admiralty Islands.[20] For just such an eventuality, Central Bureau had established a special watch solely to monitor Admiralties radio traffic. On the eve of the invasion, the electronic snoopers reported a normal flow of radio messages to and from the islands, which meant that the Japanese anticipated nothing out of the ordinary (February 29).

MacArthur and his staff had this ULTRA intelligence in hand well in advance of the Admiralties invasion. By mid-February, Willoughby had laid out a precise order of battle derived mainly from ULTRA (see Table 4.1). Just before the landings, Willoughby reported that 4,000 Japanese troops from the 51st Transport Regiment, a battalion of the 1st Independent Mixed Regiment, and units of the 38th Division were on the islands, although enemy casualties suffered in recent ship losses probably reduced the overall number of defenders (February 29). Despite the overpowering evidence Willoughby had received from the Japanese themselves, Kenney refused to believe that his pilots had not driven them from Los Negros. At most, Kenney insisted, the garrison was a handful of troops. Caught between the egos of two men, ULTRA faced its first test. The outcome hinged on the accuracy of the number of troops derived from ULTRA and would determine its future use in MacArthur's theater. If ULTRA's version of Japanese strength was hopelessly wrong, it would be discredited, thereby diminishing its usefulness to the high command. If correct, however, ULTRA's veracity would be unchallenged. Much more than the pride of two generals was riding with the 1,000 officers and men of Brewer Task Force, the codename for the reconnaissance in force.

On Los Negros, Colonel Ezaki Yoshio, commander of the 51st Transport Regiment and overall commander in the Admiralties, judged that the Allies had to

Table 4.1. Estimated and Actual Japanese Ground Order of Battle,
Admiralty Islands, January 1944

G-2 Estimate		Actual	
Unit	Men	Unit	Men
Elements, 17th Division	1,000	Service Troops	640
1st Battalion, 1st Independent Regiment	600?[a]	2d Battalion, 1st Independent Regiment	783
Elements, 38th Division	300	1st Battalion, 229th Regiment	343
Oita South Seas Detachment	300?	88th Naval Garrison[b]	680
Unidentified Antiaircraft	200	36th Antiaircraft[b]	300
51st Transport	800	51st Transport	850
Elements, 51st Field Hospital	50	Elements, 51st Field Hospital	50
Total	3,250		3,646

[a]Question marks indicate possible strength as opposed to probable strength.
[b]On Manus Island
Source: General Headquarters, Far East Command, Military Intelligence Section, General Staff, "Operations of the Military Intelligence Section GHQ, SWPA/FEC/SCAP," vol. 3, Intelligence Series (Part 1), 1950, Documentary Appendixes, appendix 1, tab 2, United States Army Military History Institute, Carlisle Barracks, Pennsylvania.

attack from the north through massive Seeadler Harbor because the entrance to Hayne Harbor on the opposite side of the cape was too narrow for a large-scale landing. Knowing that Americans never do anything in a small way, Ezaki planned for the big attack. He relegated the defense of Hayne Harbor to cover with fire. Ezaki made the most of the mixed bag of Japanese defenders. The 2d Battalion's 783-man complement included recalled reserve officers who had seen combat in China. Most of the enlisted men fell into the recalled status as well but lacked combat experience. The 1st Battalion, 229th Infantry, was a tough outfit, blooded from Hong Kong to New Georgia. However, it was short of equipment, especially its battalion artillery guns. Though Ezaki's radiograms may have betrayed him, his tactical dispositions were masterpieces of concealment, cover, and deception. Human activity in the Admiralties seemed, to the naked eye, nonexistent.[21]

General Krueger, Ezaki's opponent, also faced difficult choices. Advance scouting parties sent to Los Negros two days before the landing reported the island was "lousy with Japs." There was no turning back. MacArthur's rush to mount the reconnaissance in force meant that he had to approach Los Negros from the east through Hayne Harbor.[22] Luck, not ULTRA, brought the 1st Cavalry ashore at Hayne Harbor.

Under an overcast sky, the Americans climbed down cargo nets into landing craft bobbing slightly on the calm sea. The first wave of attackers was lucky. The cavalrymen took the Japanese by surprise and were met only by machine-gun fire. This group made it quickly to shore. The Japanese opened up on the second wave, crisscrossing the channel with their accurate 20-mm dual-purpose gunfire. The navy men in the bow of the landing craft hollered at the GIs "to keep their heads down" or risk getting them blown off. Machine-gun fire sailed over the fragile little boats. One barge turned for the beach and ran into a 20-mm shell that ripped a hole in the middle of its landing ramp. Four men disappeared in the crimson explosion.[23] Destroyers moved closer to single out targets for destruction. Heavy rain slowed the landing but also reduced visibility, rendering Japanese fire ineffective from the beaches. After four-and-a-half hours, a reinforced squadron of the 5th Cavalry Regiment was ashore. They had answered the question. The Japanese were still on the Admiralties.

ULTRA about the besieged Japanese garrison's radiograms throughout the fighting was informational rather than predictive of Japanese intentions. Decryptions available March 3, for example, described the fierce Japanese counterattack two nights earlier. A reference to Japanese strength as 2,700, down from 3,700, was picked up on March 3. Two days later another unraveled Japanese message told MacArthur that the 1st Battalion, 229th Infantry, had suffered heavy casualties and had only 142 of 700 men left the morning after the big attack (March 5). By then Japanese radio operators on the islands were tapping out their obituaries. A plain-text message melodramatically informed Eighth Area Army that "the time of the last hour is drawing near (words unintelligible). We are striving for our fatherland" (March 5).[24]

The final hour had arrived for the almost 3,300 Japanese servicemen whom the 1st Cavalry Division killed in the Admiralties. Only 75 Japanese surrendered. American ground troops then searched the hard-won battleground, gathering up discarded equipment and disposing of human remains. Picking through the debris, they uncovered 400 Japanese bunkers defending the airfield, almost seventeen times the number trained photo interpreters had pinpointed in photographs taken of the area. Willoughby was triumphant because ULTRA enabled him to list the Japanese units in the Admiralties with unparalleled accuracy.[25] Battleground verification of Japanese strength vindicated ULTRA's veracity and dispelled any suspicions about its capabilities lingering in the back of planners' minds. The Allies could prepare for the daring Hollandia invasion with full confidence in ULTRA's unequivocal picture of their adversary.

MacArthur's conquest of the Admiralties had other far-reaching repercussions as well. Seizure of the Admiralties influenced the Joint Chiefs of Staff to reassess Pacific strategy. On March 2, they directed MacArthur and Nimitz to submit their respective plans for advancing to the Luzon-Formosa–China coast triangle.[26] Three days later, MacArthur proposed to Marshall and the Joint Chiefs of Staff that two Southwest Pacific divisions, supported by the U.S. Pacific Fleet, attack

Hollandia on April 15, as a step in MacArthur's ultimate strategic goal of returning to the Philippines. His justification to General Marshall for the change in plans was based in great measure on ULTRA. MacArthur told Marshall that "the enemy has concentrated the mass of his ground forces forward in the Madang-Wewak area, leaving relatively weak forces in the Hollandia Bay area. He is attempting to concentrate land-based air forces in the area of western New Guinea and is developing additional fields in order to consolidate this area into a bulwark of air defense."[27] Only deciphered Japanese army communications could have given MacArthur such accurate intelligence about enemy deployments and intentions.

Sutherland briefed MacArthur's revised plan to strike Hollandia to the Joint Chiefs on March 8. Four days later, a Joint Chiefs of Staff directive reaffirmed the two-pronged attack strategy for the Pacific and approved MacArthur's jump to Hollandia.[28] Certainly the glaring enemy weakness at Hollandia, exposed by the Japanese themselves, swayed the Joint Chiefs to sanction MacArthur's leap far behind the Japanese front lines. Even with his extensive knowledge of his opponent's condition, MacArthur's decision to leap to Hollandia was a bold one, and it is inconceivable that the Joint Chiefs would have approved such a gamble if the general had lacked an exact appreciation of the defenses his men would storm.

Hollandia carried enormously high risks. An amphibious attack is the most complicated and dangerous of military operations. MacArthur now proposed to conduct two simultaneous amphibious assaults—later amended to three—far behind Japanese lines. It would be the largest Southwest Pacific operation to date, ultimately involving 217 ships moving 80,000 men with supplies 1,000 miles in order to bypass and isolate the Japanese Eighteenth Army. Failure would result in heavy losses and discredit MacArthur's entire bypassing strategy. A lesser commander might not have risked all on such a complex operation. But the notion of a classic envelopment of one's enemy struck a resonant chord in MacArthur. It smacked of a "Cannae by sea," and the comparison to Hannibal's great victory over the Romans did not escape his or Willoughby's attention. It appealed to MacArthur's generalship, his sense of the dramatic, and his vanity. Its spectacular scope suited the general's carefully cultivated style. MacArthur's inside knowledge of Japanese defenses, provided by ULTRA, could not, of course, be revealed. But this only added to his legend. Although Hollandia would appear to be an almost reckless gamble, it was actually a carefully planned sledgehammer blow against a known weak point of the Japanese. Its potential could put MacArthur's face and his theater on the front pages of newspapers worldwide. Victory would bring him closer to fulfilling his moral, almost megalomaniac quest to return to the Philippines.

Hollandia culminated two years of dreadful attrition warfare fought in reeking jungles and displayed MacArthur's supreme moment of generalship in the Pacific war. Besides imagination, courage, decisiveness, and the martial virtues, great soldiers also need luck. ULTRA supplied MacArthur's luck because the break into the Japanese army's mainline codes came at the most advantageous time in the New Guinea campaigns. A year earlier MacArthur's forces would have been too weak to exploit such a windfall. A month later and he might have been considering how to evacuate two divisions trapped at Hansa Bay. Instead, MacArthur learned Imperial Headquarters' most secret plans at the exact moment he was most prepared to exploit its weakness. He ensured the feebleness of Japanese defenses by severing their supply lines to Hollandia and by again smashing a resurgent Japanese army air force concentrated there.[29]

Yet another Eighth Area Army message, this one dated February 1 and issued by Central Bureau on February 5, detailed naval convoy traffic and resupply schedules from the Palaus to Rabaul, New Britain, and Wewak, New Guinea. The Eighth Area Army chief of staff reported to Eighteenth Army a list of supplies, personnel reinforcements, convoy size, escort force, and, most significant, arrival time for five convoys scheduled for Wewak from late February through late March (February 6). According to an official postwar assessment of ULTRA in the Pacific, "The messages were issued in sufficient time for our action."[30] At least twelve Japanese freighters were sunk by Allied air or naval action while en route to resupply Wewak between February 29 and March 24, 1944. Eighth Area Army's message sealed the fates of the five convoys and shows how critical ULTRA derived from the Army Water Transport Code was in anticonvoy operations.

On February 14/15, Wewak Convoy Number 19—four ships with escorts—arrived, unloaded, and departed Wewak as scheduled without incident, probably because inclement weather prevented Allied interception. Two weeks later, however, the next convoy in this series suffered serious losses. Despite three naval escorts and thirty to eighty fighter aircraft providing cover, the four ships of Wewak Convoy Number 20 fell prey to the U.S. submarine *Gato,* which torpedoed and sank the transport *Daigen* Maru Number 3 on February 26. Four hundred and four reinforcements of the 66th Infantry Regiment, 51st Division, were lost. The Eighth Area Army signal relaying this disaster did note that the regimental colors had been saved.[31] The remaining three transports arrived safely at Wewak on February 29 and departed at 1:00 A.M. on March 1 for Hollandia. After discharging aviation fuel and personnel reinforcements at Hollandia, the convoy headed back to the Palaus but may have lost a second transport to air action during its return voyage.[32]

On February 29, Hollandia Convoy Number 6, carrying the 6th South Seas Detachment, left the Palaus for Hollandia as previously announced. Alerted by submarine headquarters, Hawaii, the U.S. submarine *Peto* attacked the convoy and sank the 4,368-ton passenger cargo ship *Kayo* Maru, which exploded so violently that the Americans reported sinking an ammunition ship. The blast killed forty-five Japanese soldiers including the detachment commander, Colonel Matsuo Yutaro. The surviving 240 troops reached Hollandia on March 4 (March 14). Ironically, Willoughby commented that part of the 6th South Seas Detachment had reached Hollandia earlier on February 20 and that the ill-fated Colonel Matsuo had probably assumed command of the garrison at that time.[33]

On the night of March 15, Kenney's night air patrols, again forewarned by ULTRA, attacked a barge convoy moving from Hollandia to Wewak, sank two 1,000-ton vessels and drove another one aground (*March 13, 15*). (The italicized dates in parentheses refer to when the intelligence appeared in the War Department's MAGIC Summary—Japanese Army Supplement" [MSJAS].) The worst disaster, however, befell Wewak Convoy Number 21 on the night of March 18/19. With a March 9 water transport decryption providing revised convoy schedules, Arlington Hall had alerted the Military Intelligence Service, War Department, which in turn, by March 17, had notified Southwest Pacific Headquarters and the U.S. Navy of the schedule of the impending four-ship convoy. Two B-24s, equipped with a new radar bombsight, first discovered the convoy after midnight 60 miles northwest of Hollandia. They attacked and sank one transport, probably the *Yakumo Maru*. The remaining three ships, including two submarine chasers (auxiliary) serving as escort vessels, stood by rescuing survivors.

The rescue effort fixed the convoy's location the following morning when U.S. heavy bombers and at least eighty fighter bombers destroyed the remaining ships.[34] ULTRA confirmed the sinking of four ships whose "crews and all aboard were lost" (*March 28*). Among other losses when these freighters went down was a one-hundred-man air surveillance unit with its radar equipment that the Japanese intended to use to cover the southern and southeastern approaches to their major base of Hollandia. They were sorely missed two weeks later when massive Allied air raids against Hollandia destroyed Japanese air power in eastern New Guinea. Of more immediate importance, however, Imperial Headquarters had had enough and ordered that large-ship convoys to Wewak be suspended. It radioed Eighth Area Army that "in view of the present successively occurring losses of Wewak convoys we regret to say that it has been decided to stop for a short time the transportation by large type ships from Palaus to Wewak" (*March 31*).

The rash of sinkings did not lead the Japanese to suspect that the Americans were intercepting their ships on the basis of compromised codes. The routine night patrols Kenney's pilots conducted over Hollandia and Wewak had accustomed the Japanese to the presence of American aircraft. Furthermore, reconnaissance aircraft appeared conspicuously in sectors where ULTRA had alerted the Allies to the probable presence of Japanese convoys. The resulting aerial attacks led the Japanese to conclude that the reconnaissance planes had called for the air strikes.[35]

As for submarine attacks, at this stage of the war only about one in four Japanese merchantmen reported sighting an enemy submarine. Statistically at least, the Japanese could attribute the submarine attacks to ill fortune.

The Japanese believed that Allied scouting patrols, like the coastwatchers on New Britain, had landed from submarines and were lurking in the hills, from where they reported on convoy arrivals and departures.[36] Indeed, the Allied Intelligence Bureau constantly inserted small teams of agents behind Japanese lines and their presence probably fueled Japanese estimates of the agents' effectiveness. In any case, the result of such prohibitive losses left Tokyo no alternative but to cancel the convoy runs to Wewak, although this deprived Eighteenth Army of its major source of resupply. Advance knowledge of Japanese convoy schedules that only ULTRA could have provided had enabled the Allies to intercept and sink Japanese transports, thereby isolating Eighteenth Army from resupply by sea.

ULTRA in General Kenney's hands also played a major role in the struggle for air superiority over the northern New Guinea coast. As part of the September 1943 agreement, Imperial Headquarters had ordered the strengthening of defenses in western New Guinea, the Marianas, and the Carolines in preparation for forthcoming Allied offensives. In particular, desperately needed aircraft and pilot replacements were to augment thirty-five new airfields planned for western New Guinea. The overly ambitious projection of so many new airdromes proved impossible to achieve due to a lack of heavy construction equipment, shipping losses, and Allied air raids. These factors compelled the Japanese to concentrate their air power at Hollandia much as they had at Wewak the previous August. The evolution of the Hollandia base was a microcosm of Japanese difficulties as they tried to rebuild their air strength in New Guinea.[37]

In April 1943, Imperial Headquarters transferred Hollandia from Southern Army (Singapore, Malaya) to Eighth Area Army (Rabaul) as a rear area base. From June to November, the Japanese built two airstrips at Hollandia and constructed a road from the bay to the airfields. They also completed work on a third runway in January 1944, but the following month, without materials or equipment, they had to suspend construction of two additional strips. Nevertheless, Hollandia not only served as a base for Fourth Air Army Headquarters but also had developed into the major resupply point for Eighteenth Army operations in eastern New Guinea.[38]

In spite of the battles of attrition in eastern New Guinea in 1943, delays in the airfield construction program, and shortfalls in aircraft production, Tokyo stubbornly replaced the losses in front-line air units and, lacking alternatives, transferred existing combat air units to Hollandia. ULTRA noted the staging of these Japanese air reinforcements from Halmahera to Hollandia (February 9). A few days later, Willoughby announced that the Japanese had scheduled five new air regiments for Hollandia, including 81 bombers and 80 fighters to add to the 151 bombers and 205 fighters already in New Guinea (February 12). Washington picked up this ULTRA and reported that the realignment of the Japanese army air force in New Guinea was under way as the 8th Air Brigade (33d, 77th, and 60th Air regiments) was scheduled to arrive at Hollandia on February 15 (*February 16*). The War Department further predicted that two more fighter regiments from the Philippines would be subordinated to the 8th Air Brigade. The mission of these units was to support the defense of Hansa Bay from the Hollandia bases.[39]

By mid-February the Allies knew that approximately 150 Japanese aircraft had reinforced the fewer than 100 airplanes of Fourth Air Army. In particular they learned that the 8th Air Brigade was headquartered at Hollandia and two of its regiments, the 33rd and 75th, had a total of 56 operational aircraft (*February 18*). Willoughby reported that the five air regiments originally identified by ULTRA as potential reinforcements eleven days earlier had now arrived at Hollandia via Wakde and Halmahera (February 23). Furthermore, on February 28, responding to a February 23 inquiry, Willoughby told the War Department that "recent ultra evidence of Japanese aircraft" in New Guinea identified at least 101 aircraft at Hollandia (the 33d, 77th, and 75th Air regiments) as well as the 34th and 61st Air regiments with another 74 aircraft. On February 29, 1944, MacArthur's headquarters reported that aerial photo reconnaissance three days earlier had confirmed that hundreds of aircraft were on the island.[40]

Despite the Allied reconnaissance flights, the Japanese believed themselves secure at Hollandia because of its distance from Allied fighter bases. Although Hollandia was within the range of Allied heavy bombers, it was beyond that of the Allied fighters that had to escort the cumbersome bombers to Hollandia and back. And the Japanese judged correctly that an unescorted heavy-bomber attack would be suicidal. Learning from their bitter Wewak experience, they had located their major air base far beyond the known range of Kenney's fighters. For their part, Japanese fighter pilots planned to overcome great distances by staging from forward bases at Aitape or Wewak, thereby employing their fighters while preserving the bulk of their precious aircraft well out of range of land-based Allied fighters. Unbeknownst to the Japanese, Kenney had already identified Hollandia as a lucrative target. "The forced canalization of . . . air reserves from the west through Hollandia would probably result in a reckless and undispersed concentration of air strength taxing to the utmost the facilities of the four known Hollandia-Wakde airdromes" (March 6). On March 22 Willoughby called attention to another twenty-two Japanese aircraft reinforcing Hollandia and remarked on "the preeminence of Hollandia in the sphere of enemy air operations for New Guinea."

Another reason for the Japanese false sense of security was that, to date, no carrier aircraft had supported MacArthur's amphibious operations. Imperial Headquarters consequently ignored the possibility of carrier-based air strikes against its rear bases and believed that, as in the past, MacArthur would have to seize forward air bases somewhere between Madang and Aitape in preparation for a later invasion of Hollandia. MacArthur acknowledged the apparent validity of the Japanese estimate of the situation when he explained that without carrier support, the limit of air protection for land operations ''was the possible radius of operation of our fighter planes . . . from the actual location of our ground air bases. This required the seizing or construction of such new bases at each forward movement.''[41]

The Japanese were also confident that they could detect any Allied bombers early enough to intercept the unescorted formations before they could seriously damage the rear bases. Detection, though, depended on a reliable early warning system and accurate intelligence about Allied capabilities. The Japanese were deficient in both areas. Although they had finally installed radio intercept stations at Wewak and Hansa and had augmented coastwatchers scattered along the northern shore, they had no central air intelligence unit at Hollandia to analyze and synthesize the assembled data from field units.[42] The radar early warning unit had, of course, gone to the bottom with Wewak Convoy Number 21.

Nevertheless, the very presence of such large numbers of Japanese land-based aircraft within striking distance of his carriers was a source of much concern to Admiral Nimitz, who had agreed to provide carrier air support for MacArthur's multiple amphibious landings. At a conference on March 25 in Brisbane, Kenney promised Nimitz that he would have the aircraft ''rubbed out by 5 April.'' Since Kenney knew the location, disposition, and operational strength of the Japanese Fourth Air Army, his was not an idle boast.[43]

In February Kenney had received new P-38s modified with wing tanks to extend their range and had converted the P-38s already in the theater to equip them with wing tanks. To deceive the Japanese at Hollandia into believing they were safely beyond his fighters' range, he ordered that these modified aircraft fly no missions beyond existing ranges, thereby giving the enemy no indication of their improved range.[44] Kenney also secretly staged his heavy aircraft to forward bases undetected by the Japanese. In sum, ULTRA intelligence of the major concentration of enemy air strength allowed Kenney to plan his operation secure in the knowledge that the lucrative, unsuspecting Japanese air bases awaited him.

By Late March Kenney knew that by basing the bulk of their air strength in illusory safety at Hollandia, the Japanese probably had about 180 fighters and 130 bombers available in the New Guinea theater to combat Allied offensives. On March 30, the day of the first major Allied air strike against Hollandia, ULTRA identified 113 Fourth Air Army aircraft ''ready for action,'' including 47 fighters.[45] That day, again using a photo reconnaissance aircraft both to confirm the presence of the Japanese air units at Hollandia and to mask ULTRA, Kenney attacked the Japanese base at Hollandia with 60 B-24s escorted by 80 P-38s

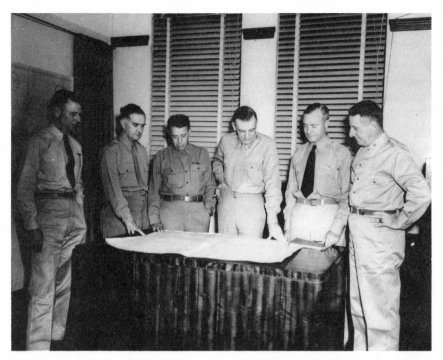

Planning the leap to Hollandia, March 1944. Photograph was taken in Brisbane where Lieutenant General George C. Kenney had promised to "rub out" the Japanese air force. Left to right: Captain Cato D. Glover, Jr., assistant plans officer, Headquarters, Seventh Fleet; Richard J. Marshall; Lieutenant General Kenney; Richard K. Sutherland; Rear Admiral Forrest P. Sherman, assistant chief of staff, Headquarters, Seventh Fleet; and Stephen J. Chamberlin. (U.S. Army Signal Corps photo, courtesy of U.S. Army Military History Institute)

equipped with the extended-range wing tanks. He continued the attacks on March 31 and, following a stand down for weather, struck again on April 3 when 63 B-24s and 171 B-25s and A-20s, escorted by 76 long-range P-38s, demolished what was left of Japanese air strength at Hollandia.

The initial flight profiles along the northern coast intentionally concealed the exact American target. At 8:45 A.M. on March 30, Hollandia scrambled 40 fighters to intercept a large formation of Allied aircraft reported by Wewak. Ten minutes later an air observer outpost at Aitape radioed Hollandia that the enemy aircraft had turned southeast, toward Allied bases, after making an attack. Hollandia then recalled its aircraft for refueling, but the American warplanes swung west again. Thus Kenney's main force surprised the Japanese as Allied aircraft formations appeared "like clouds" over the mountains, approaching Hollandia's airdromes from the south and southeast, areas the Japanese early warning system had left uncovered.[46] Kenney was replaying the Wewak raid on a grander scale.

Fifth Air Force raids made smoldering wrecks of most of the 131 operational Japanese aircraft on the ground at Hollandia and smashed forever any Japanese ambitions to regain aerial superiority in New Guinea. ULTRA had allowed Kenney the flexibility, born of awareness of his opponent's dispositions and intentions, to tailor his operational plans to deliver the most damaging attack at the time when the Japanese air force was most vulnerable parked on the ground. By early April, then, MacArthur's forces had isolated Eighteenth Army by sea and by air. The ground envelopment awaited completion as the culmination of the Hollandia operation.

ULTRA drew MacArthur and his headquarters staff a comprehensive picture of Eighteenth Army's deployments from mid-January 1944 through the Hollandia landings and beyond. The following examples of ULTRA made available to MacArthur highlight the significant decryptions and demonstrate their value to the planners. They represent only a handful of the hundreds of other decrypted messages that taken together provided a running commentary on the evolution of Japanese preparations for the defense of New Guinea.

Tokyo reacted to MacArthur's seizure of the Admiralties in early March 1944 by placing Eighteenth Army under the operational control of Second Area Army, headquartered at Davao, Philippines. ULTRA alerted the Allies to this shift as well as to the subordination of Fourth Air Army to Davao (March 13; *March 16*). Into MacArthur's hands ULTRA passed Eighteenth Army's plans and General Adachi's command relationships as he adjusted to his isolation from Rabaul after the loss of the Admiralties to the Allies. Regimental and division-level deployments such as the realignment of the 78th Infantry Regiment from a defensive line forward of Madang to its parent 20th Division at Hansa Bay also appeared in intercepted traffic. Southwest Pacific Headquarters learned of Eighteenth Army Headquarters' move to Wewak and the relocation of its forward combat command post to Hansa Bay, from where "surprise operations will be directed" (March 15, 19).

By March 20, MacArthur knew that the 41st Division had been diverted to Madang in order to be ready to counterattack and destroy an Allied landing "at any time or place." The composition of the five-thousand-man unit also appeared in ULTRA as did its mission—to hold the Madang area as an "independent fortress," thereby preventing its use by the Allies as long as possible. Aside from the valuable intelligence, analysis of the continual shifting of Eighteenth Army units indicated to MacArthur that Adachi's forces "will be in a transitory, unprepared state during March and probably most of April" (March 20). Furthermore, the Allies also knew that Eighteenth Army was short weapons and equipment from March 9 decryptions requesting two-thirds of the normal weapons allotment for a division in order to reequip the units under Adachi's command.

Members of Central Bureau's Hut 7 in April 1944. Hut 7 worked against various Japanese army codes and ciphers. This group included experts in traffic analysis, cryptanalysis, and linguistics. (Courtesy of U.S. National Security Agency)

In late March, Willoughby reviewed the Allies' knowledge to date of the missions of Eighteenth Army, Fourth Air Army, and Second Area Army. Eighteenth Army not only had to hold Wewak in strength but also had to redeploy its forces west toward Hollandia in order to secure its hold on Wewak. Fourth Air Army had to destroy Allied forces attempting to land west of Madang, support convoy escort and reconnaissance missions requested by Eighteenth Army, and deploy, as necessary, part of its strength to defend the Carolines (March 24). On March 28, decrypted signals revealed that Fourth Air Army's mission was to cooperate with Second Area Army in crushing a landing by Allied task forces in the area west of Madang, thus reconfirming Japanese intentions to defend Hansa Bay (March 28). The next day, a March 25 estimate of the Allied situation by General Anami Korechika, commander in chief of Second Area Army, became available. Anami's lengthy commentary, an unprecedented look into the Japanese commander's mind, displayed, according to Willoughby, "no serious contemplation of an Allied offensive against Hollandia, though a possibility is suggested. Attack against Carolines presumed. Our occupation of Madang and Hansa Bay are accepted as foregone conclusion. Allied advance expected after June. Conclusion: On D-day of the Hollandia operation, the bulk of 18th Army will probably be in Wewak. Transfer of a division back to Hollandia . . . is still possible prior to D-day."[47]

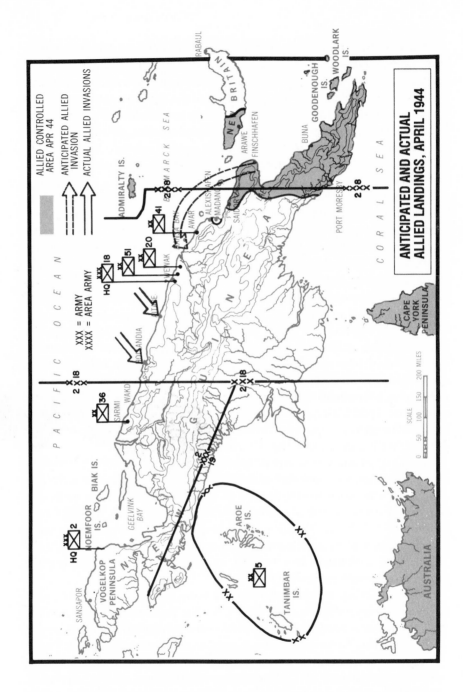

Source: Edward J. Drea, "Defending the Driniumor: Covering Force Operations in New Guinea, 1944," *Leavenworth Paper* No. 9 (Washington, D.C.: Government Printing Office, 1984).

Two days later, as intelligence analysts continued to assess Anami's estimate, they reported that in case of a landing in Hansa Bay, Eighteenth Army still laid particular stress on immediate counterattacks before the Allies could consolidate their beachhead (March 31). Washington echoed this assessment and reported that it had alerted Allied intercept stations to carefully watch radio message traffic that emanated from the Japanese 36th Infantry Division at Sarmi, about 150 miles west of Hollandia, for any indications that it might move to reinforce Hollandia. The absence of many high priority messages from Hollandia was a positive sign that the Japanese were preparing no such move at present (April 1).

As the April 22 date of the Allied landings at Hollandia and Aitape drew near, Akin and Sinkov ordered Central Bureau to give special emphasis and attention to radio communications emanating from those Japanese bases. ULTRA reported 8,647 general troops and 7,650 air troops (2,250 of whom were air duty personnel) at Hollandia. Willoughby interpreted this to mean that an aggregate 16,297 men were at Hollandia and Aitape. He estimated about 12,000 Japanese at Hollandia when, in fact, there were approximately 16,000 (April 1).[48] Despite this miscalculation, Willoughby correctly asserted that the units were overwhelmingly service, base defense, construction, and air service elements. Among the 12,000 troops he assumed to be at Hollandia, MacArthur's G-2 judged that the Japanese had perhaps one combat maneuver battalion available to defend the area. Moreover, Willoughby informed his subordinates that "in view of the pressing situation in Hollandia, it is essential to hammer away at the tactical enemy capabilities in that area, in the Special Intell as well as, guardely [*sic*], in the daily."[49] Not coincidentally, Willoughby's "suggested" comment appeared verbatim in the next day's Special Intelligence Bulletin (April 1 and 2).

The Order of Battle Section could also validate the claims of U.S. pilots on the basis of Japanese messages such as the one of April 4 stating that the airfields at Hollandia were unserviceable because of Allied air raids. Without doubt, this confirmation was a source of comfort to Admiral Nimitz. There were, however, indications that Japanese concern over a landing in Dutch New Guinea might accelerate their westward withdrawal. Reports had Eighteenth Army Headquarters moving to Hollandia by submarine, although a considerable portion of the army would remain at Wewak (April 7).

Without warning, on April 8 the Japanese army changed the key register to all its four-digit cryptologic systems. The U.S. War Department ruefully admitted that "all Japanese Army high-level cryptographic systems that the U.S. Army and Allied units have been reading were changed recently, and at the present time no messages in such systems are being read."[50] Traffic analysis filled part of this void until the codebreakers could again reconstruct readable segments of the army code. U.S. Navy ULTRA continued uninterrupted. This combination of traffic analysis and naval ULTRA led Washington to report on April 21: "Despite this [Japanese] recognition of the importance of Hollandia, a speculation by the Chief of Staff, Southwestern Area Force, that US communications might indicate a landing there, Japanese Army traffic has thus far failed to disclose that any of the three divisions under the Eighteenth Army has established either a divisional or regimental headquarters west of Wewak." Radio message traffic patterns further indicated that Second Area Army's only strategic reserve, the 36th Infantry Division, still remained immobile at Sarmi 150 miles west of Hollandia (April 21).[51]

That Adachi's three divisions remained fixed defending Hansa Bay was not accidental. A successful envelopment hinged on MacArthur's ability to maintain the element of surprise, which, in turn, depended on Southwest Pacific Headquarters' ability to conceal from the Japanese the Allies' real objective. In particular, a decrypted Japanese message, transmitted February 28/29 and available shortly thereafter, offered Allied planners unparalleled insight into the thinking of their Japanese adversaries. The message formed the core of a staff appreciation of Japanese defensive planning for New Guinea and subsequently appeared in a memorandum dated March 7 from Willoughby to Chamberlin. According to this ULTRA, which became the basis for the subsequent Allied deception plan, the Japanese anticipated that the Allies' next major amphibious operations would occur on the northern New Guinea coast between Madang and Awar. Adachi planned to counter such a landing by attacking the beachhead from the east with his 41st Infantry Division and from the west with his 20th Infantry Division, thereby "ambushing" the Allied invaders.[52]

Despite lingering bad feelings from the Fellers episode, Chamberlin approved the gist of Willoughby's recommendations for a deep envelopment of Eighteenth Army. To conceal the target of the amphibious assault from the enemy, Willoughby also devised an extensive deception plan. He suggested a strong feint and amphibious raid near Hansa Bay to hold the Japanese forces in place. He also believed that the fake landing would draw out Japanese air power and enable the Allies to destroy it. Chamberlin rejected these overly ambitious schemes. Simply stated, the Southwest Pacific theater did not have sufficient shipping to simultaneously mount the Hollandia expedition and use its ships as bait for Japanese pilots. Those points made, Chamberlin forwarded the recommendations to MacArthur, who approved the deception plan to accompany the Hollandia operation. Feeding on ULTRA revelations of what Adachi and his staff were predisposed to believe anyway, Kenney's pilots staged raids and bombed targets in the Hansa-Madang area to reinforce Japanese preconceptions of future Allied landings there. The Allies conducted conspicuous reconnaissance flights to map and photograph the Hansa Bay terrain. To further mislead the Japanese, torpedo boats were obvious off Hansa Bay. Air units dropped dummy parachutists near Hansa Point and scattered leaflets agitating Korean and Taiwanese conscripts to desert their Japanese masters. Submarines left empty rafts ashore, suggesting reconnaissance patrols had landed to scout the beaches for possible landing areas. U.S. Navy destroyers conducted deceptive feints and shelled the Hansa Bay area on April 10.[53] So successful was this deception campaign that in an April 17 signal to Marshall detailing the Hollandia operation, MacArthur stated confidently that "our feints in the Wewak–Hansa Bay front have held the mass of the enemy's forces forward, making possible the envelopment of his entire 18th Army with an estimated strength of 60,000."[54]

That same day, the Japanese naval communications center at Rabaul, reacting to radio intercepts of Allied air and naval special high-speed message traffic, issued a warning about the imminent probability of Allied landing operations along the New Guinea coast. Eighth Area Army rebroadcast the advisory to all its units. Despite sightings by Japanese naval aircraft on April 18 of the Allied naval task force near the Admiralties and a report by an Eighth Area Army reconnaissance plane of seeing the transport convoy the next day about 200 miles due north of Wewak, Imperial Headquarters was unable to forecast accurately where the Allies might land.[55] For example, on April 20, Eighth Area Army signaled all units that Allied landings would most likely be at Wewak or the Ninigo Islands north of New Guinea. Consequently, the heavy air strikes by U.S. Navy carrier-based aircraft against Hollandia on the morning of April 21 failed to alert the defenders to the approaching invasion fleet.

The deception operation did in fact mislead the Japanese. The day before the Allied landings, Eighteenth Army signaled Davao and Rabaul:

> Judging from enemy trends, there is a 90% probability that the enemy plans a new landing on the north coast line in the latter part of April. Based on the military situation, we estimate the most likely places are Madang, Hansa, or Karkar Islands. According to the general situation a landing in the Wewak sector is next in probability. In light of the recent bombings of Hansa, of reconnaissance and naval bombardment of Wewak, and the dropping of pamphlets by the enemy stating that they would land on Wewak on 24 April, it is necessary to be vigilant for it. While it cannot be said there is no possibility of a Hollandia landing, enemy submarines and destroyers have not reconnoitered the area in force. The air attack was simply a destructive measure. It is not felt these are clear indications of an imminent landing.[56]

Another U.S. deception contributed greatly to this Japanese misperception of Allied intentions. The three Allied convoys sailed on roundabout routes some 200 miles longer than a direct voyage to Hollandia required. Admiral Barbey, in command of the assault convoy, believed the northern route convinced the Japanese that the convoy was heading toward Truk in the Carolines or possibly east toward Rabaul. Regardless, the Japanese spent April 20 searching the area behind the convoy and never again made visual contact with it.[57] The final Allied deception came on the morning of the landings, April 22, when hundreds of Australian and American aircraft attacked Hollandia, Aitape, and Wakde-Sarmi in such force that the local Japanese forces of each area believed their sector was the main target for the invasion.[58]

Scarlet tracers split the blue-gray morning sky over Hollandia, and rockets rained down on the already blazing shore. Naval gunfire added to the spectacular light show, and army land-based and navy carrier aircraft roared over the beach at tree-level, strafing and bombing suspected Japanese positions. Since few of MacArthur's commanders were privy to ULTRA at this time, they were sweating out the landing. General Robert L. Eichelberger, the cantankerous I Corps commander, expected a bitter fight. "What a lucky break," he wrote to his wife about the unopposed landing. Barbey willingly offered twenty years of his life if the convoy under his care could get close enough to Hollandia to open fire without being blown out of the water.[59] Their apprehensions dissipated when the two assault battalions of the 24th Infantry Division reached Red Beach 2 in Tanahmerah Bay unopposed. Twenty-five miles to the east, at Humboldt Bay, the 162d Infantry Regiment, 41st Infantry Division, also landed without meeting any resistance.

Once ashore, the 24th and 41st divisions—moving east and west, respectively—conducted a giant pincer movement that aimed to encircle Hollandia's three airdromes. The airfields were located on a flat plain between the northern shore of Lake Sentani and the 7,000-foot-high Cyclops mountains, about midway between the two bays. Anyone approaching these flatlands had to traverse a maze of jungle trails, rain-swollen streams, and numerous hills and defiles. Terrain proved a harsher opponent than the Japanese. It punished the troops, slowed their advance, and forced them to hand-carry their supplies through the dense undergrowth. Fortunately for the Americans, Major General Inada Masazumi's forces were in total disarray and unable to coordinate any effective resistance.

Inada commanded the 6th Air Division at Hollandia, although he was an artilleryman without flight experience. His predecessor, Lieutenant General Itabana, in typical Japanese fashion, had resigned to take responsibility for the loss of his aircraft on the ground to Kenney's earlier air strikes. Inada had been in command a mere ten days when the Americans landed. His potpourri of pilots without aircraft, airfield construction units, service and supply troops, and signal units numbered more than 15,000 men. They were pitifully equipped. The service and communications units totaled nearly 7,600 men, but fewer than one in ten carried a rifle. Inada eventually gathered about 7,200 men, and on April 28 headed for Sarmi to join forces with the 36th Division. Only 1,000 men survived the terrible journey.[60]

MacArthur's troops had their own worries. Hollandia's narrow beachhead lacked adequate inland routes, so GIs piled supplies high and haphazardly around the shores. Smoldering fires from the preinvasion bombardment clearly marked the landing areas. From the moment it received word of the landings, Fourth Air Army, which had withdrawn to Menado on April 15, began planning an attack against the Hollandia beachhead. Since Kenney's earlier raids had destroyed Japanese air power, only a handful of twin-engine Type 99 bombers were available for the mission. Three Type 99s from the 75th Air Regiment flew from Ceram Island, Netherlands East Indies, to Biak Island. The Biak airstrip was pitted with bomb craters and lacked night navigation aids. Officers hurriedly mustered scores of airfield construction troops to line the runway holding flashlights to guide the intrepid pilots' landings and takeoffs. The three planes took off from Biak on April 23, but one clipped a wing on a coconut tree in a grove at the end of the runway and cartwheeled into a brilliant ball of flame. The surviving bombers flew east into the darkness toward Hollandia.[61]

It was the dark phase of the moon, and the pilots never expected to find much of a target. Fifty miles out from Hollandia they spotted flickering light and, as they came closer, they clearly saw flames from the still burning beachhead debris at Humboldt Bay. They flew in undetected and aimed their bomb loads at the middle of the fire. A massive chain reaction erupted as flames licked against American supplies stacked nearby. Tremendous explosions and pillars of flame rent the night sky. Intense heat and continued detonations made it impossible to control the inferno, although twenty-four men died and about one hundred were injured in the attempt. The conflagration burned out of control through the night and most of the next day. Fire consumed more than 60 percent of the rations and ammunition landed through D-day plus 1 and added to the logistical nightmare of resupplying through jungle terrain.[62] Two days later, ULTRA belatedly reported that "two Japanese Army medium bombers were noted returning to Biak on the night of 23-24 April after a flight to the east" (April 26).

When Southwest Pacific Headquarters planned for the leap to Hollandia, the U.S. Navy agreed to provide three days of carrier-based air support and no more. Nimitz knew from ULTRA that the Japanese were constructing a network of new air bases in western New Guinea and were staging aircraft from the Netherlands East Indies and Philippines to fill these airdromes. Without a guarantee that all the fields could be neutralized, Nimitz could not in good conscience expose his carriers like sitting ducks off Hollandia for eight long days. Denied sustained naval air support, MacArthur's staff opted to seize the three Japanese airfields at Aitape about 125 miles southeast of Hollandia. These fields could support forward bases for Fifth Air Force fighters, and American troops at Aitape could protect Hollandia's exposed eastern flank against any westward counteroffensive by Eighteenth Army.

The similarities between the Hollandia and Aitape operations were many. Tactical surprise at Aitape was as total as it had been at Hollandia. The Japanese melted into the jungle as the 163d Regimental Combat Team, commanded by Brigadier General Jens A. Doe, waded ashore. Confusion reigned on the crowded Allied beachhead, and a single Japanese bomber seriously damaged the sole U.S. Navy cargo ship, auxiliary (AK) *Etamin*, which had to scuttle its supplies in order to remain afloat. As with Hollandia, ULTRA reported after the fact on the successful Japanese raid (April 28). Hollandia developed into a massive staging base that became home to 140,000 men. Aitape was also transformed into a base, although a much smaller one. There the similarities ended. As a gatehouse for Hollandia, Aitape became the scene of one of MacArthur's hardest fought and bloodiest battles on New Guinea.

At Hollandia, though slowed by the treacherous jungle trails and reduced supplies, the American pincers finally met at the airfields on April 26. GIs found an aircraft graveyard where they counted 340 wrecked planes. Another 18 charred fighters were found at Aitape (May 16). The hunt for Japanese stragglers continued. American infantrymen killed about 3,300 Japanese and captured slightly more than 600. Intelligence teams accompanying the infantry carefully searched the abandoned Japanese airfields for discarded code and cipher materials.

One careless Japanese radioman had left 147 worksheets with key and indicator tables for the Americans. This crib was fed into the IBM machines at Central Bureau and Arlington Hall, enabling cryptanalysts to read messages enciphered in the new key. The advantage was short-lived, because the Japanese, fearing that such a security compromise had occurred on Hollandia, discontinued the key on May 10. Analysts then used the worksheets to decipher backlogged material.[63] One previously unreadable item reported that a barge sunk off Aitape had been carrying the new key registers. The codebooks presumably had been incinerated in the fire that had engulfed the ship. This assertion caught the eye of a cryptanalyst, probably one who had been assigned to burn classified documents. Books, unless burned page by page, do not disintegrate. Intense heat reduces the paper to ash, but the charred remains retain their original form, and if handled gingerly, they still give up their secrets.

Central Bureau flew a diver from Brisbane to Aitape. After several dives, literally under the eyes of Japanese hiding in the hills, he carefully salvaged the codebooks in the steel box that had become their oven. When the books arrived at Central Bureau, an Australian officer who was a cryptanalyst painstakingly separated each ashen page and mounted it on cotton backing. Next, an Australian scientist applied several chemical solutions in the hope of reviving the printed numbers. By trial and error it developed that plain rubbing alcohol worked best. Cryptanalysts broke into two-man teams. One swabbed the page and read off the numbers that briefly appeared before the alcohol evaporated. The other recorded the numbers. By this ingenious if tedious method, Central Bureau recovered 85 percent of the key register.[64] IBM technicians at Central Bureau fed these numbers into their tabulators, and by late May cryptanalysts were well on their way to breaking the Japanese army's new mainline cipher.

Eighteenth Army offered MacArthur's codebreakers another key to open its secrets. Surrounded and isolated by MacArthur's leap to Hollandia, Adachi still had sixty thousand troops. His headquarters maintained radio contact with other major Japanese commands, but because it was cut off from resupply, radiomen had to modify their (now compromised) codes to transmit messages. Central Bureau quickly broke Eighteenth Army cipher messages, and by comparing them with other army messages transmitted by different units, it reconstructed the new key registers. Adachi's radio traffic proved so lucrative a source of information, not only about Japanese plans for New Guinea but also for other theaters, that in June 1944 Marshall sent the following somewhat contradictory request to MacArthur: "So long as 18th Jap Army remains physically isolated and in radio communication with other Jap units it will continue to afford US valuable source of cryptoanalytic assistance. To the extent that it will not interfere with your present operations, it is highly desirable that this situation be preserved and fully exploited. Will advise when this advantage to us ceases."[65]

MacArthur enjoyed a tremendous intelligence advantage, but he did not always use it. For example, the general disregarded accurate and timely ULTRA to push ahead with his invasion of the Admiralties. A major staging base, Los Negros, was bought at a cheap price, but MacArthur was far luckier there than he would care to admit. His use of ULTRA to craft his Hollandia plan survives as perhaps the classic example of the application of intelligence from codebreaking to operational planning in World War II. The leap to Hollandia and Aitape with simultaneous multidivision landings caught the defenders of the Eighteenth Army totally off guard—in effect, facing the wrong direction in order to defend Hansa Bay. ULTRA alone was not, of course, responsible for MacArthur's success. He exploited his knowledge of the Japanese forces on the other side of the hill and revised operational plans to take advantage of the windfall Central Bureau brought him. Lesser (or more cautious) commanders may have vacillated and permitted the opportunity to slip from their hands. Here was MacArthur at his best: bold and resolute to seize the moment. The edge bestowed by ULTRA allowed MacArthur to select the place of battle; with this advantage, the destruction of Adachi's Eighteenth Army became a matter of time. The Hollandia operation was a masterpiece of integrating ULTRA into operational planning to deceive, outmaneuver, and isolate an opponent. It was MacArthur's finest hour in World War II and ULTRA's single greatest contribution to the general's Pacific strategy. ULTRA would score more intelligence triumphs as MacArthur drove on to the Philippines, but never again would it equal its dazzling accomplishments from February to April 1944—when ULTRA handed MacArthur the sword that cut the Gordian knot—the Bismarck Barrier.

5
Misreading ULTRA, May–September 1944

MacArthur's amphibious operations against Hollandia and Aitape had sundered Japanese ground forces in New Guinea. Although Eighteenth Army was bypassed and isolated from resupply, General Adachi still commanded sixty thousand troops whose formations he ordered to turn west toward Aitape. Japan's Second Army occupied the western end of New Guinea with its forces thinly spread across Geelvink Bay. In late 1943 the supposition was that the Wakde-Sarmi region would serve as the forward bastion for the defense of strategic Geelvink Bay, which guarded the southern flank of the major Japanese naval base in the Palaus, shielded the northern flank of the resource-rich Netherlands East Indies, and, most significant, barred the southern approaches to the Philippines to potential invaders. By January 1944, Tokyo expected the 222d Infantry Regiment, 36th Division, to defend Biak Island until a full division arrived to replace it. The 36th Division's other regiments, the 223d and 224th, were diverted to airfield and coastal defense construction duties as Second Area Army feverishly worked to develop a network of rear air bases in western New Guinea.

Since ULTRA had exposed these Japanese intentions, MacArthur was impatient to grab the enemy bases in western New Guinea before they could be developed into redoubts. He exerted tremendous pressure on his commanders to finish each successive operation in minimum time and to move swiftly to the next objective on his timetable to return to the Philippines. MacArthur's latest revised plan, RENO IV, prepared in March 1944, quickened the tempo of his advance on Mindanao to November 5, 1944. Just three months later, RENO V telescoped the invasion of Mindanao to October and promised a landing on Luzon by April 1, 1945.

The burden of implementing MacArthur's rapid-fire directives fell on the shoulders of General Krueger, who was, in effect, fighting on two fronts. On one front, Krueger had to stand firm to prevent Adachi's army from breaking through the Allied ring and rejoining Japanese units farther west. On the other, he had to advance west, away from Adachi's troops, in order to exploit the great advantage won in April 1944. His dual missions strained Sixth Army to the limit as it readied itself for the forthcoming series of amphibious assaults against enemy strongholds in western New Guinea. All the while, Krueger had to look over his shoulder at Adachi's forces, which ULTRA almost daily reported inching ever closer to the Allied coastal enclave at Aitape. Unbeknownst to Krueger, Japanese troops were also on the march against Hollandia from the west.

With his close-cropped hair, oval face, and small, neat mustache, General Anami, commander of the Second Area Army, was a man of action. He found an outlet for his tremendous physical energy in Japanese swordfighting and archery. In fact, he had had an archery range set up behind his headquarters. As a practitioner of the martial arts, the general acted emotionally, even impetuously, from sincerely held convictions, the deepest of which was his faith that a Japanese soldier's supreme duty was to serve his emperor in battle.[1] Thus when news of the Hollandia landings reached him, he refused to wait passively for MacArthur's next blow to fall. He sent two battalions from his 36th Infantry Division, then garrisoning the Sarmi-Wakde area, east to check the Allies at Hollandia.

Then in hurriedly convened planning sessions, Anami concurred with his staff's unanimous intelligence estimates that Biak was the next American objective.[2] Anami sought to strike first and so proposed to Southern Army in Singapore that a major ground and naval counterstroke be launched immediately against Hollandia. Southern Army and Imperial Headquarters vetoed Anami's counteroffensive in favor of a defense in depth. Tokyo's entire strategy hinged on how quickly the 32d and 35th Infantry divisions from China could be transferred to the threatened zone. Time was crucial because Japan's military leaders anticipated that MacArthur's next attack would fall on Second Army sometime in June. On May 2 Imperial Headquarters redefined the primary defense line as one extending to the inner part of Geelvink Bay, Manokwari, Sorong, and Halmahera. Biak would be held as long as possible, and troops from Sarmi would be withdrawn to the island.[3] Tokyo had written off the exposed salient at Sarmi in order to marshal its forces in western New Guinea to stand guard over the approaches to the Philippines.

Like Anami, MacArthur held passionate convictions. None was stronger than his quest to liberate the Philippines. Two weeks before the Hollandia landings, the Southwest Pacific commander told Admiral Barbey that he was considering an assault on Wakde immediately after the Hollandia invasion. Just four hours after the first assault wave landed at Hollandia, a jubilant MacArthur visited the beachhead. Barbey, Krueger, and Eichelberger, who was the operational commander, accompanied their chief. When they returned to the armada's flagship, the cruiser *Nashville*, MacArthur startled his subordinates by suggesting an immediate attack on Wakde while the Japanese were still off balance.[4] Barbey "was all for it," Krueger was noncommittal, and Eichelberger was strenuously opposed to diverting supply ships destined for Hollandia to Wakde on MacArthur's snap

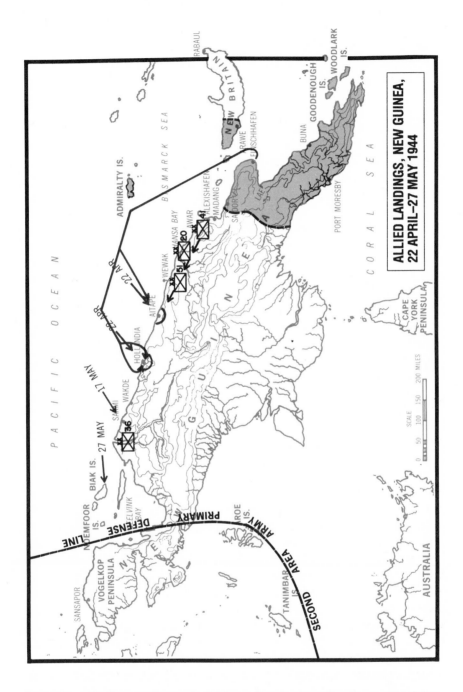

Source: Edward J. Drea, "Defending the Driniumor: Covering Force Operations in New Guinea, 1944," *Leavenworth Paper* No. 9 (Washington, D.C.: Government Printing Office, 1984).

judgment. MacArthur smiled and relented, but as Eichelberger recalled, "Mac-Arthur wanted results and quick ones. He was always impatient with failures to win objectives."[5] The Southwest Pacific commander's impetuosity asserted itself throughout the forthcoming campaigns as he drove his commanders to exploit the Hollandia advantage.

MacArthur's haste to capture Wakde stemmed in part from his passion to exploit the disorganized state of Japanese defenses in western New Guinea that ULTRA had revealed. Captured documents and ULTRA disclosed that since late 1943 the Japanese had been steadily building up their rear areas in that region. At present, a minimum of two engineer regiments and six independent engineer battalions were on the move to the Philippines, Halmahera, and western New Guinea, which suggested expanded military construction at those places. A new anchorage unit that appeared in radio communications in Halmahera in early December 1943 pointed to increased shipping to the region. Radio traffic patterns of army units and shipping messages in March foretold extensive shifting of Japanese troops already in the area and imminent ground reinforcements for western New Guinea (*February 10; March 16, 27*). According to ULTRA evidence, however, only the 36th Infantry Division defended the 300 miles of coast, islands, and bays between Wakde and Manokwari (April 21).

General Kenney was an enthusiastic supporter of MacArthur's plan to seize Wakde. The Southwest Pacific air commander always wanted more forward air bases from which to counter Japanese air reinforcements streaming into the region. ULTRA was monitoring air squadrons reinforcing the area as Biak, Noemfoor Island, and Sarmi loomed as major rear-area bases for the Japanese army air force. On April 2, Sarmi appeared on the airwaves as an operational air base, and Biak followed just ten days later (April 2, 17). From subsequent ULTRA reports, the Allies concluded three things. First, the Japanese were well ahead of schedule for their airfield construction program in western New Guinea. Second, at least 189 Japanese aircraft were capable of attacking the Allied beachhead at Wakde-Sarmi. Third, the Japanese had approximately 600 operational aircraft nearby that could quickly reinforce western New Guinea. These 400 navy and 200 army planes were deployed at airfields in an arc from the southern Philippines to the islands bounded by the Celebes, Molucca, Ceram, and Banda seas (March 27; April 2, 17, 27; *April 14*).[6] For these reasons, Kenney agreed with MacArthur that Japanese resistance in western New Guinea had to be overcome before the enemy had time to transform the region into a series of mutually supporting strongholds akin to the Bismarck Barrier, which had so long delayed the Allied advance.

On April 27, just five days after the Hollandia-Aitape landings, MacArthur committed his 41st Division to invade the Wakde-Sarmi region near Sawar airfield on May 15. The next day Willoughby estimated that 6,050 to 6,750 Japanese, anywhere from 3,950 to 6,650 of them combat troops, were dug in at MacArthur's next objective. In truth, almost 11,000 Japanese, including 6,000 combat troops, defended the locale, but numbers alone were deceptive.[7] General Tanoue Hachiro expected his 36th Division to defend Sarmi with two infantry regiments. He ended up doing it with two battalions. Second Army had deployed Tanoue's infantrymen of the 223rd Regiment farther to the west, and his 224th Infantry was hacking its way east through the jungle toward Hollandia. The dearth of roads, the numerous unfordable streams, and the incessant American air attacks on coastal barge traffic made the 224th's advance slow and grueling. At the rate of 2 miles a day, the regiment had moved roughly halfway to Hollandia by mid-May. ULTRA gave no inkling of this impending Japanese counterattack because its intercept stations did not overhear the 224th's low-powered transmissions, which soon faded away in any case, since Japanese radios frequently failed in the tropical heat and mildew.

Searching for clues about the enemy at Sarmi, cryptanalysts reexamined earlier, undecrypted Japanese army messages. A January intercept, deciphered on April 23, mentioned that 3,919 men of the 36th Division were due at Sarmi from the Palaus in mid-January 1944 (April 23). Radio messages dispatched in February spoke of accumulating sufficient ammunition stockpiles at Sarmi for an under-strength division and located the 224th Infantry Regiment in the vicinity (April 29; May 4). A Japanese prisoner of war, plucked from the sea by a U.S. Navy submarine, admitted that 36th Division Headquarters, the 224th Infantry Regiment, a battalion of the 223d Infantry, and a tankette company defended Sarmi. Another prisoner, this one seized at Hollandia, told his captors that Wakde had a 1,000-man garrison. He corroborated earlier prisoner of war revelations and the G-2's estimates of Japanese troops in that region.[8] Piecing together this mosaic, Willoughby discerned Sarmi's increasing importance "as a staging area and rendezvous" to support Japanese troops fleeing Hollandia (April 30).

This estimate dovetailed with reports from Allied pilots about extensive activity, personnel, and supply dumps in Japanese-held areas just southeast of Sarmi.[9] Methodical, heavy air strikes against Sarmi and Wakde on April 28 and 29 had flattened the Sarmi village and rendered the three airfields nearby unserviceable, but fierce antiaircraft gunfire met the attackers, who described the 10-mile stretch of coast between Sarmi and Wakde as "heavily defended."[10] While Wakde Island itself appeared deserted, naval cryptanalysts at Melbourne, reading Japanese medical returns, insisted that two naval guard divisions, or as many as 1,450 troops, might be on the tiny 1.5-square-mile atoll (April 25). Approximately 600 Japanese soldiers, including 250 combat troops, had fortified Wakde, and, like their comrades in the Admiralties, they were camera shy.[11] Photo interpreters located no human activity on Wakde in photographs taken May 2, and the invasion was less than two weeks away.[12] Monsoon weather sharply curtailed air activity, and still no one knew exactly where the Japanese were hiding. The best that Allied intelligence could offer was that the 36th Division was "somewhere in the northwest area and capable of being moved against an amphibious landing along the coast."[13]

The intelligence scenario for MacArthur's next steps portrayed Biak as weakly defended by a garrison without recent reinforcements. Accumulating evidence pointed to Sarmi as the main battleground because the 36th Division had concentrated its main defensive positions there. To accomplish this, however, the enemy had been forced to abandon Wakde. These deductions led to the bleak conclusion that American troops could expect determined opposition to their landings near Sarmi. Japanese air reinforcements and ominous naval redeployments only added to the likelihood of a tough, bloody campaign.[14]

On April 25 Central Bureau's intercept sites noted at least thirty different call signs associated with Japanese naval aircraft radio transmissions from reinforcements that were staging from Truk, Carolines, via the Palaus to western New Guinea (April 27). Shortly afterward, ULTRA made clear that Japanese naval land-based aircraft were flying from army airfields in western New Guinea and that a partial reinforcement of 57 naval aircraft had reached Halmahera (April 29; May 8). This "Z" Force totaled 261 planes—153 bombers, 99 fighters, and 9 reconnaissance aircraft. The nucleus of the force was the 23d Naval Air Flotilla, headquartered on Biak, whose three subordinate naval air groups boasted 36 bombers, 54 fighters, and 9 reconnaissance aircraft, about half of which were operational.

Every day intercept operators overheard replacement aircraft and pilots flying into western New Guinea airfields as the Japanese rebuilt their air arm after the disaster at Hollandia. In late March the Japanese were able to muster 57 aircraft scattered in several understrength air regiments dispersed throughout the region. By mid-May replacements had not only offset about forty more combat losses but also increased the 7th Air Division to 78 operational aircraft. An army-navy total of 189 planes, which included 84 bombers and 90 fighters, was available to respond to the projected Allied landings (April 27, 28).[15]

Allied planners were most disturbed by the menace of the Japanese fleet. They did not expect the Imperial Navy to intervene against the Wakde-Sarmi landings because the beachhead was within the range of Allied tactical aircraft flying from Hollandia. Biak lay 300 miles northwest of Hollandia and beyond the range of all but the largest bombers, whose weight, it had developed, was excessive for the spongy soil at Hollandia. Biak was also a mere forty hours sailing time from the major Japanese fleet anchorage at Davao where on April 1 the Combined Fleet had withdrawn from the Palaus to avoid devastating carrier aircraft attacks. Other Japanese fleet units were on the move, having sortied from Singapore to Tawitawi, the outermost island of the Sulu Archipelago, about sixty hours sailing time from Biak. The Imperial Navy thus had two fleets poised within easy striking range of a potentially vulnerable Allied beachhead at Biak. ULTRA accumulated by early

May suggested that portions of the Singapore force—twenty major warships, including five battleships and two carriers—had shifted to Davao where two carrier divisions would soon join them (April 30; May 15). Japanese intentions remained hidden, but the presence of a Japanese fleet-in-being at Davao had to be factored into any Allied plans against western New Guinea.

These unappealing assessments of Japanese strengths were instrumental in Krueger's call on May 6 for a hurried conference of the Allied air, naval, and ground commanders involved in the Wakde-Sarmi assault. A day earlier Barbey had requested Krueger to postpone the operation until May 21, at which time the moon and tide conditions would be more favorable for a landing. Keenly aware of MacArthur's "urgent desire" to advance west, Krueger replied that he was "loath to recommend your [Barbey's] proposition" by himself. The conference became the occasion for MacArthur's principal commanders to counsel delay. Krueger radioed the chief that unless strategic considerations dictated otherwise, the four-day delay would ease the logistics turmoil at Hollandia and allow additional air strikes in the target area.[16]

MacArthur approved the revised date but then recast the entire operation. His new plan was shaped by intelligence estimates that offered the prospect of severe fighting and heavy casualties for a region of questionable value as a bomber base. It appeared from the latest photographs of Sarmi that the ground was unsatisfactory for airfield development. In plain language, the place was a "mud hole," where bombers might just as likely sink to their heavy bellies as taxi on runways. Wakde alone would suffice as a forward fighter base to support the Biak operation scheduled eight to ten days after the Wakde assault. Two hours later, MacArthur fired off another cable ordering the Sixth Army commander to assemble key headquarters and operations staff at Hollandia on May 9 to develop the new guidance. Twelve hundred miles northwest of Hollandia, events originated by U.S. Navy codebreakers, then reported by U.S. Army and Navy cryptanalysts almost as they occurred, played a fundamental role in MacArthur's operational decisions.

As early as April 2, decrypted Japanese naval messages had announced an impending convoy of major proportions. Shortly thereafter, Southwest Pacific Headquarters, courtesy of naval ULTRA, reported that the 35th Infantry Division was bound for Geelvink Bay (April 13). The next day, the War Department and MacArthur's command both divulged that "navy ULTRA reports the 32d Infantry Division scheduled to move to the Philippines from Shanghai for Davao about 30 April" (April 14). Later decryptions of Army Water Transport Code messages disclosed that troops of the 35th Infantry Division were steaming toward the Palaus aboard the "TAKE" convoy. Navy traffic analysts announced that the convoy had sailed from Shanghai on April 13 and rendezvoused with its escorts south of Korea. Guided by these ULTRA disclosures, the U.S. submarine *Jack* torpedoed one transport off Luzon in late April. The sinking was a harbinger of much worse.

After the TAKE convoy departed Manila for Davao, American intercept operators plucked numerous radio transmissions related to it from the airwaves as at least 140 separate messages about the convoy were ultimately intercepted and decrypted.[17] By May 2 the War Department declared that the TAKE convoy comprised nine transports and seven escorts carrying 12,784 troops of the 32d Division as well as an unknown number of men from the 35th Division. The ships had departed Manila at 4:00 A.M. the previous day, destined for the eastern Netherlands East Indies and western New Guinea. Besides confirming that the convoy would separate north of Halmahera on May 7, deciphered Water Transport Code messages—the 2468 system—betrayed the convoy's scheduled noon positions between May 2 and 9. This extraordinary intelligence coup was "forwarded to the appropriate commands" (*May 2*).

Forewarned with precise intelligence of the convoy's route, speed, daily noon positions, and destinations, an American submarine lay in ambush about 100 miles northwest of Menado. Within ten minutes on May 6 in the Celebes Sea, the USS *Gurnard* sent three transports and 1,290 troops aboard them to their watery graves. Although escort vessels rescued 6,800 soldiers from the water, they lost almost all their equipment. Frantic Japanese radio messages validated *Gurnard's* claims, and deciphered Water Transport Code messages let cryptanalysts at Brisbane read a running commentary by the Japanese themselves on their horrendous losses. Within two days of the sinkings, Army Water Transport Code messages had revealed the names and cargoes of the six transports carrying the 32d Division and the names and tonnages of four others bringing the 35th Division (May 8).

ULTRA provided the figures that permitted the grim accountants of G-2 to fill in the columns of their ledgers. A May 7 Imperial Navy message stated that 6,800 men had been rescued from the sea. Since that number roughly doubled the capacity of the one Japanese transport known sunk at that time, War Department analysts concluded that at least two transports definitely had gone down (*May 10*). Later, ULTRA clarified the loss of three troop transports that had carried 4,670 men of the 35th and 3,420 of the 32d divisions. The War Department added the 1,290 Japanese troops who had perished to the 2,664 men of the 32d Division lost April 26 for a total of 3,954 troops with their supplies and ordnance vanished beneath the waves (May 22).

The magnitude of the TAKE debacle demanded a comprehensive analysis of this latest shipping disaster. Japanese naval staff officers congregated in Manila to examine the evidence. None considered their own codes suspect. It seemed to them more likely that bursts of increased radio messages related to coordinating the movement of the ships had alerted Allied traffic analysts that a major convoy was under way. Others hypothesized that too many staff officers in Manila knew about the convoy, resulting in a Japanese version of "loose lips sink ships." Another theory held that ubiquitous spies, lurking around Manila waterfront, had radioed messages to the Allies about the convoy's composition and departure.[18]

Southwest Pacific Headquarters actually did have a spy working as a handyman inside the Japanese Judge Advocate General's Office in Manila. Sergeant Richard M. Sakakida had convinced the Japanese military police over time that he was a disgruntled merchant seaman who had jumped ship in Manila before the outbreak of war. Sakakida used Filipino runners to carry his messages to guerrilla leaders in the hills, who transmitted his intelligence to Brisbane. The resourceful sergeant had reported the departure of the TAKE convoy, so the Japanese had some basis for their almost paranoid concern about spies, which deflected their attention from the possibility of compromised codes.[19] If Tokyo even suspected the enormity of the Allied codebreaking success, the entire radio message cipher system would have been scrapped and the Allies would have had to solve a more complex and secure encoding system. One can imagine the War Department's sigh of relief when it learned from ULTRA that the Japanese blamed spies, not broken codes, for the TAKE disaster (*June 19*).

The failure, with heavy loss of life and equipment, of the two-division Japanese reinforcement scheme left Japanese defenses in western New Guinea weak and disorganized and underscored MacArthur's insistence on striking without delay. ULTRA reports on the TAKE losses were most likely responsible for MacArthur's decision to advance D-day for Wakde to May 17, with the invasion of Biak to follow shortly after.[20] Within a week of his order, as the general's luck would have it, Central Bureau had resurrected the new key register from its ashes and was again deciphering Imperial Army codes. ULTRA handed Southern Army's new strategy to MacArthur within five days of its issuance.

Shaken by the TAKE catastrophe, Imperial Headquarters again redefined Southern Army's area of operations in western New Guinea. A Southern Army message, dispatched May 10, informed Second Area Army of the revised main defensive line that now stretched from Halmahera to Sorong. Strategic points around Manokwari, Biak, and Geelvink Bay would be held as long as possible (*May 15*). Biak now appeared to be merely a minor tactical outpost in a strategic delaying action. Even if American combat troops encountered initially determined resistance at Sarmi (as intelligence predicted), without a theater reserve, which had been sunk with the TAKE convoy, and with the equipment and supply shortages identified in ULTRA, the Japanese could not fight a protracted battle. If Biak's airfields could be taken quickly, domination of Geelvink Bay and the isolation of the 36th Division at Sarmi were guaranteed. Assured by ULTRA that no organized Japanese reinforcements were imminent, MacArthur accepted greater risks by landing his troops at places where the exact deployment and number of enemy defenders was vague. His first gamble was against Wakde Island and the New

Table 5.1. Actual and Estimated Japanese Ground Order of Battle,
Wakde-Sarmi, May 1944

Actual	SWPA Intelligence
36th Division (less 222d Infantry) Headquarters	Elements, 36th Division Headquarters
223d Infantry (reinforcements)	Elements, 223d Infantry
224th Infantry (reinforcements)	Elements, 224th Infantry
36th Division Armored Unit	Tankette Company
Division Special Troops	
Headquarters 4th Engineer Group	Unidentified Engineer Group
16th and 17th Mobile Lumber Squads	(possibly 36th Division)
20th Airfield Battalion	Elements, 20th and 31st Airfield
16th and 103d Airfield Units	Battalions
228th Independent Motor Transport Company	
53d Field Antiaircraft Battalion	
42d Field Machine Cannon Company	Elements, 42d Field Machine
4th Field Searchlight Battalion	Cannon Battery
Elements, 24th Signal Regiment	Elements, 4th Field Searchlight
11th Debarkation Unit	Battalion
54th Special Water Duty Company	Elements, 11th Debarkation Unit
91st Naval Garrison Unit	18th and 19th Guards Divisions (Naval)
Elements, 4th Army Air Ordnance Repair Unit	
104th Special Construction Duty Company	
31st and 49th Anchorage Branch	
5th Ship Transport Command Branch	
Possible Elements, 25th Base Force	

Source: Actual: Supreme Commander for the Allied Powers, *Reports of General MacArthur*, Vol. 2:
  Japanese Operations in the Southwest Pacific Area (Part 1) (Washington, D.C.: Government
  Printing Office, 1966), 277; SWPA intelligence: SWPA G-2, "Monthly Summary of Enemy
  Dispositions," No. 18, 30 April 1944, Record Group 3, Box 17, Folder 3, MacArthur
  Memorial Bureau of Archives, Norfolk, Virginia.

Guinea mainland next to it. This uncontested American landing was the result of
luck and audacity, not planning based on accurate intelligence.

On May 17 the 163d Regimental Combat Team, 41st Division, landed unopposed near Toem on the New Guinea mainland opposite Wakde. A perplexed
Willoughby commented that "in view of the importance of Wakde it is difficult to
understand the complete lack of opposition."[21] Still unaware that half the
Japanese garrison was on its way to attack Hollandia, American intelligence
speculated for the next several days that strong ground and naval counterattacks
meant hard fighting ahead.[22] General Anami might have sympathized with the

confused American intelligence estimates. He originally thought that the Americans would bypass Sarmi to attack Biak around May 20. When Wakde fell under attack, his own intelligence services failed to alert him until thirty-six hours after the American landings. The Allied naval and air bombardment had severed telephone communications between Japanese coastal observation posts and 36th Division Headquarters, so no senior officers knew what was happening. The sluggish Japanese response was a direct result of the absence of timely tactical intelligence.[23] All this was unknown to the Americans, who kept searching for enemy troops in strength when there were none.

Meanwhile, hard fighting developed on supposedly abandoned Wakde. It took two days for the 1st Battalion, 163d Infantry, to pry nearly eight hundred diehard Japanese troops from their camouflaged spider holes, coconut-log bunkers, and coral caves. The conquest of the tiny island and adjacent mainland had accomplished the task force's mission.[24] Krueger then changed the objective because of the tactical situation and faulty intelligence about the Japanese forces arrayed against them.

The New Guinea coast opposite Wakde was a morass of malarial patches. About 10 miles to the west, however, rose a 150-foot-high coral mass covered with dense rain forest and jungle scrub growth that overlooked the harbor in Maffin Bay. From this high ground, Japanese artillery could deny the Allies the use of the harbor and fire accurately on the American defensive perimeters carved out of the jungle around the village of Toem and on Wakde. Growing evidence pointed to Japanese intentions to fight for Toem. Krueger, for instance, had a decrypted Japanese navy message ordering counterattacks by two separate units against the Toem defenses.[25] Captured documents told of two battalions of the 224th Infantry Regiment near Sarmi, and Willoughby warned Sixth Army about imminent counterattacks against the beachhead.[26] Krueger was too good a soldier to stand pat and wait for a Japanese attack. The Biak invasion was less than a week away, and Adachi's steady march on Aitape threatened Sixth Army's rear area. Krueger opted to use the newly arrived 158th Regimental Combat Team to launch a spoiling attack westward against the weak Japanese force that intelligence told him held the high ground. The Americans did not know that they would be confronting three separate Japanese task forces.

While two battalions of the 163d Infantry stood guard over Toem, the 158th moved out on May 23. It took the "Bushmasters" three days to advance the 10 miles west to the base of Lone Tree Hill. Scattered but deadly Japanese delaying actions, miserable terrain, and cautious leadership of green troops had retarded the push. By May 25, brutal fighting had broken out as Japanese rifle and machine-gun teams, concealed in caves and defiles, repeatedly ambushed the GIs. The 158th called in naval gunfire and fought back with flamethrowers and tanks. Krueger, trusting intelligence reports that Japanese forces could put up only weak resistance, expected a quick end to the fighting. For that reason, he ordered two of the three battalions defending Toem to be sent to Biak. He also concurred with Chamberlin's plan to transform the Wakde-Sarmi and Maffin Bay region into a staging area for scheduled operations farther to the west. To ensure the security of the planned base, Krueger ordered the 158th to seize the high ground at Lone Tree Hill. After all, intelligence officers had spoken confidently of a single under-strength Japanese infantry regiment, short on supplies as well as ammunition, that was withdrawing slowly to the west. Krueger had no reason to suspect such a ragtag outfit was capable of obstinate resistance.

Not one American commander suspected that a second Japanese task force, the 223d Infantry, had moved east, crossed the Tor River south of the 158th's line of march, and worked its way back behind the strung-out American advance. Fur-thermore, intelligence had completely lost track of a third Japanese unit, the 224th Infantry, which had made its way back from the abortive trek toward Hollandia and was just east of Toem, poised to strike. Piecemeal attacks against the village by about 200 Japanese were beaten back. During the night of May 30/31, the 223d Infantry struck the 158th's dispersed antiaircraft emplacements between Lone Tree Hill and Toem. In the pale morning light, a GI jerked the identity disk from a Japanese corpse. It proved to be the first evidence that another infantry regiment had joined the fight and it caused U.S. field commanders to raise the number of enemy troops from 6,500 to 10,700. Willoughby insisted that the Japanese had suffered such heavy casualties that about a regiment, maybe 4,000 to 5,000 troops, were still battle worthy. Probably 8,000 Japanese were still alive and fighting, and that changed the odds considerably.[27]

Conditions on Biak, where Americans were battling fanatical opposition from the emperor's soldiers, were no better. The fighting that raged there made it impossible for the Allies to use the island's airstrips. As a stopgap measure, MacArthur ordered Sixth Army to capture an airfield on Noemfoor Island, about 60 miles west of Biak, in late June or early July. Krueger decided to use the 158th against Noemfoor. On June 14 the 20th Infantry, 6th Division, relieved the 158th and took up the fight for the high ground. Krueger expected the untried 6th Division to mount a major assault against the Vogelkop Peninsula scheduled for late July, but before that happened he wanted to blood the rookie troops in combat against the now-depleted Japanese opposition around Lone Tree Hill.[28] Ten days of hard, close-in fighting in late June achieved his purpose. The newly forged combat veterans counted nearly 1,000 Japanese bodies and sealed other Japanese soldiers forever in their fortified caves. The 6th Division held the high ground, but at heavy cost. About 150 Americans were killed, 550 wounded, and another 400 to 500 evacuated as a result of sickness, noncombat injuries, and combat fatigue. For the Japanese, the 36th Division was wrecked. It skulked about near Sarmi for the remainder of the war, incapable of offensive action. From their hard-won position on Lone Tree Hill, American GIs looked down on the key fighter base on Wakde Island and on Maffin Bay, which became the staging area for five Allied invasions—Biak, Noemfoor, Sansapor, Morotoi, and Leyte.[29]

Although no date had been set for the assault on Biak, MacArthur's staff originally envisioned it occurring in early June, just after the wrap-up of the Sarmi-Wakde operation. Intelligence about the Japanese on Biak was vague, but Central Bureau traffic analysts had discovered nothing to suggest that the Japanese were withdrawing troops from the mainland to strengthen the island's garrison (*May 21*). Based on an earlier identification, the 222d Infantry Regiment, 36th Division, was regarded as the main combat unit on the island (*May 21*). Willoughby figured that of a total of 5,000 to 7,000 Japanese on Biak, 2,300 were combat troops. He misjudged by nearly half the 12,350 Japanese servicemen—10,400 army and 1,950 navy—dug deeply into the caves of the coral isle.[30]

The Imperial Army units defending Biak did not constitute an independent army command, so signalmen enciphered their radio messages to 36th Division Headquarters in the three-digit code that Central Bureau could not decipher. Biak was nearly 700 miles west of the nearest Central Bureau intercept sites, which rendered overhearing low-powered, brief transmissions from the island nearly impossible. Available ULTRA seemingly consigned the Biak garrison to a delaying action. Collateral intelligence was sparse. The first aerial photographs were taken on April 17, but they showed little except ugly coral terrain. U.S. Fifth Air Force fighters and bombers had struck Biak repeatedly but drew little air response or ground fire.

Japanese ground forces on Biak did not overly concern Willoughby. He understood that the island was an important air base defended by a fresh infantry regiment with high morale (May 9) (see Table 5.2). ULTRA outlined Tokyo's intentions to hold Biak to the best of its ability (May 9), so the G-2 expected to encounter, in his words, "stubborn, but not serious, enemy resistance."[31] Willoughby's overarching concern was that the Japanese fleet might sortie against the stationary Allied transports in the landing area. He was reluctant to rely entirely on heavy bombers to protect the Allied invasion armada because a spell of bad weather could ground Allied air power and allow the Japanese warships uncontested passage to Biak. These concerns appear in a May 13 memorandum from Willoughby to MacArthur. The G-2 thought that the Biak operation presented the Japanese fleet in the southern Philippines with the opportunity to attack the smaller U.S. Seventh Fleet within range of Japanese air cover. Willoughby counseled delay. He wanted the Biak invasion "timed to coincide or be near a proposed Allied fleet action," thereby diverting Japanese naval attention from the island. He recommended that MacArthur postpone the occupation of the Marianas or to bring it closer to the target date of mid-June.[32]

Table 5.2. Actual and Estimated Japanese Ground Order of Battle,
Biak Island, May 1944

Actual	SWPA Intelligence
222d Infantry (less 2 companies)	222d Infantry
Army	
Elements, 36th Division	
Sea Transport Unit	
Elements, 14th Division	
Sea Transport Unit	
17th, 107th, 108th Airfield	108th Airfield Construction Unit[a]
Construction Units	
Elements, 109th Airfield	Airfield Construction Battalion
Construction Unit	
Elements, 248th Independent Motor	
Transport Unit	
15th Formosan Special Labor Group	
41st Special Land Duty Unit	
50th and 69th Construction Companies	69th Special Construction Company
3d Battery, 49th Field Antiaircraft	Antiaircraft Defense Unit (Naval)
Battalion	49th Field Antiaircraft Battalion
1st Branch, 36th Division Field Hospital	
30th Field Ordnance Depot Branch	
Elements, 24th Signal Regiment	Elements, 24th Signal Company[a]
5th, 12th Mobile Lumber Squads	
Elements, 47th Anchorage Headquarters	47th Anchorage Headquarters[a]
Navy	
Elements, 28th Naval Base Force	Elements, 28th Naval Base Force (SIB 5/16)
33d, 105th Antiaircraft Units	18th Naval Guard Division
19th Naval Garrison Unit	19th Naval Guard Division
202d Civil Engineer Unit	Minor shipping/supply units

[a]ULTRA source
Source: Actual: Supreme Commander for the Allied Powers, *Reports of General MacArthur*, Vol. 2:
    Japanese Operations in the Southwest Pacific Area (Part 1) (Washington, D.C.: Government
    Printing Office, 1966), 284, note 114; SWPA intelligence: SWPA Special Intelligence Bul-
    letin, and SWPA Military Intelligence Summary, for April-May 1944, National Archives and
    Records Administration, Washington, D.C.

But MacArthur needed Biak before that. His RENO V plan, then being devised,
envisioned a leap by the 6th Division in July to the Vogelkop Peninsula, to
Halmahera by September, and finally to the Philippines by mid-November. The
Southwest Pacific commander described the operation as "a race against hostile
defensive development, with the earliest practicable establishment of control over
Palau and Halmahera a factor of major importance."[33] Delay was unthinkable,
and he rejected Willoughby's counsel. Ever since, military strategists and historians have debated the wisdom of MacArthur's choice.[34] Barbey later speculated

that if the invasion of the Marianas had been just one week later, a Japanese naval attack may have spelled disaster for MacArthur's cruiser force at Biak. Two events in early June shaped Barbey's thoughts. First, the light cruiser *Nashville* was damaged by Japanese bombs and temporarily knocked out of action. Second, a Japanese air raid on the new American fighter base on Wakde destroyed or damaged eighty-six Allied aircraft. Without this firepower, it would have been hard to stop a determined attacker.[35]

Without minimizing the risks, MacArthur's decision was more conservative than heretofore considered. ULTRA allowed him to weigh the alternatives because he knew the locations of Japanese fleet units. He knew from ULTRA that the enemy had no ground reserve in the theater that could be rushed to Biak's aid. Expecting "stubborn but not serious" resistance on Biak, he confidently expected to conclude the operation quickly, possibly within a few days. MacArthur pressed ahead with the Biak invasion by accepting the hazards, as he had at the Admiralties, in order to meet his accelerated timetable for returning to the Philippines. Depending on one's view, it was either an example of strategic concerns overriding intelligence indications of potential disaster or an example of a clear strategic vision overcoming a cautious intelligence estimate.

Biak lies a mere 60 miles south of the equator. D-day, May 27, 1944, was one of those brilliant, tropical days when the sun's heat shimmers on calm waters. That proved the first—and last—happy impression of the coral hell. The 41st Division landed after the air and naval bombardment raised billowing smoke that blotted out the sky. At first the "Jungleers" met little resistance, but as they moved onto the island's airstrips, hope of a walkover vanished in bursts of Japanese artillery and small-arms fire. Colonel Kuzume Naoyuki, the detachment commander, had constructed a cleverly concealed defense in the numerous caves that pockmarked the cliffs overlooking the 41st's advance. It was slow going. Heavily weighted down, the Americans suffered from thirst in the stifling heat and humidity. No breeze could penetrate the thick, 12-foot-high scrub growth that covered the coral outcroppings. Japanese seemed to be everywhere, yet nowhere. The approaches to the airfields were alive with automatic-weapons fire. American infantry companies were cut off, and the beachhead itself was threatened. It might have been worse for the 41st Division had Kuzume had the time to site his interlocking defensive network.

Japanese intelligence had predicted an attack against Biak, but not until June. One day before the invasion, the Second Area Army chief of staff, Lieutenant General Numada Takezo, told Kuzume that reinforcements, then en route to Biak, would arrive before the enemy invasion. When startled soldiers saw the U.S. Fleet appear offshore the next morning, they assumed the Imperial Fleet had arrived with the promised reinforcements.[36]

The nasty surprise the Americans received was facing double the number of expected Japanese defenders. The day before the landing, troops were told that the Japanese might have shipped a battalion from Sarmi to Biak.[37] Although the Japanese garrison was in flux, the soldiers fought with the same fatalism that had become their terrifying trademark. They huddled in dark, dank caves like troglodytes, awaiting their orders to attack the invaders. One lieutenant longed for a hot bath to purify his body for the death he was sure awaited him. Allied artillery shells roaring over his cave reminded him of cars zooming along Tokyo's Ginza. Finally the Japanese left their shelters, crept cautiously into the jungle, and waited.[38] Their ambush of the 3d Battalion, 162d Infantry, forced the Americans back with heavy casualties. That night, about a mile and a half to the east, another vicious struggle erupted. In an all-out attack on the 3d Battalion, 186th Infantry, even Japanese medical personnel tied bayonets to tree limbs and joined the assault. Desperate men fought each other with rifles, machines guns, bayonets, even machetes. The Japanese screams seemed to the Americans like one extended battle cry. Some Japanese were yelling "Banzai!" as they slammed into their enemies, but many mortally wounded Japanese were crying out the names of loved ones. The attacks were broken, but the Japanese defenders were not. They persisted in their rock-ribbed determination to die in battle.[39]

Upset by the tenacious defense, MacArthur bluntly admonished Krueger about the Americans' "unsatisfactory performance" on Biak.[40] Reports from Sixth Army staff officers whom Krueger had dispatched to the island for a firsthand report on the fighting convinced him to order the I Corps commander, General Eichelberger, to take charge at Biak. Eichelberger arrived on Biak in a foul mood. He was irked at Krueger for sending him to such a tough command on such short notice. What seems to have upset Eichelberger even more was Krueger's failure to offer him dinner the night before at Sixth Army Headquarters.[41]

Eichelberger's disposition did not improve because the campaign was bogged down. The 41st Division commander made clear his displeasure at Eichelberger's appearance and requested that he be relieved of his command of the Biak task force.[42] Eichelberger forwarded the request to Krueger, who approved the relief. Replacing a general did not end the fighting, however. Inaccurate intelligence estimates misrepresenting Japanese strength on the island, coupled with his compulsion to return to the Philippines, motivated MacArthur to adhere to his unrealistic timetable. He put tremendous pressure on his subordinate commanders to conclude the campaign expeditiously. Nowhere did the Japanese cooperate. Fighting on Biak persisted despite MacArthur's public announcement of victory on June 3—only one week after the landing and twelve days before Eichelberger's arrival—and prevented the Allies from the immediate use of Biak's airdromes to support further advances toward the Marianas and the Philippines. Colonel Kuzume's protracted defense also fixed the vulnerable U.S. Seventh Fleet near

Biak where it was exposed to Japanese air and surface attacks. Japan's admirals saw the decisive fleet engagement that had so long eluded them within their grasp.

In early May Admiral Toyoda Soemu, commander-in-chief of the Combined Fleet at anchor in Tokyo Bay, issued Order A, an ambitious plan to hurl concentrated land- and carrier-based aircraft against an American fleet attacking the Palaus or the western Carolines. The Imperial Navy needed Biak's airfields to provide land-based air support for Operation A. Analysis of American naval communications in early May convinced the Japanese naval staff that American offensive operations were imminent. On May 11 the First Mobile Fleet at Tawitawi was placed on alert to launch Operation A. Five days later, however, Imperial Navy intelligence lost track of U.S. Fleet movements. The Japanese knew that "a powerful fleet" had departed Hawaii between May 11 and 17 but could only guess that the main American attack would fall on the western Caroline Islands while MacArthur continued small-scale attacks along the New Guinea front.[43]

Although the American assault on Biak on May 27 did catch the Japanese defenders unprepared, it still provoked violent Japanese air strikes against the invasion fleet. Japanese warships were also readying for battle. The commander of the Southwest Area Fleet, Vice Admiral Takasu Shiro, radioed Imperial Headquarters and the Combined Fleet recommending Biak be reinforced immediately. Similarly, Rear Admiral Sakonju Naomasa offered his powerful 16th Cruiser Division to escort the reinforcement convoy. Sakonju believed his forces could operate in Geelvink Bay under an aerial cover of Japanese fighters flying from nearby airstrips. On May 29 Tokyo approved the proposed reinforcement plan, code-named KON.[44] Within three days, decrypted Japanese radio messages had betrayed their intentions to the Americans.

A May 31 message, available June 1, from the 19th Naval Guard Division on Biak, revealed that the Japanese were planning to reinforce the island with the 2d Amphibious Brigade, then in the southern Philippines. U.S. Navy traffic analysis reported that several warships (Sakonju's 16th Cruiser Division), under cover of land-based aircraft, would escort the convoy (June 1). By June 2 Admiral Kinkaid refueled and replenished his cruiser groups and combined them into a single task force to meet the Japanese threat. The next day, Kinkaid presided over a conference of his ship commanders on proposed deployments against the Japanese.[45] Because ULTRA disclosed that four enemy warships would unload troops at Biak during the night of June 4 or 5, Kinkaid confidently advised his task force commander of the exact Japanese landing site on Biak. Even as Kinkaid prepped his officers, American pilots flying courses charted by ULTRA sighted Sakonju's fleet about the same time that Japanese lookouts spotted the B-24s. With surprise lost and a Japanese army reconnaissance pilot's erroneous report that two U.S. carriers were within range of the convoy, the Combined Fleet postponed KON operations.[46]

American soldiers had their own version of events. Word had somehow reached the infantrymen on Biak that the Japanese fleet might bombard them before the U.S. Navy could come to the rescue. Artillery units resited two batteries to fire seaward. Bulldozers and dump trucks unearthed new gun pits and revetments. The intelligence officer's tent became the most sought after place on the hot, nasty coral lump. Late that afternoon rumors spread that army bombers were attacking Japanese transports. When the men saw American cruisers and destroyers racing past Biak heading west toward the Japanese, they lined the beaches and "broke into spontaneous cheers, feelings of relief, carelessness, and a little of mightiness."[47] In this case, the rumor mill was wrong. Sakonju had reversed course before being attacked, so the GIs' celebration was premature. Still their fiction was more plausible than the truth that a handful of cryptanalysts hundreds of miles away had enabled MacArthur's air and naval commanders to deflect this first Japanese thrust.

The next day, June 4, Kinkaid knew from ULTRA the composition of Sakonju's 16th Cruiser Division, and on June 6, a decrypted Second Area Army message dated the previous day reaffirmed Japanese intentions to reinforce Biak (June 7/8). Five Japanese destroyers were expected to bring reinforcements to Biak before June 8. On the evening of June 7, Kinkaid ordered his Allied task force commander to be off Korim Bay on Biak's northern coast by 10:00 P.M. June 8. This was the location ULTRA had disclosed as the Japanese landing point (June 2, 4).[48]

With this timely warning, B-25 medium bombers attacked the Japanese convoy shortly after noon on June 8, sinking one destroyer and inflicting one hundred casualties. (ULTRA confirmed this loss three days later.) Undeterred, the Japanese pushed forward, arriving off Biak about ten hours later. They promptly encountered the waiting Allied naval task force and, following exchanges of gunfire and torpedoes, broke off their effort in the early morning of June 9 to return to their bases.

The Japanese never suspected that their codes had been broken by the Allies. They attributed the daylight bomber attacks to the persistence of Allied long-range reconnaissance patrols. Although Japanese naval officers knew that the chance of a nighttime intercept by surface vessels was remote, they believed Allied success was due not to leaky codes but to technologically superior radar equipment that had picked up the Japanese warships before Japanese radars could illuminate Allied targets.[49]

This latest setback convinced Admiral Sakonju of the futility of dispatching more reinforcements to Biak. Yet the Japanese navy still needed Biak's air bases for Operation A, which, of course, could not be launched until they located the U.S. Pacific Fleet. So KON continued by default. On June 10, the commander of the Combined Fleet, Admiral Toyoda, ordered the 1st Battleship Division added to the KON force. Its commander, Vice Admiral Ugaki Matome, expected to throw the super battleships *Yamato* and *Musashi* into KON operations. These super-dreadnaughts might have tipped the scales against Kinkaid's lighter cruiser fleet. *Yamato* and *Musashi* were each almost the length of three football fields. They displaced an extraordinary 67,000 tons and boasted 14 inches of armor protection on their sides. Giant 18.1-inch guns, capable of hurling a 3,200-pound shell nearly 30 miles, complemented these floating monsters.[50] Even with minimum air cover, they might well have reached Biak despite Allied air and naval attacks. Kinkaid's cruisers would then have been blown out of the water and the transports left helpless. Both battleships were being readied for another KON attempt when word arrived at Combined Fleet Headquarters that U.S. minesweepers, the precursors of invasions, were sighted off Saipan. KON was arbitrarily canceled in favor of launching Operation A against the Allied fleet near the Marianas.[51] MacArthur's luck held, but only by the slimmest of margins.

As late as June 14, Japanese intelligence was incapable of discerning whether the next big American strike would be at northwestern New Guinea, the Palaus, or the Marianas.[52] By contrast, ULTRA disclosed on June 15 a message dated the previous day from the commander in chief of the Southern Expeditionary Fleet to Base Force 28 on Biak announcing the end of the reinforcement effort (*June 15*). The same message made clear that the Japanese were throwing all their naval might against the American task force invading the Marianas (June 15/16, 17/18). ULTRA in late June revealed Japanese plans to evacuate Biak (June 29/30). Even though a few scattered Japanese reinforcements had landed on Biak, they contributed nothing to the battle except their lives (June 20/21). U.S. Army and Navy ULTRA was the shield U.S. commanders used against KON, allowing them to parry each Japanese thrust with well-planned air and surface interdiction attacks.

KON's termination left the Japanese defenders on Biak to their fate. Because Kuzume's doomed troops conceded nothing to the 41st Division, Biak's vital airdromes were unavailable to Kenney. As mentioned, the field on Noemfoor Island was selected as a substitute. Intelligence estimated that about 1,750 Japanese garrisoned the 15-mile-long by 12-mile-wide island. A deciphered May 31 message identified three infantry companies from the 219th Infantry, 35th Division, and one from the 222d Infantry, 36th Division, on the island (June 15/16). A provisional battalion of hodgepodge airfield construction, transport, and auxiliary formations complemented the combat troops. Another decryption mentioned sending nine coastal defense guns to Noemfoor (June 19/20). Aerial photographs showed five coastal defense positions on the island, but photo-interpreters could not tell whether or not they were occupied.

A small party of Alamo Scouts infiltrated the island from a submarine shortly before the invasion. Two hazardous days of patrolling confirmed Japanese strength, general defensive dispositions, and the unmanned state of the coastal defenses. ULTRA then reported that because Second Area Army expected another Allied landing soon (June 27/28), Japanese intercept operators were monitoring Allied radio communications concerning the invasion convoy moving along the northern New Guinea coast (July 3/4). Krueger had to seize Noemfoor's airfields before the Japanese could reinforce the garrison. With speed as the criterion, Krueger selected the teeth of the Japanese defenses near the airstrip for his landing site.[53] To compensate for an attack against fortifications, the naval and air bombardment of the landing beach was greater than in previous invasions.

Task Force Cyclone, composed of the 158th Regimental Combat Team (reinforced by more than 13,500 troops), met only desultory Japanese mortar and artillery fire as it hit the beach. Those defenders who had not been killed or fled inland during the softening-up bombardment were too stunned to put up much resistance. One dazed prisoner startled his interrogators when he off-handedly said reinforcements had raised Japanese strength on Noemfoor to between 3,500 to 4,500 troops. Previous Allied intelligence estimates that had understated Japanese strength at Sarmi were still fresh in the 158th's mind and added credibility to the lone Japanese prisoner's statement. Sixth Army knew from ULTRA about Japanese concerns over an Allied landing, so it seemed plausible that the enemy had slipped reinforcements in to Noemfoor undetected. When the task force commander called for reinforcements, Sixth Army Headquarters was predisposed to approve his request. It was an unfortunate decision because no additional Japanese troops had been sent to Noemfoor. Nearly 1,500 officers and men of the 503d Parachute Infantry were hurriedly dispatched to Noemfoor as reinforcements. They jumped from low-flying aircraft onto rugged island terrain. Tricky winds carried them to bone-cracking landings in supply dumps and vehicle parks and amid wrecked Japanese aircraft. During the parachute drop, the paratroopers suffered no casualties from Japanese guns, but 128 of them were injured in the jump, including 59 serious fracture cases. Noemfoor was rapidly secured, but more troops had been lost in the misconceived parachute drop than in the subsequent fighting to clear the island.

MacArthur's final landing on New Guinea shores took place at Sansapor on July 30 when about 7,300 men of the 6th Division went ashore unopposed thanks to ULTRA. Sansapor fell between two known Japanese strongholds: Manokwari, about 120 miles to the east, and Sorong, half that distance to the west. In mid-June, ULTRA had identified units of the 35th Division at both places (June 15/16). Later decryptions and captured documents told of about 15,000 Japanese at Manokwari and another 12,500 at Sorong (July 11/12). ULTRA further reported that the enemy expected an Allied landing against Sorong-Halmahera or Davao, Philippines, before mid-August (July 24/25). Armed with the knowledge of where the Japanese were and where they expected a landing, MacArthur sidestepped their strongholds to overwhelm a few dozen Japanese soldiers consigned to a lonely vigil as coastal outlooks. Again caught off guard, the handful of Imperial soldiers at Sansapor swiftly disappeared inland. American infantrymen fanned out to form a defensive perimeter around the coastal enclave where combat engineers would construct new airfields to support planned operations against Halmahera.[54]

The Japanese, now divided on either flank of Sansapor, were incapable of seriously threatening MacArthur's latest possession. American PT boats and Allied aircraft ruled Geelvink Bay and preyed mercilessly on Japanese resupply barges shuttling back and forth (*August 2*). They also checked any potential amphibious counterattack against the Sansapor lodgement by the nearest Japanese relief force at Sorong. Since the 35th Division's field artillery had been lost in the ULTRA-orchestrated TAKE disaster, the unit lacked the firepower to retaliate against the Americans. Sansapor's rugged mountains formed a natural barrier to an overland march by the Japanese from either side of the island, further frustrating any thought of counterattack. It proved an easy victory for the Allies, who built two airfields near Sansapor that provided valuable support in the Morotai invasion.

MacArthur's series of fast-moving amphibious assaults had cut off thousands of Japanese troops in New Guinea from their main supply lines. Strategically, the isolated Japanese formations were useless. However, they remained a tactical menace because they refused to play the role of hopelessly defeated and demoralized troops that MacArthur had assigned to them. Sixth Army's seaborne sweeps covered 1,100 miles from Saidor to Sansapor in one hundred days. It took approximately the same time for General Adachi's Eighteenth Army to trek the 280 miles overland from Madang to Aitape.

When Southwest Pacific Headquarters planned for the leap to Hollandia, the U.S. Navy, for reasons discussed earlier, agreed to provide only three days of carrier-based air support. Without sustained naval air support, MacArthur's staff opted to seize the three Japanese airfields at Aitape, about 120 miles east of Hollandia. Flying from these fields, Allied fighters could support American troops at Aitape, who were protecting Hollandia's exposed eastern flank against any westward counteroffensive by Eighteenth Army. In May the 32d Division, now reconstituted after Buna and led by Major General William H. Gill, replaced the 163d Regimental Combat Team at Aitape. Minor patrol clashes characterized the development of the Aitape perimeter as American infantry probes pushing east clashed with Japanese troops advancing west. By early June the 32d Division had established an outer defensive line, a covering force, along the Driniumor River about 15 miles east of the Aitape airfields.

After being outflanked by MacArthur's landings, Adachi had ordered his command to move west toward Aitape. Sightings by Allied pilots of Japanese forces pushing west, troop concentrations, and well-worn trails and jungle tracks confirmed Eighteenth Army's withdrawal toward Aitape. Australian traffic analysts at forward intercept sites in New Guinea followed Eighteenth Army Headquarters by taking daily bearings on its moving radio transmitter. Their electronic tracking substantiated Adachi's pullout (May 2, 9). The tough Japanese commander hoped Second Area Army forces would strike the Americans from the west while Eighteenth Army hit them hard from the east. Adachi wanted to go down fighting, and dying, for the emperor. One measure of Adachi's determination was his insistence on marching with his troops despite a painful hernia. His soul mate, General Anami, applauded from afar, declaring that Eighteenth Army's plan to attack Aitape epitomized the Imperial Army's true samurai spirit. At every opportunity Anami encouraged Adachi to smash the Americans at Aitape.[55]

Eighteenth Army made wearisome progress toward Aitape. At the beginning of the trek, its three divisions covered about 6 to 7 miles a day through dense jungle criss-crossed with streams. By the end of May, the Japanese were making barely half that distance. Painful ground, pitifully short rations, incessant Allied air attacks, and a myriad of tropical diseases plagued the marchers. Still, these battle-hardened, resourceful infantrymen were vicious fighters. A major skirmish in early June, about 20 miles east of Aitape, claimed one hundred Japanese and an equal number of American casualties. It also showed any doubters that Adachi's men had not given up.

Throughout the march, Eighteenth Army had exchanged radio messages with its higher headquarters. By late May Central Bureau, with the aid of the key register salvaged off Aitape, had solved the new cipher, and MacArthur's code-breakers were again routinely reading the Japanese army's mainline system. A steady stream of ULTRA confirming Adachi's plan to attack Aitape flowed into Allied hands. A report prepared for Sinkov in the fall of 1944 asserted: "Perhaps the most outstanding intelligence furnished by Central Bureau, Brisbane, concerned the AITAPE and WEWAK operations. . . . G-2 has said that never has a commander gone into battle knowing so much about the enemy as did the Allied commander at AITAPE on 10-11 July 1944."[56] That blanket endorsement of ULTRA was true, misleading, and, insofar as the fighting troops on July 10/11 were concerned, fatally wrong.

ULTRA did provide a cornucopia of details about General Adachi's intentions, capabilities, timetable, problems, and so forth. Enough intelligence existed to support any interpretation of events. Willoughby heralded the Japanese approach at least twenty-six times in his Special Intelligence Bulletin and forty-four times in his Daily Intelligence Bulletin—which thinly disguised ULTRA as "reliable sources"; between June 15 and July 3, he wrote six special studies about the forthcoming attack against Aitape. This intelligence bonanza was available to commanders in sufficient time for them to adjust their tactical plans to defeat the Japanese offensive.

A Central Bureau decryption of a May 28 plea from Southern Army to Tokyo to

Listening to the enemy—radio intercept operators of the 126th Signal Radio Intelligence Company at Adelaide, Australia, mid-1944. (U.S. Army Signal Corps photo, courtesy of U.S. Army Intelligence and Security Command)

rush supplies by submarine to Wewak by the end of June "due to the attack on Aitape by MO [Eighteenth Army]" was the first ULTRA evidence of Adachi's intent. ULTRA dovetailed with intelligence gleaned from documents captured in mid-May that told of plans by the 20th and 41st divisions to attack Aitape in early July (May 31). U.S. patrols along the Driniumor reported bumping into Japanese scouting parties, counterpatrols, and infantry screens, all tactical hallmarks of combat units readying for an offensive (June 2–3). Opinion was unanimous that the Japanese intended to storm Aitape. It was only a question of when Adachi would attack. The compromised Japanese codes yielded an ambiguous answer.

MacArthur's codebreakers were so proficient in June 1944 that Southwest Pacific Headquarters could eavesdrop almost at will on Japanese staff deliberations about Aitape. As the Japanese hammered out a consensus, ULTRA carried to Allied commanders a running commentary of the various Japanese options. Willoughby's analysis and integration of ULTRA into the intelligence mosaic betrayed traits reminiscent of Buna, where his first impressions shaped the intelligence assessments. His ethnocentricism and tendency to superimpose his own rationality onto his opponents, which had been so apparent at Port Moresby and Buna, reappeared at Aitape.

From the outset Willoughby saw no profit for the Japanese from an attack on Aitape because Allied forces at Hollandia would still block Eighteenth Army's supply lines and escape routes. It made better sense—or so it seemed—for Adachi to bypass Aitape and strike directly at Hollandia (April 30–May 1). That interpretation resurfaced with regularity until the Japanese offensive began (May 8/9, 25/26). Willoughby did predict an attack against Aitape, but he always cloaked his prognostication with ambiguity. For instance, a late May message from Second Area Army to Eighteenth Army about supplies for Adachi's operations was evidence that the Japanese planned to attack Aitape (June 3), but in Willoughby's eyes, the attack might be no more than a covering action to divert attention from a general Japanese withdrawal (June 5/6). Later ULTRA suggested that the Aitape attack was a diversion to permit the successful disengagement and withdrawal of Eighteenth Army (June 8/9). Shortly after that, ULTRA showed the general dispositions of the 20th and 41st divisions preparatory to an attack on Aitape (June 14/15). After a Second Area Army message, transmitted June 8, ordered attacks on Aitape and Hollandia, Willoughby admitted that the "enemy" carried out orders "regardless of the odds against him" (June 17/18). By late June a compromised Eighteenth Army message acknowledged that attack preparations were nearly completed (June 23/24). Another broken radiogram laid out the axes of advance for a Japanese attack against U.S. troops defending the Driniumor River set for around July 10 (June 24/25). Willoughby remained skeptical about a major attack because the same ULTRA describing an attack against Aitape were simultaneously portraying the Japanese army's chronic supply shortages. How, Willoughby wondered, could Adachi carry out a major offensive on such a shoestring?

Indeed, the decryption that had first mentioned the Aitape attack also bemoaned logistic difficulties. This was followed by a slew of messages describing other logistic woes, usually severe ammunition and ration shortages. Eighteenth Army, it developed, had only half the ammunition the field service regulations prescribed for a major battle, and its troops were surviving in the jungle on half rations (June 5/6). Japanese two-engine bombers, configured as cargo carriers, had been dropping supplies to Adachi's otherwise isolated army. ULTRA even told that their daring flights from the Netherlands East Indies and Halmahera were bringing only a fraction of the desperately needed medicine and stocks (June 6/7, 10/11). Japanese radio messages about units living off the land and losing precious supplies to Allied air attacks added up to a dismal logistic picture (June 8/9, 11/12). Stores at Wewak, Eighteenth Army's main supply base, were depicted as critically low (June 14/15). These repeated references to Japanese logistic and supply problems convinced Willoughby that Eighteenth Army was exhausted, ill equipped, and incapable of fighting a prolonged battle (June 17/18, 18/19, 20/21, 26/27). At the same time, ULTRA made it plain that these desperate troops were readying a massive assault against the Driniumor River line.

Eighteenth Army's two-month struggle through the jungle toward Aitape had been shadowed by ULTRA. Reports by locals of Japanese columns, sightings by pilots, prisoner of war interrogations, captured documents, and patrols augmented ULTRA and kept steady track of Japanese progress. American commanders did take the voluminous intelligence reports seriously. Because of this unfolding plan by the Japanese to attack the Allies, Krueger pressed MacArthur for, and received, additional infantry, artillery, and air reinforcements for Aitape. On June 28 Krueger created the XI Corps to oversee the more than two American divisions deployed around Aitape. The new corps commander, Major General Charles P. Hall, inherited the Driniumor River covering force and Krueger's warning that an all-out Japanese attack was likely.[57] Hall did not share Krueger's urgency because Hall had never dealt with jungle fighting or ULTRA. Unfortunately neither one was as straightforward as the new commander might have expected. As Hall looked out at the seemingly impassable jungle, he could not believe that twenty thousand men could mass there undetected. Reading the ULTRA reports, Hall discovered that they were subject to ambiguity. It was difficult to convince anyone overnight that ULTRA was the most reliable of all intelligence sources, especially when over the next two weeks a series of seemingly contradictory decryptions made ULTRA seem to Hall as tangled as the jungle itself.

On June 20 Adachi summarized his attack preparations to date for Second Area Army. Four days later, Akin handed Sutherland a deciphered copy of Adachi's message that served notice that the "entire strength" of Eighteenth Army would attack Aitape around July 10 (June 24/25). A 20th Division message, dispatched on June 24 and available three days later, bared plans for its offensive across the Driniumor on the night of June 29 (June 27/28). This apparent change in the timing of the main attack was, in fact, the 20th Division commander's recommendation to Adachi for a preliminary strike to drive back the covering force along the Driniumor. Eighteenth Army would then launch its principal offensive as planned against Aitape in July. Central Bureau's intercept operators did not pick up a later message from the 20th Division to Adachi that recommended postponing the June 29 attack because the 41st Division was unable to deploy its forces in time to support the assault.[58] Ignorant of the second message, the Americans expected a major attack along the Driniumor on June 29.

Krueger flew from Hollandia to Aitape on June 27 to confer with Hall and Major General Gill, commander of the 32d Division, about blunting the Japanese offensive ULTRA had predicted for two days hence. Gill insisted his covering force along the Driniumor was overextended and he wanted to withdraw. The demands of preparing for and conducting campaigns farther west preoccupied Krueger. The sooner Adachi was defeated, the sooner the troops waiting at Aitape could be used in western New Guinea. Rather than withdraw and thereby prolong the operation, Krueger wanted Hall to capitalize on ULTRA's warnings to smash Eighteenth Army's big attack. He ordered Hall to strengthen the covering force and be prepared to counterattack the Japanese. Hall's unfamiliarity with ULTRA complicated matters further. The XI Corps' intelligence officer revealed Hall's concern about the veracity of Sixth Army's intelligence when he questioned the source of Krueger's detailed information about the impending Japanese attack. Krueger's reply explained that the Japanese scheme of maneuver and the objectives of their June 29 attack were "based on further interpretation of ultra information."[59] The XI Corps went on full alert, and American troops on the covering force braced for an immediate attack.

The night of June 29 passed uneventfully. The frontline troops mumbled the old story of intelligence officers always crying wolf. Puzzled intelligence analysts reexamined their data and concluded that the June 29 attack had been postponed in favor of concentrating everything for the main assault still scheduled for July 10. Their interpretation fit neatly with a recently deciphered June 24 message from Eighteenth Army informing Tokyo that troops would move to their assembly areas by June 30 (*June 30*). A few days later, a prisoner of war disclosed under questioning that the attack would come during the first ten days of July. Available ULTRA forecast that the 20th and 41st divisions, about twenty thousand troops, would attack Aitape on or around July 10. Preceding that action, the 20th Division would attack the Driniumor line to secure better jump-off positions for the main assault, although supply difficulties might hamper Japanese plans (*June 27, 28*).

MacArthur was not interested in the tactical situation. The Southwest Pacific commander wanted Eighteenth Army put out of action for very personal strategic reasons. On June 12 the Joint Chiefs of Staff had notified MacArthur and Nimitz that they wanted their "views and recommendations" on expediting the Pacific campaign, which meant that the Joint Chiefs were fishing for an endorsement to bypass the Philippines in favor of an invasion of Formosa. That notion was anathema to MacArthur, who argued eloquently and vehemently that a direct invasion of Formosa was unsound because it lacked support from land-based aviation. The occupation of Luzon, he insisted, would provide a staging and air base for the Formosa operation as well as sever Japanese supply lines to the south.[60]

General Marshall disagreed and radioed MacArthur that his "personal feelings" must not override "our great objective, which was the early conclusion of the war with Japan." The army chief of staff buttressed his challenge to Mac-Arthur's concept of operations with ULTRA. Marshall warned that MAGIC/ULTRA showed a steady Japanese buildup in western New Guinea, Halmahera, and Mindanao, Philippines. He granted that the Japanese capability was limited but noted that the Imperial Army expected an early offensive by MacArthur's forces.

That gave MacArthur "less opportunity to move against his [the enemy's] weakness and to his surprise, as has been the case in your recent series of moves."[61] MacArthur's only recourse was to get his campaign moving again and thereby demonstrate that his accelerated timetable to liberate the Philippines was realistic and achievable. The pressure he began to put on Krueger to finish the Japanese at Aitape was more unrelenting than it had been a month earlier at Biak.

What MacArthur regarded in the grand scheme as a tactical nuisance, Krueger saw as a serious distraction to his ongoing operations farther west and Gill viewed as a downright danger to his covering force. Hall was the missing link. He regarded his primary mission as defense of the airfield at Aitape because its loss would have been a "considerable embarrassment to General Krueger and General MacArthur." Hall's impression was that MacArthur had "much difficulty" in convincing the Joint Chiefs of Staff of the feasibility of his bypassing strategy. If the Japanese took the Aitape airfield and then pushed toward Hollandia, the Joint Chiefs would have put a brake on MacArthur's movements and the "entire theory of bypassing would have to be discarded and MacArthur would have been somewhat discredited."[62] Krueger bombarded Hall with radio messages badgering the XI Corps commander to attack, not sit around and wait for Adachi to strike. The Sixth Army commander "kept his finger in the pot on this thing pretty closely," because he too was worried about the consequences a successful Japanese attack might have on MacArthur's overall strategy. Hall bristled at the recriminations and wrote Krueger that it never was his intention to sit tight and let the enemy come to him.[63]

While the two American commanders exchanged letters, Japanese troops were already in their assembly areas awaiting the final order to attack (*July 6*). On July 4, U.S. troops were again alerted to repel a major attack. Again nothing happened. Cynics were now convinced that the "higher brass" were gun shy. American patrols took up the intelligence slack and paid a stiff price in killed and wounded to collect information about their elusive foe. They brushed against Japanese outposts that kept the Americans from locating the main enemy concentrations.[64] Although Hall remained convinced that the Japanese could not mass troops and artillery in such rugged terrain, American soldiers on the front line were convinced that they were the targets of a brewing Japanese attack whose telltale signs they saw everywhere. The Central Bureau radio intercept company at Aitape reported a lull in low-level, three-digit Japanese radio traffic, a classic sign that preparations for a forthcoming offensive had been completed.[65] The Japanese would surely come at the Driniumor force in a terrible wave on the night of July 9/10. Again the night passed peacefully, its stillness broken by the boom of American artillery firing aimlessly into the jungle beyond the river.

Willoughby attributed this latest anticlimax to Japanese supply difficulties. As he put it in the clear morning light of July 10: "The fact that the attack scheduled to commence on 10 July has not yet been launched may indicate that he has been forced to postpone the attack until he can build up his forward supplies and until he receives urgent stores scheduled to arrived by submarine. . . . It certainly appears possible therefore that the attack has been temporarily postponed. . . . [P]resent patrol activity would not seem to point to the date of the attack being close at hand" (July 10/11). That night, ten thousand howling Japanese burst across the shallow Driniumor River.

Along the Driniumor, Companies E and F, 2d Battalion, 128th Infantry, heard muffled noises from the far bank less than 100 yards away. They were listening to Major Kawahigashi Moritoshi's 1st Battalion, 78th Infantry, spearhead Eighteenth Army's long-anticipated attack. Finally, an anonymous U.S. infantryman fired his rifle toward the sounds. Then automatic-weapons and small-arms fire lashed Kawahigashi's men like steel rain, knocking them backward. Japanese light artillery lobbed shells onto the Americans, but heavier American guns, positioned well to the rear, pounded the Japanese in return. The concentrated artillery fire splintered towering trees like matchsticks, pinning unlucky Japanese underneath.

American riflemen firing into the river saw hundreds of Japanese screaming and waving their arms as they lunged through the shallow water toward the west bank of the Driniumor. Machine-gun barrels turned red hot from constant firing, and Japanese infantrymen died in groups. But still the Japanese surged forward. Flares lit up the sky and ground. Brightly burning red and green tracers cut through the night from both sides of the river. In the end there were too many Japanese willing to take the terrible beating necessary to cross the Driniumor. They broke into and through the covering force lines and precipitated a vicious month-long battle along the river that diverted precious men and matériel from MacArthur's thrust into western New Guinea. It was a merciless struggle fought in an unrelenting jungle. During July and August 1944, American battle losses along the Driniumor amounted to 3,000 men, including 440 killed. Nearly 10,000 Japanese officers and men perished.

Willoughby reacted to the savage Japanese offensive by standing the facts on their heads. First he proclaimed that Adachi's attack on the Driniumor covering force "was not in the nature of a surprise," which somewhat stretches the definition of that word.[66] Next he put the best face on his disastrous forecast by announcing that "the enemy's attack on our Aitape positions took place as scheduled" (July 15/16). Willoughby rehabilitated his tarnished reputation by proclaiming Aitape a great intelligence coup. In large part he succeeded, abetted by Central Bureau's claim that no commander ever went into battle better armed with information about his enemy. In later years, Willoughby unabashedly touted Aitape as a model of the use of tactical intelligence for the instruction of future intelligence officers.[67] His artfully fabricated half-truths became the accepted version of events.[68] Ex post facto rationalizations could not conceal that the misinterpretation of ULTRA prolonged the bitter fighting at Aitape.

As for ULTRA, Aitape culminated nearly four months of technical and analytical frustration. On the technical side, the Japanese change of key registers in early April denied MacArthur ULTRA information about Japanese army dispositions. ULTRA derived from the Imperial Navy's ciphers and the Army Water Transport Code continued to be intelligence staples. The destruction of the TAKE convoy, which left Anami without a reserve, and the prevention of the KON reinforcement effort, which left the Biak garrison isolated, were attributable to ULTRA. By mid-May, the main army cipher system was again the source of excellent intelligence, particularly about Eighteenth Army's plans to attack Aitape. On the tactical side, the three-digit code remained unsolved and that precluded a comprehensive identification of the smaller Japanese garrisons at Wakde, Sarmi, Biak, and Noemfoor. Perhaps more important, interpretations of ULTRA and other sources of intelligence were very uneven. Coming on top of several ambiguous analyses of Japanese intentions, the Aitape blunder seemed to fit a pattern of inept intelligence assessments. Krueger suffered from faulty intelligence at Sarmi, Biak, and Aitape where these shortcomings left him wary of intelligence pronouncements, including those premised on ULTRA. From its highpoint of Hollandia, MacArthur's ULTRA had tumbled to almost a hit-or-miss proposition as the invasion of the Philippines approached.

6
The Missing Division: Leyte, 1944

During the summer of 1944, MacArthur found his drive to the Philippines hindered more by the Joint Chiefs of Staff than by Tokyo warlords. In Washington the joint planners were searching for ways to accelerate the campaign in the Pacific, which, they reasoned, could be accomplished either by advancing target dates for currently scheduled operations or by bypassing objectives previously selected. Since ULTRA had made known the Japanese buildup in the Halmahera-Mindanao area,[1] the Joint Chiefs were inclined to bypass the well-defended Philippines and strike directly at Formosa. MacArthur's success in western New Guinea and Halsey's invasion of the Marianas made the possibility of seizing Formosa next a feasible one, but MacArthur reacted indignantly to such a proposal, dismissing it as "utterly unsound" and a betrayal of the Filipino people.

General Marshall had earlier cautioned MacArthur that MAGIC/ULTRA had unmasked enemy preparations against expected Allied advances toward the Philippines. The buildup promised Sixth Army the "prospect of very heavy fighting with consequent losses and delays."[2] The Southwest Pacific commander could debate with Marshall and the Joint Chiefs over strategy, but there could be no doubt about the great numbers of Japanese reinforcements that he knew were streaming into the region.

In mid-June, ULTRA reported Japanese plans to erect a triangular defensive zone across MacArthur's axis of advance. At least three air force and four ground divisions defended the triangle that stretched from northwestern New Guinea via Halmahera and the Palau Islands to the southern Philippines. It was known that twenty thousand fresh Japanese troops were en route to the Philippines to convert the four independent mixed brigades on the islands into full divisions (June 15/16). Army Water Transport Code messages from Army Shipping Headquarters at Hiroshima detailed plans to carry still more troops to Manila (July 5). Patterns of radio message broadcasts identified MacArthur's next scheduled objective, Halmahera, as a major transshipment point between Japan and Southern Army. The Japanese had also made good their earlier aircraft losses and Halmahera now bristled with 290 planes dispersed over several fields. ULTRA gathered between mid-May and mid-June portrayed the Japanese high command massing troops, bolstering air and ground defenses, and shifting units into the Philippines and Halmahera in anticipation of the Allied attack.

The entire 2d Army Air Division, for instance, had transferred from Manchuria to the Philippines (July 7/8), and the arrival at Davao of the sixteen-thousand-man 30th Division from Korea had also been confirmed (July 8/9). By mid-July, two more air regiments from Burma had augmented the defenders in the Philippines, and Japanese naval air units had also been reinforced (July 15/16). Washington picked up the move of the 4th Army Air Division from Manchuria to the Philippines (*July 17*), and listened in as the 270 Japanese aircraft in the Philippines ballooned by more than 300 planes to 579 in just three weeks (*July 27*). Small wonder that MacArthur saw himself in a race to get to the Philippines before Japanese reinforcements converted the islands into a massive fortress.[3]

He had originally expected to use Halmahera as the staging base for the invasion of Mindanao, but the outline of the Japanese buildup on Halmahera, manifested by the discovery of the 2d Amphibious Brigade there (July 15/16), made them a less and less attractive objective for MacArthur. Although the roughly forty thousand Japanese troops on Halmahera were short of equipment and lacked mobility, they could still be counted on to fight to the death for control of the island's airfields. ULTRA also pronounced them on the alert against an American attack, which they expected before mid-August (*July 23*). MacArthur sensibly opted to sidestep Halmahera in favor of a September 15 landing on Morotai, which, according to ULTRA, was lightly defended. The island was quickly secured and an airstrip was operational in early October. ULTRA still proved valuable, especially in November and early December 1944, when it foretold Japanese air raids against Kenney's airfields on Morotai and alerted naval and air commanders to enemy attempts to run the Allied naval and air blockade isolating the garrison.

Meanwhile, the Joint Chiefs vacillated about whether to invade Luzon or Formosa and asked their Pacific commanders for more information. MacArthur responded in early July with a revised RENO V timetable that envisioned an invasion of Morotai Island on September 8; a landing on Mindanao on October 25; another on Leyte on December 20; and on April 1, 1945, his main assault on Luzon. He conceived it as the major campaign plan for the Pacific and he would need full support by all elements of the Pacific Fleet to invade Luzon.[4] MacArthur took his proposal to Hawaii where, from July 26 to 29, he and Nimitz described to President Franklin D. Roosevelt the future course of the war in the Pacific. Despite the president's endorsement of MacArthur's performance, Roosevelt made no decision about Formosa or Luzon. Further heated exchanges of radiograms from MacArthur to Marshall and the Joint Chiefs followed through August, but the Joint Chiefs could not agree on the next objective. By September 1, a compromise left both the Formosa and Luzon courses of action open contingent upon which the Joint Chiefs ordered next.[5]

During this time, an ever-confident MacArthur had crafted an overall scheme for the Philippine campaign, the MUSKETEER plan. Published on July 10, MUS-KETEER scheduled the invasion of Leyte, Philippines, on December 20. The plan underwent revisions during August in response to ULTRA's revelations of the rapidly evolving Japanese defensive preparations for a climactic battle in the Philippines. For instance, ULTRA detected the conversion (that it had predicted a month earlier) of four independent mixed brigades in the Philippines to division status (July 27/28; August 4/5). Of the estimated 176,000 Japanese defending the islands, the War Department believed that 78,000 troops were on Luzon, includ-ing the 103d and 105th divisions; 48,000 men in the central Philippines, with the 16th Division on Leyte and the 102d on Cebu; and 50,000 in the southern Philip-pines, including the 30th and 100th divisions on Mindanao (*July 24*). The numbers continued to rise.

Intercept operators overheard more references to a 100th Division (July 25/26), and in early August compromised messages told MacArthur that the 26th Divi-sion, in North China since 1939, had been transferred to Fourteenth Army at Manila (August 2/3). A broken Water Transport Code message spoke of a Lieutenant General Suzuki taking command of Thirty-Fifth Army (*August 8*). Further cryptanalysis of the message showed that Suzuki Sosaku was in command of a newly formed Thirty-Fifth Army, which was located either on Mindanao or in the Visayans (August 14/15). Suzuki's new army command presaged the creation of an area army command to control the still expanding Japanese forces. A week later, ULTRA discovered the newly created Fourteenth Area Army Headquarters in Manila (August 21/22). ULTRA uncovered both of these new headquarters less than three weeks after their July 28 activation. By mid-August, Southwest Pacific intelligence knew that there were six Japanese divisions in the Philippines with two more, the 26th and 28th, possibly en route to the area (August 15/16), although four days later ULTRA disclosed that the 28th Division had arrived on Okinawa. Shortly after, the newly identified 54th and 55th Independent Mixed brigades as well as the 18th Independent Mixed Regiment appeared in the Philippines, appar-ently to compensate for the diversion of the 28th Division (August 19/20, *30*, 30/31). In early September, telltale Water Transport Code signals betrayed the 26th Division's arrival on Luzon. That brought to seven the number of Japanese divisions in the Philippines and increased the total strength to 200,000 troops, up 50,000 men since the invasion of Saipan in June (*September 7*). Japanese deploy-ments seemed focused on the defense of Luzon. Besides being the most populous and largest of the Philippine Islands, Luzon's distance from Allied air power and shorter supply lines to Japan made it, from the Japanese point of view, the easiest to protect against potential invaders.

The loss of Saipan in mid-July had split Japan's strategic inner defensive perimeter and opened the way for an Allied thrust across the Central Pacific that threatened to cut off Tokyo from its resource-rich Southeast Asian conquests. It was the proximate cause of the downfall of Prime Minister General Tojo Hideki's cabinet. Finally, the breach in the Marianas spurred Imperial Headquarters to develop the SHO (VICTORY) operation on July 21, 1944. There were four SHO variations. SHO 1 was the plan to defend the Philippines; SHO 2, the defense of Formosa; SHO 3, the defense of southern and central Japan; and SHO 4, the defense of Hokkaido and the Kuril Islands. At that time, Tokyo and Southern Army foresaw Luzon as the site of the decisive ground battle and were hurrying divisions from Manchuria to the Philippines. These were the same units that ULTRA had been tracking into the archipelago.

A growing air arm augmented the Japanese ground forces. Japanese air commanders were consolidating their men and planes beyond the effective range of American heavy bombers but positioning them for immediate transfer to the Philippines if they were required to repel an invasion (August 13/14). The Japanese disposed their air power in the Philippines in great depth with maximum dispersion of aircraft scattered over airdromes in Mindanao and the Visayans. Under the command of Fourth Air Army, two army air divisions, the 2d and 4th, guarded the northern and central Philippines while the First Naval Air Fleet defended the southern islands. The 2d Air Division boasted almost 400 planes, and the 4th (mostly base maintenance personnel) counted perhaps 20 more aircraft.[6] About 200 of the 305 aircraft of the First Naval Fleet were operational, but the pilots were unseasoned and far below the quality of their fallen predecessors at Rabaul.[7] ULTRA enabled Washington to monitor the Japanese aerial reinforcements with impressive precision. War Department analysts were only 20 aircraft off when they declared that land-based air strength had grown by 427 aircraft, or nearly 700 total in two months, as aircraft from Manchuria, Southeast Asia, and Formosa flocked to the Philippines (*August 24*).

ULTRA continued to direct Allied submarines in their unrelenting attacks on Japanese vessels carrying fresh troops and much-needed supplies to the Philippines. A three-boat wolf pack, coached by navy ULTRA, attacked a twenty-one-ship Japanese convoy bound for Manila in mid-July. Intercepted cries for help made known the loss, by name, of three transports, and two others were thought sunk (*July 20, 23*).[8] Submarines sank a tanker, freighter, and attack transport off the northwestern coast of Luzon later that month (July 26/27). Besides identifying potential targets, ULTRA often verified the submariners' claims in the words of the Japanese themselves. Though ULTRA laid the trap for Japanese merchantmen, it was the courage of submarine commanders and sailors who pressed home attack after attack that ripped the heart from the Japanese merchant transport system. The early morning darkness of July 31 witnessed a spectacular example of such valor.

ULTRA had identified noon positions for ships of the MI 11 convoy and steered an American submarine wolf pack across its course north of Luzon. Around 3:30 A.M. the USS *Steelhead* drew first blood when it put a torpedo into a Japanese tanker. Thick black smoke surged from the stricken vessel while escorts shot off flares and signal rockets. Commander Lawson P. Ramage, skipper of the USS *Parche,* which was lurking on the surface a few miles away, saw the fireworks. Ramage charged headlong into the convoy, directing his submarine in a night surface attack. After narrowly avoiding crashing into an escort, *Parche* blew one tanker out of the water. Orchestrating the fight from the conning tower, Ramage maneuvered the submarine wildly in the middle of the wounded Japanese convoy. He climaxed *Parche's* battle with a head-on attack, a ''down-the-throat shot,'' that stopped a lumbering cargo ship dead in the water as it headed on a collision course with the submarine. ULTRA confirmed that the *Yoshino* and *Fuso* marus, laden with more than five thousand troops of the 26th Division, were among the four ships that Japan lost that night (*July 31/August 1*).[9] Ramage's intrepid attack earned him a Medal of Honor.

Clues from tattletale radio messages pinpointed still another Japanese convoy southwest of Manila, and four more marus fell to torpedoes (*August 23*). Guided into striking position by ULTRA, two U.S. submarines relied on radar to position themselves for a night torpedo attack. The first salvo exploded a tanker and sent a pillar of fire shooting 1,000 feet into the darkness. The submarines made quick work of three other ships silhouetted against the burning tanker. These attacks, and others like them, clamped an undersea vise on Luzon that was squeezing the lifeblood from Japanese resupply convoys. Convoy routes were altered and escort vessels and aircraft were added to protect the transports. Nevertheless, the fatal noon positions, broadcast in compromised ciphers, gave the submarines an insurmountable advantage because the Americans knew their quarry's path while the Japanese had little idea of where the stalking wolf packs would be. Five more merchantmen went down over the next two weeks. Tokyo ordered more daytime air patrols. Specially trained flight crews flew antisubmarine sorties by moonlight, hoping to catch American submarines napping on the surface. Nothing worked. Even persistent attacks did not drive away the submariners. The USS *Barb*, for example, was bombed several times without damage and suffered through a depth-charge attack. Still *Barb* rose from the deep, and on the night of August 31, it put its torpedoes into the *Okunia* Maru (*September 1, 9*).[10]

The slaughter of the marus continued unabated throughout September. On September 6 *Eichi* Maru, carrying men of the 31st Infantry, 8th Division, and fuel for the 2d Armored Division, went down under torpedo attack. On September 21 two ships bringing units of the 2d Armored Division were sunk. Submarine attacks on the night of October 2 sent another maru to the bottom, and distress calls to rescue 2,300 men were intercepted in Brisbane and Hawaii (*October 5*). The ULTRA that submarine commanders relied on to intercept their targets had been produced by cryptanalysts thousands of miles away from the action who then monitored the results of their work. Instead of using the ocean's vastness to hide themselves from submarines, Japanese skippers unconsciously followed predesignated courses to their destruction. As in the New Guinea campaign, they stubbornly pushed ahead with their reinforcement plans, seemingly indifferent to the terrible losses.

A ware that the Japanese desperately needed time to strengthen their Philippine defenses, MacArthur proceeded with his plans to seize Morotai, uncertain of what would follow. On September 8, one week before the scheduled invasion of Morotai, Washington ordered MacArthur to invade Leyte by December 20 so that it could become a base to support an assault either on Formosa or Luzon. The next day, Admiral William Halsey's Third Fleet carrier-borne aircraft, in support of the impending Morotai landings, struck Mindanao. Japanese air power was conspicuously absent. On September 12 and 13, Halsey's pilots followed up by hitting Leyte; again only a handful of Japanese aircraft rose to challenge the raiders. Halsey then proposed to Nimitz that the Pacific forces bypass Mindanao and converge directly on Leyte in the central Philippines, which, according to Halsey, was "wide-open" and might even be undefended.[11]

Southwest Pacific Headquarters knew Halsey's claims were wildly exaggerated. Fresh ULTRA, for example, had located the new Thirty-Fifth Army in command of the central Philippines, which meant the Japanese were strengthening not abandoning that sector (*September 11*). Reinforcements for the 30th Division in the southern Philippines and for the 16th Division on Leyte were, in Willoughby's words, "in conformity with the enemy's policy of strengthening his defenses in the southern Philippine Islands" (September 11/12, 14/15). Accumulated ULTRA showed that the Japanese had withdrawn the bulk of their air power from the southern islands to the safer environs of Luzon (September 9/10) where they were beyond the range of Allied bombers and Halsey's marauding carriers. This accounted, in part, for the feeble aerial response to U.S. carrier strikes. American ground and naval commanders had this ULTRA at their fingertips. Nonetheless, Nimitz's endorsement of Halsey's proposal did offer the Joint Chiefs the chance to accelerate the tempo of the drive toward Japan.

Marshall received Nimitz's recommendation while attending the OCTAGON Conference in Quebec. He promptly radioed MacArthur to ask his views on the drastic change of plans. MacArthur, however, was aboard the USS *Nashville* leading the invasion of Morotai. The cruiser was observing radio silence to keep its presence, and that of the invasion force, from the unsuspecting Japanese. In short, MacArthur was unavailable for one of the great decisions of the Pacific war. The responsibility fell to Sutherland, who gathered Chamberlin, Kenney, and other senior officers at Southwest Pacific Headquarters. They knew from ULTRA that there were at least twenty-one thousand Japanese on Leyte and that Japanese air power, though bruised by Halsey's recent forays, was far from broken. They also knew that no matter what ULTRA augured, Sutherland could not tell Marshall that a direct assault against Leyte was not feasible because to do so would implicitly endorse the option to invade Formosa. Sutherland radioed the chief of staff, in MacArthur's name, that intermediate operations would be dropped in favor of an invasion of Leyte.[12] Marshall was seated at a formal dinner with the Canadian prime minister, MacKenzie King, when Sutherland's answer arrived. He excused himself to confer with the other Joint Chiefs. Within ninety minutes, they issued orders to MacArthur and Nimitz canceling several scheduled operations and setting the invasion of Leyte for October 20. Not about to be overshadowed by the earlier June 6 D-day in France, MacArthur designated the invasion date A-day.

Leyte became the focal point where MacArthur's Southwest Pacific and Nimitz's Central Pacific forces converged. A mighty assault on the Philippines capped a two-and-a-half-year advance across the Pacific.[13] For Japan, the Philippines would probably offer the last chance for its army to score a decisive victory over MacArthur's forces. ULTRA accurately credited a single Japanese division—the 16th—as the defender of Leyte and confirmed the Southwest Pacific Headquarters' appreciation that the Japanese were concentrating their forces for the defense of Luzon (October 15/16). Willoughby's preinvasion intelligence estimate placed about twenty thousand Japanese troops on Leyte. The veteran 16th Division was concentrated near Tacloban and formed the backbone of the defense.[14] In early September a Japanese battle fleet was reported in Manila Bay, which foreshadowed the return of the First Striking Fleet from home waters to the Philippines. The exact locations of many major Japanese fleet units were unknown, although warships seemed to be deploying to the southwest (September 15/16). Fragmentary intercepts made mention of a "SHO" operation that analysts thought might have something to do with the defense of the Philippines. Allied intelligence about major enemy fleet units was, however, very incomplete (September 28/29; October 1/2).

For one of the few times in the Pacific war, army ULTRA about ground units in the Philippines was better than navy ULTRA about the area. By early October, Washington had identified the general locations of seven Japanese divisions in the islands. Together with four independent mixed brigades, whose exact whereabouts remained uncertain, the War Department credited 225,000 Japanese troops in the Philippines (*October 3*) (see Table 6.1). A week later, in order to account for the suspected presence of the 115th Division in the islands, Willoughby added

Table 6.1. Estimated and Actual Japanese Ground Order of Battle,
Philippine Islands, October 10, 1944

Unit	G-2 Location	Actual
Southern Army Headquarters	Luzon (Manila)	Southern Army Headquarters
Fourteenth Area Army Headquarters	Luzon (Ft. McKinley)	Fourteenth Area Army Headquarters
103d Division	Luzon	103d Division
105th Division	Luzon	105th Division
26th Division	Luzon	26th Division
		8th Division
		2d Division
Thirty-Fifth Army	Visayans	Thirty-Fifth Army
102d Division	Cebu (elements on Leyte)	102d Division
16th Division	Leyte	16th Division
30th Division	Mindanao	30th Division
100th Division	Mindanao	100th Division
54th, 55th, 58th, 61st Independent Mixed brigades and 115th Division	Unlocated	54th Independent Mixed Brigade (Mindanao) 55th Independent Mixed Brigade (south of Mindanao) 58th Independent Mixed Brigade (Luzon)

Source: G-2: SWPA, Special Intelligence Bulletin, 10 October 1944, National Archives and Records
Administration, Washington, D.C.; Actual: Maeda Toru and Kuwada Etsu, eds., *Nihon no
senso—zukai to deeta* (Tokyo: Hara shobo, 1982), plate 59.

17,000 more Japanese to his count, or approximately 242,000 total (October
10/11). A circular message from Tokyo to Manila contained twelve ground force
addresses, ten of which Central Bureau identified as divisions or larger, but Arlington Hall stuck with its earlier estimate of 225,000 troops on the islands (*October 14*). Navy ULTRA concurrently reported large numbers of planes staging
from Japan to the islands in early October. Tokyo was obviously bolstering the
archipelago's defenses against a forthcoming American invasion that several deciphered Japanese naval messages made plain it regarded as imminent (*October 7*).

Japanese deployments underscored the concern of the newly appointed commander of Fourteenth Area Army, Lieutenant General Yamashita Tomoyuki, that
the vulnerability of Leyte to overwhelming American air and naval might render it
indefensible.[15] Yamashita wanted to fight the decisive ground battle on Luzon

because the main island offered him more room to maneuver his troops and forced MacArthur to fight at the end of an extended supply line. Yamashita's sole purpose in Manila was to execute the ground phase of SHO 1 by repelling the anticipated American invasion. Additional Japanese reinforcements, notably the 1st Infantry Division, were already steaming from Korea to Manila to assist in the defense.

But Yamashita had been in command a mere eleven days before MacArthur struck. His predecessor, Lieutenant General Kuroda Shigenori, had acted more like an imperial governor than a battlefront commander, paying greater attention to his golf game than to defense of the Philippines. He enjoyed Manila's sweet life from a huge mansion well-stocked with Japanese girls from the headquarters' secretary pool. Kuroda also amused himself by reading books confiscated from MacArthur's private library.[16] Once Imperial Headquarters determined that Japan would fight the decisive battle of the Pacific in the Philippines, Tokyo could no longer wink at Kuroda's conduct. He was abruptly relieved on September 26, 1944. Yamashita, then commanding First Area Army in Manchuria, received the imperial summons and orders for Manila.

Yamashita was among the best Japanese commanders. His brilliant seventy-day campaign to seize Singapore in 1942 earned him the nickname "the Tiger of Malaya." If anyone could defeat the Americans, it was this tall, sturdily built officer. Lieutenant General Suzuki Sosaku, guarding Leyte with Thirty-Fifth Army, had served as Yamashita's chief of staff in Malaya. Suzuki enjoyed a well-earned reputation as a top-rate organizer, and his colleagues regarded him as the ideal battlefield commander.[17]

The same could not be said for Yamashita's air commander, Lieutenant General Tominaga Kyoji. Tominaga had been Tojo's henchman, serving concurrently as vice war minister and director of the powerful Personnel Affairs Bureau. Since graduating from the Imperial War College in 1923, he had amassed a paltry three-years' service with line units. The Fourth Air Army commander had no combat experience and was derided in army circles as a petty bureaucrat playing soldier. Even the emperor was taken aback by Tominaga's appointment. He asked General Sugiyama Hajime, the new war minister, if Tominaga knew anything about the air force. Sugiyama blandly responded that since Tominaga had been the personnel director on the Army General staff, he was fully acquainted with air force organization.[18] Unfortunately Tominaga was a tin soldier who loved pomp and pageantry but not danger. He prided himself on choosing appropriate names for suicide units and giving theatrical pep talks as well as send-offs to doomed kamikazes. He capped his performance in January 1945 by ordering all his surviving pilots to become suicide fliers while he escaped to Formosa on one of the few remaining Fourth Air Army transport planes in the Philippines. In between he was a constant thorn in Yamashita's side.

The Fourteenth Area Army commander selected Lieutenant General Muto

Akira for his chief of staff. They had been classmates in the 25th Academy Class and were closely associated in Tokyo during the turbulent 1930s. With his wire-rimmed glasses, Muto looked every bit the conscientious staff officer. Indeed, he was a polished military bureaucrat, but he had fallen out with Tojo in early 1942. His transfer from the directorship of the Military Affairs Bureau to command the Guards Division was more an exile than a promotion. Muto's plane landed in Manila the day the Americans stormed ashore in the Philippines. Marauding Allied fighter planes greeted the new chief of staff, who dived into the scant safety of a muddy ditch to escape the strafers. Still dressed in his soaking mud-stained uniform, Muto reported to Fourteenth Area Army Headquarters where Yamashita remarked that his old friend looked like something that had just crawled through a swamp. The two commanders then got down to business. Yamashita told Muto that the Americans had landed on Leyte. "*Ah so desu ka* [Is that right]?" Muto remarked. "But where is Leyte?"[19] Muto was not alone in his ignorance. Japanese naval intelligence had provided no advance warning of the Leyte invasion.[20]

After their assault landings on Leyte, U.S. troops moved swiftly inland against little Japanese opposition because the first part of the threefold SHO 1 for defense of the Philippines involved hurling the Combined Fleet against the American naval forces. Though Willoughby claimed prescience about Japanese intentions in his estimate of the Japanese naval reaction to MacArthur's possible landings in the Philippines, the unfolding of the Battle of Leyte Gulf was an especially complex naval engagement.[21] By October 23, when three Japanese fleets were converging on Leyte, a better picture of the Imperial Fleet's locations and intentions came from American submarine and aircraft sightings than from ULTRA. The 1st Diversion Attack Force (Second Fleet), led by Vice Admiral Kurita Takeo, had been sighted near Mindoro. Locations of Third Fleet's carrier striking force, however, were unknown, although naval intelligence believed it was at sea and proceeding to the Philippines (**October 23**). (Bold face dates in parentheses identify U.S. Navy, Joint Intelligence Center, Pacific Ocean Area, "Summary of ULTRA Traffic.")

Kurita's force split into two battle groups: Central Force, commanded by Kurita, and Southern Force, skippered by Vice Admiral Nishimura Shoji. U.S. picket submarines spotted Central Force early in the morning of October 24 and located Nishimura's smaller fleet around noon that same day. Amply forewarned by these sightings, Admiral Kinkaid positioned his battleships and torpedo forces to block the entrance to the Surigao Strait through which the Japanese Southern Force would have to pass. Early in the morning of October 25, the Americans ambushed Nishimura's fleet, sinking or seriously damaging virtually every one of his ships. At the same time, covered by darkness, Kurita steered his fleet toward the San Bernardino Strait, which opens into Leyte Gulf.

Off to the northeast, Vice Admiral Ozawa Jisaburo's Carrier Force was doing its best to lure Halsey's fleet away from the vital strait. Ozawa ordered numerous radio messages broadcast to advertise his position to the Americans, but the transmitter failed, so there were no signals for U.S. naval intercept stations to overhear. Despite Ozawa's best efforts, his decoy carrier force was neither sighted nor overheard until October 24. Once American pilots spotted the Japanese carriers, however, Halsey went after the lure and drove north to attack Ozawa. ULTRA played little role in his decision and indeed had remarkably little success during the entire massive naval battle. With Halsey gone, Kurita steamed toward Leyte Gulf to confront the U.S. Seventh Fleet's slow and vulnerable escort carrier groups, the only U.S. warships in his way. If Kurita broke through the weak American force, which given his superior firepower and speed seemed most likely, he could then smash MacArthur's fragile transports anchored off Leyte and isolate Krueger's Sixth Army on the island. Yet for reasons not satisfactorily explained to this day, after two and a half hours of fighting, Kurita broke off the engagement and withdrew. The Battle of Leyte Gulf was over and the Imperial Navy's bold gamble lost.

Japanese losses were four carriers, three battleships, six heavy and four light cruisers, eleven destroyers, and one submarine. About 500 planes were lost and some 10,500 sailors and airmen were killed. American losses amounted to one light and two escort carriers, two destroyers, one destroyer escort, and more than 200 aircraft. About 2,800 Americans were killed and another 1,000 were wounded. The Japanese reacted to this disaster by intensifying their air and ground efforts to destroy the American invaders. For the task, Fourth Air Army had about 420 aircraft of all types, a number remarkably close to Washington's running estimate of 405 planes in the Philippines (*October 12*).[22] About 150 Hayate ("Franks" to the Allies), new, easy-to-handle, single-seat fighters, augmented Japan's army air force. Naval land-based air strength under First Air Fleet Headquarters at Manila also jumped to about 400 aircraft, though only half were operational. The Second Air Fleet, which specialized in attacks against carriers, deployed to Formosa, the Ryukyu Islands, and Kyushu to counter the Philippine invasion. In Japan, an elite army-navy team, code-named T Attack Force, had organized about 100 aircraft to conduct all-weather surprise and night attacks. ULTRA made known that T Force had been ordered to Formosa in early October, and Allied intercept operators listened in as these army pilots practiced torpedo attacks in their twin-engine bombers over Kagoshima By in southern Japan (October 13/14).

The War Department credited Halsey's wide-ranging carrier strikes just before the Philippine invasion with destroying nearly 200 Japanese planes, which reduced Fourth Air Army's strength to 225 aircraft (*October 19*). In fact, Tominaga had 198 aircraft left, 104 of which were operational. The Second Air Fleet had lost about half its strength but still had about 200 planes. Willing to accept the heavy losses, the Japanese high command threw more planes and pilots into the SHO operation. About 350 planes went into action for the massive air assault of October 24; Tominaga hurled about 100 army fighters and bombers against the American fleet in Leyte Bay. Forty-five of them were lost without inflicting serious damage on the ships. For their part, naval air units resorted to kamikaze attacks. The sustained ferocity of these conventional massed army air force raids and the navy's suicide tactics against the Allies from October 27 through November 1 left the Tacloban airfield a cratered mess, sank one destroyer, and damaged five ships.[23]

Battered by incessant air attacks and in need of resupply, the U.S. carrier fleet withdrew from Leyte, leaving MacArthur to rely on ground-based aircraft to provide air support. ULTRA underlined the general's desperate need for more aircraft. Analysis of T Force's radio messages and call signs portrayed the Japanese ability to mass huge aerial formations from a web of bases in Japan, the Bonins, the Kurils, Hainan, and China that could attack Allied warships or transports on twenty-four-hours' notice. Determined Japanese pilots again and again pressed home their fearsome aerial blitz despite mounting losses (October 30). Kenney brought in the deadly P-38s to beat back the Japanese, but the northeast monsoon turned what was left of Tacloban airfield into a morass.[24] Twenty-one inches of rain fell on Leyte in November, most in short tropical cloudbursts, but three typhoons dumped heavy, long rains. These deluges and the swampy ground slowed American air base construction on Leyte, which limited the number of ground-based aircraft available at any one time. While Kenney's pilots fought rain and mud as well as the Japanese, Japanese aircrews, operating on the western side of Leyte's central mountain range, were sheltered from the worst of the monsoon. Allied ground crews had jammed P-38s together wherever dry space permitted, making them easy targets for Japanese bombardiers. A thirty-five-plane Japanese attack on November 4 destroyed two P-38s, damaged thirty-nine more, and left four men dead and 30 wounded. The same day, two suicide planes slammed into two American transports, killing 92 and wounding 156, 15 mortally.[25]

ULTRA tracked Japanese pilots from take-off to landing by reading the Japanese army air force codes. Thus MacArthur, Kenney, and Krueger knew that far from surrendering, the Japanese were stepping up their aerial onslaught. In a development that the War Department labeled "extraordinary," ULTRA detected an increase of 219 planes in the Philippines by November 2 (*November 2*). According to ULTRA, Imperial Headquarters in Tokyo was drawing on every theater except Southeast Asia for aircraft to transfer to the Philippines (November 2/3). Japanese authorities were even willing to strip homeland air defenses to gather aircraft for a climactic SHO battle in the southern skies. Large air consignments streamed into the islands throughout November. Five army air regiments, about 200 aircraft, reached Luzon by mid-November. T Force, now rebuilt and mustering 200 aircraft, had been overheard in radio communications when it deployed from Japan to Formosa (November 9/10). Willoughby predicted that the Japanese had 300 to 400 fighters and bombers within striking range of Leyte (November 10/11). Thirty-two more fighters arrived November 18 and 53 the next day as four more air regiments deployed to the Philippines. At that rate, analysts extrapolated that 1,225 aircraft would be fed into the islands during the month (November 18/19). But even the 100-to-200-plane raids against U.S. shipping and Tacloban airfield were overshadowed by the appearance of suicide attackers in even greater numbers than before.

The Japanese navy holds the dubious credit for the first "official" kamikaze attacks on October 25 when naval pilots smashed into American escort carriers off the Philippine coast.[26] The human missiles made an inferno of the *St. Lo,* which exploded and capsized. Other kamikazes rammed but did not sink five other escort carriers. More suicide attacks followed the next day, and the reported results so impressed the Imperial Navy that it expanded its euphemistically dubbed "Special Attack Corps." ULTRA available three days later disclosed that the Japanese believed three kamikazes had sunk two carriers and left a cruiser and another carrier dead in the water. In a terse comment, Willoughby predicted that the suicide attacks would only increase (October 29/30).

After the fall of Saipan in July 1944, army officers in Imperial Headquarters in Tokyo had considered using ramming tactics to improve the chances that bombs dropped by their poorly trained pilots would hit ships taking evasive action. Units had been reorganized and undergone specialized training for these missions of death. Unlike the navy, army pilots were not volunteers. Tokyo selected crews from personnel rosters of instructors at army flight training schools. In late October, one twin-engine Type 99 and one Type 4 bomber unit with three-man crews deployed to Luzon under orders to ride a 1-ton bomb into the bowels of an Allied ship. After several abortive missions, the army pilots claimed their first victim on November 27 when they rammed and sank the U.S. submarine chaser SC 744. An elated Tominaga ordered their fellow army kamikaze officers, who were waiting to fly suicide missions, to fly to Manila to join him for their macabre farewell party. The five officers selected for the "honor" flew as passengers aboard a slow-moving transport plane. American fighter pilots shot down the lumbering craft, and all five putative kamikazes died in the wreckage—a funeral pyre of sorts to Tominaga's vanity.[27]

By mid-November MacArthur's headquarters regarded the suicide attackers as "one of our current greatest threats." Willoughby's solution to these tactics of self-destruction was to let a Darwinian natural selection reduce the elite suicide units (November 9/10). In other words, the scale of kamikaze attacks might diminish as the special crews destroyed themselves (November 11/12, 15/16). By mid-December, ULTRA had shed light on the army bomber pilots' suicide plunge

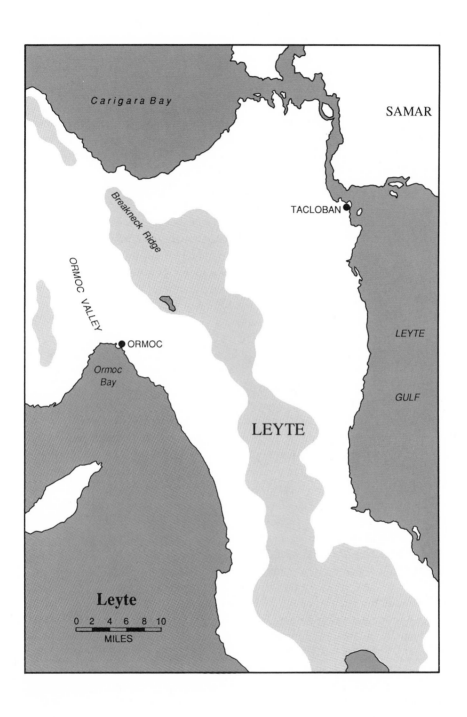

Carigara Bay

SAMAR

Breakneck Ridge

TACLOBAN ●

ORMOC VALLEY

● ORMOC

Ormoc
Bay

LEYTE

GULF

LEYTE

Leyte

0   2   4   6   8   10
MILES

into SC 744 and made it abundantly clear that the Japanese army was whole-heartedly joining in the kamikaze attacks (December 13/14). The terrifying tactics that pitted men who wanted to live against those who were willing to die became the trademark of the Pacific war in 1945.

Similar ferocity stamped the ground campaign. U.S. infantry units had advanced rapidly in a two-pronged attack until they reached Leyte's mountainous spine. Rugged terrain, torrential rains, and a skillful Japanese withdrawal to this operational high ground to await reinforcements combined to check the GIs' progress. When the Americans landed on Leyte on October 20, the Japanese high command had no intention of fighting a multidivision engagement on the island. The next day, Yamashita's immediate superior, Marshal Terauchi Hisaichi, commander of Southern Army Headquarters (located in Manila with Fourteenth Area Army Headquarters), ordered seven infantry battalions to reinforce Leyte.[28] A short, thin aristocrat, Terauchi had long advocated holding the southern and central Philippines whose possession, he believed, preserved the lines of communication between the natural resources of Southeast Asia and the Japanese homeland. He made his decision to reinforce Leyte on the mistaken assumption that the U.S. carrier force was in ruins.

From October 10, U.S. Third Fleet raids against Luzon, the Ryukyus, and Formosa had brought out the Japanese air forces. During ten days of continuous air-sea battles, the inexperienced Japanese pilots had wildly inflated their accounts of the damage they had inflicted on the American warships. The Southern Army and Tokyo had uncritically accepted the Imperial Navy's exaggerated claims of 11 U.S. carriers sunk and 1,200 American aircraft destroyed.[29] The Combined Fleet and the Navy Department of Imperial Headquarters did, in fact, reassess the alleged battle damage and had significantly downgraded the exuberant pilots' reports but did not share its new estimate with the army. Buoyed by these inflated battle claims of naval "victories," the army believed that with suitable reinforcements the Leyte defenders could annihilate the now-isolated American invaders.[30] The decision to reinforce Leyte initiated a protracted campaign that absorbed U.S. Army units already earmarked for future operations and retarded Mac-Arthur's timetable for the invasion of Luzon. As for the Allies, the Leyte operation seemed to be another steppingstone to the main battle that awaited them on Luzon.

On A-day, ULTRA correctly identified the sixteen-thousand-man 16th Infantry Division as the nucleus of the island's defense but incorrectly credited another forty-five hundred troops from the 102d Infantry Division on Leyte. Consequently, Willoughby produced an inflated intelligence estimate of twenty-seven thousand Japanese defenders on Leyte-Samar-Masabate (October 20/21). For his part, Sixth Army's G-2, Colonel Horton V. White, expected that the 16th and 102d divisions would fight a delaying defense designed to buy time until formations held in reserve could be rushed to Leyte.[31]

Table 6.2. Estimated and Actual Japanese Ground Order of Battle,
Leyte-Samar-Masabate, October 1944

SWPA Estimate		Actual
16th Infantry Division	16,000	16th Infantry Division
		(less 1 battalion on Samar)
Elements, 102d Infantry Division	4,500	102d on Cebu, Negros, Panay; 354th,
		355th Infantry Battalions on Luzon
7th Independent Tank Company	125	1 company, 6th Armored Regiment
10th Independent Tank Company	125	1 company, 10th Armored Regiment
Naval Base Troops	1,200	1,000 men
Identified Base and Support	1,750	
Unidentified Base and Support	3,300	3,000
Total	26,875	20,000 plus

Source: SWPA estimate: SWPA, Special Intelligence Bulletin, 10 October 1944, National Archives
and Records Administration, Washington, D.C.; Actual: Maeda Toru and Kuwada Etsu,
eds., *Nihon no senso—zukai to deeta* (Tokyo: Hara shobo, 1982), plate 58.

The 16th Division's three regiments had dug in along Leyte's eastern coast.
Outnumbered four to one, they could accomplish little more than to delay the
American advance westward across the island. A single company from the division's transport regiment was assigned garrison and guard duties at the western
port of Ormoc, the second largest city on the island, with a population of 86,000.
The flow of the battle during the first few days made Ormoc the natural entry point
for Japanese seaborne reinforcements to land. Operating on interior lines, they
could defend the approaches to the port, the "Ormoc corridor," a 25-mile-long
valley stretching north from the port to the ridges that overlook Carigara Bay.

Vice Admiral Mikawa Gunichi, commander of the Southwest Area Fleet,
ordered ad hoc reinforcements to Leyte on October 24. The next night, two
warships escorted five high speed naval transports carrying 2,550 troops of the
41st Infantry Regiment from Mindanao to Ormoc. Plans to embark two other
infantry regiments collapsed when planes from Rear Admiral Thomas L.
Sprague's escort carriers sank both warships and a transport on their return from
Ormoc. Meanwhile, Thirty-Fifth Army, in charge of Leyte ground operations,
dispatched two more battalions to Ormoc. Sailing separately they arrived one day
apart, but both suffered casualties along the way from attacks by roving American
fighters. Two other battalions landed at Ormoc during the next few days.[32]

Preoccupied with tracking major Japanese warships during the Battle of Leyte
Gulf on October 24/25, ULTRA provided scanty information about these first minor
reinforcements to Ormoc. For instance, the U.S. Navy's Joint Intelligence Center
for the Pacific Ocean Area recorded partially decrypted radio messages asking
about unloading two transports at Ormoc (**October 25**). The small convoys were

insignificant, but the limited ULTRA about them was ambiguous and led Willoughby to ponder the meaning of reports that the Japanese were either reinforcing or withdrawing from Leyte. He thought it likely that ULTRA references to "loading and unloading" meant that the Japanese were unloading a small force to cover the loading of base and service troops as part of a full-scale withdrawal from Leyte (October 27/28). That assessment, heavy Japanese battle casualties, and rapid U.S. advances led him to conclude "that either a last desperate stand must be made wherever he can coordinate and regroup his forces, or a determined effort to evacuate to other islands may be attempted" (October 29/30).

Willoughby's logic rested on the premise that the severe losses to the Japanese fleet and the establishment of American air bases on Leyte made it "improbable that any sizable merchant vessels will again venture into the Central P[hilippine] I[sland] area" (October 31/November 1). In other words, he assessed Japanese intentions according to what he would do if confronted by similar, seemingly hopeless circumstances. When this intelligence projection appeared, the Japanese 1st Infantry Division was secretly unloading more than eleven thousand reinforcements at Ormoc.

Tokyo had sent the 1st Division to Leyte based on mistaken intelligence and exaggerated battle claims. Army chief of staff General Umezu Yoshijiro trusted the navy's assertions about mauling the American fleet in Leyte Gulf and believed that MacArthur was trapped on Leyte.[33] On October 26, Imperial Headquarters' Twentieth Section (Wartime Guidance) confidently predicted a Japanese victory and prepared a draft radio announcement of the triumph for release on November 3 to coincide with National Foundation Day (*Meiji setsu*). ULTRA had already alerted the Americans to the mistaken estimates that were driving Japanese planning. One decryption recorded the boast of the vice chief of the Army General Staff, Lieutenant General Hata Hikosaburo, "that army and navy units had inflicted tremendous losses on the enemy in both day and night attacks." Intelligence analysts in MacArthur's headquarters commented that the "continued emphasis" on exaggerated U.S. naval losses "suggests that the Japs themselves believe that a major portion of the U.S. fleet is inoperative. This may, to a certain extent, explain the bold Jap surface action in the Philippine Island area at the present time" (*October 25;* October 25/26).[34] The assessment hit the mark but did not alter interpretations that the campaign on Leyte was all but finished.

Indeed, the continuing exaggerated battle claims convinced the commander-in-chief of the Combined Fleet, Admiral Toyoda, to reinforce Leyte. On October 27 he ordered a joint air and sea effort to transport the 1st and 26th divisions with the 68th Brigade to Leyte. He also strengthened the Southwest Area Force, designated it the controlling headquarters for the reinforcement effort, and ordered joint air elements to cover troop convoys in an operation code-named "TA" (many). The first convoy of four armed attack transports lifted the 1st

Division to Leyte. It was soon followed by three high-speed navy transports bringing advance units of the 26th Infantry Division.[35] The 1st Division's entire move from Manchuria to Ormoc Bay passed unnoticed by American codebreakers (November 7/8). Kenney's pilots, unaware of the approaching convoy, were busy attacking Japanese air bases in the central Philippines. Besides the absence of ULTRA warnings, Japanese radio deception decoyed American pilots away from the convoy.

Identifying itself as B-24 reconnaissance aircraft, the 1st Combined Signal Unit in Manila had broadcast a plain-text message in English that reported a nonexistent Japanese fleet steaming westerly toward Leyte. About one hour after the broadcast, U.S. Navy intercept operators reported that "US plain language reports of sighting of 2 BB [battleships], 3 CA [cruisers], and 8 DD [destroyers] broadcast by Nips" (**November 1**). Halsey's Third Fleet also heard reports of a large Japanese fleet approaching Leyte. Although skeptical, Halsey repositioned his forces and searched in vain for the alleged task force. With Halsey's carrier planes gone and MacArthur's air force elsewhere, the 1st Division shuttled ashore at Ormoc.[36] They unloaded most of their troops in darkness; afterward, a transport headed for Cebu where it picked up General Suzuki and his staff and promptly returned with them to Ormoc the next day.

A shipping engineer battalion at Ormoc was alloted twenty-four hours to unload the ships' cargoes, and the men were still working at dawn on November 2 when thirty-three P-38s, operating from Tacloban, peeled off in intermittent attacks that lasted through the morning. B-24s, flying from Morotai, also bombed Japanese shipping in Ormoc Bay. Coastal defense vessels and destroyers laid smoke screens and added their antiaircraft fire to the barrage put up by the eighteen antiaircraft guns and eighteen antiaircraft machine guns on the four attack transports. Japanese luck expired just after 3:00 P.M. when a stick of bombs exploded on and sank the *Noto* Maru, which was discharging its final crates of ammunition. In spite of the fury that accompanied nine hours of air strikes, the attack transports had offloaded at least 95 percent of the 1st Division and its provisions.[37]

General Krueger later estimated that "this unit, more than any other hostile unit on Leyte, was responsible for the extension of the Leyte Operation."[38] Given the importance he attached to the arrival of the 1st Division on Leyte and the criticism his generalship during the campaign has received from recent scholarship, it is worth reviewing the intelligence available to Krueger when he decided to protect the Carigara beaches instead of moving inland to seize the high ground dominating the bay.[39] On October 31 MacArthur's headquarters still insisted that the Japanese were evacuating Leyte (October 31/November 1). On November 1 Seventh Fleet radio intercept operators monitoring Japanese navy radio frequencies overheard static-filled references to a TA convoy but could make little sense of the broken exchanges. Later decryptions of messages broadcast between ships in the convoy disclosed that the commander of Thirty-Fifth Army was aboard Transport Number 9 and "had requested an immediate report on Ormoc (word missing) and the enemy situation" (**November 1**). If the Japanese were fleeing Leyte, why was an army commander arriving there?

Another Seventh Fleet decryption of a message dated October 29 from the vice chief of staff, Tokyo, stated: "Our reinforcements landed at Ormoc on the morning of 26 October." Filipino guerrillas also told of many Japanese at Ormoc. An identification tag stripped off a corpse by American soldiers established that the 30th Infantry Division was on Leyte. ULTRA confirmed that two special transports had arrived at Ormoc on the afternoon of November 1 and more were scheduled to arrive the next morning (November 1/2).

With fragments supplied by ULTRA and other sources of intelligence, the Americans were beginning to realize the scope of the Japanese reinforcement effort. Willoughby acknowledged that "the Jap evidently is determined to get in sufficient reinforcements to hold strongly on his last line in the Carigara-Ormoc sector" (November 1/2). General Suzuki's arrival lent credence to the importance of Leyte for the Japanese (November 2/3). There were reports that the 1st Division was ashore, which, if true, further underlined Japanese determination to hold Leyte. In the absence of any ULTRA about the 1st Division, however, analysts believed that it was still in Manchuria. The intelligence gap influenced controversial command decisions because ULTRA had provided no advance notification of the convoy carrying the 1st Division, none about its cargoes, and little about the Japanese at Ormoc.

ULTRA, aircraft sightings, and guerrilla reports all revealed that some Japanese reinforcements had reached Leyte. Sixth Army, following Willoughby's early lead, believed that the Japanese were withdrawing from Leyte, because otherwise "it is inconceivable that he would not have defended the Carigara area." The "hopeless tactical situation" of the Japanese meant that "the curtain is about to fall" on the Leyte operation (October 29/30).[40] This estimate of the enemy situation remained viable for Krueger until October 31 when disturbing intelligence reached him that portended massive Japanese reinforcements.

Guerrilla bands reported columns of troops and vehicles moving to the ports on Mindanao, possibly to board ships to reinforce Leyte. On November 1, MacArthur radioed Krueger that three Japanese divisions, an estimated forty-five thousand men, were bound for Manila. There were numerous aircraft sightings of the TA convoy's ships in Ormoc Bay, and P-38 pilots reported bumper-to-bumper truck traffic moving north along Highway 2 in the Ormoc corridor. The next day, the XXIV Corps forwarded to Sixth Army a captured order revealing that the entire Japanese 1st Division had landed on Leyte on November 1 and that a "grand offensive" would commence about mid-November. Viewed from Sixth Army Headquarters, the military situation had changed dramatically within a few days.

Instead of a mop-up operation, Krueger might be facing a fresh division ashore on Leyte. No one was exactly sure of the intentions of these three divisions headed for Manila, but Krueger had to consider the threat of Japanese pincers closing on him from the north (Luzon) and the south (Mindanao).[41] Was Sixth Army marching into a well-laid Japanese trap?

Krueger could not turn to ULTRA for confirmation of the 1st Division's deployment. But if the captured documents were authentic, conceivably other Japanese units, crowded into packed transports, had made it ashore undetected by ULTRA. As early as September 20, White had outlined such a reinforcement scenario in his earliest estimate of the Japanese response to MacArthur's landing on Leyte.[42]

Krueger confronted a difficult tactical decision. Bad weather and aircraft losses had deprived Sixth Army of air superiority at a time when ULTRA warned him to expect massed Japanese air attacks against Leyte. Daily torrents of rain left his forward units of the 24th Division at the wrong end of a washed-out, shell-cratered mud track looking up at the ridges and cone-shaped heights over Carigara Bay. Resupply was a torturous ordeal. Retreating Japanese troops had burned or destroyed all five bridges along the coast, and GIs had to lug food and ammunition through calf-deep mud and jungle thickets. Twelve days of combat had taken a toll of dead and wounded. Krueger's earlier requests for additional men and trained replacements had been denied, and, by early November, Sixth Army was about twelve thousand officers and men short of authorized strength.[43]

Reports of Japanese fleet and air units concentrating within easy range of Leyte were also unsettling. Sixth Army intelligence officers looked apprehensively at the possibility of an enemy landing behind Sixth Army's lines at Carigara Bay. On November 4 White handed Krueger a lengthy estimate which argued that the withdrawal of the U.S. carrier fleet and the shortage of American air bases on Leyte presented the Japanese with "a golden opportunity" to land at Carigara, outflank U.S. troops advancing into the Ormoc valley, and split Sixth Army in two.[44] Soon afterward Krueger halted the X Corps' advance south against Ormoc and ordered it to face north to defend Carigara Bay. The order made no sense to the infantrymen, who had been advancing quickly against little Japanese opposition. As late as 6 P.M. on November 4, the X Corps, whose 1st Cavalry and 24th Infantry divisions were about to collide with the Japanese 1st Division, reported, "Present Order of Battle evidence does not warrant assumption of presence of the 1st Division from Manchuria or an equivalent division as reinforcements recently landed."[45]

No single intelligence revelation determined Krueger's operational decision. He weighed available intelligence and the careful analysis of his veteran G-2 to determine the battle's course. Without ULTRA's confirmation of the other sources, the Japanese remained a shadowy force capable of attacking anywhere. Krueger made the prudent decision, but it gave the Japanese 1st Division time to dig in on the heights overlooking Carigara Bay and thereby extend the campaign. Vicious fighting for control of the ridges had uncovered the fresh Japanese divisions. Now it became a question of how many troops the Japanese would throw into the fight.

If ULTRA had noticed the 1st Division in transit to Ormoc, would Krueger have acted differently and seized the high ground? Knowing that he faced a crack division, he probably would have fought the campaign the same way. His generalship was but a single ingredient in a mixture of reactions that shaped his command decision. The mind-set at Krueger's headquarters never ruled out a Japanese amphibious attack against Sixth Army's rear. As late as November 8, Colonel White was wondering if "strong indications" (read ULTRA) of forthcoming Japanese troop movements meant that the long-awaited enemy landing at Carigara Bay was at hand.[46] Combine this enduring concern about being outflanked with the bad weather, rough terrain, rapidly shifting air-land-sea battles, limited resources, and shortage of U.S. combat troops and the complexity of Krueger's decision becomes apparent. It was probably correct, but Krueger's delay did extend the grueling campaign. Any time before November 5, American troops might have occupied the high ground without meeting serious Japanese resistance. According to the authoritative Japanese account of the action, they were most vulnerable between November 4 and 5 when the fresh 57th Infantry, 1st Division, replaced the terribly injured 34th Infantry, 16th Division. Krueger's hesitation did allow the tough 1st Division the time it needed to dig in on the ridge overlooking Carigara Bay.[47]

Within forty-eight hours the entire complexion of the battle had changed. By November 6 the War Department had confirmed Japanese reinforcements on Leyte and Samar with ULTRA gleaned from decrypting the weekly intelligence circular dispatched to Japanese military attachés. Vice Chief of Staff Hata had notified attachés that the 1st Division, five battalions of the 102d Division, and more than two battalions of the 30th Division had reinforced the 16th Division on Leyte (*November 6*). Because the three-digit regimental cipher remained unbreakable, ULTRA said little about specific Japanese tactical dispositions in the jungled hills. Instead, weekly military attaché circulars, deciphered in Washington, were a major source of intelligence about the general dispositions of Japanese troops on Leyte.

It is true that at the tactical level, this type of ULTRA "was of little value to the Sixth Army directly." Yet it did more than give some indication of Japanese morale.[48] ULTRA announced that a Japanese convoy had arrived at Ormoc on November 9 and disembarked what was later identified in captured documents as a regiment of the 26th Infantry Division (**November 10**; November 10/11). The regiment's arrival showed "the Jap's determination" to turn Leyte into the decisive battle of the war (November 15/16). ULTRA confirmed that the advance units of the

26th Division were holding the high ground in front of the U.S. 96th Infantry Division (November 13). Southwest Pacific Headquarters tallied five Japanese divisions on Leyte—the 16th, 1st, and 26th, as well as units of the 30th and 102d—and ULTRA gave Krueger their approximate locations along Breakneck Ridge (*November 14*). Later decryptions told of the 1st Division suffering three hundred dead, including sixteen officers; of Filipino guerrillas harassing Japanese supply trains with good effect; of the 26th Division shifting its location about 20 miles; and of three divisions defending the hills opposite Carigara Bay (November 15). ULTRA did not, however, forewarn MacArthur of the enemy counterattack that commenced in mid-November. Once the attacks began, ULTRA did uncover the tactical objectives of the Japanese regiments involved in the fighting (*November 18*), and it showed the confusion in Yamashita's headquarters about the fate of several major units on Leyte (November 18). Decryptions told of Japanese units cut off from supplies and provisions; of heavy equipment lost in ship sinkings or American bombings; and of casualty returns (November 19). It was of more than morale value for Sixth Army Headquarters to know the general positions of the 1st Division and that the 16th Division had lost almost all its officers in combat (*November 20*).

ULTRA derived from Fourteenth Area Army situation reports let MacArthur and Krueger read over Yamashita's shoulder as the Japanese commander assessed the course of battle. Southern Army's radio messages were also broken. MacArthur knew, for example, that Field Marshal Terauchi regarded the landing of the U.S. 77th Division at Ormoc on December 7 as a prelude to an invasion of Luzon. At the moment Terauchi was not overly concerned about such an eventuality, but he conceded that an invasion became increasingly likely after the new year (December 14). Yamashita considered the American landings on Mindoro on December 15 as ending the Leyte campaign (December 20). A later Fourteenth Area Army situation report acknowledged that the "U.S. has attained its main objective in the Leyte operations" and that an attack against Luzon was imminent (December 21).

As good as ULTRA was on Leyte, it alone could not decide the outcome of the battle. The ruthless attacks and counterattacks along Breakneck Ridge were bitter testimony to the limits of intelligence. Knowledge from ULTRA was invaluable when planning operations. However, executing the plan was another dimension of warfare. Like every other campaign, American GIs paid in sweat, pain, and blood to reap the harvest that intelligence had sown. The terrible fighting along Breakneck Ridge pushed soldiers of both armies to their limits.

The sky was black with pouring rain, and Japanese infantrymen could not see 10 feet in front at trails that were quickly obliterated. At 7:00 A.M. on November 8, in a typhoon, twelve hundred American riflemen from the 2d Battalion, 21st Infantry, assaulted Breakneck Ridge, hoping to conceal themselves behind the curtain of rain until they broke into Japanese lines. Troops from the 1st Division had converted the innumerable wooded pockets into forts that protected the rocky hills covered with grass 2 to 5 feet high. At first the GIs overwhelmed and flowed around the outer Japanese strongholds. Mortars drove Japanese out of their emplacements or deeper into spider holes and caves or blew them to pieces. Whenever the rain let up, the Americans used flamethrowers to incinerate the Japanese or to drive them flaming and screaming from their foxholes. Japanese soldiers retaliated by pouring gasoline on the grass and igniting it. Flames whipped by strong gusts of wind careened wildly back and forth, indiscriminately engulfing one side, then the other. Wounded men from both armies had crawled into the tall grass for safety. When the fire ran through them, their shrieks drowned out the clatter of machine guns. Hundreds of birds, demented by the noise and conflagration, flew wildly into the storm to escape the raging hillside. Japanese light-machine-gun teams still dominated the farther, higher ridges. Japanese mortars and artillery crashed down on the Americans. By nightfall the GIs were back at their starting point. It was a day for killing and mayhem but little else. The survivors would try again the next day.[49]

If Lieutenant General Kataoka Tadasu, commander of the 1st Division, enjoyed the same quality of intelligence about his opponents as they had about his forces, the battles on Leyte's ridge might have been even more costly for the GIs. Kataoka received his first accurate news about the fighting when his scouts ran into retreating soldiers from the shattered 16th Division.[50] He had expected to fight at Carigara but learned that the Americans had already overrun the town. Then Kataoka heard artillery firing from the north and, in a manner reminiscent of the eighteenth century, ordered his division to advance toward the sound of the guns. Japanese officers and men marched into the maelstrom to meet their opponents. As one Japanese participant recalled: "The 3d Battalion's headquarters, two infantry companies, and a machine gun company took the lead when we pursued the enemy. By that time it was pitch dark and you couldn't see your hand in front of your face. The pointmen halted at a curve in the road. The battalion commander came forward and asked them, 'What's going on?' Then we all moved forward. Enemy machine guns hit us head on, bowling men over like tenpins. The battalion commander was among the first killed."[51]

Another significant contribution of ULTRA was the advance notice it supplied to MacArthur and the U.S. Navy about the schedules of Japanese resupply convoys bound for Leyte. ULTRA detected that two convoys were scheduled to depart Manila for Ormoc on November 7. Broken codes listed the number of transports in each convoy, arrival and departure schedules, and air and surface escorts. ULTRA tracked both convoys as they converged on Ormoc Bay. At Ormoc, Allied bombs and a typhoon had wrecked the main pier so stevedores were resorting to small coastal defense vessels and navy transports to shuttle seven thousand troops ashore in the early morning darkness of November 10. Few luggers, high waves, and pitch darkness slowed the ship-to-shore unloading. As dawn approached, the veteran convoy commander ordered his ships to leave because it was suicidal to remain anchored in broad daylight as stationary targets for Allied warplanes.

On their way out of Ormoc Bay, the transports were attacked at low level by thirty B-25s. In a vicious melee, the B-25s sank one attack transport with all hands and set fire to another, which also sank, although most of its crew was rescued. In exchange, Japanese gunners shot down five of the eight B-25s in the first wave. Antiaircraft then sent two more B-25s and four P-38s plunging into the bay.[52] Naval intercept operators in Hawaii copied the Japanese version of the fighting: "Blank battle action ceased. Results: Shot down 10 large blank enemy planes. Damaged received: TAKATSU Maru sunk. CDV # 13 damaged by bomb and disabled. KA blank [*shii*] Maru (hit by bomb?) blanks" (**November 9**). In the confusion following the attacks, the surviving ships slipped safely out of the smoking bay. Shortly after noon, they passed the second convoy plowing along at 6.5 knots.

This convoy was carrying the main force of the 26th Division to Ormoc and its destruction. On the afternoon of November 10, a young intelligence officer passed Kenney a summary of the convoy's progress toward Leyte. Kenney walked across the street to MacArthur's office and asked him to request that Admiral Halsey "handle the new threat." Acting on MacArthur's plea, Halsey ordered Rear Admiral Frederick Sherman, in temporary command of Task Force 38, to cancel refueling, reverse course, and proceed west to attack the transports. Sherman reached his search position shortly after dawn on November 11 and launched reconnaissance aircraft to the area where ULTRA had told him the convoy route would cross.

The next morning, under fair skies, Sherman's air patrols pinpointed the slow-moving convoy. Then 347 aircraft launched from thirteen U.S. Navy carriers pounced on the hapless Japanese ships, sinking or damaging them and their vitally needed cargoes of replacements and ammunition. Two heavily damaged transports beached and managed to get about 2,700 troops ashore, but at the expense of their equipment. Four other ancient converted cargo or merchant ships, carrying 3,200 troops, went down forever. Only 300 survivors managed to swim to shore. The convoy commander was lost with his flagship, one of four destroyers sunk.[53] Six days later, ULTRA revealed the Japanese foreign minister's personal confirmation that five transports had been sunk with great loss of equipment and that the escorts had also suffered severe damage (*November 17*). Like the 1st Division, the 26th was a top-notch fighting force. Unlike the 1st, it never had the opportunity to deploy its full combat strength on Leyte because ULTRA revelations enabled the Americans to destroy much of its equipment and kill many of its veteran soldiers at sea. If the entire 26th Division had reached Leyte unimpeded, it likely would have extended the fighting long enough to retard, and possibly preclude, MacArthur's cherished invasion of Luzon.

As Allied air power smashed Japanese ships at Ormoc, American submarines tore at the throat of the Japanese transport fleet. ULTRA laid its now-familiar ambush for still another Japanese convoy—this one far from the Philippines. Faced with the growing number of U.S. ground troops on Leyte, Southern Army requested Imperial Headquarters to transfer the 23d Infantry Division from Manchuria to the Philippines. Tokyo concurred, so the 23d Division proceeded to Pusan, Korea, where, designated as Convoy HI 81, it was to embark in early November for the archipelago.

On November 8, Hawaii broadcast to all submarines that the 21,000-ton escort carrier *Jinyo* was about to depart on the HI 81 convoy run. Subsequent ULTRA, particularly four decryptions on November 14, kept track of the latest changes in HI 81's schedule (**November 15, 17**). Armed with these revelations, two U.S. wolf packs were waiting for the convoy as it emerged from the northern end of the East China Sea.[54] On November 15, the USS *Queenfish* torpedoed and sank the *Akitsu Maru*, which carried more than twenty-three hundred members of two infantry battalions and an artillery battalion to their watery graves. Early in the morning of November 18, the *Mayasan* Maru fell victim to *Picuda*, while *Spadefish* sank the *Jinyo* and submarine chaser SC 156. *Mayasan* Maru carried divisional headquarters and two battalions of the 72d Infantry Regiment, 23d Division. Only nine hundred of nearly twenty-three hundred troops were rescued from the sea that night. The division commander and five staff officers survived, but the remainder of the headquarters unit perished.[55]

This disaster, following news of the Ormoc convoy debacles, shocked Southern Army sufficiently for Terauchi to ask that Tokyo suspend the reinforcement effort to Leyte and brace for the defense of Luzon. Imperial Headquarters dismissed his recommendation because they accepted at face value the optimistic assessments of Tokyo staff officers who had just returned from inspection visits to Leyte. A single-minded insistence on reinforcing Leyte doomed more men and supplies to the ocean depths.

By November 17, radio traffic patterns of Army Water Transport Code messages to and from Ormoc forecast that another convoy would arrive there around November 25 (**November 17**). Notified well in advance by traffic analysis and extensive ULTRA, U.S. planes bombed and sank five transports headed for Ormoc.[56] After a two-ship convoy made it safely to Ormoc in late November, Tokyo ordered more convoys. ULTRA again betrayed the ships.

On December 4, naval intercept operators in Hawaii overheard references to a five-ship convoy scheduled to depart from Luzon the next day and arrive at Ormoc three days later (**December 4**). ULTRA detailed the convoy's composition (December 5/6) and further identified the cargo of the four marus as four thousand troops of the 68th Infantry Brigade (December 7/8). Another ULTRA decryption foretold that the convoy was scheduled to enter Ormoc Bay during the late afternoon of December 7, the scheduled date of the U.S. 77th Infantry Division's landing south of Ormoc. Shortly after 8:00 A.M., Rear Admiral A. D. Struble, commander of Amphibious Group 9, which was transporting the 77th to Ormoc Bay, received word of the approaching Japanese convoy. He called on the land-based planes to stop it.[57] Within ninety minutes the first aerial attacks began. The twelve Marine F4U Corsairs inflicted no damage on the convoy, but they lost three aircraft to enemy fire. That afternoon, one hundred fifty U.S. Army and Marine fighter-bombers overwhelmed the ships' antiaircraft defenses as stevedores unloaded the men and equipment of the 68th Brigade. A few troops, two artillery pieces, and some ordnance did get ashore, although the price was three hundred fifty more Japanese casualties. All the cargo ships were lost.

The final Ormoc resupply effort involved a total of eleven ships—six transports, three destroyers, and two submarine chasers. The cargo was the 5th Infantry Regiment, 8th Division (about four thousand men), 850 tons of military stores, and 1,400 tons of rations. A four-hundred-man Naval Special Landing Force with ten tanks was loaded onto two smaller transports. Although ULTRA exposed the impending convoy to the Americans, intelligence analysts reasoned that the 77th's landing at Ormoc would end Japanese seaborne resupply efforts (*December 8, 10, 11;* December 8/9). The Japanese, as usual, did not act predictably.

Within hours of the convoy's departure from Manila, ULTRA had recovered its schedule, a noon position report, and the ships' scheduled arrival on December 11 at Ormoc (**December 9**). The morning of November 11, Marine aircraft bombed and strafed the Japanese transports without visible success. Five hours later, nearly fifty U.S. Marine and Army warplanes sank one transport and left another burning in the water. The convoy commander ordered the surviving vessels to disperse. The two smaller transports, carrying the naval troops and tanks, managed to get most of the men and equipment ashore on December 12. Hawaii monitored Japanese reports of artillery fire from the 77th Division's guns exploding on one vessel while the other withdrew (**November 12**). In this case, ULTRA alerts cost the Japanese three more precious transports and one destroyer in order to land only four hundred soldiers.

Southern Army and Imperial Headquarters still insisted that Leyte had to be reinforced no matter what the losses. But the initiative rested with neither Tokyo nor Manila. When Japanese naval intelligence reported an American task force moving toward southern Luzon on December 14 (this was the Mindoro invasion force), the high command had to shift reinforcements intended for Leyte to the defense of Luzon. The special radio network that had served, and unwittingly betrayed, so many convoys fell silent.

Their overall reinforcement effort in the Philippines cost the Japanese forty-six merchantmen and attack transports sunk and thousands of men lost. The numerous attempts to land reinforcements at Ormoc sacrificed twenty-four ships and about 130,000 tons of shipping.[58] One light cruiser, seven destroyers, three submarine chasers, and two coastal defense vessels went to the bottom. Exact personnel losses will never be known. Approximately 38,000 Japanese reinforcements embarked for Ormoc, but at least 3,250 perished in the seas. As significant, the Allied interdiction campaign, dependent in great measure on ULTRA for pinpointing convoy routes, destroyed thousands of tons of invaluable ammunition, ordnance, rations, medical supplies, and the like before the transports even arrived at the fighting front. What would the outcome have been if all the Japanese reinforcements and their equipment had reached ashore as easily as the 1st Division? In the end, the dogged Japanese infantry would have been beaten, but only after a much longer campaign and at a much higher cost in Allied lives.

MacArthur's and Nimitz's forces had delivered crushing blows at Leyte to Japanese naval and air forces. Japan's lifeline to resource-rich Southeast Asia had been severed. Imperial Headquarters and Southern Army's determination to force a decisive ground battle on Leyte had destroyed more than five Japanese divisions. Leyte was a graveyard of Japanese hopes. It was also a great Allied victory and one achieved at proportionately low cost—15,500 army and 2,500 naval battle casualties.[59] If the Joint Chiefs' intention was to win the war against Japan quickly (which few doubted was possible) and with minimum casualties (which many doubted was possible), Leyte was a tremendous success in which ULTRA had a starring role.

MacArthur's staff put together the Leyte operation on short notice and accepted the risks that ULTRA revealed in order to telescope the general's operations from December to October and thereby gain two months in his race to liberate the Philippines. The tendency reappeared to downplay ULTRA evidence not in accord with strategic preconceptions. This was the case when MacArthur's staff made the decision to invade Leyte despite ULTRA knowledge of air, naval, and ground reinforcements flooding into the Philippines.

Before Leyte, MacArthur's staff had expected the Japanese to fight for the island, but the concentration of Japanese forces on Luzon, confirmed by ULTRA, augured that that was where they intended to make their stand. In mid-October 1944, neither MacArthur nor Yamashita foresaw Leyte as the decisive battleground of the Pacific war. The Japanese high command, operating on woefully bad intelligence, gambled all at Leyte and lost. The American high command, acting on very good intelligence, took a well-calculated risk and won. Throughout the fighting on Leyte, ULTRA's timely updates of the Japanese condition exposed the Imperial Army's intentions and weaknesses. Without ULTRA, American GIs would have had to root out five well-concealed, well-equipped, and well-supplied Japanese infantry divisions. The killing would have rivaled the scale of bloodletting on Okinawa or Iwo Jima. To ignore that fact overlooks ULTRA's contribution at Leyte.

7
The Numbers Game: Luzon, January–June 1945

Luzon is the largest of the Philippine Islands and in 1944 held about 8 million of the archipelago's 18 million people. Its largest city is Manila, capital of the Philippines, whose liberation from Japanese control drove MacArthur's strategy. Although Fleet Admiral Ernest J. King had stubbornly insisted throughout September that Formosa, not Luzon, must be the next Pacific objective, a conference with Nimitz convinced him, however reluctantly, that the Formosa route was impracticable. Shortly after, on October 3, 1944, the Joint Chiefs of Staff agreed that Douglas MacArthur would invade Luzon in late December 1944.[1] At this time, Allied cryptanalysts were routinely solving an impressive variety of Japanese codes: the army's mainline, four-digit cipher; several army air force codes; the army water transport system; the military attaché code; the navy's mainline cipher; the naval water transport system; and Foreign Ministry encryptions. Besides these ULTRA sources, MacArthur's staff had numerous, usually uneven, reports of Japanese deployments on Luzon from Filipino guerrillas as well as information from Japanese prisoners of war, captured documents, and aerial reconnaissance. One might expect that this wealth of intelligence data, leavened by years of combat experience, would yield an accurate account of the Japanese forces on Luzon. Yet the estimates of Japanese strength by MacArthur's and Krueger's headquarters differed so widely that one might wonder if they were describing the same thing.

It took longer than anyone originally expected to subdue, if not eradicate, the determined Japanese defenders on Leyte. Dragging out the fighting proved a mixed blessing. The Luzon invasion scheduled for December had to be pushed back, but, on the brighter side, planners believed that Tokyo's decision to fight the decisive engagement on Leyte would make the eventual liberation of Luzon easier. They reasoned that the massive numbers of reinforcements dispatched to Leyte had stripped Yamashita of his best units and disrupted his plans for the defense of

Luzon (December 22/23). Willoughby's estimates supported this assessment. From a high of 158,900 Japanese on Luzon in October 1944, MacArthur's G-2 counted barely 137,000 there at the end of November.[2] ULTRA was the provenance of Japanese reinforcement numbers and the names of combat units, but the divergent interpretations it drew from Southwest Pacific Headquarters, Sixth Army, and the War Department became far more important than the raw data.

A message intercepted in early November, but decrypted twenty days later, mentioned eight Japanese divisions throughout the Philippines. Willoughby identified them as the 8th, 16th, 26th, 30th, 100th, 102d, 103d, and 105th Infantry divisions. It was further known that the 2d Armored Division was on Luzon (December 1/2). Although this latest ULTRA doubled the number of divisions previously mentioned in a German report from Tokyo to Berlin in late October, it did not cause great concern. Willoughby accounted for the discrepancy by noting that the Germans had overlooked the four "100 series" divisions that had recently been converted from independent mixed brigades. He was in general agreement with War Department analysts who calculated that 239,000 Japanese, organized in eight or nine divisions, defended the entire Philippines. This figure included at least 34,000 army air force and 15,000 naval support troops (*November 4*). Washington later added another division and, after subtracting 25,000 Japanese casualties on Leyte, arrived at a total of 243,000 enemy troops throughout the archipelago (*November 9*).

The fighting on Leyte siphoned off the 1st and 26th divisions, which left two, perhaps three, infantry divisions, stiffened by an armored division, in northern Luzon where MacArthur intended to land. Elsewhere on Luzon, Yamashita had an estimated 30,000 to 40,000 combat soldiers supported by 15,000 more base defense or supply troops north of Manila. Another 40,000 to 50,000 combat troops backed by 20,000 to 25,000 support troops were scattered over the rest of the island. According to non-ULTRA sources made available for initial campaign planning purposes, somewhere between 115,000 and 140,000 soldiers and sailors guarded Luzon.[3] At this time, ULTRA specified at least four infantry divisions—the 8th, 103d, 105th, and one unidentified—along with the 2d Armored Division and a total of 158,500 Japanese (88,000 combat troops) on Luzon (November 21/22). The one-division ULTRA discrepancy was minor compared with the wide variance between MacArthur's and Krueger's headquarters over the number of Japanese defending Luzon.

Sixth Army's G-2, Colonel White, emphatically disagreed with both sets of numbers Willoughby offered. White insisted that a minimum of 234,500 Japanese were deployed throughout Luzon, of whom 107,000 were mobile combat and 127,500 support troops. His analysis was disarmingly simple. Ample reports from guerrillas regarding Japanese army activity on Luzon convinced White that enemy strength was far in excess of that identified by ULTRA. Because the Japanese had transported the 1st and 8th Infantry divisions as well as the 2d Armored Division undetected all the way from Manchuria to the Philippines, a prudent assumption was that additional Japanese formations might have reached Luzon cloaked in secrecy. White also believed that the Japanese had doubled the size of their independent mixed brigades to about 8,000 men, with a corresponding influx of additional combat reinforcements to flesh out the units. Deductions and assumptions led him to a conservative estimate of 51,000 combat troops guarding central Luzon alone. He then computed the number of support troops by multiplying each fighting soldier by a factor of 1.5 to arrive at 76,500 base and service troops, or a total of 127,500 men. White counted 30,000 troops in the rugged hills of northeastern Luzon divided equally between combat and support elements. Near Manila and points south, perhaps 77,000 Japanese soldiers were available, including 41,000 combat troops. White's figures essentially matched those of the War Department and were much closer to the actual Japanese strength than Willoughby's numbers. Southwest Pacific Headquarters' and Sixth Army's estimates of Japanese strength and the actual number of troops on Luzon are shown in Table 7.1.

Reconstructing the intelligence process in chronological fashion shows that the analysis and interpretation of data, not the data themselves, were the crux of the numerical disparity. As of December 1, 1944, ULTRA confirmed at least 153,500 Japanese on Luzon. This figure was down slightly from the November 4 estimate because ULTRA made known that Luzon-based units had been dispatched to the Leyte battleground (November 30/December 1) (see Table 7.2).

ULTRA next uncovered the 58th Independent Mixed Brigade on Luzon and hinted that the 12th Division might be moving from Manchuria to Luzon. Broken water transport messages passed the news that replacements for the 26th Division were on the way to the Philippines from Japan via Formosa (December 7/8). Claims by a Japanese prisoner of war that the 10th Division was in Manila were

Table 7.1. SWPA, G-2, and Sixth Army, G-2, Estimated Japanese Ground Order of Battle, Luzon, Compared with Actual Japanese Strength, December 1944

Area	Willoughby (November 30)	White (December 5)	Actual
Northern Luzon	33,000	30,000	30,000
Central Luzon	68,000	127,500	122,000
Southern Luzon	36,000	77,000	115,000
Total	137,000	234,500	267,000

Source: Headquarters Sixth Army, Office of the Assistant Chief of Staff, G-2, "G-2 Estimate of the Enemy Situation with Respect to 'MIKE ONE' [Luzon] Operation as of 5 December 1944." The figures in the "Actual" column are derived from Maeda Toru and Kuwada Etsu, eds., *Nihon no senso—zukai to deeta* (Tokyo: Hara shobo, 1982), plate 59.

Table 7.2. SWPA, G-2, Estimated Japanese Ground Order of Battle,
Luzon, December 1, 1944

Unit	Strength	Location
105th Division	5,000	Bicol Peninsula[a]
Base and support troops	5,000	Bicol Peninsula
Fourteenth Area Army Headquarters	500	Manila
12th Expeditionary Unit	4,000	Manila
82d Brigade	5,000	Manila
1st Field Replacement Unit	4,000	Manila
Naval troops	5,000	Manila
Base and support troops	18,000	Manila
8th Division	16,000	Batangas
Unidentified Independent Mixed Brigade	4,000	Batangas
Naval troops	1,000	Batangas
Unidentified division	16,000	Central Luzon
2d Armored Division	11,000	Central Luzon
Independent Mixed Brigade(?)	4,000	Central Luzon
Base and support troops	14,000	Central Luzon
103d Division	10,000	Northern Luzon
Base and support troops	10,000	Northern Luzon
Unidentified troops	13,000	Northern Luzon
Total	145,500	

[a]The Bicol Peninsula is the southernmost peninsula on Luzon Island.

Source: SWPA, Special Intelligence Bulletin, 30 November/1 December 1944, MacArthur Memorial
Bureau of Archives, Norfolk, Virginia.

accompanied with confirmation, courtesy of a decrypted message address, that the
2d Armored Division was bivouacked at San Miguel, Luzon (*December 10*;
December 11/12). When Filipino guerrillas first reported this powerful mobile
force in early November, ULTRA had been unable to confirm their statements.
Because armored divisions were found in faraway Manchuria and Japan, only on
rare occasions did intercept operators overhear their radio transmissions. For this
reason, the most recent ULTRA about any Japanese armored division dated from
July 27, 1944 (*November 4*; November 10/11). Meanwhile, War Department intelligence officers positively identified three infantry divisions, one armored division, and two independent mixed brigades on Luzon and predicted more units were
on the way (*December 9*). From water transport shipping messages dispatched
from Pusan, Korea, Central Bureau codebreakers discovered the loading lists of
the 23d Division's equipment destined for Manila and predicted that the division
would soon follow (December 12/13). By mid-December Willoughby wrote of the
large-scale ground reinforcement under way for Luzon that involved the 10th,

Table 7.3. SWPA, G-2, Estimated Japanese Ground Order of Battle, Luzon, December 15, 1944

Unit	Strength	Losses	Balance	Actual
103d Division	10,000	—	10,000	103d Division
105th Division	10,000	—	10,000	105th Division
2d Armored Division	11,000	—	11,000	2d Armored Division
8th Division	16,000	—	16,000	8th Division
58th Independent Mixed Brigade	4,000	—	4,000	58th Independent Mixed Brigade
61st Independent Mixed Brigade	4,000	—	4,000	61st Independent Mixed Brigade
12th Expeditionary Unit	4,000	—	4,000	19th Division
Naval troops	6,000	—	6,000	—
Headquarters, 1st FRU[a]	4,000	—	4,000	10th Division (–)
Unidentified division	16,000	—	16,000	23d Division
Total Combat	85,000	—	85,000	155,000
Base/service/air units	66,400	15,000	51,400	132,000
Total	151,400	15,000	136,400	287,000

[a]Base and service units that maintain aircraft and airfields.

Source: SWPA estimate: "SWPA G-2 Staff Study, Japanese Defensive Organization of Luzon," 15 December 1944, MacArthur Memorial Bureau of Archives, Washington, D.C.; Actual: Maeda Toru and Kuwada Etsu, eds., *Nihon no senso—zukai to deeta* (Tokyo: Hara shobo, 1982), plate 59.

23d, and 12th divisions. The only positive news was that the Japanese were gradually conceding air superiority over the Philippines (December 14/15) (see Table 7.3).

ULTRA was not omniscient. In many cases, the Allies knew that a convoy was en route to a given location but remained ignorant of the ships' cargoes. Early in the morning of November 15, for instance, the Convoy HI 81 fell victim to American submarines. Decoded army water transport messages made it plain to Central Bureau that one ship had been torpedoed and sunk and another one hit hard and badly damaged. Intercept operators also overheard numerous distress calls, broadcast in the clear, to rescue "many troops from the first vessel." Nowhere, however, did the radio messages state that this convoy was carrying the 64th and 72d Infantry regiments, 23d Division, to Luzon. Allied cryptanalysts remained ignorant that the division had lost one artillery and four infantry battalions as well as the division headquarters in the dark waters (November 17/18).[4] Similarly, ULTRA announced that a torpedoed Japanese transport had exploded off northern Luzon on December 23. No one realized that the *Ken'zui* Maru, a 4,156-ton cargo vessel, had carried three infantry battalions of the 10th Division to the bottom with it (December 25/26).[5] As a consequence, ULTRA available in early January implied that the entire 10th Division had moved safely to Luzon and was about 50 miles southeast of Lingayen Gulf where traffic analysis and direction finding had located its headquarters (*January 6*). ULTRA failed to detect the movement of the 19th Division from Korea to Luzon until three days after MacArthur's invasion of Luzon when radio transmissions from San Fernando in northern Luzon betrayed its presence (*January 11*). Only then did cryptanalysts review stacks of earlier, as yet undecoded intercepts to discover a November 13 message which disclosed that two of the 19th Division's regiments were already in transit for Luzon at that time (January 13).

Willoughby adjusted the overall enemy strength figures to account for the increased number of identified Japanese divisions on Luzon, but he did so based on fragmented information. Those gaps appeared in his year-end assessment of Japanese strength (see Table 7.4). Of this total, one tank and two infantry divisions, an independent mixed brigade, and a naval brigade—a maximum of 51,000 to 67,000 combat troops—were believed deployed north of Manila. These units presumably defended Lingayen Gulf, the site MacArthur had selected for his

Table 7.4. SWPA, G-2, Estimated Japanese Ground Order of Battle, Luzon, December 31, 1944

Unit	Strength	Losses	Balance	Actual
103d Division	10,000	—	10,000	103d Division
105th Division	10,000	—	10,000	105th Division
2d Armored Division	11,000	—	11,000	2d Armored Division
8th Division	16,000	—	16,000	8th Division
10th Division	16,000	—	16,000	10th Division (–)
23d Division	16,000	—	16,000	23d Division
12th Division	16,000?	—	16,000	—
58th Independent Mixed Brigade	4,000	—	4,000	58th Independent Mixed Brigade
61st Independent Mixed Brigade	4,000	—	4,000	61st Independent Mixed Brigade
12th Expeditionary Unit	4,000	—	4,000	19th Division
Naval troops	6,000	—	6,000	—
Headquarters, 1st FRU[a]	4,000	—	4,000	—
Corps artillery	4,000	—	4,000	—
Total Combat	121,000	—	121,000	135,000
Base/service/air units	84,800	23,400	61,400	152,000
Total	195,800	23,400	172,400	287,000

[a]Base and service units that maintain aircraft and airfields.
Source: SWPA estimate: SWPA, Military Intelligence Section, "Recapitulation of Luzon Enemy Strength and Dispositions," 31 December 1944, MacArthur Memorial Bureau of Archives, Washington, D.C.; Actual: Maeda Toru and Kuwada Etsu, eds., *Nihon no senso—zukai to deeta* (Tokyo: Hara shobo, 1982), plate 59.

invasion, and guarded the Central Luzon Plain, the main approach route to Manila from the north.

Regardless of the increase in combat troops, Southwest Pacific Headquarters overlooked or underestimated the huge number of Japanese servicemen unattached to identified units or assigned to small independent commands. The 1st Field Replacement Headquarters in Manila, for instance, directly controlled 12,000, not 4,000, men. Another 3,000 troops in various company and platoon formations provided the administrative support for the 1st Field Headquarters, and 2,000 convalescents recuperating in the city were nominally assigned to the headquarters. Where Willoughby counted 4,000 Japanese, there were probably 17,000. About 50,000 sailors were on Luzon, most of them stevedores or port personnel working on the docks, piers, and harbor installations around Manila Bay. Fourth Air Army had 55,000 airmen on the island, almost all of whom were maintenance, construction, or communications personnel: 20,400 at Clark Field, 5,000 in Manila, 10,800 with the 4th Air Division, 6,000 at the massive Manila Air Arsenal, and 3,250 in the 2d Air Communications Group. The 3d Water Transport Command had 30,000 men under its orders ranging from stevedores to three-star generals.[6] Besides major combat formations such as divisions and brigades, there were about 230 separate Imperial Army units on Luzon that ran the gamut from water purification companies to independent armored car companies. These minor units used secure telephone lines to exchange information, pass orders, and conduct routine affairs. When they did resort to radio communications, they transmitted their messages in the impenetrable three-digit code and observed strict radio discipline, which made it difficult even to detect their broadcasts. Although no one expected to pinpoint all the heterogeneous units scattered around the big island, there was a feeling at Sixth Army Headquarters that Willoughby had seriously underestimated the number of Japanese troops on Luzon.

Krueger's chief of staff, Brigadier General Clyde D. Eddleman, carried that message to MacArthur when he briefed him on Sixth Army's plans for the Luzon operation. MacArthur sat relaxed in the conference room with his familiar corncob pipe jutting from his mouth. Willoughby perched warily on the other side of the long table as Eddleman began his briefing with an intelligence summation of White's rationale for counting 234,000 Japanese on Luzon. MacArthur kept impatiently taking his pipe out of his mouth to utter, "Bunk!" Unfazed, Eddleman remarked that MacArthur apparently did not like what he was hearing. "I don't. It's too strong. There aren't that many Japanese there." Eddleman told the general that most of the intelligence came from MacArthur's headquarters. Willoughby shot to his feet, shouting, "Didn't come from me! Didn't come from me!" MacArthur ended the argument probably the same way he had ended the one about Japanese strength in the Admiralties. He ignored intelligence evidence that conflicted with his operational plan. He waved aside the almost 100,000-man discrepancy between Willoughby's and White's estimates to get to the heart of the briefing. Why, he asked, didn't Sixth Army's plan include the capture of Manila? Eddleman replied that after the landing and initial push inland, General Krueger believed he would be in a better position to reassess the Japanese response and determine how best to seize Manila. The briefing concluded, MacArthur drew Eddleman into the bedroom of the spacious two-story stucco house that had formerly served as a Japanese officers' club. He confided to Eddleman that there were only three great intelligence officers in the history of warfare "and mine is not one of them."[7]

Given MacArthur's exceptional talent at playing one general officer in his court against another, perhaps his remark should be left at that. Possibly he told Willoughby ten minutes after Eddleman departed that the Sixth Army intelligence outfit was incompetent. Though accused of many things, MacArthur was never a fool and he was a shrewd judge of men. He surrounded himself with a mixture of talented officers and sycophants. Willoughby, like his stormy disposition, functioned at the margins. He was either impressively accurate—his estimates for the Admiralties and Hollandia operations are cases in point—or he was dismally inaccurate. His "all is well" message on the eve of the Driniumor River attack would have ended the career of most intelligence officers. Perhaps what saved him was his absolute allegiance to his master, who accepted Willoughby's loyalty but never confused it with exceptional competence. In any event, the episode is another example of MacArthur's disregard for intelligence estimates that did not accord with his schemes or self-styled sense of destiny.

Audacity, calculated risk, and a clear strategic aim were MacArthur's attributes. Now so near to his goal of liberating all the Philippines and entering Manila as a conquering hero, he again cast aside counsels of caution. Sutherland had advised delay because by late November the tactical situation had turned sour on Leyte where the protracted fighting had diverted ships carrying troops scheduled to invade Luzon. Kenney had also recommended postponing the operation until he could mass enough planes on Leyte to neutralize the surviving Japanese air power on Luzon. Finally, Kinkaid had argued that Japanese air strength, especially the kamikazes, was such a serious threat to his fleet that it might make a direct assault on Luzon prohibitive.[8] Reminiscent of the western New Guinea campaigns, MacArthur responded to his lieutenants by granting them a two-week delay on the Luzon timetable. At the same time, he agreed to seize Mindoro and its air bases to support the Luzon operation.

ULTRA portrayed Mindoro as lightly defended and without combat units; it confirmed that a maximum of 1,000 Japanese base and supply troops were dispersed around the island (November 30/December 1). Japanese navy and army aircraft on their way to raid Leyte were known to stage through Mindoro's airfields. These newly operational airstrips were located in the southeastern part of the island where the Americans planned to land (December 5/6). ULTRA also monitored the Japanese response to MacArthur's December 15 assault on Mindoro and alerted his headquarters that enemy reconnaissance pilots had correctly reported only four Allied destroyers guarding the invasion transports. Echoing his predictions before the Biak operation, Willoughby warned that if bad weather grounded Allied planes, the 2d Diversion Attack Force might be handed a "golden opportunity" to attack Allied supply ships and shell the Mindoro beachhead (December 18/19). Subsequent ULTRA from a navy message intercepted on December 20 revealed the 2d Diversion Attack Force's intention to fulfill Willoughby's forecast (December 22/23). The so-called REI Operation commenced on December 26 when six Japanese destroyers and two cruisers lunged at the Allied landing area off Mindoro. They lost one destroyer en route to the island and discovered, to their disappointment, only four Allied transports anchored there. After conducting gunfire and torpedo attacks that left one transport on fire, the Japanese rapidly withdrew north. The action was notable as the last time major surface units of the Japanese fleet interfered with Allied shore operations in the Philippines.[9]

During the planning phase of the Mindoro invasion, Willoughby had speculated that the landings would expose Luzon as the next objective on MacArthur's agenda. ULTRA confirmed this when it reported Yamashita's December 17 message notifying his commanders that the Mindoro landings set the stage for an attack against Luzon. He expected the Allies to secure Mindoro within ten days and then strike Luzon. Yamashita's references to "the state of our military preparations" implied his concern that the forlorn reinforcement of Leyte had severely impaired his ability to defend Luzon (December 22/23).

Meanwhile, MacArthur had summoned his doubting commanders to explain why they had to meet the amended target date for the Luzon invasion. With considerable charm and eloquence he argued that while the Allies got stronger, so did the Japanese defenses on Luzon. The time to attack was now, before the Japanese developed their defenses. Concluding with typical rhetorical flourish, MacArthur agreed that his forces were not as fully prepared as they would like to be, but that the largest pot he ever lost in a poker game was when he held four kings in his hand.[10] This was not a commander who vacillated until the next batch of intelligence reports was delivered. He was anxious to liberate Luzon and to retake Manila.

In Manila, Yamashita was ambiguous about defending the city. Colonel Kobayashi Shujiro, Fourteenth Area Army's operations chief, wanted Yamashita to mass Japanese forces south of the city where Kobayashi expected the main American landings. Chief of Staff Muto, more realistic than Kobayashi, conceded that the Japanese could not defeat the Americans after they were ashore on Luzon. The most they could expect to accomplish was to wage a protracted campaign that at least would have the value of tying down American troops, ships, and planes that otherwise could be used against Japan's home islands. By concentrating Fourteenth Area Army's forces in a triangular redoubt in Luzon's rugged northern mountains, Muto argued, Yamashita would have a base from which to wage such a campaign. Kobayashi dismissed these Fabian tactics and insisted that if the American landings succeeded, the enemy would head for Manila. City fighting, street by street, building by building, would pin the Americans in place for Yamashita to roll up the Allies' flanks. Kobayashi dreamed of converting Manila into an oriental Stalingrad, but cooler heads—such as the Southwest Area Fleet commander, Vice Admiral Mikawa—dismissed the analogy. Mikawa dryly observed that Manila's flimsy wooden houses could not be converted into minifortresses like the solid concrete buildings of Stalingrad or Leningrad, and the city's high water table rendered constructing underground fortifications impossible. He saw no reason to bring the war to Filipino civilians and advised Yamashita to abandon the city.[11] On November 1, Mikawa was replaced by Vice Admiral Okawachi Den'shichi, who added his more hawkish views about the defense of Manila and its port to staff counsels. Shortly after, Fourteenth Area Army Headquarters officially decided not to abandon Manila.[12]

When Yamashita decided to divide Fourteenth Area Army into three main battle groups—SHOBU in the north; KEMBU around Clark Field and the Bataan Peninsula; and SHIMBU east of Manila—he did not rule out defending the city. He did announce in mid-December that the triangular grouping of forces meant that Manila would not become a battleground, but unfortunately he did not clarify his meaning of "battleground." As the clock ticked down on Luzon, no consensus on Manila emerged among the Japanese senior staff. No high-ranking army officer openly advocated abandoning the city, but no one except Tominaga urged that Manila be defended to the last man. At any rate, that man would not be Tominaga. A week after the American landings, the Fourth Air Army commander claimed illness and fled to the safety of Formosa aboard one of the few remaining army transport planes.

Although the Naval General Staff was disgruntled about Yamashita's defensive strategy for the Philippines, they did not intend to defend Manila to the last sailor. Privately, they recoiled at the thought of slinking away into the mountains with Yamashita, but they never officially advocated the Götterdämmerung recommended by one disgruntled staff officer. Upon his return to Tokyo from Manila on January 5, 1945, Captain Kami Shigetoku addressed a blunt memorandum to the naval staff that demanded a fight to the death in Manila's buildings and streets. The final act would be to burn the city.[13] Kami's irrationality was symptomatic of the sense of shame and defeat infecting the naval garrison in Manila.

Rear Admiral Iwabuchi Sanji, 31st Special Base Force commander, was responsible for the defense of Manila Bay and his command included the entire naval combat garrison in the city, upward of twenty thousand men. Because the naval

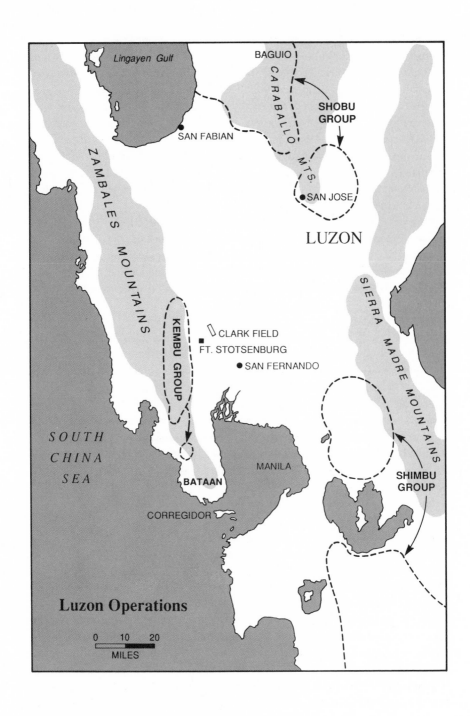

Luzon Operations

0   10   20
MILES

staff regarded the city's defense as an army affair, no one told Iwabuchi about plans for the defense of Manila.[14] Personally, Iwabuchi was a victim of repeated failure. He had captained the battleship *Kirishima*, which had gone down under American guns off Guadalcanal in November 1942. Next he had fought on New Georgia in 1943 and survived that long, terrible campaign. He had no desire to survive another defeat. Army jibes that the navy, as usual, had lost a battle and was running away added to his pent-up fury. Besides, the notion of surrendering Manila without a fight ran contrary to the grain of the military doctrine of the day. Japanese officers never abandoned anything, from a rifle stamped with the Imperial seal to a city. Iwabuchi made up his mind to fight to the death for Manila and his decision sealed the fate of a city.

Of course, ULTRA could not make Iwabuchi's frame of mind known to MacArthur. It did, however, disclose that Southern Army expected the opening Allied invasion of Luzon on the same beaches where the Japanese had landed three years earlier. Terauchi anticipated that airborne and amphibious assaults near Manila would follow shortly after the landings (December 15/16). In a rare instance, ULTRA may have let MacArthur's staff know that Fourteenth Area Army had written off Leyte before Japan's prime minister received the news. Following the Allies' seizure of Mindoro in mid-December, Yamashita had notified his commanders that Leyte might have to be abandoned in order to strengthen Luzon's defenses for the next round against the Americans (December 22/23). Prime Minister Koiso Kuniyaki heard about the shift of the so-called decisive battleground from Leyte to Luzon just before he departed for the palace on December 21 for an imperial audience. The emperor questioned Koiso about the decision, and a badly flustered prime minister stammered that he had just found out about it himself. Hirohito worried aloud that because Koiso had already proclaimed that Leyte was the climactic battle of the Pacific war, the abrupt change to Luzon might damage home-front morale and lower production.[15]

Viewed from MacArthur's headquarters, the overall intelligence picture portrayed the incomplete state of Japanese defenses on Luzon further disrupted by wholesale commitment of reinforcements to Leyte (December 22/23). One day before the Allied task force sailed into Lingayen Gulf, navy ULTRA detected that Yamashita had shifted his headquarters from Manila to Baguio (**January 5**). ULTRA available immediately after the January 9 invasion disclosed that the remaining army headquarters personnel had departed Manila where the headquarters itself had closed at midnight on January 6 (*January 11*). Within a few days, all Japanese army radio stations in Manila had ceased broadcasting and the 31st Naval Communications Unit was overheard moving north out of Manila (**January 14**). The ULTRA-acquired knowledge that Fourteenth Area Army and other important headquarters had evacuated Manila certainly hardened MacArthur's impression that the Japanese never intended to fight for the city.[16] With typical flair, Mac-

Arthur wanted to liberate Manila on January 26, to coincide with his birthday, and was planning a huge victory parade down the city's boulevards. ULTRA did seem to be underwriting his promise to the Joint Chiefs that he could secure the city within six weeks of the landings.

Allied codebreakers knew that Japanese naval intelligence had correctly deduced that an Allied invasion fleet had sailed from the Admiralties and Hollandia for the Philippines (**January 1**). They were aware that their intelligence counterparts had broadcast coded warnings about a new Allied task force on the move toward Luzon (*January 5*). They also understood that the chief of staff of the Southwest Area Fleet believed the Americans would likely land in Lingayen Gulf (**January 4**). After Japanese reconnaissance pilots spotted the huge convoy steaming north off Luzon's western coast, naval units on Taiwan and Luzon were placed on alert (*January 5*) and shortly thereafter launched a series of kamikaze attacks that punished the invasion fleet, ultimately sinking 3 ships and heavily damaging 14 others.[17] On January 6, 58 planes, including 29 kamikazes, struck with deadly accuracy, disrupting the first day of the preliminary bombardment of the Lingayen beach fortifications. The once mighty Fourth Air Army could muster only 108 aircraft, and its one-way attacks spent them quickly. The kamikaze onslaught lasted one week, which was time enough for the army to lose 79 pilots and the navy 77. On the night of the invasion, army suicide boats attacked the landing fleet. Powered by Toyota or Nissan automobile engines, 30 of these 2-man, 18.5-foot-long plywood boats sank 1 landing craft and damaged 8 others, one so severely that it had to be abandoned. Japanese records officially list 46 crewmen killed in the attacks.[18] This latest suicide tactic was an ominous foreshadowing of what potential invaders of Japan itself would face.

While MacArthur waited out the landings, ULTRA allowed him to read Yamashita's estimate of the situation. MacArthur's opponent judged that two or three divisions of Sixth Army would secure bridgeheads on both sides of Lingayen Gulf, with the main landing at San Fabian (*January 9*). The U.S. 43d Division did, in fact, hit the beach at San Fabian. Although Yamashita had predicted the invasion beaches, Krueger's infantrymen met only light Japanese ground resistance when they stormed ashore on January 9. The Japanese commander had never intended to pit his troops in a battle of maneuver on the broad central plain against superior American firepower and mobility. He realized that a set-piece battle along the beachhead would only play into MacArthur's hands and hasten the destruction of Fourteenth Area Army. Rather, Yamashita's forces, hidden in the rugged jungle-covered hills, lay waiting for the Americans to dig them out. Along the hills flanking the central plain on the east, the Tiger of Malaya had aligned about 150,000 troops. Stretching approximately 50 miles from north to south was SHOBU Group, consisting of the 19th Division, 58th Independent Mixed Brigade, 23d Division, 2d Armored Division, and 10th Division (minus). In the western hills near Clark Field was the KEMBU Group (30,000 men), and from Manila to the south and east lay the SHIMBU Group (80,000 men). The extraordinary differences between Willoughby's Southwest Pacific Headquarters' assessment of Japanese strength on Luzon and White's Sixth Army appreciation would now affect the course of the ground campaign.

Three days after Sixth Army's landings, MacArthur summoned Krueger and Eddleman to the cruiser *Boise* for a hurried conference. The Southwest Pacific commander reemphasized that Sixth Army had to take Manila quickly. Krueger was just as adamant that the Japanese on his eastern flank could counterattack his overextended formations at any moment. Besides, White still maintained that the number of Japanese on Luzon far exceeded Willoughby's estimates and further- more predicted that the Japanese would put up a desperate fight for Manila. Krueger said he needed two more divisions before he would charge hell-bent for the capital. The two senior commanders exchanged cross words. MacArthur insisted that Sixth Army had little to fear from the Japanese arrayed to its east and should head for Manila.[19] The conference resolved nothing except that U.S. theater and army commanders disagreed entirely about the size and strength of Yamashita's forces.

The day after the meeting, the War Department confirmed that the 19th Division was on Luzon (*January 13*). Shortly thereafter, a decoding of Foreign Minister Shigemitsu Mamoru's situation report, dated January 13, seemed to support Krueger's deliberate advance. Shigemitsu admitted that no large-scale engage- ments had been fought on Luzon, "although from the beginning we have occupied the hills in the rear and have been looking for a chance to counterattack" (*January 15*). The Japanese army weekly intelligence circular for January 14 waved more caution flags for Sixth Army when it warned Fourteenth Area Army commanders, whose units were attacking the Americans, to be on guard against Allied direct air support of ground units and airborne operations. The decryption declared that the 19th and 23d divisions, in concert with the 58th Independent Mixed Brigade, were already on the offensive near San Fernando. Yamashita was personally concentrat- ing Fourteenth Area Army's legions to crush the enemy (*January 15*).

This fresh evidence from ULTRA did not change Willoughby's verdict. By mid-January he said that at most 103,000 combat and 51,400 support troops, less 15 percent casualties, remained on Luzon. His attrition formula enabled Wil- loughby to factor newly discovered units such as the 19th Division and the 61st Independent Mixed Brigade into his calculations and simultaneously maintain that casualties had whittled overall Japanese strength down to 131,240 men. Like MacArthur, Willoughby believed the Japanese might delay the American libera- tion of Manila but ruled out a last-ditch stand in the city.[20] White asserted just as forcefully that at least 50,000 more Japanese were on Sixth Army's left, or east, flank than Willoughby supposed.[21] As in his earlier campaigns, MacArthur wanted to liberate his main objective (Manila) and proclaim victory in the Luzon campaign. As in the past, he continued to disregard intelligence estimates that did not fit with his operational concept. The Southwest Pacific commander did have sound strategic reasons for insisting that Krueger accelerate his methodical advance to the south, but these did not necessarily apply to rushing to Manila. For instance, Kenney needed Clark Field's airdromes for his expanding air arm, which had already outgrown the stopgap fields cut near Lingayen Gulf. Only Clark Field's paved runways and maintenance facilities could house the heavy bombers that MacArthur promised to have flying to support the Iwo Jima and Okinawa invasions set for February and March, respectively. Manila he wanted for his own satisfaction.

By this time White concluded that Yamashita had no intention of fighting for the central plain and felt certain that Allied air power could protect Sixth Army's open flank by keeping the 2d Armored Division at bay to the east. Krueger was still reluctant to drive rapidly south because he was unsure what Japanese units awaited him. Where, for instance, was the 10th Division? There were enough tantalizing hints from fleeting skirmishes to establish that the 10th had entered the fighting, but no one could locate its main force. How had the bulk of the 10th Division's sixteen thousand troops avoided American units as it pulled back to northeastern Luzon? Were other as yet unidentified combat units with the 10th Division?

Captured documents and identification tags on Japanese corpses hinted that the 11th Division had slipped undetected into Luzon. The appearance of the 1st Division on Leyte lingered as a fresh and bitter reminder of the enemy's ability to carry off a large-scale deployment in total secrecy. In the case of the 11th Division, however, the warnings proved false. The mistake arose because three hundred of the division's soldiers had been sent to Luzon to work as construction personnel. This token force was the basis for assuming the entire 11th Division was on Luzon when it was guarding the eastern Manchurian frontier with the Soviet Union.

Where were all the support and air personnel? A captured document dated January 8 mentioned an otherwise unidentified unit code-named "SHIMBU." According to a translation of the report, SHIMBU controlled Japanese forces in southern Luzon and Manila, which, if true, meant that it was at least a corps-size formation that intelligence had neither suspected nor detected. These scraps of intelligence added credence to White's original calculations. If his calculations were correct, Yamashita had one hundred thousand more troops available than MacArthur's plans and timetables had anticipated.[22] In the face of such uncertainty, Krueger thought it better to proceed slowly.

ULTRA was uneven and unable to delineate the tactical battlefield deployments. It did correctly tell of the formation of special Japanese raiding units but incorrectly reported that the 9th Division might be blocking Route 15 on Krueger's eastern flank (*January 16*). That division was on Taiwan, but Krueger had no way of confirming that fact. ULTRA did unmask the 8th Division moving north toward Krueger's approaching columns (*January 20*). It also revealed that Fourth Air Army had evacuated Manila (*January 10, 18*) and that Yamashita had transferred his headquarters to Baguio in the mountains just east of Lingayen Gulf (*January 19*). According to naval ULTRA, Yamashita's resupply route for Luzon ran from the port on the northern coast through the Cagayan Valley and had no contact with Manila (*January 22*). Another broken message spoke of preparations to burn cryptographic paraphernalia in Manila, a sure sign, intelligence analysts thought, that the Japanese were abandoning the city (*January 22*). The unthinkable truth was that the Manila-based Japanese commanders were burning their codebooks because they had no intention of leaving the city alive.

Imperial Headquarters issued a new edition of the Army Code Book effective February 1, 1945.[23] The introduction of a new codebook temporarily stymied cryptanalysts until they could recover sufficient code groups in the revised system to enable them to solve the new cipher. The time-consuming process left Krueger without army ULTRA during critical periods of the Luzon campaign. The best ULTRA sources for intelligence on Yamashita's forces became the military attaché systems and occasionally MAGIC—Foreign Ministry messages—which Allied cryptanalysts continued to read uninterrupted.

Meanwhile, Sixth Army's advance on its left flank stalled. The I Corps, composed of the 6th and 43d Infantry divisions, had been stopped by the rock-ribbed fighting of the 23d Division and 58th Independent Mixed Brigade. On the right flank, the XIV Corps, comprising the 40th and 37th Infantry divisions, was marching south against little Japanese resistance but exposing its ever-lengthening left flank. By January 17, the XIV Corps presented an open, 25-mile-long left flank seemingly ripe for a Japanese counterattack. Although Willoughby insisted that the vulnerability of Sixth Army's open flank was "more apparent than real," Krueger did not want to press his luck by extending the XIV Corps even farther south toward Manila.[24]

MacArthur was impervious to both the latest intelligence and the tactical situation. The I Corps, not the XIV, MacArthur complained, was suffering the bulk of the casualties. The XIV Corps had to get moving despite its exposed flank. He radioed Krueger on January 17, urging him forward to Clark Field. Even if the XIV Corps ran into fanatical Japanese defenders, the XI Corps' imminent landing on Luzon's western coast would cut off the enemy. The next day, MacArthur dangled the reward of a promotion and a fourth star if only Krueger would get moving. The day after, the Southwest Pacific commander visited Krueger's headquarters, which was located about 4 miles inland from the center of the U-shaped Lingayen Gulf, for a private talk about the progress of the drive south. On his way back to his own headquarters, MacArthur told an aide, "Walter's pretty stubborn. Maybe I'll have to try something else."[25]

"Something else" was MacArthur's attempt to humiliate Krueger by relocating Southwest Pacific Headquarters 25 miles nearer the front lines than the Sixth Army command post. This unprecedented military role reversal placed a theater headquarters closer to the fighting front than an army one. Sutherland made dark threats about relieving Krueger for his lack of aggressiveness. MacArthur allowed to his confidant of the moment that he was "very impatient" and "disgusted" with the Sixth Army commander.[26] MacArthur's behavior was familiar to Krueger. Southwest Pacific Headquarters had complained before that Krueger "goes in too heavy" and did not need all the troops he had had for the Hollandia through the Leyte operations.[27] MacArthur's practice of pestering his field commanders unmercifully to bring him quick victories regardless of whether or not they had the men and matériel to accomplish the goal reasserted itself. An earlier example of the mismatch of aspirations and available resources was the Buna operation. MacArthur had later hectored Krueger for the tardy pace of the Biak campaign as well as the Aitape operation. He had declared victory on Leyte before the heaviest fighting commenced and then left Krueger to make good his boasts. In the case of Luzon, Krueger had no reserve ashore after the landings, and the operations were of a much greater scale than in previous campaigns.

On January 21, the XIV Corps finally opened a rapid advance toward Clark Field 40 miles south. The sprawling air base extended along both sides of the main highway, Route 3, for almost 15 miles. It encompassed fifteen separate airstrips and Fort Stotsenburg, the prewar U.S. Army training ground. American intelligence had no clear notion of how many Japanese were defending Clark Field but guessed that somewhere between 4,000 and 8,000 were dug in there. Willoughby thought a naval brigade might be in the vicinity of Clark Field and suspected that the 19th Division was also lurking there, but he admitted that the unit remained unlocated.[28] About 30,000 Japanese, divided almost equally between sailors and soldiers, were clustered around the airfield complex. The navy contingent had only about 6,500 small arms and, except for 700 or so men, melted into the hills to form predesignated hedgehog defensive sectors. Among the 15,000 army troops, 12,000 were air force personnel cobbled together from about sixty different units of the planeless Fourth Air Army. Their common denominator was their lack of infantry training.[29]

The main Japanese defenses were dug into the mountains overlooking Clark Field where three separate detachments waited for the advancing Americans. In the hills dominating the base, 2,800 men of the Takayama Detachment anchored the left, or north, flank; 750 troops of the Takaya Detachment held the narrow center sector; and the mainstay of the defense, 4,500 men commanded by Lieutenant Colonel Eguchi Seizuke, held the right, or south, sector. American GIs fell at the rate of 100 a day for one week to drive the Japanese deeper into the mountains and secure Clark Field. More than 2,500 Japanese died, but thousands survived to slug it out in suicidal last stands deeper in the mountains. Fighting in rugged terrain continued for another month with about 800 more American and 10,000 more Japanese casualties. Krueger and White's fears about large numbers of Japanese air, naval, and service troops being thrown into the ground battle proved justified. By that time, however, the center of attention had shifted to Manila.

On February 1 Krueger launched his drive for Manila, still concerned about the exact composition of the mysterious SHIMBU unit. The newly arrived 1st Cavalry Division spearheaded the lightning advance and, against little organized resistance, covered nearly 100 miles in two days. The 37th Division also pushed south, but at a slower pace because the Japanese had demolished every bridge along the Americans' path. How many Japanese awaited the 1st Cavalry in Manila was anyone's guess. Willoughby thought somewhere between 15,000 to 18,000 troops, a figure he later reduced to 6,000 to 10,000, less casualties.[30]

ULTRA shed no light on enemy dispositions in the city or on Tokyo's intentions so once again American GIs had to check the intelligence arithmetic. By the time Sixth Army started for Manila, Iwabuchi had collected about 26,000 soldiers and sailors and was turning Manila into a fortress. His naval defense force, Iwabuchi's radiogram assured the Japanese navy minister, was ready to fight to the death to destroy the Americans. From Baguio, Admiral Okawachi wired his approval of Iwabuchi's plans, and Lieutenant General Yokoyama Shizuo, commander of the SHIMBU Group, praised the transformation of Manila into a battleground.[31] If American intercept operators overheard and copied any of these radio messages, they were apparently unable to decrypt them.

In 1945 Manila was a sprawling city that had grown out from the old Spanish walled city of Intramuros sited where the Pasig River empties into Manila Bay. The old city's 15-foot-thick and 25-foot-high stone walls made it ideal as a last redoubt. Beyond Intramuros, Iwabuchi converted any available modern, multistory, ferroconcrete structures—for example, the Agricultural Building, Manila Hotel, Army and Navy Club, Philippine General Hospital, and police station—into self-contained minifortresses. The soldiers of the Manila Defense Force were under orders to fight for and then destroy the four bridges spanning the Pasig River. The sailors were supposed to wreck the Manila pier to deny the Allies the use of Manila harbor. Iwabuchi's men were putting the finishing touches on their demolitions when the 1st Cavalry Division's advance elements roared into the Manila suburbs. ULTRA recorded a Japanese army radioman's emergency signal that "the enemy has broken into a corner of Manila City" (*February 3*).

The cavalrymen quickly liberated Bilibid Prison, which the Japanese had yet to fortify. However, just across the rubble-strewn street, Japanese soldiers fought back from prepared positions in Far Eastern University.[32] Once the fighting had started, the demolition teams began their destructive work of blasting and burning down buildings. Fires raged everywhere through the city as the Japanese systematically blew up bridges and the Manila pier and haphazardly destroyed or set ablaze any other building they took a dislike to. As explosions reverberated through the city, the Japanese started randomly shooting Filipino civilians. Terrified refugees spewed from the dying city. Looters followed in the refugees' wake, stripping shops clean of scarce goods like a horde of locusts. Japanese troops indiscriminately shot, bayoneted, or clubbed to death victims from both groups.

Each building became a Japanese stronghold that American infantrymen had to overcome. At Harrison Baseball Park, Japanese machine gunners fought from the concrete bleachers while American riflemen worked through the stands and dugouts to get at them. MacArthur had expected the Japanese to abandon Manila after token resistance. Now he watched as the city exploded and burned before his eyes. Still the Southwest Pacific commander was reluctant to use against Manila all of the massive firepower of American artillery and aircraft he had available at his fingertips. He finally authorized heavy artillery support for the infantry but rejected commanders' pleas for an aerial bombardment of the city.[33]

ULTRA placed the battle in a context that suggested the defense of Manila might be part of Yamashita's overall strategy for Luzon. According to the army's weekly intelligence circular: "14th Area Army is keeping a firm grip on the sector around Baguio, the hills east of Manila, and the hills west of the cluster of Clark Field airstrips. The plan is to draw as large a number of US troops as possible into the Central Luzon Plain and then force them into costly fighting. Thus they will prevent the enemy from using the airfields in that area or from using Manila Bay" (*February 12*). The next day, the operational unit "SHIMBU" appeared for the first time in Japanese radio traffic routings (*February 13*). Krueger may have felt that Yamashita had him just where he wanted.

In Manila, street fighting went on with its own senseless fury for three weeks. As the Japanese were gradually pushed back to Intramuros, any vestiges of discipline vanished. Perhaps one hundred thousand Filipinos perished in the terrible battle for Manila. Many, it is true, were victims of crossfires or American artillery, but the Japanese troops created their own carnage as they massacred thousands of innocent civilians. A shroud from the smoldering fires hung over the city.

Just north of the Pasig River near the Quezon Bridge, a Japanese platoon was defending the Tonan Ice Plant. One soldier looked out from his bunker on the devastated city. About a quarter mile away on the southwest side of the river, he watched the General Post Office burn. Every time fires were seemingly brought under control, indiscriminate artillery fire reignited the blazes. To the south and southwest, fires raged out of control. He watched American tanks lumber through the rubble and then fire point-blank into the post office. Supporting infantry closed in, killed his company commander, and destroyed most of his unit. The survivors escaped that night and crossed the Quezon Bridge to rejoin the squad defending the icehouse.

Inside the shell-pocked and smoldering four-story Agricultural Building, Iwabuchi radioed the high command that he had ordered some units to break out of the city, but he meant to fight to the bitter end.[34] Okawachi assured him that his inspired defense of Manila was in the highest tradition of the Imperial Navy. Early in the morning of February 25, after as many Japanese as could escaped from the doomed building, Iwabuchi stuck a pistol into his mouth and pulled the trigger.

The death of Manila did not spell the end of the Luzon campaign. There was heavy fighting in the hills east of Manila against the SHIMBU Group until late May. The bulk of Yamashita's forces, the SHOBU Group, remained in the Cagayan Valley where they fought until Japan's surrender in August 1945. According to a February army intelligence circular, Yamashita's 2d Armored Division was regrouping behind the 58th Independent Mixed Brigade and 23d Division, which were fighting east of Lingayen. American troops were driving the 10th Division back into the hills, but the Manila garrison was fighting bravely and tying down three enemy divisions (*February 18*). The next weekly installment explained that it was the 23d Division's turn to reorganize its defenses in depth to confront two Allied divisions opposite it. The 10th Division held about a 10-mile front in the hills bordering the Central Luzon Plain. Still reconstituting, the 2d Armored Division was being pestered by Filipino guerrilla ambushes (*February 26*). This ULTRA merely served to confirm what MacArthur, his staff, and Sixth Army already knew.

Neither was ULTRA instrumental in the seizure of Corregidor Island. MacArthur had earlier outlined plans for a complex simultaneous airborne and amphibious assault on the bastion, although its emotional value outweighed its strategic importance. Many officers at MacArthur's headquarters "fervently awaited the recapture of 'The Rock,' and if it could be done dramatically—by means of a parachute drop, for instance—so much the better."[35] Willoughby estimated that the Japanese garrison numbered a mere 850 men, who could be rapidly overwhelmed by 2,000 paratroopers and 1,000 infantrymen.

On February 16, air and sea attacks went off according to schedule. A combination of surprise and the death in action of the Japanese commander during the first few minutes of the fighting left the defenders disorganized and resistance sporadic. A decrypted message reported that the garrison was burning its codebooks following the Allied landings. The next day, the text of a January 21 navy message, just available, described in detail Japanese defenses on the Rock. This belated ULTRA revealed that more than 3,000 Japanese were on the tiny island, including about 1,300 laborers and 1,010 men assigned to suicide boat squadrons (*February 17*). At least 4,500 Japanese died fighting on Corregidor, while American losses were 1,005 men, including 210 killed in action. The seizure of Corregidor was a bold stroke that caught the Japanese off guard and capitalized on their confusion. The island dominated Manila Bay, so it had to be taken sooner or later to open the bay for shipping. The hastily mounted operation, relying on poor intelligence, might easily have backfired with even higher American casualties. By the time ULTRA produced accurate data, the fighting was already under way.

In MacArthur's largest campaign to date, ULTRA performed less satisfactorily than at any time since the January 1944 penetration of the army mainline cipher.[36] Its key contributions on Luzon were to the undersea interdiction campaign. On Luzon itself, Japanese formations appeared unexpectedly and in far greater numbers than ULTRA had detected. In a throwback to 1942, the most useful radio intelligence for Sixth Army's units came from the direction-finding efforts of signal radio intelligence companies rather than from ULTRA decryptions.[37] American and Australian radio direction-finding teams took cross bearings on the transmissions of Fourteenth Area Army's surviving radios and the intersection of their bearings marked the spot of likely Japanese strongholds and headquarters. Besides the codebook change, ULTRA was a victim of MacArthur's success. Much like Washington three years earlier, Tokyo regarded Luzon as a lost cause. No reinforcement convoys steamed south to relieve Yamashita's hard-pressed troops, so water transport messages disappeared from the airwaves. The radio communications of the army air force went off the air after the force was destroyed in the Philippines. Naval air force radio messages to the islands were nearly nonexistent, and radio communications between Fourteenth Area Army and Imperial Headquarters gradually decreased. For field telephones, Japanese units in the hills used landlines that ran off gasoline generators. Even Yamashita's tactical radio communications abated because radio batteries, in short supply anyway, failed repeatedly in the monsoon climate as steaming humidity drained their storage cells. The diminished volume of radio communications left intercept operators and cryptanalysts with little timely data to exploit concerning Fourteenth Area Army.

Without ULTRA's certification, flawed analyses of Japanese forces persisted throughout the long campaign. Since Willoughby never acknowledged that his original base figure of 152,000 enemy troops on Luzon was much too low, each of his subsequent estimates was consistently incorrect. By March 31 he claimed that 100,000 Japanese had been killed, leaving 51,400 troops on Luzon. In truth, there were twice that number. Krueger got revenge of sorts in a roundabout fashion. On July 1 he sent MacArthur a map of Luzon showing American and Japanese casualties to June 30, "which," Krueger added, "may be of interest to you." By that time Sixth Army counted 173,563 Japanese dead, or 20,000 more than Willoughby ever admitted were on the island.[38] And the fighting still raged.

During the Allies' unrelenting pursuit of the Japanese through Luzon's northern mountains, which led into the Cagayan Valley, four U.S. Army divisions were painstakingly closing in on Yamashita while another American division was mopping up in the southern part of the island.[39] When hostilities ceased, the enterprising Japanese general had more than 40,000 men left for a last stand. However, over 200,000 Japanese had died on Luzon. U.S. Army battle casualties amounted to 37,870 officers and men, but injury and disease claimed another 93,400 Americans.[40] Yamashita had tied down substantial American forces for seven and a half months after MacArthur's landings in Lingayen Gulf and inflicted heavy casualties on the attackers. He was still fighting when Japan surrendered, and he claimed he could have continued the uneven struggle for another month.[41] He had done all that could be expected.

Tokyo's decision to abandon the Philippines and the loss of Iwo Jima and Okinawa to the Allies left the home islands exposed to imminent invasion. Japan's military authorities rushed to bolster the threatened areas. Similarly, Allied cryptanalysts turned their attention to the final Japanese buildup. A fortuitous combination of cryptanalytic success and the capture of numerous Japanese army and navy codebooks and additive tables on Luzon and Okinawa again enabled the Allies to read all Japanese high command messages, including air force communications, in and out of Tokyo from July 1, 1945.[42] ULTRA reemerged as the definitive and, in most cases, the only source of intelligence that could identify with timely precision the scope of the massive reinforcement effort on the southernmost island of Kyushu. The gap between ULTRA data and that of other intelligence sources on the extent of the Japanese defense of the home islands was enormous.[43] ULTRA accurately portrayed a Japanese military determined to fight to the death on the sacred shores of its homeland while MAGIC told of the Japanese government and Foreign Ministry's search for ways to end the war. In this cruel paradox, ULTRA's domination of MAGIC surely influenced the American decision to use atomic weapons against Japan.

8

ULTRA as Seer: Uncovering Japanese Plans for Homeland Defense, June–August 1945

For MacArthur the reconquest of the Philippines left wide open the road to Japan. Imperial Army strategists conceded as much when they authorized planning for the defense of the home islands against imminent invasion. On January 11, 1945, just two days after MacArthur's landings on Luzon, General Umezu, the army chief of staff, ordered all directorates of the Japanese War Ministry to establish their immediate priorities for homeland defense.[1] Nine days later the emperor approved, and the army promulgated, the overall concept for the protection of Japan. From an outer defensive zone of Iwo Jima, Formosa, and Okinawa, Japanese soldiers, sailors, and airmen would wage a campaign of attrition to bleed and weaken the Americans as they approached. With the time purchased in these battles, the high command would convert the most likely landing areas—Japan's southern island of Kyushu and the Kanto (Tokyo) Plain—into bristling fortresses.

Tremendous levies of manpower and confiscation of Japan's almost exhausted resources were required for the transformation. By mid-February the army authorized a three-stage *levée en masse*. It aimed to add sixteen new divisions to the four already on Kyushu in order to concentrate twenty divisions against the likely sites of an Allied landing. Twice that number were needed. By the following week, plans emerged to mobilize sixteen divisions by the end of May alone, eight more during June and July, and sixteen more by August—or forty divisions totaling more than half a million men.[2] Four other divisions would be transferred from Manchuria to the homeland to leaven the new formations.

The first mobilization built new divisions in Japan by reactivating depot divisions and levying new formations. These "100 series" divisions were intended strictly for coastal defense, which meant the troops would fight and die near the Allied beachhead. Their purpose was to fight from static field and permanent fortifications near the landing beaches until a counterattack by mobile Japanese reserves relieved them or death overtook them. Since they were going nowhere, the 100 series divisions had little mobility or firepower—they had no trucks, carts, or artillery weapons. Of the sixteen new divisions created, three—the 146th, 154th, and 156th—were earmarked for coastal defense in Kyushu. The 25th and 57th divisions, then in Manchuria, also received orders to head for Kyushu where they would form a mobile reserve.[3] These two divisions arrived in Kyushu in early May. Around the same time, Imperial Headquarters concluded that Okinawa (which the Americans had invaded in April) was lost and that the next great Allied blow would probably fall on Kyushu, perhaps as early as June. The high command's fear of imminent invasion caused it to accelerate the buildup on Kyushu and to redouble its efforts to dispatch more men to the island.

The Joint Chiefs of Staff's directive for the invasion of Japan unintentionally followed a logic that was identical to the estimates of Imperial Headquarters. The Allied strategic concept of operations in the Pacific in February 1945 envisaged that the Okinawa operation would be followed by an assault against Kyushu after which would occur the strategically decisive invasion of the Kanto Plain. In late March the Joint Chiefs' tentative schedule for the invasion of Japan slated the preliminary assault on Kyushu (code-named "OLYMPIC") for December 1, 1945. CORONET, the main landing on the Kanto Plain, was set for March 1, 1946. Approximately one month later, the Joint Chiefs instructed MacArthur to plan and prepare for the invasion of Japan. The same April 3 directive designated him the commander in chief of United States Army Forces in the Pacific in addition to commander in chief of the Southwest Pacific Area. MacArthur was given control over all American army and air force units and resources in the Pacific except those in the inactive North and Southeast Pacific subareas and Twentieth Air Force units in the Marianas.[4] On May 25 the Joint Chiefs directed that OLYMPIC be launched on November 1, 1945.[5] MacArthur in turn selected his old warhorse, General Krueger, and Sixth Army to spearhead the invasion of Japan.

Unlike the Philippines, there were no Allied agents, spy networks, or sympathizers in Japan. Japanese prisoners of war who were captured in the outlying defenses were ignorant of the overall scale of the massive buildup on Kyushu. Aerial reconnaissance could spot some Japanese movements, but it was limited by weather, darkness, and existing technology. ULTRA was the only reliable means to assess the scope of the Japanese defenses and perhaps to gauge the enemy's determination to fight to the bitter end. ULTRA unlocked one Japanese secret after another for the Allies, and this otherwise unobtainable intelligence had significant implications even though the Allies did not have to invade Japan. For that reason, an examination of ULTRA's role in the spring and summer of 1945 is more than an exercise in antiquarian curiosity. Decisionmakers like General Marshall who were at the highest levels in Washington read ULTRA and voiced apprehension as it revealed the massive reinforcement effort on Kyushu. The ULTRA-shaped perception based on deciphered military communications superseded the MAGIC decryptions indicating that Japan's Foreign Ministry was seeking to end the war. ULTRA was a central factor in the decision to drop the atomic bomb on Japanese cities, one heretofore not fully incorporated into the historical record.

Historians have offered myriad motivations—from the altruistic to the sinister—for the controversial decision to wage atomic warfare against Japan. One strongly argued view holds that because Japan was already defeated, the needless and senseless atomic destruction of humanity was done for political ends. Such arguments rest on well-explored political and diplomatic dimensions of strategic decisionmaking concerning the use of the atomic bomb but ignore the military side of that process. ULTRA-derived knowledge of the massive buildup for a gigantic battle on Kyushu did influence American policymakers and strategists. To ignore that factor assumes that the Japanese were defeated and, more important, that they were prepared to surrender before the atomic bomb was dropped. ULTRA did portray a Japan in extremity, but it also showed that its military leaders were blind to defeat and were bending all remaining national energy to smash an invasion of their divine islands.[6] From that perspective, the Imperial Army was as defeated and in as hopeless a situation as Adachi was at the Driniumor, as Yamashita on Luzon, as Suzuki on Leyte, and as Kuzume on Biak. Everywhere in the Pacific, cut-off, outnumbered, and defeated Japanese garrisons had continued fighting to the death. Given that bitter legacy, it was not difficult for American military planners and political decisionmakers to believe that the Japanese stood ready to defend their sacred homeland with equal or greater suicidal ardor than the emperor's soldiers throughout the Pacific war.

By April 25 Willoughby had produced an initial assessment of the enemy defenses Sixth Army would likely encounter on Kyushu. Every trend in troop movements and unit dispositions highlighted preparations for a desperate fight for the home islands. MacArthur's G-2 predicted that a Kyushu garrison of at least six combat and two depot divisions would expand to a maximum of ten combat divisions by the time of the invasion. Since the Japanese would be ignorant of the exact landing beaches, they would have to protect the island's entire coastline, most likely by dividing combat divisions equally between the northern and southern parts of Kyushu. Available ULTRA confirmed that Sixteenth Area Army Headquarters at Fukuoka in northern Kyushu controlled the approximately 224,200 to 229,200 Japanese troops on the island. In the northern sector, the 57th Division, 18th Armored Regiment, and 6th and 56th Depot divisions formed the backbone of the defense. When one included three major fortress commands at Hoyo, Iki, and Nagasaki in northern Kyushu, there were about 64,000 combat troops in the area.

Willoughby's figures showed that the 86th Division at Miyakonojō defended Kyushu's southern half. Altogether 88,700 troops (25,700 combat, 5,000 naval ground, 45,000 air ground, and 8,000 support) were available to fight in southern Kyushu, although Willoughby forecast that two more Japanese combat divisions

The underground radio communications center of 86th Division Headquarters near Ariake Bay in southern Kyushu. A radio message transmitted by the division on July 9, 1945, betrayed its deployment from Miyakonojō to southern Kyushu to the Americans. (Courtesy of National Institute for Defense Studies, Tokyo)

would be deployed there by the November 1 D-day. About 1,000 Japanese combat aircraft of all types stood ready to strike an approaching fleet, and this figure was expected to rise to between 2,000 and 2,500 aircraft by the eve of the invasion. Granting that half the airplanes might be obsolete or trainers, they were a serious threat, especially if used as kamikazes. The remnants of the once invincible Imperial Fleet were dismissed as insignificant because Allied air superiority over southern Kyushu and the overwhelming power of the U.S. Navy's main carrier and battle fleets could destroy any Japanese warship foolish enough to contest the invasion beaches.[7]

As Allied intelligence shifted its focus to Kyushu, ULTRA was the premier source of enemy intentions. A navy message of April 7 ordered obvious counterinvasion measures such as the evacuation of civilians from coastal areas and the mining of several Kyushu bays "as soon as possible" (*April 9*). Messages of April 9 and 11 were evidence of large troop movements from the Asiatic mainland to Japan as somewhere between thirty thousand and sixty thousand Japanese troops were embarking from Korean ports for Kyushu (*April 13*). A vice chief of staff message predicted an American invasion of Kyushu sometime after the middle of the year (*April 15*) and accounted for the urgency of Chief of Staff Umezu's directive to army commands to discover the time, place, and scale of the Allied invasion of Japan for a KETSU ("decisive") operation. In similar fashion, Southern Army had alerted its subordinate units to gather intelligence on an Allied invasion of Japan (April 27/28).

Domei, the official Japanese news agency, reported the organization of two general armies, which was confirmed by decoded messages transmitted April 14 and 16 that identified First General Army at Tokyo and Second General Army at Hiroshima (*April 17*; April 19/20). Army water transport decryptions of troop manifests revealed that the 57th Division had arrived on April 13 at Hakata, Kyushu (April 20/21). Its presence prompted Washington to call attention to the large-scale movement of troops from Korea to Japan (*April 18*). Anchorage command messages in the Army Water Transport Code disclosed the impending withdrawal of the 3d Amphibious Brigade, specially designed for counteramphibious operations, from the northern Kurils to somewhere in Japan. Broken addresses on army air force radio messages mentioned a new General Army Air Command in Tokyo that was designed to centralize aerial operations nationwide (*April 20, 21*).

This ULTRA was incorporated into the original ground order of battle that located one combat and two depot divisions as well as a parachute and an armor regiment on Kyushu (April 20/21). At first the Americans did not realize the significance of what they were overhearing—that these initial deployments were only the first stage of a general mobilization for the homeland battle. The reinforcements were predictable for the threatened areas, and their numbers, though large, were not extraordinary. However, as ULTRA ferreted out other units on Kyushu, Willoughby became more concerned about what was shaping up on the island.

Japanese reinforcements seemed to blossom with the warm May weather in Kyushu. Central Bureau and Arlington Hall first spotted the new units through deciphered message addresses. For example, a badly garbled, fragmentary message addressed to a Fifty-Eighth Army in Korea was the first reference to that formation, and it was the highest numbered Japanese army discovered to date. This suggested that other newly formed armies might exist (*May 3*). Naval ULTRA dealing with the creation of a commander in chief of Combined Naval Forces reflected the integration of all naval forces under a unified commander to counter any invasion (May 6/7). As for air power, by May 8 there were 705 Japanese tactical aircraft within striking range of southern Kyushu beaches, although fewer than half were operational on any given day (May 8/9). Ten days later, large numbers of aircraft that had withdrawn from southern Kyushu and harm's way when American carriers appeared returned in force to the vacated fields (May 18/19). The fly-away recalled Japanese tactics employed earlier in the Philippines.

Tokyo's continuing apprehensions about an imminent invasion surfaced in the exchange of radio messages during mid-May. Japanese signal intelligence analysts, for example, had detected a sudden increase in the number of Allied merchant ships in the Central Pacific, which implied that a new and fairly large-scale operation, such as the invasion of Kyushu, was close at hand (*May 14*). A fresh and consistent stream of radio message traffic emerged from an unidentified army unit in central Kyushu. The sender employed an army-level code to communicate with headquarters of the same or higher echelon throughout Japan. Sixteenth Area Army was the only identified major command on Kyushu, but this new unit had all the electronic fingerprints of a high-level headquarters (May 13/14; *May 16*). The only known formation nearby was the previously identified 86th Division, but if a newly formed army headquarters was there, then two or three additional, but undetected, Japanese divisions might conceivably be somewhere in southern Kyushu. Direction-finding techniques located 57th Division Headquarters' radio transmitter in northwestern Kyushu, indicative of Japanese intentions to fend off invasion from that direction (May 16/17). Then radio messages of the 3d Amphibious Brigade disclosed that it had moved to the southern part of the island near Kagoshima Bay (*May 18;* May 21/22). The brigade, however, had suffered heavy losses to submarine attacks while displacing from the Kurils and when it arrived on Kyushu, it was absorbed by the newly formed 125th Independent Mixed Brigade.[8] ULTRA never identified the new brigade, perhaps because it retained the call sign that previously belonged to the 3d Amphibious Brigade. A few days later, messages passed back and forth from Manchuria to central Kyushu betrayed the 25th Division's deployment to southern

Japan (*May 25*). Meanwhile, the 1st Armored Division, another vintage Manchurian formation, was discovered near Tokyo. Its compromised code name, TAKU, was the giveaway (May 24/25).

In light of Japanese nervousness over a forthcoming invasion, the "feverish effort to reinforce the homeland" by drawing men and matériel from Manchuria, Korea, and North China was still within the bounds of a predictable development (May 31/June 1). ULTRA now confirmed at least three combat and two depot divisions on Kyushu. According to Japanese military doctrine, an area army normally controlled two numbered armies, which in turn controlled two or three divisions each, so Allied cryptanalysts searched for Sixteenth Area Army's subordinate entities as army-level headquarters. If the two army headquarters did exist, then the command structure could accommodate perhaps three to five more combat divisions, a total of six to eight total combat divisions. The evolving command structure, revealed by ULTRA, so far supported Willoughby's earlier contention that six combat divisions would garrison Kyushu.

The hasty Japanese buildup during May was premised on Second General Army Headquarters' expectation that the next Allied objective after Okinawa would be southern Kyushu. Staff officers believed that an enemy landing was possible any time after the end of June and were rushing reinforcements, which ULTRA was reporting, to the threatened areas.[9] In the meantime, the army had already entered stage two of its mobilization scheme, which coincided with the May strengthening of Kyushu. Reservists and youngsters caught in the net of the April 2 call-up were organized into "200 series" divisions. After four to six weeks of minimum basic training, they were sent to operational commands. These divisions were supposed to be the counterattack units that Imperial Headquarters expected to break into and destroy the Allied beachhead. Consequently, they were more heavily armed with field artillery guns, mortars, and automatic weapons and had more engineer troops than the corresponding 100 series divisions of the first mobilization.[10] On May 10, three of the 200 series divisions—the 206th, 212th, and 216th—came under Sixteenth Area Army's control. A few weeks later, the third phase of general mobilization commenced.

ULTRA enabled American planners to discern the outline of the reinforcement effort for Kyushu. A May 27 message describing antiaircraft installations had as an addressee a Fifty-Seventh Army, which identified the suspected army-level unit in central Kyushu (*June 1*). Army message routings exposed another headquarters in northern Kyushu that was tentatively identified as Fifty-Sixth Army and established that the 25th Division was in central Kyushu (*June 7*). Unit code name ASO 33406 surfaced in southern Kyushu. The previous highest unit code number had been 23109, which implied that another major unidentified combat unit was in southern Kyushu (June 10/11). On June 5 and 7, radio operators in southern Kyushu transmitted messages addressed to units code-named "NEN 9254" and

"NEN 9260." Analysts already knew that NEN 9254 was Headquarters, 77th Division, so this data pointed to the shift of that unit from northern Japan to Kyushu (June 13/14).

ULTRA from naval and air force messages conjured up still raw memories of massed suicide attacks off the Philippines and Okinawa. The commanding officer of the 12th Naval Air Flotilla in Kyushu described the dispositions at air-staging bases and his intentions. In case of an Allied landing on Kyushu, the flotilla's 900 obsolete planes and trainers would be hurled into battle, many equipped as kamikazes (*June 11*; June 11/12). An earlier message had ordered naval air depots throughout Japan to prepare suicide equipment and night gear for 417 biplane trainers, which bespoke a desperate effort to throw anything that could fly into the climactic battle (June 9/10). The commander of Sasebo Naval Base described his progress on suicide-boat construction as well as measures to disperse and conceal the deadly boat-bombs that had hurt MacArthur's navy in Lingayen Gulf. A subsequent decoded order disclosed a *kaiten* (the naval version of a piloted torpedo) base on the southeastern tip of Kyushu (*June 17*). U.S. Navy intelligence foresaw the Japanese extensively employing suicide craft in their defense of the empire (June 13/14). Allied strategists were also aware that Japanese naval chieftains had convened a major conference on May 17 to discuss KETSU-GO, the code name for the defense of the home islands (June 18/19).

Japanese army air force communications told of the consolidation of two air armies from overseas and an air division in Tokyo under the General Army Air Command (June 7/8). This was further evidence of Japanese willingness to concede air superiority in all theaters outside the main islands in favor of mustering all available aircraft within striking distance of southern Kyushu under a single command (June 15/16). Allied intelligence disclosed fourteen hundred suicide trainers in Japan augmented by four thousand other aircraft of questionable efficiency, leading to predictions of a continuing and bitter air war over the home islands for the next four to five months. ULTRA highlighted underground aircraft hangar construction and new, concealed dispersal airfields on Kyushu designed for such operations (June 6/7, 8/9). ULTRA exposed daily the high command's hurried efforts to transform Kyushu into a mighty stronghold. Nowhere could one detect pessimism or defeatism. According to ULTRA, Japan's military leaders were determined to go down fighting.

This ULTRA testimony of Japanese capabilities was available to the Joint Chiefs of Staff and President Harry S. Truman when they met at the White House on June 18, 1945, to discuss the human toll of an invasion of Japan. To prepare for the meeting, Marshall had requested that MacArthur provide a casualty estimate for OLYMPIC from the invasion through the first ninety days of fighting. A curious exchange of top secret cables ensued. Southwest Pacific Headquarters responded with an estimated total of 105,050 battle and 12,600 nonbattle casualties for the period. Marshall's return radiogram to MacArthur expressed the president's great concern over casualties in OLYMPIC and implied that his headquarters' estimate was too high to be acceptable. A second MacArthur cable dismissed the first estimate as "purely academic and routine." In fact, the commander of army forces in the Pacific did not expect such a high loss rate. Besides, he argued, a Soviet attack against Japanese forces in Manchuria would lessen the hazards of invading Kyushu. For these reasons, MacArthur continued, "I most earnestly recommend no change to OLYMPIC."[11] Left unsaid was that any change to OLYMPIC would deny MacArthur his role in history as the commander of the greatest invasion force ever assembled.

At the White House session, Truman candidly voiced his concern about the bloodbath that had drenched Okinawa—more than 46,000 battle casualties in seventy-nine days—and wanted the Joint Chiefs' assurance that an invasion of Kyushu would neither repeat that savagery nor degenerate into a race war. Figuring that Kyushu would be defended by eight divisions and relying on MacArthur's reassurances, Marshall extrapolated from known Japanese defenses and American losses on Luzon that U.S. battle casualties would run slightly more than 1,000 a day for the first thirty days of the fighting, or 31,000 total.[12] Fleet Admiral William D. Leahy, chairman of the Joint Chiefs and the president's personal representative to the service chiefs, thought Marshall's number was too low. American troops on Okinawa, he said, suffered 35 percent casualties. Should not this same percentage apply to the American troops waiting to invade Kyushu? Marshall allowed that 766,700 assault troops would be employed against Kyushu. Although unstated, a 35 percent casualty rate translated to more than a quarter-million American casualties.[13]

Marshall observed that divisions were, of course, still being raised in Japan, but, all things considered, the deadly American air and naval attacks made reinforcement of Kyushu a dangerous and difficult business for the Japanese. When the president questioned whether Japanese reinforcements could move into Kyushu from the other home islands, Marshall replied that the Joint Chiefs expected Allied air and naval might to sever all communications between Kyushu and potential sources of reinforcement and resupply. Marshall seems to have thought that the Japanese forces on Kyushu, like Yamashita's on Luzon, would receive no further reinforcements and be left to fend for themselves. No consideration was given to the likelihood that Tokyo would dispatch substantial reinforcements to Kyushu between June and the November invasion date. However, if the Japanese did throw more men and matériel into Kyushu, one logically would expect casualties to rise in proportion to the number of Japanese defenders.

A terrible irony surrounded Truman's concern about what he termed "creating another Okinawa closer to Japan." As the eminent Japanese historian Fujiwara Akira pointed out, Imperial Headquarters never expected to repel an American assault on Okinawa. Instead, Okinawa was considered the front line of the defense of the homeland and their strategy amounted to nothing more than a protracted battle of attrition in expectation of inflicting as many casualties as possible on American troops. To serve notice to the Americans of what awaited invaders on Kyushu, they sacrificed the Okinawan people, two hundred thousand of whom perished in the horrible battle.[14] A trio of Okinawa-born historians maintain that the Japanese military deliberately prolonged the hopeless struggle solely to impede an American invasion of the main islands. By doing so, the Japanese military sacrificed thousands of civilians whom they herded together indiscriminately with soldiers.[15] When images of suicide planes, Japanese soldiers who preferred death to surrender, and mass military and civilian suicides on Saipan and Okinawa were combined with a carefully cultivated official image of a samurai nation blindly devoted to military victory, it added up to a chilling prospect for American invaders of the Land of the Gods.[16] The conduct of Japanese soldiers provided enough evidence of their willingness to fight to the death and conditioned the Allies to accept at face value their bombastic public announcements of a last-ditch stand. Even their confidential messages revealed by ULTRA gave no hint of surrender. Quite the opposite, they foreshadowed another bloody battle. By accurately tracking the swelling flood of reinforcements that poured into Kyushu through the end of June and into July 1945, ULTRA made OLYMPIC seem very costly indeed.

While the Joint Chiefs and president talked, so did the emperor and his military chieftains. At a June 8 Imperial Conference, Japan's top admirals and generals reported to his majesty that Kyushu or Shikoku might be invaded any time after June 20.[17] Since the third and final stage of mobilization had just been completed in late May, eleven coastal defense divisions (the "300 series") and fifteen independent mixed brigades were newly available for homeland defense. Among the divisions, the 303d went to Fortieth Army and the 312th and 351st to Fifty-Sixth Army. Three of the newly formed independent mixed brigades—the 118th, 122d, and 126th—found themselves heading south to Sixteenth Area Army, and another, the 125th, ended up with Fortieth Army.[18] ULTRA uncovered Japanese dispositions near the very beaches that Krueger would have to seize and the fact was that the defenders outnumbered projected attackers at the critical landing sites.

Along with ground reinforcements, Imperial Headquarters was carefully hoarding aircraft for the decisive struggle. The army air force expected to marshal 5,400 aircraft of all types, including 2,800 trainers, while the navy promised another 5,040, including 2,100 trainers. Of these, about 2,000 planes, mainly trainers, were designated suicide attackers. Trainers were selected as kamikazes because they were simple and cheap to manufacture, did not require much gasoline (which was critically short in Japan), and were easy to learn to fly. By July Sixth Air Army, headquartered at Fukuoka in northern Kyushu, boasted 1,000 suicide planes and 400 other aircraft to defend southern Japan. In early July American pilots flew hundreds of reconnaissance sorties to photograph every one of the 243 known airfields in Japan. Photo interpreters peering through their stereoscopes counted a grand total of 8,010 Japanese aircraft of all types. On Kyushu, 1,807 airplanes appeared on film against the ULTRA-derived total of 1,885 (July 7/8). Japan's military preparations signaled a resolution to fight to the death, especially the rapidity of the buildup on Kyushu, which caused the Allies the most immediate concern.

ULTRA detected repeated messages about construction of concealed bases for suicide aircraft, and the commander of the 72d Naval Air Flotilla ordered airfields in northeastern Kyushu to provide basing and maintenance for at least 140 of his kamikaze planes (July 10/11). A week earlier, 90 aircraft had arrived in eastern Kyushu from Osaka (June 30/July 1). Pilots, aircraft mechanics, technicians, and equipment were being ferried on small boats from Honshu and Korea to Kyushu (*July 7*). On July 4 the 13th Naval Air Flotilla in Osaka was ordered to move about 3,800 base personnel and its estimated 600 suicide trainers to 29 air bases in southern Japan (July 21/22). Two army air force brigades—twin-engine bombers and fighters, respectively—staged from Honshu to southwestern Kyushu. The same broken code portrayed 14 "partially trained" suicide units, each with 10 aircraft, deploying to the southern island (*July 9*). The main concentrations of these suicide attackers were also known through ULTRA, as was the navy's decision to abandon air bases close to the coastline for fear of losing men and planes to offshore naval bombardment.[19]

Of course, Kenney did not allow the Japanese airmen to redeploy with impunity. His bombers, together with navy carrier aircraft and the mighty B-29s of the Twentieth Air Force, ranged over the Japanese homeland, attacking targets almost at will. A spectacular example of the combination of ULTRA and air power followed a decryption about the lack of dispersal facilities for 170 aircraft crammed into a northern Kyushu airfield. Far Eastern Air Force bombers promptly attacked the field, and subsequent ULTRA told of the "tremendous damage" from an air strike on July 25 that left 57 planes in ashes (July 31/August 1). However, there were so many Japanese aircraft, small boats, and men coming into Kyushu that air power could not dam the flow.

The panoply of Japanese suicide weapons was another source of worry for the Allies. Besides the kamikaze aircraft, there were flying bombs (*oka*), human torpedoes (*kaiten*), suicide attack boats (*koryo*), midget suicide submarines (*kairyu*), motorboat bombs (*unyo*), and navy swimmers transformed into human mines (*fukuryu*). Japanese ingenuity seemed channeled to invent engines of self-destruction. Since March 1945, for instance, Nakajima Aircraft was engaged in building a prototype designed to carry a 1,000-pound bomb solely for suicide crashes. The novel feature was the plane's reusable landing gear, which separated from the aircraft on takeoff. It ensured a one-way flight and conserved scarce rubber. Furthermore, these weapons were not flights of Japanese fantasy. With the exception of the Nakajima design, all had been used at Okinawa and the Philippines with lethal results. ULTRA unveiled locations on Kyushu of suicide motorboats, fuel allocations for *kairyu* and *kaiten*, and the composition of suicide assault units (**June 23, 27**). A conference on training suicide swimmers in methods of attacking targets occurred in early July (**July 8**). The consolation of learning from ULTRA that an accidental explosion and fire had destroyed twenty suicide boats in their tunnel hideout and that bombs stored in an underground magazine had accidently exploded (June 20/21); **July 14**) was balanced by the Fifth Naval Air Fleet's request for sixty *oka* in July and one hundred fifty thereafter for bases in northern Kyushu (**July 21**, 29/30).

Another consideration was the military potential of auxiliary ground forces organized from a *levée en masse* of Japanese civilians (**July 2**). Willoughby expected this National Volunteer Corps to form military labor groups that would be converted to combat status as the occasion demanded (June 30/July 1). ULTRA made known that the volunteers had paramilitary duties during the intensified Allied air raids and preparations for the "fast-approaching" decisive battle of the homeland (June 27/28). In less lofty terms, these woefully untrained children, old men, and women were beasts of burden who cleaned debris after air raids, portered supplies on their backs, and, armed with bamboo spears, were used as cannon fodder. Americans had witnessed them in all these roles on Okinawa.

ULTRA also revealed Japanese defensive intentions. Imperial Headquarters conceded Allied control of the air and sea during an invasion of Kyushu but planned a stubborn defense along the few beaches large enough to support a massive amphibious force. Heavy artillery was installed in caves to cover the approaches to the principal landing areas. Soldiers, conscripted civilians, and gangs of children and old men and women labored through the stifling summer heat to construct a web of bunkers, field fortifications, and connecting tunnels along the shoreline. When available, scarce concrete was poured into permanent bunkers that housed observation teams and artillery just to the rear of the beaches. Fixed fortifications, well dug in and camouflaged, complemented these ugly concrete pillboxes and served as the main line of defense. Behind them, still more Japanese toiled to dig bunkers and tunnels to protect the forces destined to counterattack the invaders. Kyushu's heavily forested mountains lent themselves perfectly to such a defensive scheme.

Tokyo's aim was to inflict such severe damage and casualties on the attackers that the Allies would be convinced of the futility of further fighting and of the wisdom of a negotiated peace. A mid-June intelligence circular from the army vice chief of staff laid out a strategy for the defense of Kyushu that counted heavily on suicide weapons to destroy the invaders at sea or on an unrelenting full-scale counteroffensive to annihilate them on the beaches (*June 29*). The theme of bold aggressive action reappeared a few weeks later when air and naval forces were called on to smash the Allied armada at sea while ground troops destroyed invaders on the beaches. Transports and landing craft packed with soldiers were prime targets (July 15/16). ULTRA also reported that the crews of float reconnaissance planes were training to smash into transports and strafe and bomb landing beaches (**July 14**). If the Americans did gain a beachhead, mobile troops covered by coastal divisions would counterattack and destroy the Allied lodgement (*July 12*).[20]

ULTRA did, of course, reassure MacArthur that the Japanese military confronted serious difficulties. Incessant air raids and naval bombardments against Kyushu had disrupted the rail movement of fuel, ammunition, and equipment from north to south, thereby slowing scheduled troop deployments (**July 6**). Fuel was in such critically short supply that naval headquarters even suggested that whenever practicable, commanders should drain fuel from the tanks of sunken vessels within their jurisdiction (**July 19**). Air fleets were diluting aviation gasoline with alcohol because of shortages. The food situation was desperate, in part because railway tie-ups resulting from repeated Allied air attacks made distribution of foodstuffs difficult. A grimmer statistic was that the June wheat and barley crops were 20 percent below normal. Japan's leaders believed that if air raids destroyed the fall rice crop, the nation might face starvation (**July 24**). There were also peace overtures. The first hint of such sentiment in Japan itself appeared in an April message deciphered in early July (**July 7**). Earlier decryptions of Japanese Foreign Ministry telegrams exposed Japanese peace initiatives through Sweden, Switzerland, and the Soviet Union (**July 28**).[21] As far as Allied military intelligence was concerned, the Japanese civil authorities might be considering peace, but Japan's military leaders, who American decisionmakers believed had total control of the nation, were preparing for war to the knife. ULTRA testified that from mid-July, the number of troops in Kyushu had skyrocketed.

First mention of a "200 series" division, the 206th in southern Kyushu, became available in early July (July 8/9). Four days later, ULTRA pinpointed the 212th Division on Kyushu's eastern coast, the sixth combat division thus far identified on the island (*July 13*). Intelligence experts then located two new armored regiments—the 37th and the 40th—in southern Kyushu. Because the 30th Armored Regiment was the highest numbered armored regiment known to date, the implication was that as many as ten more tank regiments might exist (*July 16*). Next ULTRA identified the 154th Division on the south-central Kyushu coast. Cryptanalysts picked up the code names of two more divisions as well as the 1st Artillery Command, betrayed by its code number 3870 (July 6/7, 15/16). Willoughby sounded the alarm that military strength in Japan proper had doubled to 1,865,000 troops between January and July 1945, resulting in the "tremendous influx and organization of combat units" in Kyushu (July 15/16).

Intercept operators tuned into the new radio frequencies provided for freshly minted Japanese units whose messages lit up the frequency bands like so many fireflies. A Sixteenth Area Army radio message verified another new formation in Kyushu—the 126th Independent Mixed Brigade. This ULTRA awareness inspired Washington's new estimate that 380,000 soldiers and sailors defended Kyushu, an increase of about 100,000 men since early June (*June 7; July 20*). A day later that figure leaped to 455,000 men when Arlington Hall accepted three new division code names, originally identified by Central Bureau, as valid division formations (*July 21*). Shortly afterward, the 156th Division's name appeared on the airwaves, along with the 122d Independent Mixed Brigade (July 23/24). A few days passed and two more divisions popped up in communications. One ULTRA spoke of personnel transfers to Kyushu to join the 146th Division; another mentioned the 203d Division (July 25/26). The former's presence was confirmed in extreme southern Kyushu shortly after (July 28/29). ULTRA's discovery of a newly formed Fortieth Army was "the outstanding single event" of late July because it foretokened still more Japanese forces on Kyushu (July 31). Cryptanalysts deduced Fortieth Army's existence from myriad radio messages sent in June and July. A request for one officer from the Fortieth Army Ordnance Depot to report to Kyushu seemed linked to messages from Formosa to a unit in southwestern Kyushu with the characteristics of an army headquarters. The clincher was a Sixteenth Area Army circular addressed to Fifty-Sixth, Fifty-Seventh, and Fortieth armies that numerically distinguished the unidentified formation (July 28/29). Traffic analysis of radio call signs also discovered otherwise unsuspected units.

Address routings of the May radio message, recovered in mid-July, included the code name "TO," which direction finding located in the mountain fastness near Mount Kirishima in southern Kyushu (July 11/12). A review of May intercepts unearthed another message referencing the TO unit (July 15/16). Direction finding isolated an unidentified radio transmitter in the same area as the mysterious TO, which broadcast that the 37th and 40th Armored regiments were under "our command" (July 21/22). With two regiments, TO was probably the code name for an armored brigade. A mid-July message from TO to Manchuria was signed by one Major Ushio Heiji, who mentioned in passing that he had arrived safely at the new post (July 27/28). Ushio, it developed, had been the adjutant at an armor school in Manchuria in March 1943. His past experience with tank units, and the connection of TO with two tank regiments, made it likely that TO was indeed an armored brigade. Address routings on another message included three armored brigades, the 4th, 5th, and 6th, numbering perhaps 480 tanks and all stationed in Kyushu (*July 30*). With this confirmation, cryptanalysts reviewed old, previously unbroken message traffic and turned up an April radiogram from the Army Mechanized Maintenance School in Tokyo to Kyushu asking where the new commanders of the 5th and 6th Armored Brigade maintenance units should report (August 1/2).

Further analysis revealed that TO was the code name for the 6th Armored Brigade (which actually had about 70 tanks) whose headquarters was located near Mount Kirishima.

Only two years earlier, the identification of TO by such means would have been impossible. In July 1943 no army messages had ever been solved, and something as rudimentary as the code name "TO" might have remained hidden from cryptanalysts' prying eyes. Direction finding, it is true, could have isolated major units and suggested likely unit subordinations based on the pattern of TO's radio network. It could not, however, have identified the exact type of unit transmitting the message. Without breaking the cipher, no one could know that a Major Ushio signed a message. Armed with Ushio's name, intelligence officers checked him against the roster of Japanese officers (captured in April 1943) and connected him with tanks. A deceptively simple unit identification like TO was the end product of the talent and energy of countless men and women. The TO case illustrates how cryptanalysts, traffic analysts, intercept operators, intelligence analysts, technicians, and a host of others all contributed to the war effort.

From the ULTRA these experts produced, it became abundantly plain to MacArthur's staff that the original appraisal of six to ten Japanese divisions on Kyushu by X-day had seriously underestimated Japanese determination to fight for the homeland. Since the April estimate, ULTRA had already confirmed seven additional divisions, one amphibious brigade (the 125th Independent Mixed Brigade, in fact), one independent mixed brigade, and three armored regiments on Kyushu. ULTRA had located more than ten Japanese divisions and the end of the reinforcement effort was nowhere in sight. Navy, air force, and base and service troops augmented the fighting units. Japanese mobile combat strength alone had almost tripled between April and July, from 80,000 to 206,000 troops. According to Willoughby, "this threatening development, if not checked, may grow to a point where we attack on a ratio of one (1) to one (1) which is not the recipe for victory."[22] The probability that other units, as yet unidentified or unlocated, were on Kyushu added to the grimness of Willoughby's conclusions.

MacArthur's G-2 observed that air strikes had failed to prevent the Japanese from staging large-scale reinforcements from northern to southern Kyushu. The deployments revealed in ULTRA showed that the enemy had correctly estimated southern Kyushu as the probable invasion site. It seemed likely that Imperial Headquarters would move even more units in the target area before X-day and tip the balance of the attack in Japan's favor. Allied intelligence did allow that some of the new units in southern Kyushu were neither fully assembled nor completely equipped, but it still conceded that a formidable and unexpectedly large force blocked the selected invasion beaches.[23]

No intelligence coup guided the hand devising the Japanese designs for beachhead defense. A terrain analysis by any competent staff officer reduced to a handful the number of beaches in southern Kyushu that were capable of supporting the massive ground force MacArthur was set to hurl at Japan. With the invaders' options restricted, Imperial Headquarters sited their defenses in the right places by a process of exclusion, not deduction. With three months until X-day, Japan's military masters seemed determined to stack troops into the likely invasion beach areas at whatever cost. As the fighting on Okinawa had demonstrated, the fate of Japanese civilians was of small consequence compared with the general's grandiose notions of Japan's latest war goal. By inflicting unacceptable casualties on the Americans, they expected to gain a negotiated peace. It was as brutally simple as it was simply unrealistic. From Pearl Harbor to Tokyo Bay, the Japanese high command had consistently underestimated the hate sowed at Pearl Harbor that now fueled America's determination to smash Japan at almost any cost. Imperial Headquarters' inability to comprehend the raw, driving motivations of its major enemy was about to reap the whirlwind.

While the Japanese operational commands prepared for battle, so did General Krueger's Sixth Army. On July 1, Sixth Army turned over the Luzon campaign to Eighth Army so that Krueger's staff could devote full time to planning and preparing for the invasion of Kyushu. The OLYMPIC scenario called for a three-pronged simultaneous assault on Kyushu from the east, south, and west. Two U.S. Army corps (a total of six divisions) and the V Marine Amphibious Corps (three U.S. Marine divisions) were slated for the massive assault. Another army corps of two divisions was in follow-up reserve; an army division was poised to attack the small chain of islands just south and west of Kyushu; and still another would be held in strategic reserve. In all, 650,000 troops backed by more than 100,000 sailors and airmen were being readied for the greatest amphibious operation in history.[24] From west to east, the OLYMPIC sequence of invasion and the ULTRA-detected opposition were as follows:

1. The V Marine Amphibious Corps (the 3rd, 4th, and 5th Marine divisions) would assault the western side of the Satsuma Peninsula and then drive east toward Kagoshima Bay. It would meet, according to Willoughby, the 77th and 146th divisions as well as the 3rd Amphibious Brigade (the 125th Independent Mixed Brigade) and assorted naval and replacement units—as many as fifty-two thousand Japanese defenders.

2. The XI Corps (the 1st Cavalry, Americal, and 43d divisions) would storm Ariake Bay, capture Kanoya, advance to Kagoshima Bay, and then turn northwest. It would first encounter the 86th Division and later perhaps two more divisions— the 25th and 156th—and an armored brigade—an estimated fifty-five thousand Japanese troops.

3. The I Corps (the 25th, 33d, and 41st divisions) would go ashore at Miyazaki and then move southeast. It would have to fight the 154th and 212th divisions and a parachute brigade—perhaps sixty-one thousand Japanese troops.

As ULTRA had foretold, the Japanese high command wanted to fight the battle on the beaches. Imperial Headquarters expected the mobile combat reserves, which were concentrated in the forested mountains of south-central Kyushu, to move 8 to 12 miles at night and arrive at predesignated assembly areas ready to attack and destroy the American beachhead. Coastal divisions had to hold the first assault waves in check on or near the beaches until these mobile divisions could counterattack. Variations of the basic plan were labeled I, RO, and HA (A, B, and C) for operations against landings at Miyazaki, Shibushi, and the Satsuma Peninsula, respectively.

The composition of the mobile force would vary, depending on which beach the Americans chose for their landings. At a minimum, the force always included the three tank brigades and the 25th, 57th, and 216th Infantry divisions. Thus the I Corps, landing at Miyazaki, would face the 212th, 154th, and 156th divisions; the XI Corps at Shibushi would face the 86th Division and the 98th Independent Mixed Brigade; and the V Amphibious Corps on the Satsuma Peninsula would face the 146th, 206th, and 303d divisions and the 125th Independent Mixed Brigade.[25]

In retrospect, the counterattack scheme seems wildly ambitious, but Japanese willingess to persevere despite seemingly overwhelming odds meant that their announced intentions could not be dismissed out of hand. More telling, however, was Imperial Headquarters' concept of the defense of Kyushu. Japan's military leaders premised the giant counterstroke against one, not multiple, invasion beaches. Given the wretched state of communications, the devastated railway network, Allied mastery of the air and sea, and the lack of fast-moving motorized and mechanized combat formations, Japan's last legions might have been able to wreck havoc against one beachhead, but American troops on the other two beaches would have secured their objectives, though probably with high casualties. The result—the American conquest of Kyushu—was inevitable.

Any estimate of the human toll of an invasion of Japan is conjecture, but two novelists, one American and the other Japanese, have given us an idea of "what might have been" had Operation OLYMPIC been launched.[26] David Westheimer's hypothetical campaign carries OLYMPIC through December 30, 1945, or forty-eight days after the landings. For that period, American casualties are 71,000, including 17,500 killed in action. Japanese losses were conjectured at 194,000 soldiers and sailors killed, 19,000 wounded, and 2,100 captured. Civilian volunteer losses were 143,000: 40,000 killed, 50,000 wounded, and 53,000 captured. Total Japanese combatant losses amounted to 338,000 in about one and a half months of fighting. Hiyama Yoshiaki's fictional vision is apocalyptic. Japanese casualties alone exceed 2,675,000 from November 1, 1945, to January 15, 1946. Hiyama writes of 615,000 Japanese servicemen and 260,000 civilian volunteers killed. Unceasing B-29 Superfortress saturation bombing attacks, constant aerial strafing by fighter aircraft, naval bombardment, and indiscriminate American artillery fire account for 1,800,000 civilian, noncombatant casualties. American losses are equally grim: 187,000 battle casualties with another 23,000 cases of battle fatigue. In either portrayal, the Americans achieve all their objectives and southern Japan is in ashes.

Unbeknownst to MacArthur and his headquarters, on July 16, 1945, the first atomic bomb was successfully tested near Alamogordo, New Mexico. On July 25, President Truman approved dropping an atomic bomb on Japan as soon after August 3 as the weather would permit visual bombing of the selected target. Neither MacArthur nor Nimitz were told about the actual target until two days before the Hiroshima attack. In later years, MacArthur criticized the use of the atomic weapon and claimed it was unnecessary from a military standpoint.[27] ULTRA reports that the general received between July 29 and August 5 (the day before the Hiroshima attack) about the state of Kyushu defenses make his assertion suspect.

There were definitely three Japanese armies—Fifty-Sixth, Fifty-Seventh, and Fortieth—on Kyushu and another was expected (July 28/29). From a Fortieth Army message, dated July 27, ULTRA ascertained two new divisions—the 216th and 303d—in Kyushu (July 29/30). On July 30, Washington concurred that the first radio network of a 300 series division was broadcasting in southern Kyushu (*July 30*). The new divisions were still unlocated, but other ULTRA stated that the 145th Division was thought to be moving from Hiroshima to Kyushu while the 7th Division's radio messages hinted that it was deploying south from northeastern Japan. ULTRA had uncovered the locations of eleven divisions, two depot divisions, two independent mixed brigades, and one unidentified armored brigade under Sixteenth Area Army's command. Electronic clues strongly suggested that at least two more divisions and two more armored brigades were somewhere on Kyushu (July 31/August 1).

Deciphered messages in early August also referred to 300 series divisions. ULTRA disclosed the presence of the 312th Division from a July 26 message, which caused Washington to raise Japanese strength on Kyushu by 20,000 men—to 545,000 (*August 2*). Ultra also tracked the 206th Division deploying into southwestern Kyushu to strengthen the defenses of the western coast under Fortieth Army's guidance (*August 4*). New units sprang up seemingly overnight. Three days later, Washington positively identified the 216th and 303d divisions in Kyushu and raised the number of defenders there to 560,000 troops (*August 7*). ULTRA also revealed the location of the newly identified 4th Artillery Command in southern Kyushu (August 4/5). On August 6, ULTRA confirmed the existence of the 312th Division and uncovered yet another formation—the 351st Division (August 5/6). On the eve of atomic warfare, ULTRA painted a menacing picture of a Kyushu transformed into an island bastion.

Table 8.1. ULTRA-Estimated and Actual Japanese Ground Order of Battle, Kyushu, July 1945

ULTRA		Actual	
Unit	Location	Unit	Location
86th Division	Ariake Bay	86th Division	Ariake Bay
3d Amphibious Brigade	Satsuma Peninsula	125th Independent Mixed Brigade	Satsuma Peninsula
25th Division	Kobayashi	25th Division	Kobayashi
77th Division	Kagoshima Area	77th Division	Kagoshima Area
154th Division	Miyazaki	154th Division	Tsuma
212th Division	Miyazaki Plain	212th Division	Tomitake
6th Armored Brigade	Kagoshima	6th Armored Brigade	Kagoshima
156th Division	Miyazaki Area	156th Division	Honjo
146th Division	Satsuma Peninsula	146th Division	Satsuma Peninsula
206th Division	Izaku	206th Division	Izaku
57th Division	Sasaguri	57th Division	Senzoku
303d Division	unidentified	303d Division	Kawauchi
312th Division	unidentified	312th Division	Karatsu
216th Division	unidentified	216th Division	Kumamoto
		351st Division	Tsuyazaki
145th Division	in transit[a]	145th Division	Ashiya
Fortieth Army	Izuku	Fortieth Army	Izuku
Fifty-Sixth Army	Izuka	Fifty-Sixth Army	Izuka
Fifty-Seventh Army	Miyakonojō	Fifty-Seventh Army	Miyakonojō
Sixteenth Area Army	Fukuoka	Sixteenth Area Army	Fukuoka

[a]The War Department carried the 145th at Senzoku, confusing it with the 57th, which it incorrectly placed at Sasaguri. SWPA believed the 145th was moving from Hiroshima to Kyushu.

Source: ULTRA: SWPA, Special Intelligence Bulletin, and War Department, Military Intelligence Summary, for 1–31 July 1945, National Archives and Records Administration, Washington, D.C.; Actual: Boeicho, Boei kenshujo, ed., *Senshi sosho,* Vol. 57: *Hondo kessen jumbi: Kyushu no boei* (2) (Tokyo: Asagumo shimbunsha, 1972), plate 13.

ULTRA had correctly identified thirteen of the fourteen Japanese divisions defending Kyushu and located their major concentrations. Only ULTRA accurately portrayed the general dispositions of enemy forces and presented MacArthur with the overall Japanese plan of defense along the beaches. Only ULTRA gave MacArthur a straightforward accounting of Japanese forces, doctrine, and intentions for the great battle. It did not, however, assess the wretched state of Japanese equipment. Deciphered diplomatic cables revealed the deterioration of Japan's food stocks and concerns that if the Allies somehow destroyed the fall rice crops, the resulting famine would leave Japan unable to continue the war (July 15/16). Planners also recognized through ULTRA that the strategic naval blockade, the mining of Japanese ports, and the systematic aerial destruction of Japan's cities were hurting the homeland (June 15/16; July 15/16). These measures were viewed as preparatory to an invasion of Japan, not as ends in themselves.

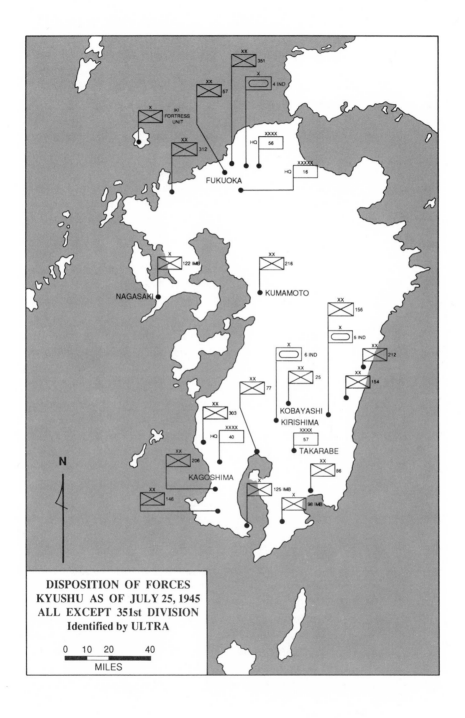

N

DISPOSITION OF FORCES
KYUSHU AS OF JULY 25, 1945
ALL EXCEPT 351st DIVISION
Identified by ULTRA

0   10   20   40

MILES

This left decisionmakers with only the yardstick of total numbers to measure the capability of Japanese ground forces. Those figures said that 600,000 Japanese soldiers and sailors with perhaps 6,000 to 7,000 aircraft stood ready to fight to the death for Kyushu against the 650,000 Americans readying to invade Japan. There were, in fact, approximately 900,000 soldiers assigned to Sixteenth Area Army defending Kyushu. Three air armies—First, Fifth, and Sixth—had 3,300 aircraft, including 2,100 kamikazes, ready to strike the invaders. Another 5,225 navy aircraft, almost 4,000 dedicated to suicide roles, complemented the force.[28]

ULTRA's steady revelations of the large Japanese buildup of air and ground forces on Kyushu deeply troubled the men responsible for the decision to drop the atomic bomb. Secretary of War Henry L. Stimson foresaw any invasion producing a bitter struggle, heavy American losses, and a Japan laid waste.[29] The day the atomic bomb was successfully tested, Stimson's memorandum to the president expressed his belief that "our newer weapons" and possibly Soviet entry into the war might be necessary to subdue Japan. Later reports about the devastating power of the atomic bomb convinced Stimson that Soviet participation was no longer needed to conquer Japan.[30] Marshall was less certain, and MacArthur, still not privy to the nuclear secret, wanted the Soviets to enter the Pacific war.[31]

During the final week of July, Marshall told the president at Potsdam, Germany, that OLYMPIC and CORONET would cost a minimum of a quarter-million and possibly a million American casualties.[32] It seems likely that the wave of reinforcements that ULTRA spotlighted played heavily on Marshall's mind and caused him to revise his earlier casualty projection dramatically upward. Unlike Stimson, Marshall continued to worry about American losses during an invasion of Japan; his concern did not dissipate in the vision of a radioactive cloud over Japan.

The day after Hiroshima was obliterated, Marshall sent an "Eyes Only" message to MacArthur about problems he had with the OLYMPIC objectives. Intelligence reports available to both commanders, and Marshall certainly was referring to ULTRA, showed a vast enemy buildup in southern Kyushu, including "a large component of suicide planes." If the Japanese were deployed in such force on the invasion beaches, then Sixth Army faced the possibility of heavy losses when it stormed Kyushu. Marshall asked MacArthur for his "personal estimate of Japanese intentions and capabilities" and possible alternative objectives to OLYMPIC such as Tokyo proper, Sendai, and Ominato.[33]

MacArthur's response typified his attitude about intelligence data that conflicted with his concept of operations. ULTRA, the general believed, had greatly exaggerated the Japanese air threat; therefore, he dismissed that source out of hand. Neither did he believe the reports of greatly increased strength in southern Kyushu. Besides, if the Japanese units were there, the ever-growing American air and naval forces would cripple the defenders before OLYMPIC commenced. The same air forces that Willoughby had insisted did not prevent Japanese reinforcement of Kyushu, MacArthur assured Marshall would destroy all enemy air potential in southern Kyushu and immobilize ground forces. Echoing his June plea, MacArthur emphatically rejected the "slightest thought of changing the Olympic operation." His concluding passage encapsulated his esteem for intelligence: "Throughout the Southwest Pacific Area campaigns, as we have neared an operation, intelligence has invariably pointed to greatly increased enemy forces. Without exception, this buildup has been found to be erroneous. In this particular case, the destruction that is going on in Japan would seem to indicate that it is very probable that the enemy is resorting to deception."[34]

The one failing of which Willoughby was never guilty was overestimation of Japanese forces. From Buna to Luzon, intelligence was exceptionally accurate on four major occasions: the Admiralties, Hollandia, the Driniumor River, and Leyte. On two of those instances—the Admiralties and Driniumor—MacArthur ignored intelligence revelations to pursue the operation. In other instances— Buna, Lae, Saidor, Wakde-Sarmi, Biak, and Luzon—Willoughby's intelligence estimates fell far short of actual Japanese strength. Like the charismatic figure he was, MacArthur took greater heed of his own counsels than those of his staff. The notion of leading the greatest amphibious assault in history—fourteen divisions versus nine at Normandy—held overwhelming appeal to MacArthur's vanity. Fortunately, the general was not permitted to test this egotistical ambition against the realities of OLYMPIC.

Initial ULTRA reports of the atomic destruction of Hiroshima were inconclusive. Washington reported that, with one exception, no Hiroshima army radio station was on the air from the time of the bombing until noon (*August 7*). Willoughby maintained, however, that the normal transmissions of the army radio station in the city were not interrupted (August 7/8). Landlines were disrupted because the atomic blast had blown down telephone poles like matchsticks, forcing Japanese broadcasters to switch from secure phone lines to radios for plain-language transmissions of weather reports. A message to the navy minister from the giant Kure Naval Base, just across the bay from Hiroshima, reported a "terrific explosion" about 1,000 feet above the ground. "The concussion was beyond imagination, demolishing practically every house in the city. About 80 percent of the city was wiped out, destroyed or burned. Casualties alone have been estimated at 100,000 persons (**August 8**). Excited messages ordered pilots to shoot down Allied B-29 bombers or, failing that, to destroy the parachute that retarded the atomic bomb's fall. Japanese signal intelligence correctly identified the weather observation plane as belonging to the 313th Bomber Wing on Tinian because it had broadcast coded messages directing the attack from thirty minutes to one hour before the bombing (**August 9**). Some Japanese interrogators, however, were willing to accept almost any story in order to file their reports with Tokyo. A decryption described such a tale, likely told by First Lieutenant Marcus McDilda whose P-51 fighter Japanese gunners had downed near Osaka.

McDilda had withstood random beatings inflicted by Japanese civilians as his captors marched him through Osaka streets to military police headquarters. Several hours of questioning got him more punches, slaps, and abuse, especially when he said he knew nothing about the atomic weapon. Around midnight a high-ranking Japanese officer appeared in McDilda's cell and threatened to cut the American's head off if he did not tell about the bomb. ULTRA recorded McDilda's life-or-death improvisation as later reported to Tokyo. He claimed that the bomb atomized an area of 6 square miles with a searing blast and a flash, described a fictitious bomb's dimensions, and assured his captors that it could not be dropped at night or during rainfall. Hiroshima had been an experiment, he lied, and Tokyo was the next atomic bomb target. McDilda's clever fabrication satisfied his tormentors and enabled him to survive the war (August 10/11; **August 11**).[35]

Japanese officials did not have to rely on make-believe accounts for their assessments. ULTRA provided eyewitness versions of the devastation at Hiroshima from messages that were sent to the chief of staff of the General Army Air Command in Tokyo. "There was a blinding flash and a violent blast (over city center, flash and burst were almost simultaneous but in the vicinity of the airfield blast came 2 or 3 seconds later), and a mass of white smoke billowing up into the air," one report stated (August 9/10). The now ominously familiar description of the mushroom cloud had made its initial appearance in ULTRA.

Eyewitnesses then described the results of the searing heat and atomic concussion. As far as 2 miles away from the center of the explosion, the heat burned exposed parts of people's bodies and ignited their thin summer clothing. Within the same 2-mile radius of death, the blast leveled, either completely or partially, sixty thousand buildings. A conflagration spread, consuming vast areas of the city. Almost all government buildings were obliterated. Terrible burns or lacerations from flying shards of glass injured thousands of residents (*August 9;* August 9/10). Army ULTRA also revealed that the atomic bomb had killed 30 percent of the army personnel at Second General Army Headquarters in Hiroshima and wounded another 30 percent. Life ceased in the city as overwhelming destruction and roaring spontaneous fires transformed Hiroshima into hell (*August 10;* **August 10**). A later report from Hiroshima concluded pathetically, "There is practically no defense measure" (*August 15*).

The next atomic bomb attack against Nagasaki in western Kyushu on August 9, 1945, passed unnoticed in ULTRA channels. Hiroshima monopolized attention, and the war had not ended. Despite the two atomic attacks, American intelligence's study of Japanese naval radio messages for August 15 left the impression that the Japanese were still planning and executing wartime operations with air,

surface, and underwater suicide units (**August 15**). Willoughby was more gener-
ous. He argued that there was nothing contradictory in Japanese field commanders
urging their troops to greater efforts as Japanese diplomats scurried about seeking
peace. Such confusion, Willoughby believed, was a natural outgrowth of the
disorder involved in preliminary peace negotiations (August 15/16). Furthermore,
broken codes illuminated the emperor's indispensable role in compelling Japan's
armed forces to lay down their weapons of war.

ULTRA picked up the navy minister's account of the Imperial Council where the
final problem of peace or war was submitted to the emperor. " 'His and only his'
decision was to accept the Potsdam Declaration, 'on the condition that the structure of the nation be left intact' " (**August 18**). Deciphered message after deciphered message testified to the force of the Imperial Rescript (*shosho*) of August
14, 1945, as radio messages of compliance poured into Tokyo from units strewn
from Java to North China. Southern Army's case exemplified the emperor's unique
position in Japanese society. On August 15 Southern Army informed all its subordinate units, which stretched from Rabaul to Burma, that although an imperial
statement accepting the Potsdam Declaration had been issued, all Japanese forces
would continue to fight. "So long as the Southern Army has no orders, you are not
to enter into any negotiations with the enemy, but are to continue to repel him"
(August 15/17). Late the next day, after receiving imperial orders, Southern Army
instructed all units to obey the emperor's edict. Officers and men were ordered "to
observe strict discipline and obey orders to the last, thus proving to the world their
fidelity to the Emperor." Other combat formations signaled that "the only road to
follow now is united obedience to the Emperor" (August 18/19). This impressive
display of authority surely made an indelible impression not only on MacArthur
but also on leaders in Washington. One may speculate that it was instrumental in
the later American decision to retain the emperor and imperial institution as
symbols of the Japanese state despite vociferous calls from other Allies for his
indictment as a war criminal.[36]

As Japan's legions stacked their arms in surrender, the former great stream of
military radio communications declined to a trickle, mainly directing units to burn
codebooks and cryptanalytic paraphernalia. The Pacific war had ended with the
same suddenness with which it had begun. An unstable postwar world subsequently consigned ULTRA's accomplishments in the Southwest Pacific to a limbo
of secrecy for thirty years.

9
Conclusion

On a warm summer day in February 1988, Dr. Abraham Sinkov unveiled a modest plaque on the wall of a private residence at Twenty-one Henry Street, Brisbane. It read: "Central Bureau, an organisation comprising service personnel of Australia, U.S.A., Britain, Canada, and N.Z., both men and women, functioned in this house from 1942 till 1945. From intercepted radio messages the organisation provided intelligence which made a decisive contribution to the allied victory in the Pacific War." This brief public tribute left Central Bureau's exact, extensive contributions to the war against Japan wrapped in obscurity. The code-breaking successes on the Southwest Pacific front rivaled similar efforts in any theater during World War II. Although trial and error characterized Central Bureau's first year, the grueling labor during those lean months laid the foundation for subsequent progress. Central Bureau and the Signal Intelligence Service together solved the Japanese Army Water Transport Code in April 1943, working on purely cryptanalytic principles. This success ensured Central Bureau's reputation as a decryption center, because it gave the Allies a general picture of Japanese army deployments throughout the Pacific. That knowledge guided the aerial and submarine interdiction effort against the Japanese transport fleet.

The watershed for Central Bureau was the capture of the Imperial Army Code Book and cipher paraphernalia at Sio in January 1944. This fortuitous event enabled MacArthur's codebreakers to penetrate the final mystery of the army's mainline code and transformed Central Bureau overnight into a first-rate crypt-analytic center capable of reading thousands of enemy radio messages. By imaginative use of state-of-the-art technology, such as early model IBM equipment, and the application of ingenuity and creativity, Allied cryptanalysts were able to keep pace with subsequent Japanese changes to these army codes and to read hidden messages with regularity. There were occasional blackouts of the Imperial Army's four-digit system—for example, when the Japanese introduced new key

A representative of each of the services at Central Bureau, August 1945. Top row, left to right: Sergeant David Eunson, Royal Air Force, Great Britain; Corporal William Sanders, Australia Militia Forces; Technician 5th Grade (T/5) Bud Curtner, U.S. Army; Sergeant Dennis Olmstead, Canada; Warrant Officer Richard Bellingham, Great Britain; and Corporal Ross Rampling, Royal Australian Air Force. Bottom row, left to right: T/5 Stella Kurkul, Women's Army Corps, U.S.A.; Corporal Cynthia Hickey, Women's Auxiliary Australian Air Force; and Corporal Dorothy Hilliard, Australian Women's Army Service. (Courtesy of U.S. National Security Agency)

registers (April-May 1944) or new Army Code Books (January-June 1945)—but Central Bureau maintained technical mastery over a variety of army codes. Besides the Water Transport and four-digit army codes, Central Bureau was routinely solving several Japanese army air force ciphers. Central Bureau regularly dispatched cryptanalytic data to Washington and received, in turn, cryptanalytic intelligence derived from the Japanese Foreign Ministry and military attaché codes. The rulers of this bureaucratic game demanded that a first-level, independent player (MacArthur's own requirement) generate high-quality intelligence.

Despite the frustration caused by its inability to penetrate lower-level, three-digit tactical codes, Central Bureau's contributions to codebreaking during the Pacific war were as significant as they were extensive. The Allied solution of the four-digit cipher complemented the data gleaned from the Imperial Navy's compromised main operational code and was one of the greatest Allied triumphs of

World War II, as authentic a battlefield victory as Midway or Hollandia. In short, Central Bureau produced ULTRA, the interception, decryption, and translation of Japanese radio messages.

ULTRA provided Allied commanders with an astonishing range of data about the Japanese army and army air force. An effective distribution system was used to disseminate ULTRA data in a secure manner to MacArthur and his staff and to commanders in the field who needed the intelligence to craft their operations. Akin had the authority to disseminate perishable and critical ULTRA immediately to the commands, where it could be turned to quick advantage. Otherwise, the dissemination of ULTRA evolved over the course of the Pacific war. In 1942 dissemination was typically loose and haphazard; in 1943 security tightened considerably and the distribution list for ULTRA was restricted to a select few in Southwest Pacific Headquarters. At that time, neither Washington nor Brisbane could generate much ULTRA about the Japanese army, so the increased restrictions did not affect operational planning very much. When copious ULTRA became available in early 1944, the network of commanders who received it grew apace with the steady expansion of MacArthur's forces. The distribution of ULTRA was institutionalized, going to Sixth Army, Fifth Air Force, and Seventh Fleet and later to the various army corps that were organized under Sixth and Eighth armies. Washington's regulations and requirements were enforced by dispatching special security officers to these commands. The dissemination system moved intelligence efficiently from Southwest Pacific Headquarters to the major field commanders, who would have ULTRA in hand when making their plans or decisions. It did make possible the widespread distribution of ULTRA so that MacArthur and his chief lieutenants usually had ULTRA when it was most needed. Of course, how they used ULTRA involved generalship.

Generalship—a commander's use of ULTRA in strategic or operational planning and decision—was the most complex ingredient in the ULTRA mixture. I began this book with the expectation that ULTRA would fill in puzzling gaps or explain the motivations behind certain command decisions that historians have debated since the end of World War II. In some cases, ULTRA did provide clear answers to thorny questions. MacArthur's sudden decision to leap to Hollandia was neatly explained by the heretofore missing dimension of ULTRA. But the intelligence component did not resolve other questions. For example, why did MacArthur decide to attack the Admiralties in spite of ULTRA warnings that the islands had not been abandoned? Why did Krueger decide to attack west toward Lone Tree Hill or defend the Carigara beaches instead of the ridge? The Southwest Pacific commander often ignored ULTRA—most notably in pushing for the Biak and Leyte invasions and, potentially the most ominous, in decisions about the projected invasion of Kyushu. As the climactic invasion of Japan neared, MacArthur bluntly told Marshall that he did not believe ULTRA forecasts of Japanese numbers gathering to contest the Allies. In MacArthur's defense, the inconsistent performance of ULTRA in his theater may account for the general's skeptical attitude. For long periods MacArthur had no reliable ULTRA about the Japanese army. From April 1942 until January 1944, army ULTRA was very spotty, and during this twenty-one-month period its value was usually to confirm, not to reveal, Japanese ground and air dispositions. From January 1944 until April 1945, periodic blackouts made reading the army's mainline code a fragile intelligence source. ULTRA's importance was recognized, but so too was its fickleness.

If the boldness that characterized MacArthur's campaigns from January 1944 on was directly attributable to success in breaking the Japanese army code, a reevaluation of his generalship could have proceeded from that premise. However, this hypothesis proved incorrect because Allied ability to read the Japanese army codes waxed and waned and MacArthur sometimes pushed ahead with scheduled operations using minimal or even contradictory intelligence. ULTRA cannot fully account for the motivations behind MacArthur's decisionmaking. One searches in vain for that "ULTRA state of mind" commanders fighting the war against Germany are alleged to have possessed.[1]

For MacArthur, ULTRA was sometimes available and sometimes not. Planning for the western New Guinea campaigns was done without ULTRA, and, indeed, the Southwest Pacific Area witnessed the evolution of a much different pattern of Japanese army ULTRA than was yielded by its decrypted German counterpart in the European war. As pointed out earlier, from about February 1941 the flow of decrypted German messages was sufficiently reliable to require round-the-clock shifts, and output progressively increased with only rare and brief interruptions.[2] MacArthur never enjoyed a rich, steady flow of information and, indeed, fought the first half of his war with very limited army ULTRA. The unique development, use, and inconsistency of Japanese army ULTRA in the Southwest Pacific and Philippines make MacArthur's uneven exploitation of ULTRA more understandable.

Even fifty years later, ULTRA does not fully reveal the connection between intelligence evaluation and strategic or operational planning. A possible reason for that involves *how* people dealt with intelligence data. MacArthur and his senior staff and commanders—Willoughby, Krueger, Kenney, Hall, Kinkaid, and so forth—each read and evaluated translated Japanese messages in light of their own preconceptions, military expertise, and personalities. A message that triggered a red flag for one officer might pass unnoticed by another. Willoughby, for instance, was habitually more cautious than MacArthur in his prognostications about Japanese defenses in the Admiralties, Sarmi, Biak, Leyte, and Kyushu. In each case, he candidly told MacArthur about his concerns. He never overstated enemy strength but, rather, always erred on the side of underestimation. Still, in early 1944 this cautious officer brought to MacArthur's attention the ULTRA revelations that ultimately canceled the Madang plan in favor of the bold leap to Hollandia. Kenney provides another example. He relied heavily on ULTRA to target Japanese airfields and shipping for his airmen. He enjoyed great success and presumably regarded ULTRA as authentic and reliable. Yet when ULTRA challenged Kenney's cherished belief that air power alone could force the enemy to desert the Admiralties, he simply disregarded the evidence. Krueger used ULTRA in planning and operational estimates. Sixth Army naturally wanted to know the Imperial Army's latest tactical dispositions, but it was foiled by the unbreakable three-digit code. Krueger found himself surprised by Japanese strength at Sarmi and Leyte and his seemingly lukewarm attitude about ULTRA may stem from these experiences. At another level, Hall at the Driniumor River battle was caught in the confusion of contradictory and ambiguous ULTRA and wasted an intelligence windfall.

Other operations were botched despite advance warnings from ULTRA. When naval ULTRA tipped off Southwest Pacific Headquarters about the impending Buna invasion, MacArthur vacillated while the Japanese landed unimpeded and turned Buna into a stronghold whose elimination cost hundreds of Allied lives. The Southwest Pacific commander's insistence that his field commanders rapidly conclude operations glossed over ULTRA-derived estimates that accurately depicted the enemy's strength. MacArthur was also willing to press ahead without accurate intelligence. The campaigns on Luzon and the planning for Kyushu illustrate the former, and Krueger's attack against Saidor and MacArthur's exasperation with his Sixth Army commander at Biak, Leyte, and Luzon exemplify the latter. At root was MacArthur's tendency to ignore Japanese capabilities when formulating his timetables for victory.

MacArthur consistently dismissed ULTRA evidence that failed to accord with his preconceived strategic vision. Nothing influenced him more than his desire to liberate the Philippines from Japanese occupation and thereby erase the stain on his military reputation. MacArthur thought in strategic terms and was willing to take calculated operational risks to achieve higher goals. Likewise, he was willing to ignore intelligence that contradicted that strategic appreciation to which he was committed. Paradoxically, such steadfastness of purpose is essential for a successful commander. ULTRA was normally ambiguous and to use it effectively, a commander had to be straightforward and clear about his plans and objectives.

What remains is a striking impression that MacArthur did not rely heavily on ULTRA either to frame his strategic concept of the war in the Southwest Pacific or to devise operational plans to implement the strategy. A sense of destiny, not revelations from ULTRA, propelled MacArthur through his Southwest Pacific campaigns. The Hollandia operation of April 1944 was the exception where MacArthur relied on accurate intelligence to accelerate his campaign. Elsewhere he ignored intelligence, ULTRA or otherwise, that might have interfered with his determination to return to the Philippines. He disregarded Willoughby's precise ULTRA estimate of Japanese troops in the Admiralties and risked an invasion that might have turned to disaster. He pushed his forces into Wakde, Sarmi, and Biak (where ULTRA did reveal that Japanese rear areas were weak and disorganized) on the barest intelligence appreciations of Japanese defenses there. For his Leyte operation, strategic considerations overrode intelligence realities as MacArthur disregarded timely and accurate ULTRA about reinforcements pouring into the islands in order to steal a march on the Philippines. Luzon was another case in which MacArthur willed away about one-third of the Japanese garrison to craft an overly ambitious operational plan. MacArthur's curious attitude toward the invasion of Japan affords still another instance in which he dismissed, by a wave of the hand, exceptionally accurate ULTRA regarding the Japanese buildup on the Kyushu front. These points lead inexorably to the conclusion that intelligence assessment depends on the beholder's prejudices, underscoring the eternal, basic problem of evaluation.

If no one could be forced to use ULTRA, neither could ULTRA alter the personalities of those who made decisions about its utility. As always, a commander's personality filtered his perception of ULTRA. An aggressive, driven general was not transformed overnight into a timid, cautious one because of ULTRA's revelations. Indeed, ULTRA appears to have reinforced basic personality traits. It convinced forceful commanders to take risks and push forward, just as it persuaded prudent ones to go even more slowly. The personalities of MacArthur, his staff, and his army commanders colored the manner in which they employed ULTRA for campaign planning and during their operations. MacArthur used ULTRA most effectively when its revelations were in harmony with his fixed ideas of strategy. Put differently, intelligence that augured against the liberation of the Philippines received less consideration than that which enabled the Southwest Pacific chieftain to accelerate his advance toward this strategic goal. In operational terms, when MacArthur used ULTRA's disclosures to plan the isolation and bypassing of Japanese strongholds, he was an exceptional practitioner of the art of war—then he reached Luzon where the Japanese could not be bypassed. In strategic terms, on the other hand, MacArthur seemed to be so captivated by the allure of a triumphant return to the Philippines that he was willing to disregard or at least downplay ULTRA or, for that matter, any intelligence that indicated that the risks might outweigh the potential advantages.

What did ULTRA accomplish in MacArthur's theater? Its impact on the air and sea dimensions of the war profoundly affected the conduct of operations. ULTRA immeasurably simplified the interdiction of enemy air and sea resupply routes because it foretold with exactitude the locations and times Japanese ships and aircraft would appear. Japanese radio operators were inadvertently betraying the convoys as they tapped out their dispatches in supposedly unbreakable codes. Using this data, U.S. submarines could be positioned to patrol Japanese convoy routes, and Allied reconnaissance planes could fly over areas of enemy activity. Allied fighter pilots were programmed, without their knowledge, to fly missions over locations where their quarries were likely to be. Once detected visually or by radar, Japanese transports and warships suffered merciless air, submarine, and surface attacks.

Kenney and his air commanders used ULTRA with deadly effectiveness. Kenney began with small attacks against Japanese naval resupply convoys around Buna but quickly moved to orchestrate the Battle of the Bismarck Sea with the intelligence he derived from naval ULTRA. The near annihilation of the 51st Division at sea marked the strategic turning point of the New Guinea operation and enabled MacArthur's 1943 ground campaign to push forward. Kenney also capitalized on ULTRA sources to pinpoint and strike Japanese airdromes from Rabaul to Hollandia with massed air assaults. His attacks against Wewak in August 1943 made possible MacArthur's landings near Lae; his war of attrition against Rabaul made possible the Admiralties invasion; and his destruction of Japanese air power at Hollandia in March and April 1944 made possible MacArthur's greatest leapfrog operation along the northern New Guinea coast. ULTRA handed Kenney the times and routes of the Japanese resupply convoys at Leyte and allowed his airmen to exact a terrible price in Japanese ships and men. In the summer of 1945, Kenney was using ULTRA revelations for his bombing campaign on Kyushu. Clearly, ULTRA guided Kenney's air operations with a higher degree of consistency than it did the ground campaigns.

Naval ULTRA, whether obtained from the Army Water Transport Code or from naval decipherments, was also of great value, especially in the submarine war against the Japanese empire. With chilling regularity, American and Allied submarines rose from beneath the waves to launch torpedoes into unsuspecting Japanese merchantmen and warships. The destruction of the TAKE convoy, bound for western New Guinea with men and supplies, served as an outstanding example of the interplay between ULTRA and operations. Guided by ULTRA, these incessant submarine attacks sent hundreds of ships and thousands of men to the ocean floor. From the *Tenryu* going down off Madang to the 23d Division convoy being torpedoed off Luzon, Allied submarines used ULTRA with deadly effect. The interdiction campaign not only thwarted Japanese efforts to bolster their Southwest Pacific defenses but also forced abandonment of large garrisons that could no longer be resupplied without prohibitive losses. ULTRA's operational worth was manifested off Biak when Admiral Kinkaid used its revelations to position his fleet to intercept the approaching KON force.

Allied ability to read Japanese army radio messages definitely shortened the ground war in the Pacific. When ULTRA was available, MacArthur's staff was able to plan operations confidently because of their accurate understanding of the enemy situation. ULTRA had a major role in the manner and timing of MacArthur's great victories at Hollandia and in western New Guinea, which were achieved at comparatively little cost in Allied casualties, but only because it meshed with his desire to propel his forces toward the Philippines. As luck or fate would have it, ULTRA identified the operational flaw in MacArthur's New Guinea campaign by exposing Japanese intentions to defend Hansa Bay in strength. If MacArthur had become bogged down fighting Adachi's three divisions there, the course of the Pacific war would probably have been very different. The Central Pacific drive likely would have bypassed the Philippines in favor of Formosa. ULTRA underwrote MacArthur's carefully calculated leap to Hollandia, a maneuver that not only escaped the trap at Hansa Bay but also broke the back of Japan's defenses on New Guinea. Seizing Hollandia split the Japanese forces on the island and shattered Japanese timetables for stiffening their defenses. ULTRA next revealed the extent of the TAKE disaster, which assured MacArthur that no strategic reserve waited in western New Guinea to block his path to the Philippines.

One might argue that ULTRA did not matter because American matériel superiority sooner or later would have crushed the Japanese. This is true but irrelevant. Without ULTRA the cost in Allied casualties would have been much higher, the Pacific war much longer, and the shape of the postwar world much different. In the final analysis, the American GIs and Australian infantrymen who moved forward against yet another Japanese-held ridge, pillbox, or bunker won the ground war. But without the access MacArthur had to ULTRA, enabling him on occasion to choose the time and place of his battles, their suffering would have been far greater. ULTRA was no substitute for matters that only armed men could decide in battle, but its revelations did give commanders an inestimable advantage over their opponents. During peak periods of ULTRA output, such as late January through April 1, 1944, MacArthur possessed unparalleled insight into Japanese intentions. With the strategic initiative firmly in hand, ULTRA enabled MacArthur to select the Imperial Army's weakest points and then strike at the emperor's troops with overwhelming local superiority. Similarly, a technologically and numerically superior Allied Air Forces seized the skies because ULTRA made known the Imperial Air Force's whereabouts.

However, MacArthur's decisions about Leyte and Luzon were amalgams of several elements, and ULTRA was not high among them. By fall 1944, the conjunction of the Central and Southwest Pacific drives at Leyte assured MacArthur overwhelming naval might. In such favorable conditions, ULTRA was a less important factor than might be expected. ULTRA was also not instrumental in the decision to accelerate the advance on the Philippines. Quite the opposite. MacArthur pressed ahead in liberating the archipelago despite General Marshall's cautions about the Japanese air and naval buildup uncovered by ULTRA. In this instance, by deprecating ULTRA, MacArthur shaved another two months from the schedule for his counteroffensive. With the Philippines liberated and his reputation in the islands restored, MacArthur turned his attention to OLYMPIC and the invasion of Japan. Once again, after plans were finalized, he dismissed ULTRA's accurate revelations of a massive Japanese buildup on Kyushu in July 1945. MacArthur's reasons for not relying on ULTRA intelligence concerning the scope of the Kyushu buildup—intelligence was not reliable enough and Allied air and naval power would weaken the enemy—had an eerie ring when the same arguments were used five years later on Wake Island. At that time, of course, MacArthur was assuring President Truman that the Chinese were incapable of intervening against United Nations forces in northern Korea. Clearly, MacArthur's successes were due less to solid ULTRA intelligence than to the circumstances that obviated the need for ULTRA.

I did not discover an intelligence template to place over MacArthur's campaigns that would outline a pattern of ULTRA cause and operational effect and serve to measure his generalship. Instead, I found a situational use of ULTRA, one dependent upon MacArthur's assessment of the strategic condition of the moment. When ULTRA fit into the general's plans, it was employed. When it did not, it was relegated to a minor role. ULTRA was only one of many ingredients in MacArthur's complex approach to decisionmaking.

MacArthur's generalship and to an even greater degree his personal leadership suffered because of ULTRA's disclosures. He pressured his subordinates unmercifully to pull off victories when ULTRA made plain that the Japanese were present in greater numbers than MacArthur was willing to accept. One also thinks of his and Kenney's reaction to ULTRA's testimony of the Bismarck Sea losses. MacArthur's carefully constructed persona as a daring gambler was diminished because ULTRA showed that as often as not he was betting on a sure thing. ULTRA's portrayal of the opponent's condition was the ace up MacArthur's sleeve. In most showdowns with the Japanese, he held the winning cards. MacArthur was perhaps not as daring as he may have wished others to believe, but he was willing to take risks—such as the Admiralties, Sarmi, Biak, Leyte, Luzon, and ultimately Kyushu—to achieve the overriding strategic goal. Although certain of his personality traits may have been distasteful, Douglas MacArthur was an aggressive, brilliant leader and surely one of the top two or three military commanders of World War II.

One must be wary of generalizations about ULTRA in MacArthur's theater. What was true in 1942 was false in 1944. What may have been approved procedure in 1943 was not the way it was done in 1945. The production, dissemination, and use of ULTRA was always evolving. To generalize for the entire war from particularistic assertions confuses issues already shrouded in conflicting and incomplete evidence. Similarly, because ULTRA made known Japanese intentions, to assume that a corresponding action resulted from this knowledge founders on examples such as the Japanese breakthrough on the Driniumor River in July 1944. ULTRA and other intelligence abounded concerning an impending attack, but the Japanese assault still caught Willoughby and others off guard. To solve even a part of this puzzle, one must study what ULTRA was available, who received it, and what, if anything, was done with it.

Postwar chroniclers of the Pacific war have highlighted ULTRA's spectacular successes—the discovery of the TAKE convoy, the Driniumor decryptions, the shooting down of Admiral Yamamoto's plane, the Admiralties' order of battle, and the Hollandia coup—at the expense of operational context and rigorous analysis. They have overstated ULTRA's accomplishments and skewed a proper understanding of its role in the Pacific during World War II. By making the extraordinary appear commonplace, ambiguous and often contradictory ULTRA data were transformed into a perspicacious source for posterity. This representation of the role of ULTRA intelligence in MacArthur's theater was misleading, for it grossly oversimplified the complex process of intelligence evaluation and its relationship to operational planning. The reality of ULTRA was more mundane. It was a cumulative process, a series of victories that added up to a general picture of Japanese capabilities and forces. However, even though the breaking of Japanese army codes became routine, it should not obscure the fact that ULTRA was an intellectual, technological, and military triumph.

Notes

Abbreviations

AAF	Allied Air Forces
ATIS	Allied Translator and Interpreter Section
DI	Directorate of Intelligence
FEC	Far East Command
GHQ	General Headquarters
GS	General Staff
FRUMEL	Fleet Radio Unit, Melbourne (code name)
MID	Military Intelligence Division
MIS	Military Intelligence Service
MMBA	MacArthur Memorial Bureau of Archives, Norfolk, Virginia
NARA	National Archives and Records Administration, Washington, D.C.
NIDS	National Institute of Defense Studies, Tokyo
NPM	Pearl Harbor (code name)
NSS	Washington (code name)
OPD	Operations Division
SWPA	Southwest Pacific Area
T2W	Melbourne (code name)
USAMHI	United States Army Military History Institute, Carlisle Barracks, Pennsylvania
WNRC	Washington National Records Center, Suitland, Maryland

*Documents in Record Group 457, U.S. National Archives
and Records Administration, Washington, D.C.*

SRH-005	Use of (CX/MSS ULTRA) by the United States War Department (1943–45)
SRH-011	The Role of Communications Intelligence in Submarine Warfare in the Pacific (Jan. 1943–Oct. 1943), 7 vols.

SRH-012	The Role of Radio Intelligence in the American Japanese Naval War (August 1941–September 1942), 4 vols.
SRH-026	Marshall Letter to Eisenhower on the Use of ULTRA Intelligence (15 March 1944)
SRH-027	MAGIC Background of Pearl Harbor
SRH-029	A Brief History of the Signal Intelligence Service
SRH-032	Reports by U.S. Army ULTRA Representatives with Field Commands in the Southwest Pacific, Pacific Ocean, and China-Burma-India Theaters of Operation, 1944–1945
SRH-035	Marshall Letter to MacArthur on Use of ULTRA, 23 May 1944, and Related Correspondence
SRH-035	History of Special Branch, MIS, War Department, 1942–1944
SRH-036	Radio Intelligence in World War II: Tactical Operations in the Pacific Ocean Area, January 1943
SRH-038	A Selection of Papers Pertaining to Herbert O. Yardley
SRH-041	MID Contribution to the War Effort, MIS, WDGS, December 1945
SRH-044	Regulations Governing the Dissemination and Security of Communications Intelligence, 1943–1945
SRH-045	Reminiscences of Lieutenant Colonel Howard W. Brown
SRH-059	Selected Examples of Commendations and Related Correspondence Highlighting the Achievements of U.S. Signal Intelligence during World War II
SRH-062	History of the Military Intelligence Service
SRH-066	Examples of Intelligence Obtained from Cryptanalysis
SRH-090	Japan's Surrender Maneuvers
SRH-107	Problems of the SSO System, World War II
SRH-111	MAGIC Reports for the Attention of the President, 1943–1944
SRH-116	Origin, Functions, and Problems of the Special Branch
SRH-117	History of the Special Branch, MIS, June 1944–September 1945
SRH-127	Use and Dissemination of ULTRA in the Southwest Pacific Area
SRH-134	Expansion of the Signal Intelligence Service from 1930 to 7 December 1941, by William F. Friedman
SRH-135	History of the Second Signal Service Battalion, 1939–1945
SRH-136	Radio Intelligence in World War II Tactical Operations in the Pacific Ocean Area, December 1942
SRH-140	History of the "Language Liaison Group," MIS, War Department, 22 September 1945
SRH-144	Radio Intelligence in World War II Tactical Operations in the Pacific Ocean Area, February 1943 (2 parts)
SRH-146	Handling of ULTRA within the Military Intelligence Service, 1941–1945
SRH-149	A Brief History of Communications Intelligence in the United States, by Laurance F. Safford, Captain, USN (Ret.)
SRH-152	History Review of OP-20-G, United States Navy
SRH-169	Centralized Control of U.S. Army Signal Intelligence Activities
SRH-180	U.S. Naval Pre–World War II Radio Intercept Activities in the Philippine Islands
SRH-200	Army-Navy Collaboration, 1931–1945

SRH-203   Special Intelligence Bulletins, Military Intelligence Section, General Staff, GHQ, SWPA
SRH-207   Evacuation of USN COMINT Personnel from Corregidor in World War II
SRH-211   Japanese Radio Communications and Radio Intelligence
SRH-219   ULTRA Material in the Blamey Papers
SRH-222   OP-20 Report of Japanese Grand Fleet Maneuvers, May-June 1930
SRH-223   Various Reports on Japanese Grand Fleet Maneuvers, June-August 1933
SRH-224   Various Reports on Japanese Grand Fleet Maneuvers, August-October 1934
SRH-225   Various Reports on Japanese Grand Fleet Maneuvers
SRH-227   Unit History, 126th Signal Intelligence Company, February 1941–September 1945
SRH-254   The Japanese Intelligence System
SRH-266   The Japanese Signal Intelligence Service, 3d edition
SRH-269   U.S. Army COMINT Policy, Pearl Harbor to Summer 1942
SRH-280   An Exhibit of the Important Types of Intelligence Recovered through Reading Japanese Cryptograms
SRH-284   Radio Intelligence in World War II: Submarine Operations in the Pacific Ocean Areas, November 1943
SRH-285   Radio Intelligence in World War II: Submarine Operations in the Pacific Ocean Areas, December 1943
SRH-286   Radio Intelligence in World War II: Submarine Operations in the Pacific Ocean Areas, January-February 1944
SRH-287   Radio Intelligence in World War II: Tactical Operations in the Pacific Ocean Areas, March 1943
SRH-288   Radio Intelligence in World War II: Tactical Operations in the Pacific Ocean Areas, April 1943
SRH-306   OP-20-G Exploits and Commendations in World War II, 1942–1948
SRH-307   GHQ, SWPA, Special Intelligence Précis, G-2 GHQ, South-Southwest Pacific Area, 22 February 1943–22 November 1943
SRH-318   U.S. Navy Reports on Japanese Grand Fleet Maneuvers, 1936
SRH-319   Various Reports on Japanese Grant Fleet Maneuvers, 1937
SRH-320   Various Reports on Japanese Grand Fleet Maneuvers, 1927 to 1929
SRH-349   The Achievements of the Signal Security Agency in World War II
SRH-355   Naval Security Group History to World War II
SRH-361   History of the SSA, Vol. 2: The General Cryptanalytic Problems, 15 January 1947
SRH-362   History of the SSA, Vol. 3: The Japanese Army Problem: Cryptanalysis, 1942–45
SRH-391   American Signal Intelligence in Northwest Africa and Western Europe
SRMD-007   JICPOA Summary of ULTRA Traffic, 11 September 1944–30 June 1945 (4 vols.)
SRMD-009   JICPOA/F22 File of Administrative Letters/Correspondence, January 1942–September 1945
SRMD-015   Reports and Memoranda on a Variety of Intelligence Subjects
SRMD-017   Fundamentals of Traffic Analysis (Radio-Telegraph), October 1948

SRMN-008	CINCPAC and COMFOURTEEN CI Bulletins/Radio Digests, 1 March–31 December 1942
SRMN-009	CINCPAC Fleet Intelligence Summaries, 22 June 1942–8 May 1943
SRMN-012	Combat Intelligence Unit, Fourteenth Naval District, Traffic Intelligence Summaries with Comments by CINCPAC, War Plans/Fleet Intelligence Sections, 16 July 1941–30 June 1942
SRMN-013	United States Navy, CINCPAC Intelligence Bulletins 78–345 (10 parts), 1 June 1942–23 September 1945
SRMN-016	U.S. Navy COMINCH (F-22) File of Intelligence and Liaison, Pacific Area "BESAW," 10 September 1943–21 November 1945
SRS-01–547	"MAGIC" Summaries, Japanese Army Supplement/Far East Summaries, 19 September 1944–2 October 1945
SRS-170–182	"MAGIC" Far East Summaries, 12 February 1944–18 September 1944
SRS-549–823	"MAGIC" Summaries, 20 March 1942–31 December 1942
SRS-1534–1837	"MAGIC" Diplomatic Summaries, 1 January 1945–3 November 1945

Preface

1. GHQ, FEC, Military Intelligence Section, GS, "Operations of the Military Intelligence Section, GHQ, SWPA/FEC/SCAP," vol. 3, Intelligence Series (part 1), 1950, 29, USAMHI.

2. Rear Admiral John Godfrey, director of Naval Intelligence, Royal Navy, in early 1940 warned his commanders that if information decrypted from German signals did become available, it would be signaled to them with the security prefix "HYDRO." On 13 May 1940, this prefix was changed to ULTRA, the first use of the code word, which now has far wider, if erroneous, application. Patrick Beesly, *Very Special Intelligence* (New York: Ballantine, 1981), 43, note 3. Michael J. Parrish, *The Ultra Americans: The U.S. Role in Breaking the Nazi Codes* (New York: Stein and Day, 1984), 127, relates how the classification ULTRA SECRET evolved to plain ULTRA.

3. Ralph Bennett, *Ultra in the West: The Normandy Campaign of 1944–45* (New York: Charles Scribner's Sons, 1979).

4. Peter Calvocoressi, *Top Secret Ultra* (New York: Ballantine, 1980), 3.

5. Bennett, *Ultra in the West,* 10.

6. GHQ, SWPA, Special Intelligence Bulletin 465, 14/15 August 1944, in SRH-203, part 4.

7. Calvocoressi, *Top Secret Ultra,* 3, notes that certain German messages were broken within hours in the West. The same was true, as I show in this book, about certain Japanese codes in the Southwest Pacific theater.

Chapter 1. MacArthur's Codebreaking Organization

1. On codes and ciphers, see David Kahn, *The Codebreakers: The Story of Secret Writing* (New York: Macmillan, 1967), chapter 1. Also refer to David Kahn, "The Code Battle," in Kahn, ed., *Kahn on Codes: Secrets of the New Cryptology* (New York: Macmillan, 1983), 42–43.

2. Information on Japanese army codes may be found in Kamaga Kazuo, "Nihon rikugun ango wa 'antai' datta" [The Japanese army codes were secure], *Shogen: Rekishi to jimbutsu* (September 1984): 270–281 (hereafter cited as "Antai"), and Kamaga Kazuo, Fujiwara Kuniki, and Yoshimura Akira, "Zadankai: Nihon rikugun ango wa naze yaburarenakatta" [Discussion: why couldn't the Japanese army codes be broken?], *Rekishi to jimbutsu* (December 1985): 150–165 (hereafter cited as "Naze"). Kamaga and Fujiwara are former Imperial Army signal officers who devised army codes. Later in the war the Japanese army adopted repeated changes and innovations to their cryptographic systems. SRH-349, 27. A double encipherment system employed for some Japanese codes is described in Alan J. Stripp, *Codebreaker in the Far East* (London: Frank Cass, 1989). Stripp served as a British cryptanalyst in Burma during World War II.

3. Alan J. Stripp, "Breaking Japanese Codes," *Intelligence and National Security* 2, no. 4 (October 1987): 145.

4. SRH-362, 79.

5. ATIS, SWPA, "The Exploitation of Japanese Documents," ATIS Publication No. 6, 14 December 1944, 1, USAMHI.

6. The *"kaisen"* example is taken from Nakamuda Ken'ichi, *Joho shikan no kaiso* [Memoirs of an intelligence officer] (Tokyo: Asahi sonorama, 1985), 315–316.

7. Theodore M. Hannah, "The Many Lives of Herbert O. Yardley," 5–13, in SRH-038. Herbert O. Yardley, *The American Black Chamber* (New York: Ballantine, 1981; reprint of 1931 edition). Ronald Lewin, *The American Magic: Codes, Ciphers, and the Defeat of Japan* (New York: Farrar Straus Giroux, 1982), 19–23 and 31–34. David Kahn, "Herbert O. Yardley: A Biographical Sketch," in Kahn, ed., *Kahn on Codes*, 63.

8. Hannah, "Many Lives of Herbert O. Yardley," 10–11. The assistant chief of staff, G-2 (Intelligence), of the War Department exercised staff supervision over SIS. SRH-361, vol. 2: 28–29. The War Department emphasized that the decryption was for training, not intelligence, purposes. See also Kahn, *Codebreakers*, chapters 1 and 12. A less satisfactory account of Friedman is found in Ronald W. Clark, *The Man Who Broke Purple* (London: Weidenfeld and Nicolson, 1977). Thomas Parrish, *The Ultra Americans: The U.S. Role in Breaking the Nazi Codes* (New York: Stein and Day, 1984), 39.

9. SRH-361, 2:25. Parrish, *Ultra Americans*, 39–40.

10. Kahn, *Codebreakers*, 14.

11. SRH-361, 2:29–30. Parrish, *Ultra Americans*, 36–37. Kahn, *Codebreakers*, 26. Interview with Dr. Abraham Sinkov, February 23, 1989. Information from a former officer who served in Central Bureau, 14 March 1987.

12. SRH-361, 2:46.

13. Spencer B. Akin, "MacArthur's Signal Intelligence Service, World War II," manuscript, MMBA, RG 15, Box 11, Folder 4, "Papers of Major General B. H. Pochyla," 3. General Pochyla was Akin's deputy in SWPA during World War II.

14. SRH-269, 9; Parrish, *Ultra Americans*, 56; Edwin T. Layton, *"And I Was There"*: *Pearl Harbor and Midway—Breaking the Secrets* (New York: William Morrow, 1985), 81. Layton was a naval intelligence officer before and during the Pacific war.

15. Kahn, *Codebreakers*, 26.

16. Dundas P. Tucker, "Rhapsody in Purple: A New History of Pearl Harbor (1)," *Cryptologia* (July 1982): 204.

17. Akin, "MacArthur's Signal Intelligence Service," 6.

18. SRH-207, 1; D. M. Horner, "Special Intelligence in the South-West Pacific Area in World War II," *Australian Outlook* 32, no. 3 (December 1978): 311–312; Akin, "Mac-Arthur's Signal Intelligence Service," 19.

19. Jack Finnegan, "Grim Fate for Station 6," *Military History* (October 1986): 10; Akin, "MacArthur's Signal Intelligence Service," 7; SRH-045, 11 and 13. SRH-269, 10; Lewin, *American Magic,* 129.

20. SRH-045, 15. George R. Thompson et al., *United States Army in World War II: The Technical Services: The Signal Corps: The Test (December 1941 to July 1943)* (Washington, D.C.: Government Printing Office, 1957), 10–15, describes the signal warning system in the Philippines at the outbreak of the war.

21. SRH-045, 4–7.

22. Edwin T. Layton, trans., "America Deciphered Our Code," *United States Naval Institute Proceedings* (June 1979): 98–100. Kamaga et al., "Naze," 157–158, compares the Japanese army and naval encipherment systems. In "Antai," 277, Kamaga equates the degree of sophistication of the Japanese naval coding system to a sixth-grade primary-school level and the army's to a university one.

23. For examples of the U.S. Navy's efforts targeted against the Imperial Navy during the interwar years, see SRH-223–225 and SRH-318–320; SRH-180. Ellis M. Zacharias, *Secret Missions* (New York: G. P. Putnam Sons, 1946), offers the inside perspective of a naval intelligence officer. More sensational and less reliable is Ladislas Farago, *The Broken Seal: "Operation Magic" and the Secret Road to Pearl Harbor* (New York: Random House, 1967). W. J. Holmes, *Double-Edged Secrets: U.S. Naval Intelligence Operations in the Pacific during World War II* (Annapolis, Md.: U.S. Naval Institute Press, 1979), 23, sets the number of naval officers knowledgeable in Japanese at forty. Holmes also served as a naval intelligence officer in the Pacific war.

24. SRH-355, 398; Layton, *"And I Was There,"* 78.

25. Nakamura Fumio, "Rikugun ni okeru COMINT no hoga to hatten" [The germination and development of communications intelligence in the Imperial Army], *Shinboei ronshu* 16, no. 1 (June 1988): 84–88; Sanematsu Yuzuru, *Nichi-Bei joho senki* [Record of the Japanese-American intelligence war] (Tokyo: Tosho shuppansha, 1985), 44. Nakamuda, *Joho shikan,* 142.

26. SRH-045, 18, 22, 25. Thompson et al., *Signal Corps: The Test,* 12.

27. SRH-045, 34, 36–37, and GHQ, FEC, MIS, GS, "Operations of the Military Intelligence Section, GHQ, SWPA/FEC/SCAP," vol. 3, Intelligence Series (part 1), 1950, 41, USAMHI (hereafter cited as "MIS 3"). Michael Maslak, "Signalman's Odyssey," 138–140, in Diane L. Hamm, ed., *Military Intelligence: Its Heroes and Legends* (Washington, D.C.: Government Printing Office, 1987). Maslak was an intercept operator with Station 6 who endured three years of Japanese captivity.

28. Ann Bray, "Undercover Nisei," in Hamm, ed., *Military Intelligence,* 29–35. Joseph D. Harrington, *Yankee Samurai: The Secret Role of Nisei in America's Pacific Victory* (Detroit: Harlo Press, 1979), 50–51. "MIS 3," 37.

29. "MIS 3," 40. GHQ, FEC, MIS, GS, "A Brief History of the G-2 Section, GHQ, SWPA, and Affiliated Units," introduction, Intelligence Series, 1948, 6 (hereafter cited as "Brief History").

30. SRH-207, 1–5. Fleet Radio Unit, Melbourne, was officially designated as radio message address FRUMEL in January 1943. Previous designations were BAKER,

BELCONNEN, MELBOURNE, and T2W. I have used the anachronistic FRUMEL throughout for convenience.

31. Finnegan, "Grim Fate." Maslak, "Signalman's Odyssey." SRH-045, 41–47.

32. Supreme Commander for the Allied Powers, *Reports of General MacArthur*, Vol. 1: *The Campaigns of MacArthur in the Pacific* (Washington, D.C.: Government Printing Office, 1966), 31.

33. These observations are from D. Clayton James, *The Years of MacArthur*, Vol. 2: *1941–1945* (Boston: Houghton Mifflin, 1975), 78–79; William M. Leary, "Walter Krueger: MacArthur's Fighting General," in William M. Leary, ed., *We Shall Return! MacArthur's Commanders and the Defeat of Japan, 1942–1945* (Lexington: University Press of Kentucky, 1988), 251, note 21; John Miller, Jr., *United States Army in World War II: The War in the Pacific: Cartwheel: The Reduction of Rabaul* (Washington, D.C.: Government Printing Office, 1959), 20, note 2; George C. Kenney, *General Kenney Reports* (Washington, D.C.: Office of Air Force History, 1988; reprint of 1949 edition), 26–27; Charles A. Willoughby and John Chamberlain, *MacArthur: 1941–1951* (New York: McGraw-Hill, 1954); 35; Jay Luvaas, ed., *Dear Miss Em: General Eichelberger's War in the Pacific, 1942–1945* (Westport, Conn.: Greenwood Press, 1972), 28, 99–100, 186, 188. Weldon E. ("Dusty") Rhoades, *Flying MacArthur to Victory* (College Station: Texas A&M University Press, 1986), 204–205, 521–527.

34. "Memorandum for Colonel Clarke and Colonel McCormack," 20 January 1944, SRH-127, 23, mentions this proclivity of Willoughby.

35. James, *Years of MacArthur*, 79–80. Roger A. Beaumont, "Flawed Soothsayer: Charles A. Willoughby, MacArthur's G-2," *Espionage*, n.d. I am indebted to Professor Beaumont for providing me a draft copy of his article. Willoughby's sentiments are well documented in his papers at MMBA. Conversation with Mr. Taro Yoshihashi, who served in Willoughby's Order of Battle Section.

36. Willoughby and Chamberlain, *MacArthur*, 22. George R. Thompson and Dixie Lee Harris, *United States Army in World War II: The Technical Services: The Signal Corps: The Outcome (mid 1943 through 1945)* (Washington, D.C.: Government Printing Office, 1966), 242. Former Central Bureau officer interview. Sinkov interview.

37. Douglas MacArthur, *Reminiscences* (New York: McGraw-Hill, 1964), 168.

38. D. M. Horner, "Blamey and MacArthur: The Problem of Coalition Warfare," in Leary, ed., *We Shall Return!* 27–28, 57–59.

39. See the provocative and insightful essay by Stanley L. Falk, "Douglas MacArthur and the War against Japan," in Leary, ed., *We Shall Return!* 1–22. Eichelberger's letters to his wife frequently refer to MacArthur as "Sarah Bernhardt." See Luvaas, ed., *Dear Miss Em.*

40. MacArthur to Marshall, 31 December 1942, OPD Exec. 10, Item 23a, RG 165, NARA. Cited in Horner, "Special Intelligence," 313.

41. SRH-269, 11–12.

42. "MIS 3," 76. Sinkov interview. The information on Kullback comes from a former Central Bureau officer.

43. T. A. Blamey to General Douglas MacArthur, " 'Y' Intelligence: Central Bureau," 26 August 1942, in MMBA, RG 4, Box 6, Series 2, "Correspondence Allied Air–Allied Naval," 13. Hereafter cited as "Correspondence Allied."

44. Finnegan, "Grim Fate," 66; Horner, "Special Intelligence," 313; SRH-269, 12; "MIS 3," 69.

45. Akin, "MacArthur's Signal Intelligence Service," 9.

46. Interview with a former officer in Central Bureau. Akin, "MacArthur's Signal Intelligence Service," 11. Akin's corrections to "A History of the Signal Corps—Interview Transcript," Office of the Chief of Military History Collection, USAMHI. Lieutenant Colonel James Ashby, Jr., to Colonel [Carter] Clarke, 24 October 1944, in SRH-127, 127. Ashby was a War Department special security officer in SWPA. On 18 April, when SWPA opened, Akin was a brigadier general and Willoughby was a colonel. Akin's date of rank to brigadier general was 18 December 1941 and to major general 3 November 1943. Willoughby was promoted to brigadier general on 20 June 1942 and to major general 17 March 1945.

47. SRH-117, 7.

48. Interview with a former Central Bureau officer.

49. "Memorandum for Colonel Clarke and Colonel McCormack, Subject: Special Security Officer, SWPA," 20 January 1944, in SRH-127, 9–10. Interview with a former Central Bureau officer.

50. Correspondence with Mr. Taro Yoshihashi. Yoshihashi is the UCLA-educated nisei who worked in the Order of Battle Section. SWPA's Battle Order Section of 1942 became its Order of Battle Section in 1944. For consistency, I use the latter term throughout.

51. Akin, "MacArthur's Signal Intelligence Service," 11. Refer also to Thompson and Harris, *Signal Corps: The Outcome*, 242. Special Intelligence Bulletin 329, 31 March 1944, in SRH-203, part 2.

52. See, for example, Willoughby's remarks in "MIS 3," 29.

53. Willoughby's allegation is found in "Affidavit by MG C. A. Willoughby," 8 May 1945, *Pearl Harbor Attack*, part 35, 87, cited in Horner, "Special Intelligence," 317. On the liaison arrangement, see Blamey to MacArthur, 26 August 1942, "Correspondence Allied."

54. "Memorandum for Director Naval Communications," 9 March 1943, 1. This memorandum is attached as an enclosure to "Memorandum Admiral E. J. King, U.S.N., Subject: Merger of Army and Navy Radio Intelligence Activities," 10 March 1943, in SRH-200, 155, 157. King was the commander of the U.S. Fleet.

55. Horner, "Special Intelligence," 317. Clay Blair, *Silent Victory: The U.S. Submarine War against Japan* (New York: Harper and Row, 1975), 304. Fabian's name was provided by the former officer in Central Bureau.

56. SRH-200, 156; Horner, "Special Intelligence," 317.

57. Blamey to MacArthur, 26 August 1942, "Correspondence Allied."

58. Sinkov interview.

59. Finnegan, "Grim Fate," 66; Horner, "Special Intelligence," 313; SRH-045, 52.

60. Sinkov interview.

61. Desmond J. Ball, "Allied Intelligence Cooperation Involving Australia during World War II," *Australian Outlook* 32, no. 3 (December 1978): 302. Interview with Mr. Joseph E. Richard, a former member of Central Bureau, January 29, 1989.

62. MacArthur to Blamey, 11 September 1942, "Correspondence Allied."

63. Cited in Horner, "Special Intelligence," 317. MacArthur to Blamey, 11 September 1942, "Correspondence Allied." American security derelictions are noted by Horner, "Special Intelligence," 319, who describes an incident in which GHQ, G-3, improperly

disclosed signals intelligence to Headquarters, I Corps, U.S. Army, in November 1942. See also Sutherland to Blamey, 3 December 1942, "Correspondence Allied." U.S. Navy concerns appear in paragraph 6 of "Memorandum for Director Naval Communications," 9 March 1943, SRH-200, which complains about "the total lack of security in the Army intelligence activities in that [security] area."

64. Sutherland to Blamey, 6 February 1943, "Correspondence Allied."

65. From War Department to CINC, SWPA, CG, NATO, ETO, "Intercept Directive," 26 March 1943, in SRH-391, appendix B; Akin, "MacArthur's Signal Intelligence Services," 11.

66. Sutherland to Marshall, 22 July 1944, RG 4, Box 17, Folder C-N-C, USAF, PAC, War Department 701-800, 2 April 1944–6 August 1944, MMBA.

67. Marshall to MacArthur, 31 July 1943; MacArthur to War Department, 4 August 1943; Marshall to CINC, SWPA, 5 August 1943; and MacArthur to War Department, 2 September 1943, RG 4, Box 16, Folder C-N-C, USAF, PAC, War Department, 13 May 1943–1 September 1943 and 1 September 1943–1 December 1943, MMBA.

68. "Memorandum for Colonel Clarke and Colonel McCormack: Subject: Special Security Officers, SWPA," 20 January 1944, in SRH-127, 20–21, 23, 26; Major Thomas E. Ervin, "Memorandum for Colonel Clarke: Subject: Points to Be Discussed with General Sutherland," 8 February 1944, in SRH-127, 30–31. Ervin worked in Special Branch, Military Intelligence Division. First Lieutenant Francis A. O'Connell, Jr., to Colonel Clarke, 21 March 1944, in SRH-127, 39. O'Connell was the assistant special security officer. Clarke to Major General Richard J. Marshall, 28 April 1944, and "G-2 (Willoughby) to C/S (Sutherland), Subject: Handling of ULTRA Intelligence," 27 May 1944, in RG 4, Box 17, Folder C-N-C, USAF, PAC, War Department 701-800, 2 April 1944–6 August 1944, MMBA.

69. Marshall to MacArthur, 23 May 1944, RG 39, Box 11, Papers of Lieutenant General Richard Sutherland, "Correspondence with War Department," MMBA.

70. Ashby to Clarke, 24 October 1944, in SRH-127, 127, and Special Branch, MIS, War Department to CINC, SWPA, 3 November 1944, in SRH-127, 137.

71. Correspondence with Brigadier General Carter W. Clarke, U.S. Army (Ret.), 17 June 1987.

72. "Memorandum for General Bissell, Subject: Security of Special Intelligence in SWPA," 21 December 1944, in SRH-127, 141.

73. SRH-117, 10.

74. For Willoughby's remarks, see "Brief History," 36, and "MIS 3," 31. Memorandum, Bissell to Marshall, 10 July 1945, in SRH-169, 76.

Chapter 2. ULTRA's Trials and Errors, 1942

1. D. Clayton James, *The Years of MacArthur*, Vol. 2: *1941–1945* (Boston: Houghton Mifflin, 1975), 117–120.

2. SRMD-017, 2–3.

3. SRH-349, 15, and interview with Dr. Abraham Sinkov, February 23, 1989.

4. Mr. Joseph E. Richard interview, January 29, 1989, and correspondence, May 10, 1989.

5. "COMZAC to CINCPAC," 16/10551 April 1942, SWPA, MIS, Daily Summaries, March-April 1942, RG 3, MMBA (hereafter cited as SWPA, MIS, and date); SWPA, MIS, 20 April 1942; D. M. Horner, "Special Intelligence in the South-West Pacific Area in World War II," *Australian Outlook* 32, no. 3 (December 1978): 314; and Edwin T. Layton, *"And I Was There": Pearl Harbor and Midway—Breaking the Secrets* (New York: William Morrow, 1985), 390–391.

6. "Memorandum to: Chief of Staff, G-3, 'Subject: Japanese offensive expected end of April/early May,' " 21 April 1942, in Charles A. Willoughby Papers, USAMHI; "G-2 Information Bulletin," 5 May 1942, Willoughby Papers, USAMHI.

7. "CINCPAC to COMSOUWESTPAC," 22/05411 April 1942, in RG 3, Box 9, Folder 4, Richard J. Sutherland Papers, MMBA.

8. "12 May—Results of conference with Naval Intelligence regarding 'AF' (Midway) and 'AOB' (Kiska)," COMSUBFOR, 18 May 1942, in SRMD-009, 15; Ronald Lewin, *The American Magic: Codes, Ciphers, and the Defeat of Japan* (New York: Farrar Straus Giroux, 1982), 182. A FRUMEL intercept on 18 May spoke of a land route to Port Moresby (SRH-012, 1:281). "Commander Rochefort's Estimate," SRMD-009, 24.

9. SRH-012, 1:53–54.

10. Richard interview and correspondence; Forrest R. ("Tex") Biard, "The Pacific War through the Eyes of Forrest R. 'Tex' Biard," *Cryptolog: Naval Cryptologic Veterans Association* 10, no. 2 (Winter 1989): 20–22.

11. SRH-349, 15, and SRH-362, 31, 34; Richard interview; "Memorandum for Director Naval Communications," 9 March 1943, SRH-200, 3.

12. SRH-012, 4: 2, 584; SWPA, MIS, 5/6 November 1942; SWPA, MIS, 12/13 November 1942; SWPA, MIS 21/22 December 1942. Akatsuki code numbers appear in War Department, MID, *Order of Battle of the Japanese Armed Forces* (Washington, D.C.: Government Printing Office, 1 March 1945), 732–739.

13. SWPA, MIS 29/30 December 1942.

14. Samuel Milner, *U.S. Army in World War II: The War in the Pacific: Victory in Papua* (Washington, D.C.: Government Printing Office, 1957), 43.

15. Boeicho, Boei kenshujo [Japan, Japan National Institute for Defense Studies], ed., *Senshi sosho,* Vol. 14: *Minami Taiheiyo rikugun sakusen: Pooruto Moresubi—Ga shima shoki sakusen* (1) [Official military history, Vol. 14: Army Operations in the South Pacific: Port Moresby—first stage operations at Guadalcanal (book 1)] (Tokyo: Asagumo shimbunsha, 1968), 172–175. Hereafter cited as MTRS (1).

16. SWPA, MIS, 1 July 1942. GHQ, SWPA, MIS, GS, "G-2 Information Bulletin, Enemy Ground Dispositions in Front Areas," 2 August 1942, 15 August 1942, 15 September 1942, and 1 October 1942, RG 3, GHQ, SWPA, Box 15, SWPA G-2 Correspondence—Guerrilla Resistance in Philippines, MIS, Enemy Dispositions July 1942–June 1943, MMBA (hereafter cited as "Enemy Dispositions").

17. Lewin, *American Magic,* 184; W. J. Holmes, *Double-Edged Secrets: U.S. Naval Intelligence Operations in the Pacific during World War II* (Annapolis, Md.: U.S. Naval Institute Press, 1979), 118. SRH-012, 3:57, and ibid., 3:145, FRUMEL, 10/0914 July 1942. SWPA, MIS, 11 July 1942.

18. SWPA, MIS, 13 July 1942, and 115, 16 July 1942.

19. SRMN-009, 23, Fleet Intelligence Summary, 11 July 1942. James, *Years of MacArthur,* 2:193.

20. James, *Years of MacArthur,* 2:191–192; SWPA, MIS, 18 July 1942.

21. SRH-012, 3:232, FRUMEL, 18/0732 July 1942. SRMN-009, 36, Fleet Intelligence Summary, 21 July 1942.

22. SWPA, MIS, 22 July 1942; SRMN-009, 61, Fleet Intelligence Summary, 25 July 1942, 40, and 13 August 1942.

23. SRH-012, 3:264–265 and 325, OPNAV 22/1801 July 1942 and OPNAV 26/1635 July 1942, respectively. SWPA, MIS, 26/27 July 1942. On Willoughby's stubbornness, see "Enemy Dispositions," 2 August 1942, 15 August 1942, 15 September 1942, and 1 October 1942. A good summary of the battle is found in Samuel Milner, "The Battle of Milne Bay," *Military Review* 30 (April 1950): 18–29.

24. MTRS (1), 194.

25. George C. Kenney, *General Kenney Reports* (Washington, D.C.: Office of Air Force History, 1988; reprint of 1949 edition), 65, mentions that "some information came in" about impending Japanese reinforcements for Buna. The phrase "clients of ULTRA" was coined by Professor Harold Deutsch.

26. Ibid., 65. MTRS (1), 335. SRMN-009, 66, Fleet Intelligence Summary, 18 August 1942.

27. COM-14, 17/0658 August 1942, and FRUMEL, 18/0713 August 1942, in SRH-012, 4:492 and 493. Also ibid., 521.

28. For the U.S. Navy's view, see SRH-012, 2:162–283 and 233, 248–249. These pages were declassified after the original SRH-012. For the Japanese contention, see Inagaki Takeshi, " 'Chie no tatakai' ni mo yabureta Taiheiyo senso" [Even the Battle of Wits was lost in the Pacific war], in Hasegawa Keitaro, ed., *Nihon kindai to senso,* Vol. 1: *Johosen no haiboku* [Japan's modernity and war, Vol. 1: Defeat in the intelligence wars] (Tokyo: PHP kenkyujo, 1985), 186.

29. Milner, *Victory in Papua,* 70–71; SWPA, MIS, 17/18 August 1942.

30. MacArthur to Marshall, 2 August 1942, RG 4, USAFP, Box 15, USAFFE—War Department, 200, MMBA. SWPA, MIS, 12 July 1942, voices concern about the Japanese reading American codes.

31. SWPA, MIS, 13 July 1942. Supreme Commander for the Allied Powers, *Reports of General MacArthur,* Vol. 1: *The Campaigns of MacArthur in the Pacific* (Washington, D.C.: Government Printing Office, 1966), 66 (hereafter cited as *MacArthur* 1). Willoughby probably based his deduction on U.S. Navy decryptions found in SRH-012, 3:165–166, FRUMEL, 10/0914 and 10/0718 July 1942. Also MTRS (1), 185. For premature Allied assessments of an attack on Milne Bay, see SRMN-009, 46–47, Fleet Intelligence Summary, 31 July and 1 August 1942 (see also MTRS [1], 184). Okishu sakumei ko dai 10 go [Oki force operations order number 10], dated 18 July 1942, mentioned a separate, one-battalion-force attack against Samarai on the tip of Milne Bay. See also MTRS (1), 195. Willoughby specifically mentions special intelligence as a basis for his interpretation in MIS, 13 July 1942 above, and SWPA, MIS, 29/30 July 1942.

32. SRH-012, 3:264, FRUMEL, 21/1505 July 1942; SWPA, MIS, 4/5 August 1942. Milner, *Victory in Papua,* 40–43. MacArthur to Marshall, 2 August 1942.

33. MTRS (1), 195, 216–217, 223, 362. Japanese pilots had reported strong antiaircraft defenses at Milne Bay.

34. Milner, *Victory in Papua,* 76–77; "Douglas MacArthur to Chief of Staff, Washington," 2 August 1942, RG 4, USAF, PAC, Box 15, USAFFE–War Department, 200, MMBA. SWPA, MIS, 24/25 August 1942. Kenney, *General Kenney Reports,* 76, uses the term "special intelligence."

35. Kenney, *General Kenney Reports*, 82–83. SRH-012, 4 (part 2):674, FRUMEL, 21/0740 August 1942. MTRS (1), 364.

36. SRMN-009, 74, Fleet Intelligence Summary, 25 August 1942. Nakamuda Ken'ichi, *Joho shikan no kaiso* [Memoirs of an intelligence officer] (Tokyo: Asahi sonorama, 1985), 279.

37. Dudley McCarthy, *Australia in the War of 1939–45: Army: South-West Pacific Area—First Year: Kokoda to Wau* (Canberra: Australian War Memorial, 1959), 175.

38. MTRS (1), 365, 367. "GHQ, SWPA, G-3 Daily Reports," Nos. 139–143, 25–29 August 1942, "Sutherland Papers, RG 3, Box 9, Folder 4, MMBA, records the Allied air attacks. *MacArthur* 1, 66–70; see 67, note 37, for the Allied assessment of Japanese staff work for Milne Bay.

39. Report of Commander Yano Minoru, Commanding Officer, 3d Kure Special Naval Landing Force, cited in MTRS (1), 370.

40. This intelligence from "most secret sources" is cited in Milner, *Victory in Papua*, 87, note 36, and also in D. M. Horner, "Special Intelligence in the South-West Pacific Area in World War II," *Australian Outlook* 32, no. 3 (December 1978): 315. The intercepts may be those available as "Eighth Fleet to Landing Force," 4 September 1942, and "18th Squadron to Special Landing Party," 3 September 1942. Both cited in MTRS (1), 374. According to Alan J. Stripp, *Codebreaker in the Far East* (London: Frank Cass, 1989), 67, the Allies were reading JN-14 or JN-25, which disclosed Japanese plans for the attack on Milne Bay. Unfortunately, he adduces no documentation to support his contention.

41. Vice Admiral Ugaki Matome, diary entry for 5 September 1942. Cited in MTRS (1), 376.

42. SRMN-009, 104, Fleet Intelligence Summary, 17 September 1942. United States Navy, Commander in Chief, Pacific Intelligence Bulletins, 18 September 1942 in SRMN-013 (hereafter cited as SRMN-013, CINCPAC Bulletin, and date). "CINC COM-SOWESPAC to MARSHALL," 27/0800 September 1942, RG 4, Box 4, Folder 17, August 1942–12 December 1942, War Department, C-N-C, USAF, PAC, MMBA.

43. MTRS (1), 518. Boeicho, Boei kenshujo, ed., *Senshi sosho*, Vol. 28: *Minami Taiheiyo rikugun sakusen: Gadarukanaru-Buna sakusen* (2) [Official military history, Vol. 28: Army operations in the South Pacific: Guadalcanal and Buna operations (book 2)] (Tokyo: Asagumo shimbunsha, 1968), 111 (hereafter cited as MTRS [2]).

44. SRMN-013, CINCPAC Bulletin, 13 October 1942; MTRS (2), 324.

45. SWPA, MIS, 5/6 November 1942.

46. "Strong Cable; G-2 War Dept. No: 3214 Nov. 1st," in ibid.

47. Milner, *Victory in Papua*, 138–139; SWPA, MIS, 12/13 November 1942, and 14/15 November 1942.

48. SWPA, MIS, 15/16 November 1942.

49. SWPA, MIS, appendix, 17/18 November 1942; SRMN-013, CINCPAC Bulletin, 17 November 1942; MTRS (2), 324–325.

50. SWPA, MIS, 18/19 November 1942.

51. Cited in Milner, *Victory in Papua*, 175. The impressions are those of Major David B. Parker, an engineer-observer who was present at Buna.

52. Lieutenant Colonel Imoto Kumao, diary entry for 20 December 1942. Cited in MTRS (2), 335. Imoto was a staff officer assigned to Eighth Area Army. He was at Buna to provide the Eighth Area Army commander with a firsthand assessment of the fighting.

53. Kamagawa Kazuo, "Nihon rikugun ango wa 'antai' datta" [The Japanese army codes were secure], *Shogen: Rekishi to jimbutsu* (September 1984):281.

54. SRMN-013, CINCPAC Bulletin, 29 November 1942 and 30 November 1942. SWPA, MIS, 4/5 and 5/6 December 1942.

55. SRMN-013, CINCPAC Bulletin, 26 November 1942. MTRS (2), 330.

56. MTRS (2), 330–331, 338–339. Captured documents misled G-2 into believing that seven hundred officers and men of the 3d Battalion, 170th infantry, had landed.

57. SRH-012, 2:233, 240.

58. Eric A. Feldt, *The Coastwatchers* (Oxford: Oxford University Press, 1947), chapters 8, 15, and 16.

59. Willoughby doubted special intelligence reports of a Yokohama fighter bomber squadron at Gasmata. He wrote, "Present report is strikingly at variance with previous negative sightings, since special intelligence is hitherto accepted as infallible." See his comments in SWPA, MIS, 16 July 1942.

60. SRMN-013, 234–235, CINCPAC Bulletin, 4 and 5 December 1942; SRMN-009, 224, Fleet Intelligence Summary, 12 December 1942. MTRS (2), 340. Milner, *Victory in Papua*, 217.

61. SRMN-009, 222, Fleet Intelligence Summary, 10 December 1942. Kenney, *General Kenney Reports*, 165, reports no damage. SRMN-009, 228, Fleet Intelligence Summary, 14 December 1942, mentions five destroyers; MTRS (2), 341.

62. MTRS (2), 333, 362.

63. SRMN-013, 253–254, CINCPAC Bulletin, 15 December 1942; SRH-136, 455–457, 16 December 1942 report of 14 December 1942 message. SRH-136, 457, R[adio] I[ntercept] U[nit] CACTUS (Guadalcanal) to COMSOPACFOR, 18/0444 December 1942. SRH-144, part 2, CINCPAC to COMINCH, 15/0239 February 1943, reports the sinking of *Tenryu*. SRMN-013, CINCPAC Bulletin, 15 February 1943, reporting the decryption of 19 December 1942 message. MTRS (2), 364–365; SRH-136, 459–461, MacArthur to War Department, 20/1045 December 1942; NPM (Pearl Harbor), 14/1038 February, 459–461.

64. SRH-136, T2W (Melbourne), 18/0213 December, 518. SRMN-013, 260, CINCPAC Bulletin, 19 December 1942.

65. SWPA, MIS, 15/17 December 1942; SWPA, MIS, 18/19 December 1942; SRH-136, 349, T2W (Melbourne), 14/0221 December 1942, and SRH-136, 514, T2W, 18/0056 December 1942. SWPA, MIS, 21/22 December 1942, and 25/26 December 1942.

66. Kimata Jiro, *Rikugun koku senshi: Mare sakusen kara Okinawa tokko made* [History of the army air force: From the Malaya operation to the Okinawa special attack corps] (Tokyo: Keizai oraisha, 1982), 69, 71. Boeicho, Boei kenshujo, ed., *Senshi sosho*, Vol. 54: *Nansei homen kaigun sakusen* [Southwest Area Fleet operations] (Tokyo: Asagumo shimbunsha, 1972), 69; SRH-136, 347, shows that the U.S. Navy believed the carrier that reached Truk was the *Otaka*. See also SRH-136, 515, NPM (Pearl Harbor), 18/0056 December 1942, and CINCPAC Chronological Dispatch File, 24 December 1942. There were actually two light carriers involved in the transport.

67. SRH-136, 601–606, NPM (Pearl Harbor), 23/2032 December 1942.

68. "Memorandum for Director Naval Communications," 9 March 1943, SRH-200, 2.

69. Ibid. My explanation of the first technique is taken from Lewin, *American Magic*, 88.

70. Kenney, *General Kenney Reports*, 61. For SWPA strength in early 1942, see "G-2

Information Bulletin; Subject: General Review of Probable Enemy Plans," 5 May 1942, Willoughby Papers, USAMHI. For the 1943 figures, refer to "Employment of Forces under the Southwest Pacific Command" *United States Strategic Bombing Survey Reports: Pacific War,* No. 65 (Washington, D.C.: Government Printing Office, 1947), 18.

Chapter 3. Breaking into the Japanese Army Codes,
January 1943–January 1944

1. SRH-361, 81.

2. John Miller, Jr., *United States Army in World War II: The War in the Pacific: Cartwheel: The Reduction of Rabaul* (Washington, D.C.: Government Printing Office, 1959), 36.

3. Imai Sei' ichi, ed., *Taiheiyo senso,* Vol. 5: *Taiheiyo senso* (II) [History of the Pacific war, Vol. 5: The Pacific war (part 2)] (Tokyo: Aoki shoten, 1973), 47–48. Tsunoda Fusako, *Sekinin Rabauru no shogun Imamura Hitoshi* [The general responsible for Rabaul: Imamura Hitoshi] (Tokyo: Shinchosha, 1984), 150, 158, 189–190.

4. Supreme Commander for the Allied Powers, *Reports of General MacArthur,* Vol. 2: *Japanese Operations in the Southwest Pacific Area* (part 1) (Washington, D.C.: Government Printing Office, 1966), 189 (hereafter cited as *MacArthur 2*). Boeicho, Boei kenshujo [Japan, Japan National Institute for Defense Studies], ed., *Senshi sosho,* Vol. 40: *Minami Taiheiyo rikugun sakusen: Munda Saramoa* (3) [Official military history, Vol. 40: Army operations in the South Pacific: Munda Salamaua (book 3)] (Tokyo: Asagumo shimbunsha, 1970), 17 (hereafter cited as MTRS [3]).

5. Boeicho, Boei kenshujo, ed., *Senshi sosho,* Vol. 7: *Tobu Nyuginia homen rikugun koku sakusen* [Official military history, Vol. 7: Army air operations on the eastern New Guinea front] (Tokyo: Asagumo shimbunsha, 1967), 112–115. Hereafter cited as TNKS.

6. SRH-036, 9–11.

7. George C. Kenney, *General Kenney Reports* (Washington, D.C.: Office of Air Force History, 1988; reprint of 1949 edition), 175. MacArthur to War Department, 07/1046 January 1943, Urgent, SRH-036, 221, is MacArthur's first report of sighting the convoy. TNKS, 117. The quotations are from HQ, AAF, SWPA, DI, Intelligence Summary 77, 13–15, cited in SRH-036, 234, 236–237.

8. NSS-08/1603-January-DI, in SRH-036, 218. A U.S. Army pilot reported seeing a submarine surface after depth-charge attacks and Japanese destroyers firing into it. See CTF 42 to COMSOPAC/COMSOWESPAC, 19/0731 January 1942, in SRH-036, 45. Japanese destroyers rescued 739 of 1,100 troops aboard the sunken transport. See *MacArthur 2*, 190, note 67.

9. Kimata Jiro, *Rikugun koku senshi: Mare sakusen kara Okinawa tokko made* [History of the army air force: From the Malaya operation to the Okinawa special attack corps] (Tokyo: Keizai oraisha, 1982), 74–75. TNKS, 118–119.

10. SRH-036, 12. CINCPAC Bulletin 306, 16 January 1943, in ibid., 360; and T2W-14/1254-January-DI, in ibid., 370.

11. NSS-23/2215–23/2228-January-DI, in ibid., 502. T2W-23/0703–January-DI and NPM-30/1058-January-DI, in ibid., 505 and 676, respectively.

12. Tsunoda, *Sekinin Rabauru no shogun Imamura Hitoshi,* 45, 57–58, 65. When

Adachi learned of his daughter's death in 1945, he burned all his *tanka*. Tanaka Kengoro, "Adachi Hatazo," in Imai Takeo and Terasaki Ryuji, eds., *Nihongun no kenkyu shikkikan (jo)* [Japanese army studies: The commanders (vol. 1)] (Tokyo: Hara shobo, 1980), 57–58, 65.

13. MTRS (3), 28, 31–33. TNKS, 164.

14. TNKS, 169–170. MTRS (3), 35.

15. HQ, AAF, SWPA, DI, Intelligence Summaries 76 and 78, 10 and 13 February 1943, respectively.

16. "Memorandum for Director Naval Communications," 9 March 1943, SRH-200, 1–2. NSS-17/0036-February-DI, SRH-144, part 2, 446. SRMN-013, CINCPAC Intelligence Bulletin 339, 19 February 1943. SRH-144, part 1, 63. U.S. naval intelligence was unaware that the 51st Division had moved to Rabaul. Analysts therefore suggested that the numeral "5" might be an originator's error for "4" because the 41st Division had been confirmed in decrypted messages.

17. SWPA, MIS, 22/23 February 1943. CINCPAC, February 26, 1943, SRMN-013, part 2, NSS-24/1920-February-DI, SRH-144, part 2, 565. Supreme Commander for the Allied Powers, *Reports of General MacArthur*, Vol. 1: *The Campaigns of MacArthur in the Pacific* (Washington, D.C.: Government Printing Office, 1966), 110; hereafter cited as *MacArthur* 1. Kenney, *General Kenney Reports*, 198–201. Donald M. Goldstein, "Ennis C. Whitehead: Aerial Tactician," in William M. Leary, ed., *We Shall Return! MacArthur's Commanders and the Defeat of Japan, 1942–1945* (Lexington: University Press of Kentucky, 1988), 187, and Herman S. Wolk, "George C. Kenney: MacArthur's Premier Airman," in ibid., 101, attributes the signal intelligence to Headquarters, Fifth Air Force, resources. This is incorrect.

18. On Willoughby's analyses, see SWPA, MIS, 24/25 and 27/28 February 1943, respectively.

19. Kimata, *Rikugun koku senshi*, 80.

20. The first two quotations are cited in "Headquarters, Advance Echelon, Fifth Air Force: Report on Destruction of Jap Convoy in Bismark [*sic*] Sea, March 1 to 5, 1943 (incl.)," dated 6 April 1943, SRH-144, 2:578–579. The next quotation appears in the U.S. Navy's version of the Fifth Air Force's 6 April report, ibid., 569.

21. D. Clayton James, *The Years of MacArthur*, Vol. 2: *1941–1945* (Boston: Houghton Mifflin, 1975), 294. Martin Cadin, *The Ragged, Rugged Warriors* (New York: Bantam, 1979), 24, quotes Major Edward F. Hoover, 5th Bomber Command: "This was the dirty part of the job. We sent out A-20s and Beaufighters to strafe the lifeboats. It was rather a sloppy job, and some of the boys got sick." John Dower, *War without Mercy: Race and Power in the Pacific War* (New York: Pantheon, 1986), 67, cites the same quotation as evidence that the strafing was a war crime. For an opposite view—that shooting survivors in the water was a military necessity—see Samuel Eliot Morison, *History of United States Naval Operations in World War II*, Vol. 6: *Breaking the Bismarck Barrier* (Boston: Little, Brown, 1957), 62.

22. "Oka ho sanichi den dai 564 go, dai 565 go" [Eighth Area Army chief of staff messages 564 and 565], 4 March 1943, cited in MTRS (3), 58. The 115th's losses are in ibid., 59. To this day, there is no consensus among Japanese historians on how many troops were loaded aboard the transports. An Eighteenth Army order says 5,916; a Southeast Pacific Fleet document gives 6,912; and an Eighth Area Army staff officer's notes record

about 7,500. Ibid., 53. The report to the emperor is found in Sanbohonbu [Chief of staff], ed., *Sugiyama memo* (ge) [The Sugiyama memo (vol. 2)] (Tokyo: Hara shobo, 1967), 19–20. General Sugiyama Hajime was the chief of staff of the Imperial Army from October 1940 to February 1944.

23. SRH-144, 2: 571. James, *Years of MacArthur*, 295–303. Japanese losses were seven transports (*Ryokusei, Oigawa, Teiyo, Shinai, Aiyo, Taimei, and Kembu*), a naval transport (*Nojima*), and four destroyers.

24. *MacArthur* 2, 205, has a translation of the document.

25. Kojima Noboru, *Taiheiyo senso* (ge), [The Pacific war (vol. 2)] (Tokyo: Chuo koronsha, 1965), 18–21.

26. SRH-288, 1–7, and Kojima, *Taiheiyo senso*, 22.

27. The decryption of Yamamoto's itinerary is found in SRH-288, 336. See also NSS-30/2220-March 1943; NSS-31/1944-March 1943; CINCPAC to COMSOPAC, 04/2255 April 1943; CINCPAC Bulletin 390, 10/0257 April 1943; and CINCPAC to COMSOPAC, 10/2031 April 1943, in SRH-288, 47–48, 59, 62, 84–86, 148–149, 245–247, 258, and 289–291, respectively. NSS-14/2157-April 1943 is a decryption of a message from an unknown originator to several addresses that amplifies details of Yamamoto's schedule first reported by naval codebreakers in Hawaii.

28. *MacArthur* 2, 111, note 20. A slightly different version is found in MIS, 3:1, appendix 16.

29. Correspondence with Mr. Taro Yoshihashi, UCLA-educated Nisei who worked in the Order of Battle Section. ATIS, "The Japanese Army List (15 October 1942)," ATIS Publication No. 2, May 1943. Copy at USAMHI.

30. Inagaki Takeshi, " 'Chie no tatakai' ni mo yabureta Taiheiyo senso" [Even the Battle of Wits was lost in the Pacific War], in Hasegawa Keitaro, ed., *Nihon kindai to senso*, Vol. 1: *Johosen no haiboku* [Japan's modernity and war, Vol. 1: Defeat in the intelligence wars] (Tokyo: PHP Kenkyujo, 1985), 188, asserts that Allied divers salvaged the Army Water Transport Code books. Interviews with Dr. Abraham Sinkov, February 23, 1989, and Mr. Joseph E. Richard, a former member of Central Bureau, January 29, 1989, refute the Japanese claim.

31. SRH-349, 26. SRH-280, 1, 2.

32. MacArthur could act on Central Bureau–produced ULTRA while forwarding a copy of the intercepted signal and its decryption to the Signal Security Agency. For security reasons, such data in microfilm form was couriered by air to Arlington Hall during 1943. The following year, improved teletype facilities enabled the information to be passed within twenty-four hours of interception.

33. SRH-349, 28.

34. SRH-280, 12.

35. See "Berlin (Oshima) to Tokyo," No. 1349, 10 November 1943, in SRH-111, 4–8. It is also reproduced in SRH-059, 5–9. A translation of this lengthy signal was available 12 November 1943.

36. GHQ, SWPA, MIS, GS, "G-2 Information Bulletin, Enemy Ground Dispositions in Front Areas," 30 April 1943, RG 3, GHQ, SWPA, Box 15, MMBA (hereafter cited as "Enemy Dispositions"). Ibid., No. 7, 31 May 1943.

37. MTRS (3), 227–228.

38. Ronald H. Spector, *Eagle against the Sun* (New York: Free Press, 1985), 232. James, *Years of MacArthur*, 316–317.

39. Weldon E. ("Dusty") Rhoades, *Flying MacArthur to Victory* (College Station: Texas A&M University Press, 1986), 204–205. Also William M. Leary, "Walter Krueger: MacArthur's Fighting General," in Leary, ed., *We Shall Return!* 60–62.

40. Paolo E. Coletta, "Daniel E. Barbey," in Leary, ed., *We Shall Return!* 211–212.

41. William F. McCartney, *The Jungleers: A History of the 41st Infantry Division* (Washington, D.C.: Infantry Journal Press, 1948), 53. MTRS (3), 327. TNKS, 312.

42. David M. Horner, "Blamey and MacArthur: The Problem of Coalition Warfare," in Leary, ed., *We Shall Return!* 42–43.

43. Kimata, *Rikugun koku senshi,* 87.

44. Kenney, *General Kenney Reports,* 255, 274.

45. TNKS, 78–79. On prewar Japanese intelligence training, see Hayashi Saburo, "Senjika no rikugun chuobu" [Army central headquarters in wartime], *Rekishi to jimbutsu* (Winter 1986): 249–250. Kimata, *Rikugun koku senshi,* 72. Boeicho, Boei kenshujo, ed., "Koso chosa 'Nihon rikukaigun no joho kiko to sono katsudo,' " *Kenkyu shiryo* 84RO—2H [Basic research: The intelligence organizations and activities of the Japanese army and navy, Research document 84RO—2H] (Tokyo: Boei kenshujo senshibu, 1984), 144–145 (hereafter cited as 84RO-2H).

46. Kimata, *Rikugun koku senshi,* 88–89.

47. TNKS, 389–394. Kenney, *General Kenney Reports,* 276. Kenney claimed eleven Japanese bombers and three fighters destroyed; actual Japanese losses were six bombers and three fighters.

48. Willoughby's Special Intelligence Bulletin (SIB) 109 for 19 August 1943 reported ULTRA that Akin had already passed to Kenney by 15 August.

49. TNKS, 395, and 84RO-2H, 182.

50. Kimata, *Rikugun koku senshi,* 90–91. SIB 108, 18 August 1943.

51. Kojima, *Taiheiyo senso,* 50–51. MTRS (3), 373.

52. Kojima, *Taiheiyo senso,* 53. Allied radio direction finders noted both major Japanese radio stations on the move, which confirmed their overland withdrawal. See SIB 134, 14 September 1943. Majime Mitsuru, *Jigoku no senjo: Nyuginia senki* [Hell's battleground: New Guinea war record] (Tokyo: Kojinsha, 1988), 115. Majime's first-person account is based on his service with the 30th Independent Engineer Regiment in New Guinea.

53. MTRS (3), 440.

54. Ibid., 430.

55. Ibid., 517, 520. Takagi Sokichi, *Taiheiyo kaisenshi* [A naval history of the Pacific war], rev. ed. (Tokyo: Iwanami shinsho, 1977), 86–87.

56. *MacArthur 2,* 226. Takagi, *Taiheiyo kaisenshi,* 88.

57. MTRS (3), 520–521. COMINCH to CINCPAC, 12 November 1943, BESAW and CINCPAC to COMSOUWESTPAC, 16 November 1943, in SRMN-016, 13 and 14, respectively.

58. MTRS (3), 443–444.

59. David Dexter, *Australia in the War of 1939–45: Army: The New Guinea Offensives* (Canberra: Australian War Memorial, 1961), 445–446.

60. SWPA, "Enemy Dispositions," No. 10, 31 August 1943. Dexter, *Australia in the War of 1939–45,* 447.

61. James, *Years of MacArthur,* 337; Miller, *Reduction of Rabaul,* 230; Kenney, *General Kenney Reports,* 313–314.

62. SIB 187, 8 November 1943. Wesley Frank Craven and James Lea Cate, eds., *The*

Army Air Forces in World War II, Vol. 4: *The Pacific: Guadalcanal to Saipan, August 1942 to July 1944* (Chicago: University of Chicago Press, 1950), 326. Kenney, *General Kenney Reports,* 319. On page 320, Kenney says that six B-25s were lost.

63. James, *Years of MacArthur,* 337.

64. "G-2 Estimate of the Situation," in SWPA, "Enemy Dispositions," No. 15, 31 January 1944.

65. Letter, Colonel H. Bennett Whipple, GSC (Brisbane), to Colonel S. D. Sturgis (Milne Bay), 5 October 1943, Folder 1944, Box 1943–1951, postwar, undated, Richard J. Marshall Papers, USAMHI.

66. *MacArthur* 2, 130, plate 38. Boeicho, Boei kenshujo, ed., *Senshi sosho:* Vol. 58: *Minami Taiheiyo rikugun sakusen: Fuinshehaahen Tsurubu Tarokin* (4) [Official military history, Vol. 58: Army operations in the South Pacific: Finschhafen-Tsurubu-Tarokina (book 4)] (Tokyo: Asagumo shimbunsha, 1973) 262 (hereafter cited as MTRS [4]). SWPA, "Enemy Dispositions," No. 13, 30 November 1943.

67. GHQ, FEC, MIS, GS, "A Brief History of the G-2 Section, GHQ, SWPA, and Affiliated Units," introduction, Intelligence Series, 1948, 53–56, has an account of the Arawe action. Eric A. Feldt, *The Coastwatchers* (Oxford: Oxford University Press, 1947), 218.

68. MTRS (4), 369, 383.

69. SRH-362, 139.

70. SRH-362, 139–141; Richard interview and correspondence: Forrest R. ("Tex") Biard, "The Pacific War through the Eyes of Forrest R. 'Tex' Biard," *Cryptolog: Naval Cryptologic Veterans Association* 10, no. 2 (Winter 1989): 20–22.

71. Sinkov interview.

72. SRH-140, SRH-280, 1A.

Chapter 4. ULTRA*'s Great Victory:*
The Hollandia Operation, January–April 1944

1. GHQ, FEC, MIS, GS, "G-2 Estimate of the Situation," in GHQ, SWPA, Box 15, SWPA G-2 Correspondence—Guerrilla Resistance in Philippines, MIS, Enemy Dispositions July 1942–June 1943, MMBA. Hereafter cited as SWPA, "Estimate of Enemy Situation."

2. Stanley L. Falk, "Douglas MacArthur and the War against Japan," in William M. Leary, ed., *We Shall Return! MacArthur's Commanders and the Defeat of Japan, 1942–1945* (Lexington: University Press of Kentucky, 1988), 15.

3. U.S. Department of State, "Employment of Forces under the Southwest Pacific Command," *United States Strategic Bombing Survey Reports: Pacific War,* No. 65 (Washington, D.C.: Military Analysis Division, 1947), 27.

4. Ibid., 29. D. Clayton James, *The Years of MacArthur,* Vol. 2: *1941–1945* (Boston: Houghton Mifflin, 1975), 366, 368.

5. Robert Ross Smith, *United States Army in World War II: The War in the Pacific: The Approach to the Philippines* (Washington, D.C.: Government Printing Office, 1953), 4–6.

6. OPD, Top Secret Message File (1–29 February 1944), SWPA to War [Department], 2 February 1944, in RG 165, A 48-12, Box 5, NARA. The Operations Division was the main

war planning agency and central command post to assist Marshall in his strategic direction of the military forces in the various theaters of war.

7. SWPA, "Estimate of the Enemy Situation," 31 December 1943.

8. BESAW, 12 and 16 November 1943, and MacArthur to War [Department], 17 January 1944, in SRMN-016, 13, 14, and 31, respectively; GH, FEC, MIS, GS, "Operations of the Military Intelligence Section GHQ, SWPA/FEC/SCAP," vol. 3, Intelligence Series (Part 1), 1950, Documentary Appendixes, appendix 1, tab 4 (hereafter cited as MIS 3). SWPA, "Estimate of the Enemy Situation," 31 January 1944.

9. GHQ, Far East Command, MIS, GS, "A Brief History of the G-2 Section, GHQ, SWPA, and Affiliated Units," introduction, Intelligence Series, 1948, 25 (hereafter cited as "Brief History"); Smith, *Approach to Philippines,* 4–7; James, *Years of MacArthur,* 444–445. The original Japanese signal appears as "Oka ho sanden dai 284 go" [Eighth Area Army chief of staff message no. 284], 19 January 1944, in *Nanto Taiheiyo homen (dai 8 homengun, dai 17 gun, dai 18 gun, dai 4 kokugun) kankei denpo tsuzuri* [Southeast Pacific front (Eighth Area Army, Seventeenth Army, Eighteenth Army, Fourth Air Army) related miscellaneous signals], Showa 19 nen 1 gatsu [January 1944], 131, in NIDS (hereafter cited as NT with date).

10. Supreme Commander for the Allied Powers, *Reports of General MacArthur,* Vol. 2: *Japanese Operations in the Southwest Pacific Area* (Part 1) (Washington, D.C.: Government Printing Office, 1966), 136–137; "Brief History," 25; MIS 3 (1), appendix 1, tab 4.

11. George C. Kenney, *General Kenney Reports* (Washington, D.C.: Office of Air Force History, 1988; reprint of 1949 edition), 353.

12. SWPA, "Estimate of the Enemy Situation," 30 November 1943, 31 December 1943, and 31 January 1944; Sanbo honbu senshishido han [Army General Staff, War Guidance Office], ed., "Daihon'ei kimitsu senso nisshi" [Confidential war diary of Imperial General Headquarters], 26 January 1944 entry, in *Rekishi to jimbutsu* (October 1971): 300.

13. Wesley Frank Craven and James Lea Cate, eds., *The Army Air Forces in World War II,* Vol. 4: *The Pacific: Guadalcanal to Saipan, August 1942 to July 1944* (Chicago: University of Chicago Press, 1950), 558.

14. MIS 3 (1), 1. John Miller, Jr., *United States Army in World War II: The War in the Pacific: Cartwheel: The Reduction of Rabaul* (Washington, D.C.: Government Office, 1959), 320; Kenney, *General Kenney Reports,* 358–360.

15. Kenney, *General Kenney Reports,* 353, 358. MIS 3 (1), 1–3.

16. MTRS (4), 416–420.

17. At 1:50 P.M. on 14 January 1944, *Whale* received *Seawolf*'s dispatch giving information on the convoy. NARAE to Various Addresses, 10/1640 January 1944, HOMI 9 to WOI 7 et al., 10/1820 January 1944, in SRH-286, 138–139.

18. SWPA, "Estimate of the Enemy Situation," 31 October 1943, 31 December 1943, and 31 January 1944.

19. G-2 to C/S (and C/S Sixth Army), 10 February 1944, in SRH-203, part 2, 569.

20. G-2 to C/S (radio Sixth Army), 27 February 1944, in ibid., 587, notes Japanese detection of Allied signals.

21. Miller, *Reduction of Rabaul,* 319; MTRS (4), 429–430.

22. William C. Frierson, *The Admiralties: Operations of the 1st Cavalry Division (29 February–18 May 1944),* American Forces in Action Series (Washington, D.C.: War Department, 1946), 15–17.

23. My account is adapted from ibid., 24.

24. SRH-219, 11, has a compendium of deciphered Japanese messages about the Admiralties from 25 January through 5 March 1944. The document was prepared 6 March, therefore much intelligence was not available in a timely manner.

25. MIS 3 (1), 2.

26. James, *Years of MacArthur*, 391.

27. OPD, Top Secret Message File, (1–15 March 1944), CG, Rear Echelon, SWPA to War [Department], 5 March 1944, in RG 165, A48-12, Box 5, NARA. A slightly abbreviated version of this message may be found in Supreme Commander for the Allied Powers, *Reports of General MacArthur*, Vol. 1: *The Campaigns of MacArthur in the Pacific* (Washington, D.C.: Government Printing Office, 1966), 142 (hereafter cited as *MacArthur 1*).

28. Smith, *Approach to Philippines*, 10. James, *Years of MacArthur*, 392–393.

29. For a more detailed account of air and sea interdiction operations against the Japanese at Hollandia, see Edward J. Drea, "ULTRA Intelligence and General Douglas MacArthur's Leap to Hollandia, January-April 1944," *Intelligence and National Security* 5, no. 2 (April 1990): 330–336.

30. U.S. War Department, Office of the Assistant Chief of Staff, G-2 Special Branch, Military Intelligence Division, "MAGIC Summary—Japanese Army Supplement," 31 March 1944, SRS-01-547 (hereafter cited as MSJAS and date). "Oka ho san ni dai 276 go" [Eighth Area Army chief of staff signal no. 276], 2 February 1944 NT (February 1944), 17–19, in NIDS. SRH-059, 26.

31. "Oka ho san ni den dai 459 go," 28 February 1944, Ji Showa 19 nen 1 gatsu itaru Showa 19 nen 12 gatsu Dai 8 homegun hatsuden tsuzuri (yon kan) [Miscellaneous Eighth Area Army signals: January-December 1944], vol. 4, 1340, in NIDS, identifies *Daigen Maru Number 3* as the torpedoed vessel. Theodore Roscoe, *United States Submarine Operations in World War II* (Annapolis, Md.: U.S. Naval Institute Press, 1949), 318, identifies *Gato* as the U.S. submarine.

32. The fate of the second transport, allegedly sunk by air action, is not clear. MSJAS, 13 March 1944, reported the loss of two transports on 29 February, one to air and one to submarine. SWPA's Fifth Air Force, however, recorded no successful convoy attacks that day. See Kit C. Carter and Robert Mueller, comps., *The Army Air Forces in World War II: Combat Chronology, 1941–1945* (Montgomery, Ala., and Washington, D.C.: Albert F. Simpson Historical Research Center Air University and Office of Air Force History, Headquarters, USAF, 1973), 281–282.

33. Boeicho, Boei kenshujo [Japan, Japan National Institute for Defense Studies], ed., *Senshi sosho*, Vol. 75: *Daihon'ei rikugunbu: Showa 19 nen 7 gatsu made* (8) [Official military history, Vol. 75: Imperial General Headquarters: To July 1944 (book 8)] (Tokyo: Asagumo shimbunsha, 1974), 214 (hereafter cited as *Daihon'ei rikugunbu* [8]). Roscoe, *United States Submarine Operations in World War II*, 544. The U.S.S. *Peto* recorded the date of the sinking as 4 March. The Japanese reported that the submarine attack commenced at 11:00 P.M. on 3 March.

34. ULTRA confirmed the sinking of four ships, including two escorts, although operational reports claimed five ships were sunk. See Kenney, *General Kenney Reports*, 374–375; *Daihon'ei rikugunbu* (8), 218, 234. "Yon ko gun sanden dai 2841 go [Chief of staff, Fourth Air Army message, 2841], 25 March 1944, NT (March 1944), 263, in NIDS.

35. SRH-349, 22, states that SWPA regulations prescribed such tactics. Evidence that

the Japanese were growing conditioned to the presence of American aircraft on night patrol over Hollandia and Wewak may be found in "Mogo sanden dai 771 go" [Eighteenth Army (rear) staff message number 771], 22 February 1944, in NT (February 1944), 137. The message relates the nightly raids by B-24s and B-25s.

36. *MacArthur* 1, 116, note 26.

37. *MacArthur* 2, 58–260; Kimata Jiro, *Rikugun koku senshi: Mare sakusen kara Okinawa tokko made* [History of the army air force: From the Malaya operation to the Okinawa special attack corps] (Tokyo: Keizai oraisha, 1982), 88–89.

38. Boeicho, Boei kenshujo, ed., *Senshi sosho*, Vol. 22: *Seibu Nyugineya homan rikugun koku sakusen* [Army air force operations on the western New Guinea front] (Tokyo: Asagumo shimbunsha, 1969), 255; Kimata, *Rikugun koku senshi*, 96. Southern Army moved from Singapore to Manila in May 1944.

39. *Seibu Nyugineya*, 205–208; *Daihon'ei rikugunbu* (8), 21–22, has the Imperial Headquarters' order.

40. Rear Echelon, GHQ, SWPA to War [Department], 28 February 1944, OPD, Top Secret Message File, NARA. The results of the aerial reconnaissance were reported in Willoughby's Special Intelligence Bulletin (SIB) 298 for 29 February 1944.

41. *MacArthur* 2, 263. MacArthur's views may be found in Letter, General Douglas MacArthur to Major General A. C. Smith, Chief, Military History, Department of the Army, 5 March 1953, RG 10, "Personal Correspondence, March 1953," MMBA.

42. *Seibu Nyugineya*, 256, and Kimata, *Rikugun koku senshi*, 97. "Nihon Rikukaigun no joho kiko to sono katsudo" [The intelligence structure of the Japanese army and navy and its activities] *Kenkyu shiryo* 84SRO-2H [Research document 84SRO-2H], mimeo, 180–185, in NIDS.

43. Kenney, *General Kenney Reports*, 377.

44. Ibid., 373–374.

45. A 29 February Fourth Air Army signal reported 133 operational aircraft, although errors in encoding make the 113 figure more reliable. See "Yon ko gun sanden dai 3018 go" [Chief of staff, Fourth Air Army message 3018], 29 February 1944, NT (February 1944), 136, in NIDS.

46. Kenney, *General Kenny Reports*, 379–381; 84 SRO-2H, 184–185; *Seibu Nyugineya*, 263–266; and SRH-266, 20. Eighteenth Army had a signal intercept detachment at Wewak and the 20th Division had one at Hansa.

47. See "Hi san ni den dai 262/263 go," 26 March 1944, Nanpogun (reika butai) kankei denpo tsuzuri [Miscellany of signals related to Southern Army (and subordinate units)], 32–34, in NIDS. Anami's lengthy signal appears in full in SIB 327 for 29 March 1944.

48. SWPA, "Estimate of the Enemy Situation," 31 March 1944; *MacArthur* 2, 265.

49. Willoughby's handwritten note is appended to SIB 330 for 1 April 1944.

50. SWPA's SIB 327 for 29 March 1944 announced that it was believed that the Japanese changed their code on 26 March after the loss of Wewak Convoy Number 21.

51. This bulletin refers to a "Southwestern Area Force" that may be the Southwest Area Fleet. The Ninth Fleet, the main Japanese naval headquarters in New Guinea, passed from Southeast Area Fleet Headquarters, Rabaul, to Southwest Area Fleet in March 1944. The Southwest Area Fleet controlled all naval units in the Netherlands East Indies and was directly subordinate to the Combined Fleet. Smith, *Approach to Philippines*, 95.

52. "Brief History," 25–28, Plate 9, and accompanying text.

53. Ibid. *MacArthur* 1, 144–145.

54. CG, Rear Echelon, SWPA, Brisbane, Australia, to WD, "MacArthur Eyes Alone Marshall," 17 April 1944, OPD, Top Secret Message File, NARA.

55. *MacArthur* 2, 266.

56. My translation of "Mo sanden dai 489 go" [Eighteenth Army staff message 489], 22 April 1944, in Ji Showa 19 nen 3 gatsu itaru Showa 19 nen 12 gatsu Dai juhachi gun hatsuden tsuzuri (fu 20D/51D) kan go [Miscellany of Eighteenth Army signals (appendix 20 and 51 divisions) from March 1944 to December 1944, vol. 5], in NIDS. A slightly different version of this message may be found in "Brief History," 28.

57. Daniel E. Barbey, *MacArthur's Amphibious Navy: Seventh Amphibious Force Operations, 1943–45* (Annapolis, Md.: U.S. Naval Institute Press, 1969), 167.

58. *MacArthur* 2, 266.

59. William F. McCartney, *The Jungleers: A History of the 41st Infantry Division* (Washington, D.C.: Infantry Journal Press, 1948), 77. Eichelberger wrote on 23 April 1944: "Our route was such that our arrival was a complete surprise. . . . While we are not out of the woods, we are a long way on the road to victory. Had expected more Japs and a bitter fight. What a lucky break!" The following day he wrote: "A week ago if I could have anticipated conditions as good as they are today I would have been very happy" (in Jay Luvaas, ed., *Dear Miss Em: General Eichelberger's War in the Pacific, 1942–1945* [Westport, Conn.: Greenwood Press, 1972], 107). Barbey, *MacArthur's Amphibious Navy*, 170.

60. Kimata, *Rikugun koku senshi*, 95–100. Takahashi Masatoshi, "Dai juuyon hikodan no kaimetsu" [The destruction of the 14th air brigade], *Rekishi to jimbutsu* (August 1980): 129; Smith, *Approach to Philippines*, 101. Tanaka Kengoro, "Adachi Hatazo," in Imai Takeo and Terazaki Ryuji, eds., *Nihongun no kenkyu shikkikan* [Japanese army studies: The commanders], vol. 1 (Tokyo: Hara shobo, 1980), 85.

61. Boeicho, Boei kenshujo, ed., *Senshi sosho*, Vol. 7: *Tobu Nyuginia homen rikugun koku sakusen* [Official military history; Vol. 7: Army air operations on the eastern New Guinea front] (Tokyo: Asagumo shimbunsha, 1967), 338. Hereafter cited as TNKS.

62. Smith, *Approach to Philippines*, 78–79.

63. SRH-362, 147, interview with Mr. Joseph E. Richard, a former member of Central Bureau, 29 January 1989.

64. Richard interview.

65. "For MacArthur from Marshall," 11 June 1944, Chief of Staff Record Files, CINC, USAF, PAC RG4, Box 14, MMBA.

Chapter 5. Misreading ULTRA, *May–September 1944*

1. Tsunoda Fusako, *Sekinin Rabauru no shogun Imamura Hitoshi* [The general reponsible for Rabaul: Imamura Hitoshi] (Tokyo: Shinchosha, 1984), 102.

2. "I butai sosanbocho" ["Chief of staff, Southern Army"], I san den 87 go [Southern Army chief of staff signal no. 87], 27 April 1944, in *Nanto Taiheiyo homen denpo tsuzuri: ji Showa 19 nen 4 gatsu itaru Showa 19 nen 5 gatsu* [Miscellaneous signals of southeastern Pacific front forces: April-May 1944], in NIDS.

3. Supreme Commander for the Allied Powers, *Reports of General MacArthur*, Vol. 2: *Japanese Operations in the Southwest Pacific Area* (Washington, D.C.: Government Printing Office, 1966), 274. Hereafter cited as *MacArthur* 2.

4. Paolo E. Coletta, "Daniel E. Barbey: Amphibious Warfare Expert," in William M. Leary, ed., *We Shall Return! MacArthur's Commanders and the Defeat of Japan, 1942–1945* (Lexington: University Press of Kentucky, 1988), 227–228.

5. Robert Eichelberger Papers, Box: "Memoirs and Dictations on Career; done 1954–1961," 1–167, USAMHI.

6. HQ, AAF, Allied Air Forces Intelligence Summary 205, 6 May 1944, in Papers of Lieutenant General Richard K. Sutherland, RG 30, Box 41, MMBA.

7. Robert Ross Smith, *U.S. Army in World War II: The War in the Pacific: The Approach to the Philippines* (Washington, D.C.: Government Printing Office, 1953), 235. Daihon'ei rikugunbu [Imperial General Headquarters, Army Division], " 'Biaku' shima oyobi 'Sarumi' chiku ni oekru Yuki heidan no sento" [Combat operations of the Yuki (36th Division) group in the Biak Island and Sarmi area], *Sen'kun tokuho* dai 33 go [Special bulletin, lessons learned no. 33], October 1944, in *Dai ni gun kimitsu sakusen nisshi shiryo tsuzuri* [Miscellaneous documents of the classified operations diary of Second Army], in NIDS (hereafter cited as "Yuki heidan").

8. Daily Intelligence Summary 24/25 May 1944, SWPA, MIS, Daily Summaries, RG3, MMBA. Hereafter cited as SWPA, MIS, and date.

9. Ibid., 2/3 May and 3/4 May 1944.

10. Ibid., 28/29 April 1944.

11. Boeicho, Boei kenshujo [Japan, Japan National Institute for Defense Studies], ed., *Senshi sosho*, Vol. 21: *Gohoku homen rikugun sakusen* [Official military history, Vol. 21: army operations north of Australia] (Tokyo: Asagumo shimbunsha, 1968), 469. Hereafter cited as *Gohoku sakusen*.

12. Wesley Frank Craven and James Lea Cate, eds., *The Army Air Forces in World War II*, Vol. 4: *The Pacific: Guadalcanal to Saipan, August 1942 to July 1944* (Chicago: University of Chicago Press, 1950), 625.

13. SWPA, MIS, 2/3 May 1944.

14. AAF Intelligence Summary 205. SWPA, MIS, 7/8 May 1944.

15. Compare ULTRA reports with Boeicho, Boei kenshujo, ed., *Senshi sosho*, Vol. 22: *Seibu Nyuginea homen rikugun koku sakusen* [Official military history, Vol. 22: army air force operations on the western New Guinea front] (Tokyo: Asagumo shimbunsha, 1969), 384.

16. Radio CTF 76 [Barbey] 042354Z to Alamo [HQ, Sixty Army] 5 May 1944, in Alamo G-3 Journal Wakde-Biak, 1–7 May 1944, in RG 94, Box 1488, WNRC. Radio Krueger 052709Z to CTF 76, 5 May 1944, in ibid.

17. SRH-280, 30, 31.

18. Boeicho, Boei kenshujo, ed., *Senshi sosho*, Vol. 54: *Nansei homen kaigun sakusen* [Official military history, Vol. 54: Southwest Area Fleet operations] (Tokyo: Asagumo shimbunsha, 1972), 402. Hereafter cited as NHKS.

19. Ann Bray, "Undercover Nisei," in Diane L. Hamm, ed., *Military Intelligence: Its Heroes and Legends* (Washington, D.C.: Government Printing Office, 1987), 41.

20. The decision to fix the invasion for May 17 was made at Hollandia by MacArthur's staff. Krueger 091700K to CTF 76, 9 May 1944, in Alamo G-3 Journal Wakde-Biak, 8–13 May 1944, in WNRC. GHQ, SWPA, "Operating Instruction 51/1," 10 May 1944, ibid., set the invasion date.

21. SWPA, MIS, 16/17 May 1944.

22. Ibid., 16/17, 17/18, 18/19, and 19/20 May 1944.

23. *Gohoku sakusen*, 427.

24. Robert Ross Smith, *U.S. Army in World War II: The War in the Pacific: The Approach to the Philippines* (Washington, D.C.: Government Printing Office, 1953), 237.

25. CTF 76 191645K to CG Alamo 200407K, May 1944, in Alamo G-3 Journal Wakde-Biak, 14–19 May 1944, in WNRC.

26. SWPA, MIS, 19/20 May 1944.

27. Ibid., 1/2 June 1944, and Smith, *Approach to Philippines*, 259–260.

28. General Clyde D. Eddleman Oral History, USAMHI. Eddleman was Krueger's G-3, or operations officer. He related that "as we moved up from New Guinea, General Krueger wanted to 'blood his troops' as much as possible so he liked to bring in a new division that was going into one of the later operations and have them go in and clean out the residue of the Japanese forces."

29. D. Clayton James, *The Years of MacArthur*, Vol. 2: *1941–1945* (Boston: Houghton Mifflin, 1975), 456; Smith, *Approach to Philippines*, 279.

30. SWPA, MIS, 17/18 and 21/22 May 1944.

31. Ibid., 17/18 May 1944.

32. Memorandum, Lieutenant Commander T. E. L. McCabe to General Willoughby, 13 May 1944, and attachment in Sutherland Papers, Miscellaneous Records, 1943–1945, RG 30, Box 10, Folder 5, MMBA.

33. GHQ, SWPA, "RENO V Outline Plan for Operations of the Southwest Pacific Area to Include the Reoccupation of the Philippines," 1 June 1944, 3, USAMHI.

34. Most recently, Ronald H. Spector, *Eagle against the Sun* (New York: Free Press, 1985), 293, comments negatively on MacArthur's Biak operation.

35. Daniel E. Barbey, *MacArthur's Amphibious Navy: Seventh Amphibious Force Operations, 1943–45* (Annapolis, Md.: U.S. Naval Institute Press, 1969), 203.

36. *Gohoku sakusen*, 497, 505.

37. SWPA, MIS, 26/27 May 1944.

38. "Ko rikushukei Asano Hiro no nikki" [Diary of the late intendance First Lieutenant Asano Hiro], entries for 30 May and 2 June 1944, in Toyohashi Fusataro et al., eds., *Gohoku o seiku* [The subjugation of the front north of Australia] (Tokyo: Gohuku homen ikotsu hikiageru sokushinkai, 1956), 502, 504. Asano was killed in action on Biak.

39. Sugihara Yotaro, "Nakiyobu Biaku shitai" [Echoing cries: The Biak detachment], in ibid., 340.

40. MacArthur to Krueger, 5 and 14 June 1944, RG 4, Box 14, Folder 3, MMBA. MacArthur tersely stated, "The situation on Biak is unsatisfactory."

41. Eichelberger papers, USAMHI.

42. James, *Years of MacArthur*, 459–460, discusses the relief of Major General Horace H. Fuller, commander of the 41st Infantry Division at Biak.

43. NHKS, 399, 404. *Gohoku sakusen*, 470.

44. *MacArthur* 2, 288–289. NHKS, 405.

45. Samuel Eliot Morison, *History of United States Naval Operations in World War II*, Vol. 8: *New Guinea and the Marianas, March 1944–August 1944* (Boston: Little, Brown, 1964), 122–123.

46. *Gohoku sakusen*, 506.

47. William F. McCartney, *The Jungleers: A History of the 41st Infantry Division* (Washington, D.C.: Infantry Journal Press, 1948), 110–111.

48. SIB 394 for 4 June 1944 named Wardo Bay as the Japanese landing area, and the

same day Kinkaid advised his subordinate commanders that the enemy would land at Wardo Bay. See Morison, *History of United States Naval Operations in World War II*, 124.

49. *Gohoku sakusen*, 526–528; NHKS, 410; *MacArthur* 2, 291.

50. Yoshida Mitsuru, *Requiem for Battleship Yamato*, trans. Richard H. Minear (Seattle: University of Washington Press, 1985), xv and xvi.

51. *Gohoku sakusen*, 517, 542, 545; *MacArthur* 2, 291.

52. *Gohoku sakusen*, 552–553.

53. Walter Krueger, *From Down Under to Nippon: The Story of Sixth Army in World War II* (Washington, D.C.: Combat Forces Press, 1953), 108.

54. GHQ, SWPA, "Outline Plan: Occupation of Cape Sansapor (Northwestern Vogelkop), 24 June 1944, 1, USAMHI.

55. Tsunoda, *Sekinin Rabauru*, 102.

56. Central Bureau, Brisbane, "Intelligence Derived from ULTRA," 21 December 1944, SRH-059, 25.

57. U.S. Army, 32d Infantry Division, Persecution Task Force, "Report after Action, 28 June to 25 August 1944, Aitape, New Guinea," 1, microfilm copy at USAMHI.

58. Kengoro Tanaka, *Operations of the Imperial Japanese Armed Forces in the Papua New Guinea Theater during World War II* (Tokyo: Japan–Papua New Guinea Goodwill Society, 1980), 203.

59. Krueger 1017K to G-2, XI Corps 1127K, 27 June 1944, in U.S. Army, 32d Infantry Division, Persecution Task Force, "G-3 Reports, G-3 Journal and File, 32d Infantry Division, Aitape Campaign," cited in Edward J. Drea, "Defending the Driniumor: Covering Force Operations in New Guinea 1944," *Leavenworth Paper* No. 9 (Washington, D.C.: Government Printing Office, 1984), 39.

60. James, *Years of MacArthur*, 522.

61. Chief of Staff, War Department, to CINCSWPA, 24 June 1944, in GHQ, FEC, MIS, Historical Division, "Historical Record Index Cards," mimeo, n.d., copy at USAMHI. James, *Years of MacArthur*, 522–526, has an excellent summary of the events.

62. "Comments and Off-the-Record Remarks on Interview with Gen. Hall," in Robert Ross Smith material, USAMHI.

63. Letter, Hall to Krueger, 10 July 1944, in Smith material.

64. Letter, Hall to Krueger, 8 July 1944, in Smith material.

65. Colonel John W. Patton, A[ssistant] C[hief of] S[taff], G-2 [XI Corps] to CO, Det[achment] 126th Sig[nal] Rad[io] In[tercept] Co[mpany], 14 August 1944, in SRH-227.

66. SWPA, MIS, 12/13 July 1944.

67. See GHQ, FEC, MIS, GS, "Operations of the Military Intelligence Section, GHQ, SWPA/FEC/SCAP," vol. 3, Intelligence Series (part 1), 1950, inserts 5 and 17, USAMHI.

68. See Ronald Lewin, *The American Magic: Codes, Ciphers, and the Defeat of Japan* (New York: Farrar Straus Giroux, 1982), 252–253, and Spector, *Eagle*, 456.

Chapter 6. The Missing Division: Leyte, 1944

1. Grace Person Hayes, *The History of the Joint Chiefs of Staff in World War II: The War against Japan* (Annapolis, Md.: U.S. Naval Institute Press, 1983), 604.

2. CS to CINCSWPA, 24 June 1944, in GHQ, FEC, MIS, Historical Division, "Historical Record Index Cards," mimeo, n.d., copy at USAMHI.

3. GHQ, SWPA, "RENO V Outline Plan for Operations of the Southwest Pacific Area to Include the Reoccupation of the Philippines," 1 June 1944, 3. Copy at USAMHI.

4. Hayes, History of the Joint Chiefs of Staff, 608.

5. Ibid., 608–620, has an excellent description of the high-level strategy deliberations.

6. Supreme Commander for the Allied Powers, Reports of General MacArthur, Vol. 2: Japanese Operations in the Southwest Pacific Area (Washington, D.C.: Government Printing Office, 1966), 331. Hereafter cited as MacArthur 2.

7. Takagi Sokichi, Taiheiyo kaisenshi [A naval history of the Pacific war] (Tokyo: Iwanami shoten, 1977; reprint of 1949 edition), 118.

8. W. J. Holmes, Doubled-Edged Secrets: U.S. Naval Intelligence Operations in the Pacific during World War II (Annapolis, Md.: U.S. Naval Institute Press, 1979), 186.

9. Theodore Roscoe, United States Submarine Operations in World War II (Annapolis, Md.: U.S. Naval Institute Press, 1949), 343–346.

10. Ibid., 352.

11. D. Clayton James, The Years of MacArthur, Vol. 2: 1941–1945 (Boston: Houghton Mifflin, 1975), 537; Ronald H. Spector, Eagle against the Sun (New York: Free Press, 1985), 419.

12. James, Years of MacArthur, 538.

13. The best single-volume treatment of the air, ground, and naval aspects of the struggle for Leyte is Stanley L. Falk, Decision at Leyte (New York: W. W. Norton, 1966).

14. GHQ, SWPA, "G-2 Estimate of the Enemy Situation with Respect to an Operation against the Leyte Gulf Area," 30 September 1944, MMBA.

15. Boeicho, Boei kenshujo [Japan, Japan National Institute for Defense Studies], ed., Senshi sosho, Vol. 41: Shogo rikugun sakusen: Reite kessen (1) [Official military history, Vol. 41: SHO ground operations: The decisive battle of Leyte (book 1)] (Tokyo: Asagumo shimbunsha, 1970), 205, 208. Hereafter cited as Shogo rikugun sakusen.

16. Maebara Toru, "Manira boeishi: Nihongun no toshi to tatakai" [The defense of Manila: Japanese army and city fighting], Kenkyu shiryo 82RO-7H (mimeo) (Tokyo: Boeikenshujo, 1982), 12–13; Falk, Decision at Leyte, 41–42.

17. Yamashita is one of the few Japanese general officers to receive book-length treatments in English. See John Deane Potter, The Life and Death of a Japanese General (New York: Signet, 1962), and A. J. Barker, Yamashita (New York: Ballantine, 1973). Falk, Decision at Leyte, 33–40, has an excellent brief description. On Suzuki, see Watanabe Rikaku, "Suzuki Sosaku taisho" [General Suzuki Sosaku], in Imai Takeo and Terasaki Ryuji, eds., Nihongun no kenkyu shikkikan (ge) [Japanese army studies: The commanders (vol. 2)] (Tokyo: Hara shobo, 1980), 33, 55–60.

18. Ooe Shinobu, Showa no rekishi, Vol. 3: Tenno no guntai [History of the Showa reign, Vol. 3: The emperor's army] (Tokyo: Shogakkan, 1982), 300–302. The emperor's question is found in Ikuta Makoto, "Dai yon kokugun sakusen no temmatsu" [Facts about Fourth Air Army's operations), Bessatsu Maru, "Taiheiyo senso shogen shirizu" [Pacific war testimony series], 4, "Nichi-Bei sen no Tennozan Fuiripin kessenki" [The climactic Japanese-American battle; record of the decisive battle of the Philippines] (November 1986):204.

19. Ishikawa Kikuo, "Yamashita Tomoyuki taisho" (General Hamashita Tomoyuki), in Imai and Terasaki, Nihongun no kenkyu shikkikan (jo) [vol. 1], 298. Muto's remark about Leyte is related in John Toland, The Rising Sun: The Decline and Fall of the Japanese Empire, 1936–1945 (New York: Random House, 1970), 543.

20. Nakamuda Ken'ichi, *Joho shikan no kaiso* [Memoirs of an intelligence officer] (Tokyo: Asahi sonorama, 1985), 265–266.

21. See Supreme Commander for the Allied Powers, *Reports of General MacArthur,* Vol. 1: *The Campaigns of MacArthur in the Pacific* (Washington, D.C.: Government Printing Office, 1966), 205–212 (hereafter cited as *MacArthur 1*), for Willoughby's self-serving account of G-2 prescience about Leyte Gulf. A review of available ULTRA does not support his selective use of the evidence.

22. *MacArthur 2,* 331, gives the 420 figure.

23. Compare Kimata Jiro, *Rikugun koku senshi: Mare sakusen kara Okinawa tokko made* [History of the army air force: From the Malaya operation to the Okinawa special attack corps] (Tokyo: Keizai oraisha, 1982), 203–204, with Wesley Frank Craven and James Lea Cate, eds., *The Army Air Forces in World War II,* Vol. 5: *The Pacific: Matterhorn to Nagasaki, June 1944 to August 1945* (Chicago: University of Chicago Press, 1953), 370–371.

24. George C. Kenney, *General Kenney Reports* (Washington, D.C.: Office of Air Force History, 1988; reprint of 1949 edition), 471–472.

25. Craven and Cate, eds., *Army Air Forces in World War II,* 5: 370–371.

26. Denis Warner and Peggy Warner, with Sadao Seno, *The Sacred Warriors: Japan's Suicide Legions* (New York: Van Nostrand Reinhold, 1982), 84–94. Imai Sei'ichi, *Taiheiyo senso,* Vol. 5: *Taiheiyo senso* (II) [The History of the Pacific war, Vol. 5: The Pacific war (part 2)] (Tokyo: Aoki shoten, 1973), 260.

27. Kimata, *Rikugun koku senshi,* 221–222. Warner and Warner, *Sacred Warriors,* 323–334, has a list of the victims of Japanese special attack aircraft. Tominaga's folly appears in Ooe, *Tenno no guntai,* 301–302.

28. *Shogo rikugun sakusen,* 282.

29. Ibid., 234. Three former Fourteenth Area Army staff officers discuss the assessments in Akieta Shigeharu et al., "Danwakai Hito kessen o ayamaraseta mono" [Discussion: Things mistaken in the decisive battle of the Philippines], *Rekishi to jimbutsu* (Summer 1986): 133–138.

30. Imai, *Taiheiyo senso,* 5 (part 2): 258. Hori Eizo, "Reite kessen kara Ruson jikyu made Yamashita Tomoyuki taisho kujyu nichikan kuno" [From the decisive battle of Leyte to the protracted fighting of Luzon—General Yamashita Tomoyuki's ninety days of suffering], *Rekishi to jimbutsu* (Winter 1986): 324–329, offers a Fourteenth Area Army staff intelligence officer's insights into Yamashita during the Leyte fighting.

31. Headquarters Sixth Army, Office of the Assistant Chief of Staff, G-2, "G-2 Estimate of the Enemy Situation with Respect to 'KING TWO' Operation," 20 September 1944, 10–11, MMBA.

32. *Shogo rikugun sakusen,* 310–315. Falk, *Decision at Leyte,* 221. Tanaka Ken'ichi, *Reite sakusen no kiroku* [Record of Leyte operations] (Tokyo: Hara shobo, 1980), 61. Tanaka fought on Leyte as a member of the Second Raider Unit.

33. *Shogo rikugun sakusen,* 313, 315–316. Falk, *Decision at Leyte,* 60–61.

34. Intercepted and decrypted messages from the German air and naval attachés in Tokyo provided this intelligence.

35. Boeicho, Boei kenshujo, *Senshi sosho,* Vol. 56: *Kaigun shogo sakusen: Fuiripin oki kaisen* (1) [SHO naval operations: The naval battle of the Philippine Sea (book 1)] (Tokyo: Asagumo shimbunsha, 1970), 515–517. Hereafter cited as *Kaigun shogo sakusen.*

36. Kusumi Tadao, "Nansei homen kantai" [Southwest Area Fleet], *Rekishi to jimbutsu*

(Winter 1985): 119, and Ooka Shohei, *Reite senki* [Military record of the Leyte operation] (Tokyo: Chuo koron, 1971), 119. Samuel Eliot Morison, *History of United States Naval Operations in World War II*, Vol. 12: *Leyte: June 1944–January 1945* (Boston: Little, Brown, 1963), 345–346.

37. *Kaigun shogo sakusen*, 510. Ooka, *Reite senki*, 276–278. Craven and Cate, *Army Air Forces in World War II*, 5:376–377.

38. Sixth United States Army, *Report of the Leyte Operation*, 17 October 1944–25 December 1944, 41. Copy at USAMHI.

39. Spector, *Eagle*, 513–514. For another viewpoint, see William M. Leary, "Walter Krueger: MacArthur's Fighting General," in Leary, ed., *We Shall Return! MacArthur's Commanders and the Defeat of Japan, 1942–1945* (Lexington: University Press of Kentucky, 1988), 74–76.

40. Sixth Army, KING II Operations, G-2 Journal and File No. 1 (Folder 1), 24 October–3 November 1944, Headquarters Sixth Army, Assistant Chief of Staff, G-2, "G-2 Periodic Report," 27–31 October 1944, Nos. 309–313, respectively, RG 94, Box 2425, WNRC.

41. Sixth Army, "G-2 Periodic Report," 1–4 November 1944, Nos. 314–318, respectively. See also items 387, MacArthur to Ad[vanced] Ech[elon], GHQ CG Sixth Army (TOR [time of receipt] 011124 Nov.); 423, Fertig to Krueger (TOR 212251 Oct.); 522, CG XXIV Corps to CG Sixth Army (TOR 022246 Nov.). The X Corps' account of Krueger's order is found in Headquarters X Corps, "A History of X Corps in the Leyte-Samar-Philippine Island Operation," 19 November 1945, 25 USAMHI. Item 423 was a signal from Colonel Wendell W. Fertig, an American officer who became a guerrilla leader in southern Mindanao rather than surrendering.

42. Headquarters Sixth Army, "G-2 Estimate of the Enemy Situation, 'KING TWO,' " 20 September 1944, 11, MMBA.

43. Leary, "Krueger," 76.

44. Sixth Army, "G-2 Periodic Report," 4 November 1944, No. 317.

45. Headquarters X Corps, "G-2 Periodic Report, No. 14, 031800 to 041800, Nov. 44," in Thomas F. Hickey Papers, USAMHI. I am indebted to Dr. Richard J. Sommers for making me aware of this collection.

46. Sixth Army, "G-2 Periodic Report," 8 November 1944, No. 321.

47. Ooka, *Reite senki*, emphasizes that the 57th Infantry, 1st Division, moved into the vital heights on November 4 and 5. Ooka himself was a replacement on Mindoro when the Americans invaded Leyte. After his capture, he met soldiers and sailors who told him of the Leyte fighting. His book is a brilliant account of the 1st Division on Leyte and a model of the genre.

48. General Clyde D. Eddleman Oral History, USAMHI.

49. My version is a composite of accounts by Ooka, *Reite senki*, 238, and Jan Valtin [Richard J. Krebs], *Children of Yesterday* (New York: Readers' Press, 1946), 187.

50. Tanaka, *Reite sakusen*, 68.

51. Tomita Seinosuke, *Dai ichi shidan Reite kessen no shinso* [The truth about the 1st Division's decisive battle on Leyte] (Tokyo: Asagumo shimbunsha, 1987), 116.

52. Craven and Cate, *Army Air Forces in World War II*, 5:378, and Kenney, *General Kenney Reports*, 475. Compare SRMD-007, JICPOA Summary of ULTRA Traffic, 11 September 1944–30 June 1945, Summary for 10 November 1944, with *Shogo rikugun sakusen*, 430, and *Kaigun shogo sakusen*, 532.

53. Federick C. Sherman, *Combat Command: The American Aircraft Carriers in the Pacific War* (New York: E. P. Dutton, 1950), 318. The Japanese version of these attacks is in *Kaigun shogo sakusen*, 538–539.

54. Holmes, *Double-Edged Secrets*, 194, and *Shogo rikugun sakusen*, 437.

55. Roscoe, *United States Submarine Operations*, 401–402, 416. *Shogo rikugun sakusen*, 470.

56. ULTRA reports of the convoy were numerous. See the War Department's daily ULTRA summaries 245, 247, 248, 249, and 250 (*November 20, 22, 23–25*), JICPOA, (**November 20, 22, 24**), and SIB (November 21/22, 23/24). *Shogo rikugun sakusen*, 494, 499; *Kaigun shogo sakusen*, 554; Craven and Cate, *Army Air Forces in World War II*, 5:379.

57. Morison, *History of United States Naval Operations*, 12:380.

58. *Shogo rikugun sakusen*, 203.

59. Falk, *Decision at Leyte*, 316–317, discusses the relatively cheap victory.

Chapter 7. The Numbers Game: Luzon, January–June 1945

1. Grace Person Hayes, *The History of the Joint Chiefs of Staff in World War II: The War against Japan* (Annapolis, Md.: U.S. Naval Institute Press, 1983), 623.

2. GHQ, SWPA, MIS, GS, "G-2 Staff Study Japanese Defensive Organization of Luzon," 15 December 1944, in RG 4, USAFPAC, Intelligence, General, MMBA.

3. GHQ, SWPA, MIS, GS, "G-2 Estimate of the Enemy Situation with Respect to an Operation against Lingayen Gulf and the Central Plain of Luzon," 22 November 1944, in ibid.

4. W. J. Holmes, *Double-Edged Secrets: U.S. Naval Intelligence Operations in the Pacific during World War II* (Annapolis, Md.: U.S. Naval Institute Press, 1979), 194. See also SRMD-007, JICPOA Summary of ULTRA Traffic, 11 September 1944–30 June 1945, Summary for 15 and 17 November 1944.

5. Boeicho, Boei kenshujo [Japan, Japan National Institute for Defense Studies], ed., *Senshi sosho*, Vol. 60: *Shogo rikugun sakusen: Ruson kessen* (2) [Official military history, Vol. 60: SHO ground operations: The decisive battle of Luzon (book 2)] (Tokyo: Asagumo shimbunsha, 1972), 26. Hereafter cited as *Ruson kessen*.

6. Maebara Toru, "Manira boeishu: Nihongun no toshi to tatakai" [The defense of Manila: Japanese army and city fighting], *Kenkyu shiryo* 82 RO-7H (mimeo) (Tokyo: Boeikenshujo, 1982), 33, 46, 53.

7. General Clyde D. Eddleman Oral History, USAMHI.

8. Robert Ross Smith, *United States Army in World War II: The War in the Pacific: Triumph in the Philippines* (Washington, D.C.: Government Printing Office, 1963), 22–23.

9. Discrepancies exist in accounts of the REI operation. For the American version, see Supreme Commander for the Allied Powers, *Reports of General MacArthur*, Vol. 1: *The Campaigns of MacArthur in the Pacific* (Washington, D.C.: Government Printing Office, 1966), 1, 251 (hereafter cited as *MacArthur 1*). A Japanese version of events may be found in Hoshino Seizaburo, "Mindoro shima totsunyu 'REI' sakusen shimatsuki" [A record of the circumstances surrounding the thrust at Mindoro Island: The REI operation], *Bessatsu Maru*, "Taiheiyo senso shogen shirizu" [Pacific war testimony series], 4, "Nichi-Bei sen no Tennozan Fuiripin kessenki" [The climactic Japanese-American battle; record of the decisive battle of the Philippines] (November 1986): 204.

10. Eddleman Oral History, USAMHI.

11. Maebara, *Manira boeishu*, 6–7. Maebaru Toru, "Manira boei no higeki rikukaigun no tairitsu" [The tragedy of the defense of Manila—The opposition between the army and navy], *Rekishi to jimbutsu* (September 1982): 102–103.

12. *Ruson kessen*, 10.

13. Maebara, "Manira boei no higeki," 106.

14. Ibid., 103–104.

15. Kojima Noboru, *Tenno*, Vol. 5: *Teikoku no shuen* [The emperor, Vol. 5: Death of the empire] (Tokyo: Bungei shunju, 1974), 252.

16. Smith, *Triumph in Philippines*, 141. Walter Krueger, *From Down under to Nippon: The Story of Sixth Army in World War II* (Washington, D.C.: Combat Forces Press, 1953), 227–228.

17. Gerald E. Wheeler, "Thomas C. Kinkaid: MacArthur's Master of Naval Warfare," in William M. Leary, ed., *We Shall Return! MacArthur's Commanders and the Defeat of Japan, 1942–1945* (Lexington: University Press of Kentucky, 1988), 149–150. *MacArthur* 1, 258.

18. Compare accounts of the action in Samuel Eliot Morison, *History of United States Naval Operations in World War II*, Vol. 14: *The Liberation of the Philippines: Luzon, Mindanao, the Visayans, 1944–45* (Boston: Little, Brown, 1959), 138–140; and Gido Tamotsu, *Ruson no ishibumi* [Tombstones of Luzon] (Tokyo: Kojinsha, 1981), 53–57. Gido served in the 2d Surface Raiding Regiment, the official designation for the suicide boat units, on Okinawa.

19. Eddleman, Oral History, USAMHI, noted the cross words exchanged. Krueger, *From Down under to Nippon*, 227–228, is the Sixth Army commander's account of the meeting.

20. GHQ, SWPA, MIS, GS, "Recapitulation of Luzon Enemy Strength and Dispositions," 15 January 1945, in RG-4, USAFPAC, Intelligence, General, MMBA.

21. Compare SWPA G-2 15 January estimate with White's in Smith, *Triumph in Philippines*, 141.

22. Sixth United States Army, "Report of the Luzon Campaign, 9 January 1945–30 June 1945," vol. 3, 17, MMBA. SWPA, G-2, MIS, 14/15 January 1945.

23. *Rikugun angosho* 4 [Army codebook, 4th edition] was valid from 1 June 1943 to 31 January 1945. SRH-362, 3: 139. Interview with Joseph E. Richard, a former member of Central Bureau, 29 January 1989.

24. Willoughby's comments appear in SWPA, G-2, MIS, 21/22 January 1945.

25. Cited in William M. Leary, "Walter Krueger: MacArthur's Fighting General," in Leary, ed., *We Shall Return!* 79.

26. D. Clayton James, *The Years of MacArthur*, Vol. 2: *1941–1945* (Boston: Houghton Mifflin, 1975), 625.

27. Eddleman Oral History, USAMHI.

28. *Ruson kessen*, 163. SWPA, G-2, "Periodic Summary of Enemy Trends," No. 26, 21 January 1945, RG 3, Box 41, MMBA.

29. *Ruson kessen*, 165.

30. SWPA, G-2, MIS, 11/12 February 1945.

31. Maebara, *Manira boeishu*, 107–108. *Ruson kessen*, 177.

32. B. C. Wright, comp., *The 1st Cavalry Division in World War II* (Tokyo: Toppan Printing, 1947), 128–130.

33. James, *Years of MacArthur*, 640, 643.

34. *Ruson kessen*, 245.

35. Smith, *Triumph in Philippines*, 335.

36. "History of the Special Security Officer, Headquarters Sixth Army, 6 October 1944–8 August 1945," SRH-032, 22.

37. Ibid.

38. SWPA, G-2, "Monthly Summary of Enemy Dispositions," 31 March 1945, RG 3, Box 19, and Memorandum, Krueger to MacArthur, 1 July 1945, RG 30, Box 25, MMBA.

39. Smith, *Triumph in Philippines*, 651.

40. Ibid., 652.

41. Robert Ross Smith, "Luzon versus Formosa," in Kent Roberts Greenfield, ed., *Command Decisions* (Washington, D.C.: Government Printing Office, 1960), 170–172.

42. Memorandum, Lieutenant Colonel A. W. Sanford, GS, to C-in-C, Australian Military Forces (Blamey), 30 June 1945, in SRH-219, 64. Sanford was one of the Australian directors of Central Bureau.

43. "History of the Special Security Officer, Headquarters Sixth Army," SRH-032, 23.

Chapter 8. ULTRA *as Seer: Uncovering Japanese Plans for Homeland Defense, June–August 1945*

1. Tanemura Suketaka, *Daihon'ei kimitsu nisshi* [Confidential war diary of Imperial Headquarters] (Tokyo: Fuyo shobo, 1985; reprint of 1952 edition), 256.

2. Ibid., 258–259, 261–262.

3. Boeicho, Boei kenshujo [Japan, Japan National Institute for Defense Studies], ed., *Senshi sosho*, vol. 57: *Hondo kessen jumbi: Kyushu no boei* (2) [Official military history, Vol. 57: Preparations for the decisive battle of the homeland: Defense of Kyushu (book 2)] (Tokyo: Asagumo shimbunsha, 1972), 213. Hereafter cited as *Kessen*.

4. Grace Person Hayes, *The History of the Joint Chiefs of Staff in World War II: The War against Japan* (Annapolis, Md.: U.S. Naval Institute Press, 1983), 690–693.

5. Ibid., 707–710.

6. Louis Morton, "The Decision to Use the Atomic Bomb," in Kent Roberts Greenfield, ed., *Command Decisions* (Washington, D.C.: Government Printing Office, 1960), 504 U.S. Department of Defense, *The Entry of the Soviet Union into the War against Japan: Military Plans, 1941–1945* (Washington, D.C.: Government Printing Office, 1955), 85. Leon V. Sigal, *Fighting to a Finish: The Politics of War Termination in the United States and Japan, 1945* (Ithaca, N.Y.: Cornell University Press, 1988), is a good synthesis of decisionmaking in 1945 but slights the ULTRA contribution to the American side.

7. GHQ, USAFPAC, MIS, GS, "G-2 Estimate of the Enemy Situation with Respect to an Operation against Southern Kyushu in November 1945," 25 April 1945, MMBA.

8. Supreme Commander for the Allied Powers, *Reports of General MacArthur*, Vol. 1: *The Campaigns of MacArthur in the Pacific* (Washington, D.C.: Government Printing Office, 1966), 415; ibid., Vol. 2: *Japanese Operations in the South-West Pacific Area*, part 2, 622, note 42. *Kessen*, 365.

9. *Kessen*, 275.

10. Ibid., 279.

11. Marshall to MacArthur, WD 1050, 16 June 1945; MacArthur to Marshall, WD 1052, 17 June 1945; Marshall to MacArthur, WD 1056, 19 June 1945; MacArthur to Marshall, WD 1057, 19 June 1945; and Marshall to MacArthur, WD 1060, 19 June 1945, in RG 4, USAFPAC, Folder 4 (War Department 1001–1095, 29 April –2 August 1945), MMBA.

12. U.S. Department of State, *Foreign Relations of the United States: Diplomatic Papers: The Conference of Berlin (the Potsdam Conference), 1945*, vol. 1 (Washington, D.C.: Government Printing Office, 1960), 905, 907–908 (hereafter cited as *FRUS*). Rufus E. Miles, Jr., "Hiroshima: The Strange Myth of Half a Million American Lives Saved," *International Security* 10, no. 2 (Fall 1985): 134–138, critically analyzes the projected numbers of U.S. casualties for the Kyushu operation. He did not, however, use available ULTRA materials for his study.

13. *FRUS*, 907.

14. Fujiwara Akira, *Taiheiyo senso shiron* [A historical interpretation of the Pacific war] (Tokyo: Aoki shoten, 1982), 175, 178.

15. Shinzato Keiji, Taminato Tomoaki, and Kinjo Seitoku, eds., *Kenshi no shiriizu*, Vol. 47: *Okinawa no rekishi* [Prefectural history series, Vol. 47: A history of Okinawa] (Tokyo: Yamakawa shoten, 1980), 215. I am indebted to Professor Steve Rabson of Brown University for locating this information for me.

16. Gordon Daniels, "The Great Tokyo Air Raid," in W. G. Beasley, ed., *Modern Japan: Aspects of History, Literature, and Society* (Tokyo: Charles E. Tuttle, 1976), 130. Kojima Noboru, *Tenno*, Vol. 5: *Teikoku no shuen* [The emperor, Vol. 5: Death of the Empire] (Tokyo: Bungei shunju, 1974), 5, 323. On Marshall's impressions of Japanese homeland defense, see Forrest C. Pogue, *George C. Marshall: Statesman, 1945–1959* (New York: Viking Press, 1987), 19.

17. Kojima, *Tenno*, 5:430.

18. *Kessen*, 283.

19. Various references to such measures appear in the Special Intelligence Bulletin, in SRH-203, part 4. See, for example, July 10/11, 19/20, and 25/26 1945.

20. Compare with plans described in *Kessen*, 465.

21. See U.S. War Department, Office of the Assistant Chief of Staff, G-2 Special Branch, Military Intelligence Division, "MAGIC Summary—Japanese Army Supplement," SRS-01–547, for 5 and 18 May, 5, 6, 14, 22, 25, and 30 June, and 11 and 18 July 1945, for descriptions of Japanese Foreign Ministry peace efforts.

22. GHQ, USAFPAC, MIS, GS, "Amendment No. 1 to G-2 Estimate of the Enemy Situation with Respect to Kyushu (Dated 25 April 1945)," 29 July 1945, 1, MMBA.

23. Ibid.

24. Special Staff, U.S. Army Historical Division, "Sixth Army Occupation of Japan," 1946. Copy at the U.S. Army Center of Military History, Washington, D.C.

25. *Kessen*, 467–468.

26. David Westheimer, *Downfall: The Top-Secret Plan to Invade Japan* [originally published as *Lighter than a Feather*] (New York: Bantam, 1972), and Hiyama Yoshiaki, *Nihon hondo kessen* [The decisive battle of the Japanese homeland] (Tokyo: Kobunsha, 1981). Westheimer's overlooked novel is a model of the historical "what if" genre, with insights about Japanese thinking rarely found elsewhere in English.

27. D. Clayton James, *The Years of MacArthur*, Vol. 2: *1941–1945* (Boston: Houghton Mifflin, 1975), 772–775. COMGENUSASTAF, Eyes Only to MacArthur and Nimitz, 25

July 1945, RG 30, Box 7, Folder 7, MMBA, gave the first warning that the bomb would be used after 3 August. A later message, dated 4 August, identified Hiroshima as the target for an atomic attack scheduled for 06/0945 August 1945.

28. *Kessen,* 597. Hayashi Saburo, *Taiheiyo senso rikusen gaishi* [An overview of army operations in the Pacific war] (Tokyo: Iwanami shoten, 1951), 258–259.

29. "Henry L. Stimson Diaries," entry for 2 July 1945, Papers of Henry L. Stimson, microfilm copy at Library of Congress, Reel 9.

30. Ibid., 23 July 1945. "Memorandum for the President: The Conduct of the War with Japan," 16 July 1945, Stimson Papers, microfilm copy at Library of Congress, Reel 113.

31. MacArthur to Marshall, WD 1057.

32. Miles, "Hiroshima," 137. Wesley Frank Craven and James Lea Cate, eds., *The Army Air Forces in World War II,* Vol. 5: *The Pacific: Matterhorn to Nagasaki, June 1944 to August 1945* (Chicago: University of Chicago Press, 1953), between pages 712 and 713 is a photocopy of Truman's letter to the authors on Marshall's Potsdam estimate.

33. Marshall to MacArthur, War 45369, 7 August 1945. I am indebted to Professor Ray Skates of the University of Southern Mississippi for sharing with me this document and the one cited in note 34.

34. MacArthur to Marshall, War 31897, 9 August 1945.

35. John Toland, *The Rising Sun: The Decline and Fall of the Japanese Empire, 1936–1945* (New York: Random House, 1970), 795 (note). See also William Craig, *The Fall of Japan* (New York: Dial Press, 1967), 73–74.

36. D. Clayton James, *The Years of MacArthur,* Vol. 3: *Triumph and Disaster* (Boston: Houghton Mifflin, 1985), 105–108. Robert Butow's classic *Japan's Decision to Surrender* (Stanford, Calif.: Stanford University Press, 1954), remains the standard depiction of the tortuous path that led the Japanese leadership to capitulate.

Chapter 9. Conclusion

1. Peter Calvocoressi, *Top Secret Ultra* (New York: Ballantine, 1980), 127.

2. Ralph Bennett, *Ultra and Mediterranean Strategy* (New York: William Morrow, 1989), 402.

A Note on Sources

Major General Charles A. Willoughby was the earliest exploiter of ULTRA as history, although security considerations prevented him from using the code word. Originally classified "Secret," the multivolume Intelligence Series—an introduction and nine volumes (June 1947–June 1948)—compiled under Willoughby's editorship, was a collection of case studies about the use of all types of intelligence in General Douglas MacArthur's Pacific operations. Willoughby envisaged the series as a practical teaching tool in the U.S. Army Command and Staff College. He discussed Central Bureau and radio intelligence in general terms and used the Admiralties and Hollandia as examples of the importance of radio intelligence. Indeed, a reproduction of the translation of a decrypted Japanese army radio message complements the text. Willoughby's subsequent book, *MacArthur, 1941–1951* (1954), also discussed the value of radio intelligence during the Pacific War. Until the declassification of the ULTRA documents in the mid-1970s, it was impossible to judge whether Willoughby's assertions were the rule or the exception.

From 1945 to 1951, during the Allied occupation of Japan, Willoughby also oversaw the writing of MacArthur's official history. Because of its uncritical approach and selective use of documentation, the multivolume *Reports of General MacArthur* (2 vols. in 4 parts, 1966) remained unpublished for fifteen years. Scattered throughout these volumes are references to an otherwise unidentified "Special Intelligence Bulletin" (SIB). Willoughby was the editor-in-chief, so the writers extolled the role of intelligence in MacArthur's campaigns. All of the materials upon which the *Reports* were based, however, present a skewed appreciation of MacArthur's use of intelligence by making the exceptional appear commonplace.

Authors of the U.S. Army's official account of the war in the Southwest Pacific, *U.S. Army in World War II: The War in the Pacific* (1953–1963), occasionally referred to intelligence obtained from radio intercepts of Japanese communications. These historians, however, did not have unrestricted access to ULTRA-level materials, so no systematic account of the role of ULTRA emerged. Similarly, former high-ranking officers like George C. Kenney (1949) or Walter Krueger (1953) wrote in their memoirs of "getting some intelligence" about the enemy. Today we understand that they meant ULTRA, but their reminiscences do not tell a comprehensive tale of using it. Nonetheless, by matching these first-person accounts with the official histories of Japan and the United States and available ULTRA evidence, one may make reasonable inferences about a commander's reliance on ULTRA.

David Kahn wrote his trailblazing book *The Codebreakers* (1967) long before the release of the ULTRA materials and concentrates on the naval aspects of the Pacific war. Following the release of the ULTRA documents in the mid-1970s, a spate of monographs and articles appeared. Several—for example, those by Ralph Bennett (1979, 1989), Peter Calvocoressi (1980), and Patrick Beasley (1977) and the official volumes by F. H. Hinsley (1979)—were of high quality but dealt exclusively with the European war. John Costello's *The Pacific War* (1981) opted to sensationalize ULTRA, whereas Ronald Spector's *Eagle against the Sun* (1985) was a thoughtful effort to include the ULTRA evidence available to him. In the latter two cases, ULTRA was woven into the fabric of the narrative, not treated as a separate, specialized subject. Accounts such as Jasper Holmes's *Double-Edged Secrets* (1979) or the more controversial *And I Was There* (1985) by Rear Admiral Edwin T. Layton, concentrate on naval ULTRA and rarely touch on MacArthur's war. Both books rely heavily on memory. The compartmentalized nature of special intelligence leaves us with necessarily incomplete first-person accounts by former cryptanalysts who worked on solving Japanese codes, such as Alan Stripp's *Codebreaker in Burma* (1989) or Edward Van Der Rhoer's *Deadly Magic: A Personal Account of Communication Intelligence in World War II in the Pacific* (1978). Both contain much valuable detail but make no pretense of being inclusive.

With the exception of an excellent article about MacArthur and ULTRA by David M. Horner, "Special Intelligence in the Southwest Pacific Area in World War II" (1978), and Edward J. Drea, "Ultra Intelligence and General MacArthur's Leap to Hollandia, January-April 1944" (1990), little has appeared about MacArthur's ULTRA in the ground or air war against Japan. The late Ronald Lewin was the only author to attempt a comprehensive history of ULTRA in the Pacific. His *The American Magic: Codes, Ciphers, and the Defeat of Japan* (1982) is frankly a disappointing book. In this largely concocted interpretation, Lewin relies on his unfavorable interpretation of MacArthur to hold together his uncritical acceptance of ULTRA's assertions. Because Lewin did not verify the claims made for ULTRA, the book is more a series of impressionistic essays or glosses of declassified ULTRA materials. No comprehensive history of the role of ULTRA in America's Pacific campaigns exists in either monograph or document form.

Information about Japanese codebreaking and special intelligence is similarly fragmented. The reaction provoked among former Japanese army cryptanalysts by claims by Japanese scholars of ULTRA's effect on the Pacific fighting has enabled scholars to sketch the broad outlines of Japan's special intelligence system. Documentary evidence is almost nonexistent—much having gone up in smoke following Japan's surrender. Memoirs and accounts from memory suffer the same failings as their English-language counterparts.

As for the campaigns themselves, little has been written in the United States since the appearance of the official histories. Later American efforts to describe the fighting in New Guinea have produced only a handful of monographs, such as Lida Mayo's *Bloody Buna* (1974) and Edward Drea's "Defending the Driniumor," *Leavenworth Paper No. 9* (1983). The Australian contribution about New Guinea, from the three excellent official histories of the land campaigns (1959–1963) to substantive secondary accounts, gives perspective to otherwise parochial American views of that theater. On the Japanese side, six volumes of the official military history are devoted to New Guinea ground operations (1969–1975).

Numerous secondary works on the topic remain popular in Japan, at least if judged in terms of book sales. Stanley L. Falk's *Decision at Leyte* (1966) treats the ground fighting on that island. Its Japanese equivalent is the late Ooka Shohei's masterpiece, *Reite senki* (Military record of the Leyte operation) (1971). Aside from the U.S. Army's official account (1963), there is no comprehensive history of the fighting on Luzon in 1945.

Two factors may account for this general neglect of MacArthur's campaigns. First, historians have focused on General MacArthur, who so dominates the historical landscape that he overshadows his campaigns in the Southwest Pacific. Autobiography, biography, and memoirs are the staple for these operations. Second, in a historiographical sense, the Central Pacific offensive (broadly used to include the Solomons) has overwhelmed the one in the Southwest Pacific. Books about Guadalcanal, Tarawa, Iwo Jima, Okinawa, and so forth appear with regularity, but one searches in vain for a similar outpouring about MacArthur's theater.

The basic primary-source materials for this book are found in the U.S. National Archives and Records Administration (NARA), Record Group (RG) 457, in Washington, D.C. These documents consist of cryptologic materials declassified by the National Security Agency. The documents do not provide a definitive history of the use of ULTRA in the Pacific or of its use in other operations. Many reports require a healthy skepticism, many a historical context. Much work remains to be done with this archival treasure. (The reports used in this study are listed at the beginning of the notes section.)

World War II U.S. Army unit records are at the Washington National Records Center, Suitland, Maryland. Most helpful were army, corps, and division G-2 and G-3 journals and files in RG 94 (Alamo Force [Sixth Army] records). Also useful for this work was RG 165 (Operations Division, War Department, files), NARA. Any study about MacArthur must begin at the MacArthur Memorial Bureau of Archives, Norfolk, Virginia. For this book, RG 3 Records of Headquarters, South West Pacific Area (SWPA), 1942–1945 (199 boxes); RG 4, Records of General Headquarters, United States Army Forces, Pacific (USAFFE), 1942–1947 (57 boxes); RG 23, Papers of Major General Charles A. Willoughby, USA, 1947–1973 (23 boxes); and RG 30, Papers of Lieutenant General Richard K. Sutherland, USA (45 boxes), proved most useful. I also made extensive use of various archival collections housed at the U.S. Army Military History Institute, Carlisle Barracks, Pennsylvania. In Japan I conducted research at the military archives of the Japan Self-Defense Forces located in the National Institute for Defense Studies, Military History Archives, Tokyo. In the United States, the Japanalia Division, Library of Congress, Washington, D.C., is a mine of secondary works in Japanese on the Pacific war.

Selected Bibliography

Public Documents

Allied Translator and Interpreter Section (ATIS). South West Pacific Area. "The Exploitation of Japanese Documents." ATIS Publication No. 6. 14 December 1944. Copy at United States Military History Institute, Carlisle Barracks, Pennsylvania.

———. "The Japanese Army List (15 October 1942)." ATIS Publication No. 2. May 1943. Copy at United States Military History Institute, Carlisle Barracks, Pennsylvania.

General Headquarters. Far East Command. Military Intelligence Section. General Staff. *A Brief History of the G-2 Section, GHQ, SWPA and Affiliated Units.* Introduction to Intelligence Series. 1948. Copy at United States Military History Institute, Carlisle Barracks, Pennsylvania.

———. *Operations of the Military Intelligence Section, GHQ, SWPA/FEC/SCAP.* Vol. 3 of Intelligence Series (part 1). 1950.

———. Historical Division. "Historical Record Index Cards." Mimeo. N.d. Copy at United States Military History Institute, Carlisle Barracks, Pennsylvania.

Sixth United States Army. *Report of the Leyte Operation.* 17 October 1944–25 December 1944. Copy at United States Military History Institute, Carlisle Barracks, Pennsylvania.

United States. Department of Defense. *The Entry of the Soviet Union into the War against Japan: Military Plans, 1941–1945.* Washington, D.C.: Government Printing Office, 1955.

———. Department of State. *Foreign Relations of the United States: Diplomatic Papers: The Conference of Berlin (the Potsdam Conference), 1945.* Vol. 1. Washington, D.C.: Government Printing Office, 1960.

———. "Employment of Forces under the Southwest Pacific Command." *United States Strategic Bombing Survey Reports: Pacific War,* No. 65. Washington, D.C.: Military Analysis Division, 1947.

———. War Department. Military Intelligence Division. *Order of Battle of the Japanese Armed Forces.* Washington, D.C.: Government Printing Office, 1 March 1945.

Secondary Sources

Agawa, Hiroyuki. *The Reluctant Admiral: Yamamoto and the Imperial Navy*. Trans. John Bester. New York: Harper and Row, 1979.

Alperovitz, Gar. *Atomic Diplomacy: Hiroshima and Potsdam*. New York: Vintage, 1967.

Ball, Desmond J. "Allied Intelligence Cooperation Involving Australia during World War II." *Australian Outlook* 32, no. 3 (December 1978): 299–309.

Barbey, Daniel D. *MacArthur's Amphibious Navy: Seventh Amphibious Force Operations, 1943–45*. Annapolis, Md.: U.S. Naval Institute Press, 1969.

Barker, A. J. *Yamashita*. New York: Ballantine, 1973.

Beasley, W. G., ed. *Modern Japan: Aspects of History, Literature, and Society*. Tokyo: Charles E. Tuttle, 1976.

Beesly, Patrick. *Very Special Intelligence*. New York: Ballantine, 1981.

Bennett, Ralph. *Ultra and Mediterranean Strategy*. New York: William Morrow, 1989.

———. *Ultra in the West: The Normandy Campaign of 1944–45*. New York: Charles Scribner's Sons, 1979.

Biard, Forrest R. ("Tex"). "The Pacific War through the Eyes of Forrest R. 'Tex' Biard." *Cryptolog: Naval Cryptologic Veterans Association* 10, no. 2 (Winter 1989): 1–27.

Blair, Clay. *Silent Victory: The U.S. Submarine War against Japan*. New York: Harper and Row, 1975.

Butow, Robert. *Japan's Decision to Surrender*. Stanford, Calif.: Stanford University Press, 1954.

Cadin, Martin. *The Ragged, Rugged Warriors*. New York: Bantam, 1979.

Calvocoressi, Peter. *Top Secret Ultra*. New York: Ballantine, 1980.

Cannon, M. Hamlin. *United States Army in World War II: The War in the Pacific—Leyte: The Return to the Philippines*. Washington, D.C.: Government Printing Office, 1954.

Carter, Kit C., and Robert Mueller, comps. *The Army Air Forces in World War II: Combat Chronology, 1941–1945*. Montgomery, Ala., and Washington, D.C.: Albert F. Simpson Historical Research Center Air University and Office of Air Force History, Headquar ters, USAF, 1973.

Clark, Ronald W. *The Man Who Broke Purple*. London: Weidenfeld and Nicolson, 1977.

Costello, John. *The Pacific War*. New York: Rawson and Wade, 1981.

Craig, William. *The Fall of Japan*. New York: Dial Press, 1967.

Craven, Wesley Frank, and James Lea Cate, eds. *The Army Air Forces in World War II*. Vol. 4: *The Pacific: Guadalcanal to Saipan, August 1942 to July 1944*. Chicago: University of Chicago Press, 1950.

———. *The Army Air Forces in World War II*. Vol. 5: *The Pacific: Matterhorn to Nagasaki, June 1944 to August 1945*. Chicago: University of Chicago Press, 1953.

Dexter, David. *Australia in the War of 1939–45: Army: The New Guinea Offensives*. Canberra: Australian War Memorial, 1961.

Dower, John. *War without Mercy: Race and Power in the Pacific War*. New York: Pantheon, 1986.

Drea, Edward J. "Defending the Driniumor: Covering Force Operations in New Guinea, 1944." *Leavenworth Paper* No. 9. Washington, D.C.: Government Printing Office, 1984.

———. "ULTRA Intelligence and General Douglas MacArthur's Leap to Hollandia, January-April 1944." *Intelligence and National Security* 5: no. 2 (April 1990): 323–349.

Dull, Paul. S. *A Battle History of the Imperial Japanese Navy (1941–1945)*. Annapolis, Md.: U.S. Naval Institute Press, 1978.

Falk, Stanley L. *Decision at Leyte*. New York: W. W. Norton, 1966.

———. "Leyte Gulf: A Bibliography of the Greatest Sea Battle." *Naval History* (Fall 1988): 60–61.

Farago, Ladislas. *The Broken Seal: "Operation Magic" and the Secret Road to Pearl Harbor*. New York: Random House, 1967.

Feis, Herbert. *The Atomic Bomb and the End of World War II*. 2d, rev. ed. Princeton, N.J.: Princeton University Press, 1966.

Feldt, Eric A. *The Coastwatchers*. Oxford: Oxford University Press, 1947.

Finnegan, Jack. "Grim Fate for Station 6." *Military History* (October 1986): 10, 63–66.

Frierson, William C. *The Admiralties: Operations of the 1st Cavalry Division (29 February–18 May 1944)*. American Forces in Action Series. Washington, D.C.: War Department, 1946.

Greenfield, Kent Roberts, ed. *Command Decisions*. Washington, D.C.: Government Printing Office, 1960.

Hamm, Diane L., ed. *Military Intelligence: Its Heroes and Legends*. Washington, D.C.: Government Printing Office, 1987.

Harrington, Joseph D. *Yankee Samurai: The Secret Role of Nisei in America's Pacific Victory*. Detroit: Harlo Press, 1979.

Hayes, Grace Person. *The History of the Joint Chiefs of Staff in World War II: The War against Japan*. Annapolis, Md.: U.S. Naval Institute Press, 1983.

Herken, Gregg. *The Winning Weapon*. New York: Knopf, 1980.

Holmes, W. J. *Double-Edged Secrets: U.S. Naval Intelligence Operations in the Pacific during World War II*. Annapolis, Md.: U.S. Naval Institute Press, 1979.

Horner, D. M. "Special Intelligence in the South-West Pacific Area in World War II." *Australian Outlook* 32, no. 3 (December 1978): 310–327.

James, D. Clayton. *The Years of MacArthur*. Vol. 2: *1941–1945*. Boston: Houghton Mifflin, 1975.

———. *The Years of MacArthur*. Vol. 3: *Triumph and Disaster*. Boston: Houghton Mifflin, 1985.

Kahn, David. *The Codebreakers: The Story of Secret Writing*. New York: Macmillan, 1967.

———, ed., *Kahn on Codes: Secrets of the New Cryptology*. New York: Macmillan, 1983.

Kenney, George C. *General Kenney Reports*. Washington, D.C.: Office of Air Force History, 1988; reprint of 1949 edition.

Krueger, Walter. *From Down Under to Nippon: The Story of Sixth Army in World War II*. Washington, D.C.: Combat Forces Press, 1953.

Layton, Edwin T. *"And I Was There": Pearl Harbor and Midway—Breaking the Secrets*. New York: William Morrow, 1985.

———, trans. "America Deciphered Our Code." *United States Naval Institute Proceedings* (June 1979): 98–100.

Leary, William M., ed. *We Shall Return! MacArthur's Commanders and the Defeat of Japan, 1942–1945*. Lexington: University Press of Kentucky, 1988.

Lewin, Ronald. *The American Magic: Codes, Ciphers, and the Defeat of Japan*. New York: Farrar Straus Giroux, 1982.

Luvaas, Jay, ed. *Dear Miss Em: General Eichelberger's War in the Pacific, 1942–1945*. Westport, Conn.: Greenwood Press, 1972.

MacArthur, Douglas. *Reminiscences*. New York: MacGraw-Hill, 1964.

McCarthy, Dudley. *Australia in the War of 1939–45: Army: South-West Pacific Area— First Year: Kokoda to Wau*. Canberra: Australian War Memorial, 1959.

McCartney, William F. *The Jungleers: A History of the 41st Infantry Division*. Washington, D.C.: Infantry Journal Press, 1948.

Miles, Rufus E., Jr. "Hiroshima: The Strange Myth of Half a Million American Lives Saved." *International Security* 10, no. 2 (Fall 1985): 121–140.

Miller, John, Jr. *United States Army in World War II: The War in the Pacific: Cartwheel: The Reduction of Rabaul*. Washington, D.C.: Government Printing Office, 1959.

Milner, Samuel. "The Battle of Milne Bay." *Military Review* 30 (April 1950): 18–29.

———. *U.S. Army in World War II: The War in the Pacific: Victory in Papua*. Washington, D.C.: Government Printing Office, 1957.

Morison, Samuel Eliot. *History of United States Naval Operations in World War II*. Vol. 6: *Breaking the Bismarck Barrier*. Boston: Little, Brown, 1957.

———. *History of United States Naval Operations in World War II*. Vol. 8: *New Guinea and the Marianas, March 1944–August 1944*. Boston: Little, Brown, 1964.

———. *History of United States Naval Operations in World War II*. Vol. 12: *Leyte: June 1944–January 1945*. Boston: Little, Brown, 1963.

———. *History of United States Naval Operations in World War II*. Vol. 14: *The Liberation of the Philippines: Luzon, Mindanao, the Visayans, 1944–45*. Boston: Little, Brown, 1959.

Morton, Louis. *United States Army in World War II: The Pacific: The Fall of the Philippines*. Washington, D.C.: Government Printing Office, 1953.

Parrish, Thomas. *The Ultra Americans: The U.S. Role in Breaking the Nazi Codes*. New York: Stein and Day, 1984.

Pogue, Forrest C. *George C. Marshall: Statesman, 1945–1959*. New York: Viking Press, 1987.

Potter, John Deane. *The Life and Death of a Japanese General*. New York: Signet, 1962.

———. *Yamamoto, the Man Who Menaced America*. New York: Viking Press, 1965.

Rhoades, Weldon E. ("Dusty"). *Flying MacArthur to Victory*. College Station: Texas A&M University Press, 1986.

Roscoe, Theodore. *United States Destroyer Operations in World Wra II*. Annapolis, Md.: U.S. Naval Institute Press, 1953.

———. *United States Submarine Operations in World War II*. Annapolis, Md.: U.S. Naval Institute Press, 1949.

Sherman, Frederick C. *Combat Command: The American Aircraft Carriers in the Pacific War*. New York: E. P. Dutton, 1950.

Sherrod, Robert E. *History of Marine Corps Aviation in World War II*. Washington, D.C.: Combat Forces Press, 1952.

Sherwin, Martin J. *A World Destroyed: The Atomic Bomb and the Grand Alliance.* New York: Knopf, 1975.

Sigal, Leon V. *Fighting to a Finish: The Politics of War Termination in the United States and Japan, 1945.* Ithaca, N.Y.: Cornell University Press, 1988.

Smith, Robert Ross. *United States Army in World War II: The War in the Pacific: The Approach to the Philippines.* Washington, D.C.: Government Printing Office, 1953.

———. *United States Army in World War II: The War in the Pacific: Triumph in the Philippines.* Washington, D.C.: Government Printing Office, 1963.

Spector, Ronald H. *Eagle against the Sun.* New York: Free Press, 1985.

Stimson, Henry L. "The Decision to Use the Atomic Bomb." *Harper's* (February 1947): 97–107.

Stripp, Alan J. "Breaking Japanese Codes." *Intelligence and National Security* 2, no. 4 (October 1987): 135–150.

———. *Codebreaker in the Far East.* London: Frank Cass, 1989.

Supreme Commander for the Allied Powers. *Reports of General MacArthur.* Vol. 1: *The Campaigns of MacArthur in the Pacific.* Washington, D.C.: Government Printing Office, 1966.

———. *Reports of General MacArthur.* Vol. 2: *Japanese Operations in the Southwest Pacific Area* (Part 1). Washington, D.C.: Government Printing Office, 1966.

Tanaka, Kengoro. *Operations of the Imperial Japanese Armed Forces in the Papua New Guinea Theater during World War II.* Tokyo: Japan–Papua New Guinea Goodwill Society, 1980.

Thompson, George R., et al. *United States Army in World War II: The Technical Services: The Signal Corps—The Test (December 1941 to July 1943).* Washington, D.C.: Government Printing Office, 1957.

Thompson, George R., and Dixie Lee Harris. *The United States Army in World War II: The Technical Services: The Signal Corps: The Outcome (mid 1943 through 1945).* Washington, D.C.: Government Printing Office, 1966.

Toland, John. *The Rising Sun: The Decline and Fall of the Japanese Empire, 1936–1945.* New York: Random House, 1970.

Tucker, Dundas P. "Rhapsody in Purple: A New History of Pearl Harbor (1)." *Cryptologia* (July 1982): 193–228.

Valtin, Jan [Richard J. Krebs]. *Children of Yesterday.* New York: Readers' Press, 1946.

Van Der Rhoer, Edward. *Deadly Magic: A Personal Account of Communication Intelligence in World War II in the Pacific.* New York: Charles Scribner's Sons, 1978.

Warner, Denis, and Peggy Warner, with Sadao Seno. *The Sacred Warriors: Japan's Suicide Legions.* New York: Van Nostrand Reinhold, 1982.

Westheimer, David. *Downfall: The Top-Secret Plan to Invade Japan* (originally published as *Lighter than a Feather*). New York: Bantam, 1972.

Willoughby, Charles A., and John Chamberlain. *MacArthur: 1941–1951.* New York: McGraw-Hill, 1954.

Wright, B. C., comp. *The 1st Cavalry Division in World War II.* Tokyo: Toppan Printing, 1947.

Yardley, Herbert O. *The American Black Chamber.* New York: Ballantine, 1981; reprint of 1931 edition.

Yoshida, Mitsuru. *Requiem for Battleship Yamato*. Trans. Richard H. Minear. Seattle: University of Washington Press, 1985.

Zacharias, Ellis M. *Secret Missions*. New York: G. P. Putnam Sons, 1946.

Japanese-Language Sources

Akieta Shigeharu et al. "Danwakai Hito kessen o ayamaraseta mono" [Discussion: Things mistaken in the decisive battle of the Philippines]. *Rekishi to jimbutsu* (Summer 1986): 132–146.

Boeicho. Boei kenshujo. [Japan. Japan National Institute for Defense Studies], ed., "Kiso chosa 'Nihon rikukaigun no joho kiko to sono katsudo.' " *Kenkyu shiryo* 84RO—2H. [Basic research: The intelligence organizations and activities of the Japanese army and navy. Research document 84RO—2H]. Tokyo: Boei kenshujo senshibu, 1984.

———. *Senshi sosho* [Official military history]. Vol. 7: *Tobu Nyuginia homen rikugun koku sakusen* [Army air operations on the eastern New Guinea front]. Tokyo: Asagumo shimbunsha, 1967.

———. Vol. 14: *Minami Taiheiyo rikugun sakusen: Pooruto Moresubi—Ga shima shoki sakusen* (1) [Army operations in the South Pacific: Port Moresby—First stage operations at Guadalcanal (book 1)]. Tokyo: Asagumo shimbunsha, 1968.

———. Vol. 21: *Gohoku homen rikugun sakusen* [Army operations north of Australia]. Tokyo: Asagumo shimbunsha, 1968.

———. Vol. 22: *Seibu Nyugineya homan rikugun koku sakusen* [Army air force operations on the western New Guinea front]. Tokyo: Asagumo shimbunsha, 1969.

———. Vol. 28: *Minami Taiheiyo rikugun sakusen: Gadarukanaru-Buna sakusen* (2) [Army operations in the South Pacific: Guadalcanal and Buna operations (book 2)]. Tokyo: Asabumo shimbunsha, 1968.

———. Vol. 40: *Minami Taiheiyo rikugun sakusen: Munda Saramoa* (3) [Army operations in the South Pacific: Munda Salamaua (book 3)]. Tokyo: Asagumo shimbunsha, 1970.

———. Vol. 41: *Shogo rikugun sakusen: Reite kessen* (1) [SHO ground operations: The decisive battle of Leyte (book 1)]. Tokyo: Asagumo shimbunsha, 1970.

———. Vol. 54: *Nansei homen kaigun sakusen* [Southwest Area Fleet operations]. Tokyo: Asagumo shimbunsha, 1972.

———. Vol. 56: *Kaigun shogo sakusen: Fuiripin oki kaisen* (1) [SHO naval operations: The naval battle of the Philippine Sea (book 1)]. Tokyo: Asagumo shimbunsha, 1970.

———. Vol. 57: *Hondo kessen jumbi: Kyushu no boei* (2) [Preparations for the decisive battle of the homeland: Defense of Kyushu (book 2).] Tokyo: Asagumo shimbunsha, 1972.

———. Vol. 58: *Minami Taiheiyo rikugun sakusen: Fuinshehaahen Tsurubu Tarokina* (4) [Army operations in the South Pacific: Finschhafen-Tsurubu-Tarokina (book 4)]. Tokyo: Asagumo shimbunsha, 1973.

———. Vol. 60: *Shogo rikugun sakusen: Ruson kessen* (2) [SHO ground operations: The decisive battle of Luzon (book 2)]. Tokyo: Asagumo shimbunsha, 1972.

———. Vol. 75: *Daihon' ei rikugunbu: Showa 19 nen 7 gatsu made* (8) (Imperial General Headquarters: To July 1944 (book 8)]. Tokyo: Asagumo shimbunsha, 1974.

————. Vol. 84: *Minami Taiheiyo rikugun sakusen: Aitape-Puriaka-Rabaaru* (5) [Army operations in the South Pacific: Aitape–Empress August Bay–Rabaul (book 5)]. Tokyo: Asagumo shimbunsha, 1973.

Fujiwara Akira. *Taiheiyo senso shiron* [A historical interpretation of the Pacific war]. Tokyo: Aoki shoten, 1982.

Gido Tamotsu. *Ruson no ishibumi* [Tombstones of Luzon]. Tokyo: Kojinsha, 1981.

Hasegawa Keitaro, ed. *Nihon kindai to senso.* Vol. 1: *Johosen no haiboku* [Japan's modernity and war. Vol. 1: Defeat in the intelligence wars]. Tokyo: PHP kenkyujo, 1985.

Hata Ikuhiko. *Showashi no gunjintachi* [Military men of the Showa era]. Tokyo: Bungei shunju, 1982.

Hayashi Saburo. "Senjika no rikugun chuobu" [Army central headquarters in wartime]. *Rekishi to jimbutsu* (Winter 1986): 248–261.

————. *Taiheiyo senso rikusen gaishi* [An overview of army operations in the Pacific war]. Tokyo: Iwanami shoten, 1951.

Hiyama Yoshiaki. *Nihon hondo kessen* [The decisive battle of the Japanese homeland]. Tokyo: Kobunsha, 1981.

Hori Eizo. "Reite kessen kara Ruson jikyu made Yamashita Tomoyuki taisho kujyu nichikan kuno" [From the decisive battle of Leyte to the protracted fighting of Luzon—General Yamashita Tomoyuki's ninety days of suffering]. *Rekishi to jimbutsu* (Winter 1986): 324–339.

Imai Sei'ichi. *Taiheiyo senso.* Vol. 5: *Taiheiyo senso* (II) [History of the Pacific War. Vol. 5: The Pacific War (part 2)]. Tokyo: Aoki shoten, 1973.

Imai Takeo and Terasaki Ryuji, eds. *Nihongun no kenkyu shikkikan* [Japanese army studies: The commanders]. 2 vols. Tokyo: Hara shobo, 1980.

Kamaga Kazuo. "Nihon rikugun ango wa 'antai' datta" [The Japanese army codes were secure]. *Shogen: Rekishi to jimbutsu* (September 1984): 270–281.

Kamaga Kazuo, Fujiwara Kuniki, and Yoshimura Akira. "Zadankai: Nihon rikugun ango wa naze yaburarenakatta" [Discussion: Why couldn't the Japanese army codes be broken?]. *Rekishi to jimbutsu* (December 1985): 150–165.

Kimata Jiro. *Rikugun koku senshi: Mare sakusen kara Okinawa tokko made* [History of the army air force: From the Malaya operation to the Okinawa special attack corps]. Tokyo: Keizai oraisha, 1982.

"Kimitsu senso nisshi" [Confidential war diary]. *Rekishi to jimbutsu* (September–November 1971): 333–373, 272–309, and 280–309, respectively.

Kojima Noboru. *Taiheiyo senso* [The Pacific war]. 2 vols. Tokyo: Chuo koronsha, 1965.

————. *Tenno.* Vol. 5: *Teikoku no shuen* [The emperor. Vol. 5: Death of the empire]. Tokyo: Bungei shunju, 1974.

Kusumi Tadao. "Nansei homen kantai" [Southwest Area Fleet]. *Rekishi to jimbutsu* (Winter 1985): 115–119.

Maebara Toru. "Manira boei no higeki rikukaigun no tairitsu" [The tragedy of the defense of Manila—The opposition between the army and navy]. *Rekishi to jimbutsu* (September 1982): 110–113.

————. "Manira boeishi: Nihongun no toshi to tatakai" [The defense of Manila: Japanese army and city fighting]. *Kenkyu shiryo* 82RO-7H (mimeo). Tokyo: Boeikenshujo, 1982.

Maeda Toru and Kuwada Etsu, eds. *Nihon no senso—zukai to deeta* [The wars of Japan—Illustrated maps and data). Tokyo: Hara shobo, 1982.

Majime Mitsuru. *Jigoku no senjo: Nyuginia senki* [Hell's battleground: New Guinea war record]. Tokyo: Kojinsha, 1988.

Nakamuda Ken'ichi. *Joho shikan no kaiso* [Memoirs of an intelligence officer]. Tokyo: Asahi sonorama, 1985.

Nakamura Fumio. "Rikugun ni okeru COMINT no hoga to hatten" [The germination and development of communications intelligence in the Imperial Army]. *Shinboei ronshu* 16, no. 1 (June 1988): 84–88.

Ooe Shinobu. *Showa no rekishi.* Vol. 3: *Tenno no guntai* [History of the Showa reign. Vol. 3: The emperor's army]. Tokyo: Shogakkan, 1982.

Ooka Shohei. *Reite senki* [Military record of the Leyte operation]. Tokyo: Chuo koron, 1971.

Sanbohonbu [Chief of staff], ed. *Sugiyama memo* (ge) [The Sugiyama memo (vol. 2)]. Tokyo: Hara shobo, 1967.

Sanematsu Yuzuru. *Nichi-Bei joho senki* [Record of the Japanese-American intelligence war]. Tokyo: Tosho shuppansha, 1985.

Shinzato Keiji, Taminato Tomoaki, and Kinjo Seitoku, eds. *Kenshi no shiriizu.* Vol. 47: *Okinawa no rekishi* [Prefectural history series. Vol. 47: A history of Okinawa]. Tokyo: Yamakawa shoten, 1980.

"Taiheiyo senso shogen shirizu" [Series of testimonies about the Pacific war]. *Bessatsu Maru* [Special series Maru]. 10 vols. Tokyo: Ushio shobo, 1987–1988.

Takagi Sokichi. *Taiheiyo kaisenshi* [A naval history of the Pacific war]. Tokyo: Iwanami shinsho, 1977; reprint of 1949 edition).

Takahashi Masatoshi. "Dai juuyon hikodan no kaimetsu" [The destruction of the 14th Air Brigade]. *Rekishi to jimbutsu* (August 1980): 122–129.

Tanaka Ken'ichi. *Reite sakusen no kiroku* [Record of Leyte operations]. Tokyo: Hara shobo, 1980.

Tanemura Suketaka. *Daihon'ei kimitsu nisshi* [Confidential war diary of Imperial Headquarters]. Tokyo: Fuyo shobo, 1985; reprint of 1952 edition.

Tomita Seinosuke. *Dai ichi shidan Reite kessen no shinso* [The truth about the 1st Division's decisive battle on Leyte]. Tokyo: Asagumo shimbunsha, 1987.

Toyohashi Fusataro et al., eds. *Gohoku o seiku* [The subjugation of the front north of Australia]. Tokyo: Gohoku homen ikotsu hikiageru sokushinkai, 1956.

Tsunoda Fusako. *Sekinin Rabauru no shogun Imamura Hitoshi* [The general responsible for Rabaul: Imamura Hitoshi]. Tokyo: Shinchosha, 1984.

Index

Adachi Hatazo, 53, 54, 79, 91, 94, 96, 112, 121, 143, 204: and Aitape attack, 123–124, 133, 143–144; and Bismarck Sea debacle, 71; and defense of Lae, 67, 85; at Finschhafen, 85, 87; personality, 67; and plan to ambush Allies at Hansa Bay, 97, 116, 233

Admiralty Islands, 86, 96, 98, 127, 137, 223, 228, 230, 235: Allied air raids on, 98–99; Japanese defenses in, 99–100; Japanese reaction to loss of, 112; Kenney proposes seizure of, 99; strategic value of, 98, 121; ULTRA reports on, 97, 101–104

Aitape, North-East New Guinea, xiii, 56, 110, 111, 115, 118, 133: Allied operations, 119–120, 147–151

Aiyo Maru (ship), 70

Akatsuki, 38–39, 59. *See also* Japan, army

Akin, Spencer B., 13, 14, 16, 23, 27, 62, 228: and Admiralties, 101; and Aitape, 147, 149; differences with Signal Intelligence Service, 28, 31; as director of Central Bureau, 19–21, 26–28, 30; and Hollandia, 115; and Japanese Army Water Transport Code, 75–76; personality, 18; prewar career, 9–11; relationship with Clarke, 30; relationship with special security officers, 28–29; relationship with Willoughby, 20–21

Akitsu Maru (ship), 76

Alamo Force. *See* U.S. Army, Sixth Army

Alamo Scouts, 87, 141–142

Albacore (ship), 55

Allied Air Forces, 16

Allied Intelligence Bureau (AIB), 54, 91, 108

Allied Land Forces, 16, 78

Allied Naval Forces, 16, 78

Allied Translator and Interpreter Section (ATIS), 21, 73

Alphabetical List of Japanese Army Officers, 73, 216

Ambon, Netherlands East Indies, 82

American Black Chamber, The (Yardley), 8

Anami Korechika, 132–133: and Aitape attack, 144; estimate of Allied situation, 113–114; personality, 124

Arawe, New Britain, 90, 100

Argonaut (submarine), 65–66

Arlington Hall Station, Arlington, Va., 6, 28, 130, 207: and Aitape, 120; breaks Japanese address code, 38; breaks Japanese Army Water Transport Code, 62, 75–76; breaks Japanese military attaché code, 62, 77; evaluation of (1942), 57, 59; exchanges data with Central Bureau, 20–21, 23, 25, 38, 75, 92–93; and Kyushu, 215; mission, 21; and Philippines, 159; and Wewak Convoy Number 21, 107. *See also* Central Bureau; Signal Intelligence Service; Signal Security Agency

Army Code Book (*Rikugun angosho*). *See under* Japan, military codes

Army-Navy Central Agreement: March 1943, 72; September 1943, 86–87

Army Water Transport Code. *See under* Japan, military codes

Ascot Park, Brisbane, Australia, 25–26

Atomic bomb, xiii, 201, 219: historical controversy over, 204; ULTRA influence in decision to use, 219, 222; ULTRA reports of destructive effect, 223–224

Australian Army: Australian Special Wireless Group, 20; 7th Infantry Division, 63; 9th